Texts by

GEOFFREY BARRACLOUGH · WILLIAM H.C. FREND
JOACHIM GAEHDE · IAN N. WOOD
STEVEN RUNCIMAN
COLIN MORRIS · MARGARET ASTON
HANS HILLERBRAND · J. WILLIAM T. YOUNGS
JUDITH HOOK · OWEN CHADWICK
PAUL A. CARTER
ADRIAN CUNNINGHAM

*With 353 illustrations, 85 in color,
268 photographs, drawings
and maps*

EDITED BY GEOFFREY BARRACLOUGH

THE CHRISTIAN WORLD

*A social and cultural history
of Christianity*

Thames & Hudson

PAGE ONE
Mosaic from the baptistery of Albenga Cathedral with triple Chi-
Rho and Alpha and Omega, probably symbolizing the Trinity.

Editor and publisher wish to acknowledge the generous advice given by all the authors
on the selection of the illustrations and the wording of the captions; it must
be made clear, however, that final responsibility for these picture
sections remains entirely with the publisher.

Part of Chapter 8 by J. William T. Youngs has appeared in *American Realities:
Historical Episodes from the First Settlements to the Present*,
Little, Brown & Co., Boston, Massachusetts, 1980.

Designed and produced by THAMES & HUDSON LTD, LONDON
MANAGING EDITOR: Ian Sutton DESIGN: Ian Mackenzie-Kerr
EDITORIAL: Marcy Bourne PICTURE RESEARCH: Georgina Bruckner
Map on page 89: Shalom Schotten

Published in paperback in the United States of America in 2003 by
Thames & Hudson Inc., 500 Fifth Avenue, New York, New York 10110

thamesandhudsonusa.com

Library of Congress Catalog Card Number 2002107853
ISBN 0-500-28398-2

Printed and bound in Slovenia by Mladinska Knjiga

CONTENTS

IN PRINCIPIO ERAT VERBUM ...
'In the beginning was the Word'. The opening of the Gospel
according to St John. Adapted from the *Codex Aureus* or Golden Gospel
of Echternach, 10th century.

PRINCIPIO

THIS BOOK will be concerned with the way Christianity has affected the lives of men and women during the two thousand years of its existence. By way of prologue, this introductory section presents three of Christianity's most fundamental ideas, which typically are three Persons – God the Father, the Virgin Mary and Jesus Christ. Theologians today take a broader view than their predecessors did, and these three figures are no longer represented or believed in with quite the literalness of the past. But the imagery of the past is still useful in understanding how Christian doctrine has evolved and what meaning it can have in the modern world.

To most Westerners, 'Christianity' and 'religion' have become so synonymous that we tend to forget how extraordinary Christianity is. Imaginatively, it asks more of its believers than any other world faith, since it is founded on a miracle, the incarnation of God in Christ, and – for Catholics at least – continues to subsist on a daily miracle, the Eucharist; it makes the supernatural not merely an idea but a historical fact; and it postulates a cosmic framework of original sin, divine sacrifice and eternal salvation for which the evidence outside revelation is, to say the least, tenuous. All this is hard for reason to accept. On the other hand, it has been, at every level, all-inclusive. Many beliefs, often apparently contradictory, shelter within the Christian fold. Socially, it seems to be both egalitarian – though rarely to the point of disturbing the ruling class – and hierarchical; politically, it has justified both revolution and repression; intellectually, it has accommodated almost every philosophical theory and scientific discovery; ethically, its emphasis on personal responsibility allows an almost infinite range of behaviour; psychologically, it places supreme value on the uniqueness of each individual while offering an interpretation of the human condition that is universally applicable. Such inclusiveness has not made for unity, and, as we shall see, the history of Christianity has been a history of quarrels and secessions, with their tragic corollaries: intolerance, persecution and war. Yet the way it has for so long embodied and expressed all our highest ideals of universal love and self-sacrifice makes it hard to believe that our civilization would have been better off without it.

The message of redemption
has always been central to the church's teaching.
Until modern times this has been taken completely literally: without Christ's
vicarious suffering on behalf of mankind, everybody would spend eternity in hell.
The image of the Harrowing of Hell was therefore both a literal truth and an
allegory. According to tradition, as embodied in the Apostles' Creed, between
Christ's burial and resurrection he descended into hell and released all the
virtuous who had lived up to that time. In this spirited rendering in alabaster,
made in Nottingham in the 15th century, he is shown taking Adam by the hand
and leading him out of hell's jaws. Eve follows, then John the Baptist and then all
the patriarchs and prophets who foretold Christ's coming. Allegorically, it is a
picture of every soul's rescue, since original sin – let alone the sins that we
actually commit – would justly condemn us
to everlasting punishment. (1)

God the Father

To represent God in visible form is to the other mono-theistic religions – and, it must be said, to many Christians, too, at various times – a blasphemy. Yet we accept it without shock, a convention so familiar that it no longer seems extraordinary. In art, the problem of illustrating the Trinity – Father, Son and Holy Ghost, three Persons but one God – has produced a range of different solutions. *Top:* Lucas Cranach's Trinity, 1516, with the Father as ruler of the universe, the Son as sacrificial victim, the Holy Ghost as dove. *Above:* three details from 15th-century paintings – God as a papal figure holding the orb; the Trinity as three identical faces on a single body, from a Tyrolean folk painting; God as a Jove-like deity wielding thunderbolts. *Opposite:* the most traditional representation – the atavistic, all-powerful image of authority, which Freud and Jung have taught us to look for deep in our own subconscious. (2–6)

Virgin Mother

The image of Mary emphasized her state of sinlessness and her motherhood. Historically this has had the effect of exalting woman as virgin and as mother, but implicitly condemned her sexuality.

The happy mother nursing the infant Jesus is a perennial symbol of hope and renewal. In 15th-century Flanders (*above* by Gerard David), Mary became the typical bourgeois housewife. (7)

The Queen of Heaven – a gilded Virgin by J. L. Saler of Augsburg (*above right*), 1750. (8)

The mourning mother: Mary with her dead son (*right* by Sebastiano del Piombo) is another universal image. The bleak landscape conveys despair; but Mary's pose embodies a faith that reaches beyond death. (9)

Mother Church: in the image of the Virgin of Charity, Mary came to represent the church itself, sheltering mankind within her all-enfolding cloak. This painting (*opposite*) is by Jean Mirailhet, 15th century. (10)

Jesus the Man

For the first thousand years of Christianity, Christ the Saviour was a remote figure, a divinity rather than a man. But towards the end of the Middle Ages emphasis began to be placed on the humanity of Christ, in particular on his sufferings at the Passion. As God identified himself with man, now man could identify himself with God.

Faces of Christ. *Opposite:* detail of a terracotta figure by Giovanni della Robbia, *c.* 1500. *Above:* Christ taking leave of the three Marys, an incident not mentioned in the Gospels, showing him as a man with family and friends. *Above right:* detail from *Christ Crucified* by Rembrandt, the moment of death, the supreme act of identity between God and man. *Right:* Christ's moment of human despair on the Mount of Olives, by Goya: 'Father, if thou art willing, remove this cup from me.' (11–14)

INTRODUCTION

The risen Christ is for most Christians the conclusive
reason for believing. By conquering death Christ both
vindicated his own claims to be the Messiah and led the way
for mankind to conquer death also. This has certainly been
the prevailing view throughout most of Christianity's
history. This float from a Sicilian Holy Week procession is
still firmly rooted in such a mode of thought. The
triumphant Christ welcomes man to eternal life, while in
front an angel holds a scroll bearing the answer given to the
women when they came to anoint his body: 'He is not here,
for he is risen even as he said.' (15)

The spiritual complexion of different Christian churches is often clearly recognizable in their art. The stern 12th-century Byzantine Christ from the baptistery of Monreale contrasts with the almost contemporary Christ of Chartres, where the tenderness of the western tradition is already apparent.

Introduction: a Christian world?

GEOFFREY BARRACLOUGH

WHAT DO WE MEAN when we speak of a 'Christian world'? How is it to be defined and delimited? All the great world religions have a universal message; but all, except Buddhism and Christianity, are associated also with a particular people or region. Hinduism is the religion of the peoples of India; Taoism never extended beyond the frontiers of China; and inherent in Judaism is the belief that the Jews, though dispersed over the four quarters of the world, are the Chosen People. Islam, on the other hand, is one of the great missionary religions, spread far and wide; but it also is associated primarily with the Arabs, and has a spiritual home in Mecca, just as Judaism has a home and base in Jerusalem. Christianity is different, and this difference may help to define its special place in the sequence of world religions.

Because it originated as a Jewish sect in Asia Minor, a splinter group with no firm spiritual anchorage, Christianity became almost from the start a missionary religion, conveying God's message to the Gentiles and the peoples beyond. This was the essence of Pauline Christianity, and it is the essence of Christianity as it appears in history. Only Buddhism, which began as a reformist movement in Hinduism, much as Christianity began as a reformist movement in Judaism, has a similar story to tell. Buddhism also spread – and continues to spread – through its missionary activity, and today, paradoxically, has almost no adherents in its Indian homeland. The history of Christianity is not very different.

The origins are not irrelevant because they conditioned much of the subsequent history. Once it had shaken free from its Jewish roots, Christianity embarked on its missionary career, seeking to convert the pagans to the Christian faith and to a Christian way of life. This, it might almost be said, is one explanation of its survival. Rejected by the Jews, its only prospective field of activity was among the Gentiles. First, it permeated, and eventually conquered, the Mediterranean world of Rome; indeed, in Christian eschatology it was soon believed that God had only created the Roman Empire in order to provide a field for the expansion of Christianity. Then, it turned to the pagan peoples on the confines of Rome: the Goths, whom Ulfilas set out to convert in the middle of the 4th century, the Irish, converted by St Patrick a century later, then the Anglo-Saxons, later the continental Saxons and their neighbours, the Frisians and Hessians, and later still the Scandinavian peoples, the Slavs of Russia, Bohemia and Poland and the Magyars of Hungary. The process was completed, so far as Europe was concerned, when heathen Lithuania was converted in 1387. But scarcely more than a century elapsed before it began again in the newly discovered Americas, and later it continued wherever Christian Europe set its foot. The pastoral visits of Pope John-Paul II to Latin America and to Africa in 1980 are a testimony to the world-wide impact of Christianity.

But how deep does that impact go? How far has a Christian ethic succeeded in capturing a nominally Christian world? Pope John-Paul II's far-flung journeying, unprecedented in the whole long history of the Catholic church, may be seen, from another angle, as a spectacular Christian counter-offensive, a reinvigoration of its evangelizing mission, in a world where Christianity has been losing ground and influence. It raises, inevitably, the further question, how far, after nearly two thousand years, the message of Christianity permeates contemporary society. Indeed, we may go further and ask how far, historically, it has ever shaped and permeated the lives and cultures of the peoples who, often (it must be remembered) through the decision of rulers who were more concerned with politics than with ethics or religion, were propelled willy-nilly into the Christian world. These are some of the questions implicit in this book. We shall not attempt to answer them directly, preferring to leave the reader to draw his or her own conclusions. But it is important to bear them in mind because they define to some degree the scope, character and content of this book and what it sets out to achieve.

It is not, to begin with, a history of Christianity, though the different chapters follow each other in a more or less chronological order. Its subject – narrower, perhaps, in scope, but broader, perhaps, in implication – is the impact of the Christian religion on the lives and cultures of the peoples who, voluntarily or by superior command, entered the Christian fold. Histories of Christianity abound. Our concern is different from theirs, and excludes many subjects they

Throughout most of its history, Christianity has confidently expected that one day it would conquer the world. This Spanish woodcut of 1578 is particularly pointed, coming only decades after the expulsion of the Moors from Spain.

deal with at length. We are not concerned with theology or dogma, for example, nor with the history of the different Christian churches or ecclesiastical institutions. Admittedly this distinction is not always easy to maintain. At many periods abstruse ecclesiological and Christological questions had wide popular repercussions, stirred passions and influenced attitudes in a way it is difficult for anyone in a less doctrinally minded age to comprehend. It would be absurd and misleading to ignore them; but they are not our main concern.

The impact of Christianity and its effects on society and culture have, of course, been much discussed in the past. Here also there is a large body of writing, much of it polemical or apologetic. Gibbon in the 18th century assigned Christianity a leading role in the decline and fall of the Roman Empire; for him its impact was negative. Later, in a famous epigram, Marx described religion (including, needless to say, the Christian religion) as the opium of the people. On the other hand, the 19th-century · Romantics, including writers like Novalis in Germany and Chateaubriand in France, viewed Christianity as the very keystone of Western civilization; indeed Chateaubriand's *Génie du Christianisme*, published in 1802, may be regarded as the symbol of the Christian revival after the deism of the Enlightenment. In our own day, similar views have been put forward, with great learning and eloquence, by Christopher Dawson.

It is hardly necessary to say that the purpose of this book is neither polemical nor apologetic. The historians who have contributed to it include both Christians and non-Christians, all scholars of high standing whose first commitment is veracity. Their aim is not, like that of so much of the earlier literature, to record a verdict, but to describe how things were.

This is an old precept, going back to the father of modern historiography, Leopold von Ranke. But its realization has been made more easy by recent developments in the writing of history, in particular by the trend among historians to pay more attention, at all periods of history, to the lives of ordinary people and less to the elite at the head of the social hierarchy. The study of 'popular culture' is relatively new, scarcely more than thirty or forty years old, but it has already produced striking, almost revolutionary results in the history of Christianity. It has shown, for example, that even in what are sometimes called 'the Christian centuries' thousands of ordinary people and sometimes whole districts in nominally Christian countries lived lives virtually untouched by the Christian church. Only five per cent of the population of the United States professed any religion at all in 1790, as Professor Carter points out in a later chapter, although the New England colonies had been founded as Puritan settlements. There is, it would seem, a non-Christian and sometimes overtly anti-Christian stream – a stream sometimes

Recent research is discovering that at certain periods and in certain areas Christianity was only skin deep. Country people who believed that witches could bring rain (a German woodcut of 1489) were living in a fundamentally non-Christian world.

exemplified by sorcery, heathen practices and witch-craft – running parallel with the Christian stream from Roman times through the Middle Ages into modern industrial society. The 'Christian world' apparently was never more than partly Christian.

These new insights, the achievement of the new generation of historians which has done so much to unravel the secrets of the lives and mental processes of ordinary people, are perhaps the ultimate justification for this book. No serious attempt to assess the social and cultural influence of Christianity can leave them out of account. They explain why the older literature and the older approach, with its concentration on the literate classes and on the evidence they have left behind, are no longer adequate. In fact, they never were adequate; that is to say, they always left an uneasy impression that an important dimension was missing, but no one knew quite how to fill the gap. The historians who have brought to life the anonymous masses have added the missing dimension and at the same time have changed the content and outline of the picture. That is why a new attempt to assess the social and cultural impact of Christianity is necessary. This book, in intention at least, may be regarded as a step in that direction.

At the same time, all who have contributed to it are aware of the problems and difficulties involved in any such assessment. Only those who have never had to do the spadework themselves will be tempted to think that the social and cultural impact of Christianity can be described in simple or straightforward terms, and it would be misleading if this book were to leave that impression. It had its shadows as well as its light, and both are part of the picture.

There is also the question of the interpretation of the evidence. This is a technical question, and there is no reason to burden the reader with it. But it is something the historians who have contributed the following chapters have had to grapple with at every step. As I have indicated, we have done our best to take into account the findings of recent work on 'popular culture'. But this work is still in an early stage, and there are many empty spaces. The annals of the poor, as the poet Gray observed long ago, are short and simple, or, as Margaret Aston puts it: 'The religion of the people belongs to the unscripted history of the church.' Our knowledge – for example, our knowledge of witchcraft or of the popular religion of the Middle Ages – comes almost without exception from hostile witnesses. To discover what ordinary people thought about Christi-anity requires a long and difficult distillation; it is not written out for all to see. For some twelve centuries, from the beginning of the 5th century until the 17th century, in Europe at least, our primary literary sources

A friar preaches to Muslims, Barcelona, c. 1500. Peaceful persuasion was always preferable to more violent methods.

are Christian writers. This had not been the case in the Roman Empire where there was a voluble and spirited anti-Christian literature, at least until the reign of the Emperor Theodosius; and a new, more critical spirit entered again in the 18th century, with Voltaire and the Encyclopædists. But in between we have to allow for a Christian bias which – without malice, no doubt – had an inherent tendency to emphasize, if not to magnify, Christian influences, and to put them in the best light. We know a great deal more about what Christian leaders, saints, popes and bishops, thought and set out to do, about their ideals and plans and policies, than about what they actually achieved.

Similar problems arise in connection with the artistic evidence. Here, people say, is a direct witness which cannot deceive. For them, Christian art is the clearest, most vivid representation of Christian civilization. Its reality is visible in the Gothic cathedrals of 13th- and 14th-century Europe, and in the Baroque churches of the 17th century which span the Christian world in a great arc extending from St Florian and Melk in Austria, on the very confines of the hostile Ottoman Empire, to the dazzlingly beautiful Dominican church at Oaxaca in Mexico. But here again there are questions of interpretation which can only be hinted at. First and foremost, perhaps, is the need to make allowance for the effects of patronage. Once the Christian church became a great and wealthy property owner – as it did at a remarkably early stage – it was able, through

Coptic Christianity became cut off from Europe at an early date and evolved in its own way. This 5th–6th-century gravestone comes from Fayum in Egypt: Mary suckling the infant Jesus.

patronage, to impose its own image and to give art and architecture a Christian imprint which, perhaps, is larger than life. There was, indeed, secular art throughout – brooches, ornaments, caskets, ivory carvings, and other embellishments of everyday life. But until the appearance of lay patrons, princes and bourgeois, in considerable numbers during the Renaissance, 'great' art was religious art, commissioned by or on behalf of the church. This does not imply that the depth of artistic feeling in triptychs, altarpieces, or sculptures of Christ or the Virgin was not profound or genuine. But the artists who painted scenes from the Bible or from the life of Christ were working for a patron and reproducing the vision of reality the patron expected of them. When taste changed, they could just as easily paint scenes from pagan mythology.

This does not mean that the impact of Christianity on society was not real, only that we must be careful how we evaluate it. The fact that every parish had its church, sometimes simple and unembellished, sometimes large and imposing, but all imbued with the spirit of Christianity, is eloquent testimony enough. It means that Christian influence was inescapable. But does it follow that the prevalence of Christian art necessarily implies that the world it portrays was a Christian world? It is only necessary to contrast the Christian and Islamic architecture of Spain, where the two civilizations existed side by side, to see that each represented not merely a different architectural style but also a different perception of divine truth. When we pass beyond this crude and simple contrast, however, complications immediately arise. The Christian art of Egypt, before the Arab conquest, is extraordinarily powerful and impressive; but it is not the art of western Europe and its Christian vision is not the western vision. It is certainly not inferior, and some might think it superior; in any case, it is indubitably different. It represents a different interpretation of Christ's message.

Much the same conclusion is driven home in Joachim Gaehde's chapter, in which he traces the evolution of Christian art between approximately the third and the eighth century. It is a significant story, because the changes express so clearly the rise of a specifically Christian civilization, and one has only to compare the artistic forms at the beginning and at the end of the period to see the magnitude of the transformation. By AD 800 we are in a different spiritual world. But it is equally important to see that the evolution, though always within a Christian framework, was not uniform. It was to follow a different course in the Greek or Byzantine half of the Christian world, and in the Latin or western half, and the outcome was two different medieval styles which, we can safely say, reflected two different versions of the Christian faith.

The last thing we should wish to do, in this book, is to adjudicate between them, or to suggest which of the two is nearer to Christ's message. Personally, I suspect that each incorporates an element of the truth. But what seems to follow – and this is perhaps a first conclusion we should draw – is that we might do better to speak, not of a 'Christian world', but rather of a number of Christian worlds. Because it was addressed to all mankind, Christ's message has always been able to tolerate many different forms of expression. The rise of the African churches during the last century – churches stemming from those brought by Christian missionaries from the West, but rapidly assuming their own distinctively African character – is evidence of its ability to accommodate itself to different social and cultural environments. Christian Armenia, one of the most remarkable of all Christian communities, with a capacity for survival in the face of adversity only matched by that of Judaism, is almost a Christian world on its own. But even in the heartland of Christendom, in Christian Europe, diversity, or the coexistence of different Christian worlds, is one of its most striking features. The most obvious example is the differentiation between eastern, or Greek, and western, or Latin, Christianity. But the differences between north and south are scarcely less noteworthy than those between east and west. Gothic architecture, though it was carried south to Spain by French monastic orders, and later, as at Assisi, to Italy, is essentially an expression of the Christianity of north-western Europe, and as such is distinct from the Christian art of the Mediterranean lands. Here in the south, the bonds of the Roman heritage link east to west. Ravenna is the classical example of the persistence of Greek artistic forms west of the Adriatic; but even in far away Spain Christian art was visibly affected by Byzantine influences.

All this makes the study of the impact of Christianity more fascinating; it also makes it more complicated. An earlier generation of historians was apt to assume that, once a people had become Christian, Christianity became the dominant element in its civilization. Over the long run that is doubtless true. We can see, for example, how a Christian sexual ethic gradually pushed back and defeated a pagan sexual ethic in barbarian Europe between the 8th and 11th centuries, and we have seen the same thing happening in Africa during the present century. But it was always a long struggle and a hard-won victory. It is no secret in Africa today that many political leaders have one wife married according to traditional African custom and another married in accordance with Christian precept. It was little different in early medieval Europe. The great Frankish emperor, Charlemagne, was the offspring of what, in the eyes of the Christian church, was an 'irregular' marriage, though it was perfectly normal in Frankish customary law. Four centuries later, by which time the law of the church had been codified and expounded by the Bolognese monk Gratian, the Christian ethic was triumphant, and it would be hard after that time to find instances of a ruler succeeding to the throne who was not the offspring of a Christian marriage.

Sexual morality is, perhaps, the clearest – but not the only – example of the way Christian standards penetrated and shaped society. Another is the curbing of the blood-feud, and the control of warfare through the truce of God. Sometimes, no doubt, only lip-service was paid to Christian teaching; but the very fact that

Armenia was another 'Christian world' with a distinctive character of its own. The church of the Holy Cross at Aghtamar (now in Turkey) contains this typical relief of the Virgin and Child.

people found it necessary to pay lip-service is a measure of the church's success, and in fact most people paid more than lip-service. But success was purchased at a price. Because Christianity came from outside, its arrival meant everywhere a clash of cultures and of ethical standards, in a way that Hinduism, for example, did not – a clash between Christian ethics and the traditional ethical standards of the peoples who encountered it. This was true of ancient Rome and of the Germanic peoples of medieval Europe, and it is also true today of modern Africa. The result was a psychological tension which sometimes found bizarre outlets, seen perhaps most vividly in the lives and legends of desert fathers such as St Anthony. It also engendered a pervading sense of guilt and sin, springing from failure to live up to Christian standards, which has been the mark of many, though not all,

Christian communities. Baroque churches, with their glittering golden high altars, their marble columns and their lavish use of colour, celebrate the joy and wonder of Christianity and the sublimity of God's omnipotence. But elsewhere, particularly in Lutheran Europe but also in North America, emphasis has tended to fall on insufficiency and sinfulness, with consequences that have not always been desirable or healthy.

What this suggests is that the social impact of Christianity is, and always has been, equivocal. Its advance is indubitable. Its values, even when they have been debased and secularized, are embedded in Western civilization. Whether they are aware of it or not, the peoples of Europe and the Americas, of Australia and New Zealand live in a Christian environment, their education and their ways of thought shaped and coloured by Christian assumptions. Christianity has also been a potent influence in Africa, helping Africans to discover themselves as individuals in the face of God. But the Christian inheritance has certainly produced no uniformity of response among the peoples it has encountered. Greek and Russian Christianity have a different emphasis from Latin or western Christianity and provoked a different response. Here the testimony of Christian art is eloquent. One has only to compare the commanding figure of Christ Pantocrator, the Mighty Judge, in the 12th-century baptistery of the cathedral of Monreale with the tenderness and love so visible in the almost contemporary sculptures at Chartres to perceive the difference. But the Christian religion served as a bond between the peoples of eastern Europe in the same way as it did in the west, and the missionary activity of the Russian church in Siberia in the 17th century was (in the words of the British historian B. H. Sumner) 'a gigantic frontier expansion of Christianity', comparable with anything achieved by Catholic or Protestant missions.

If Orthodox and Catholic Christianity are expressions of different facets of a single faith, may not the same be said of Catholicism and Protestantism? The differences are not simply doctrinal or institutional. No one today would speak, as some German writers did a generation ago, of a specific 'Germanic Christianity'; but it would be hard to deny, with all due allowance for the obvious exceptions, such as Catholic Ireland, that Protestantism and Catholicism reflect, in the broadest of terms, the different reactions of different peoples, those of northern Europe and of Mediterranean Europe, to the Christian challenge, and it would be hard also to deny that those differences reflect to some considerable (though not easily measurable) extent differences in their pre-Christian past and in their subsequent historical development. In the course of its history, Christianity has come to terms, almost of

necessity, with the habits, beliefs and traditions of the peoples with whom it has had dealings. The course was set, as early as the close of the 6th century, by Pope Gregory the Great, who instructed the bishop of London not to suppress the sacrifice of oxen 'to the devils' but instead to convert and continue it 'to the praise of God'. Just as many of the church's festivals in Europe are pagan festivals thinly disguised under a Christian veneer, so many of its saints are successors of local pagan deities, whose attributes they not infrequently inherited.

What this means, from a Christian point of view, is that the struggle to create a Christian world is unending, that the reality is always less than perfect, that the dichotomy between an ideal Christian world and a world which is part Christian and part the heir of a pre-Christian morality still remains to be solved. This explains why Christianity remains in essence a missionary, evangelizing, proselytizing religion, as it has been ever since Paul set out to preach to the Gentiles. Since then its missionary activities have reached out, with varying degrees of success, to peoples far beyond the fold: to Africans, to Latin American Indians, to Chinese and Japanese. But its main field of action has always been at home, within Christian Europe, among people who formally are Christians but who live their lives on a different plane, reaching out also to those, like the new industrial proletariat of the 19th century, whom the advance of Christianity had largely bypassed. Ever since the 17th century this has been the first concern of the Christian churches of the West, Catholic and Protestant alike, just as it was the first concern of St Francis of Assisi in the 13th century when the spread of urbanization was creating similar problems.

This is another important fact in the history of Christianity. Ideally the Christian world has no limits, it encompasses the congregation of the faithful everywhere and at all times, past, present and future. But there is no doubt that historically its links have associated it pre-eminently with Europe. Where it has spread, notably in the Americas, it has been in the wake of European conquest and settlement. That is why the chapters that follow are concerned first and foremost with Christianity's impact upon European civilization, in both the eastern and western halves of the continent and in the areas of European settlement overseas. Some readers may think that the balance is slanted too heavily towards Europe. If so, it is not because of an inherent Eurocentrism, but because that is the direction in which the historical record points. It is in Europe that Christian influence has been most continuous, most pronounced and most visible.

When one considers that Christianity is in origin an Asian religion with its roots in Asia Minor, its close association with Europe is one of the paradoxes of history. It did not have to be so, and for many generations it was not so. In its earlier centuries Christianity was certainly as vigorous and active in Asia as in Europe, probably more so. The great churches of the east, Jacobites and Nestorians, carried Christ's message to Persia, across the mountains and deserts of central Asia to China, and through the Persian Gulf to the Malabar coast of India; the Coptic Christians of Egypt carried it far south to the Horn of Africa. By the end of the first Christian millennium the Nestorian church was probably more numerous and more influential than any other Christian church in the world. If this book were a history of Christianity, it would certainly be necessary to give as much weight to Asia as to Europe. The spread of Asian Christianity is a remarkable story; but its impact on culture and society, on the way people lived and thought, so far as we can judge, was surprisingly small. This is still another paradox. The Christian community on the coast of Malabar has apparently survived in unbroken succession, perhaps from apostolic times (if we can believe the legend that it was founded by St Thomas) to the present, but it would be hard to show that it has made any meaningful impact on its Hindu environment. Even the great Coptic church of Egypt, for all its proud traditions and its astounding capacity for survival, is surrounded by an Islamic world. And the Christian churches of further Asia have vanished almost without trace. Only in Europe and the lands settled by Europeans has Christianity shaped and coloured the values of the whole of society.

There are, no doubt, many reasons for the relative failure of Christianity to impose its image outside Europe. The most important, probably, is that the Asian churches, though tolerated and sometimes even encouraged, were never given official status as established religions of state. They lacked, in short, the support of the civil power, which Christianity in Europe had possessed since the time of Constantine, and had to compete on an equal footing with other religions. In the capital city of China in the 8th century, for example, there were 91 Buddhist temples, 16 Taoist places of worship, 4 Zoroastrian temples and 2 Christian churches. Christ's message might, and did, reach a substantial minority; but what chance had Christianity, in such circumstances, of influencing and changing social and cultural values? Furthermore, it is impossible to overlook the difficulties and setbacks the Christian churches seem to encounter whenever they are confronted by the other great world religions. These are not easy to explain, but they are more fundamental. If we examine Christianity's triumphs, it seems that they have occurred where it has come into

The Irish church was a lonely outpost of Christianity, tenuously connected with Coptic monasticism. It survives today in a few splendid manuscripts and in its Celtic crosses, large stone monuments with encircled crosses and wealth of spiral and interlace ornament.

contact with animistic cults, with tribal deities, sacred trees, spells, curses, spirits. Here its success can be explained by the superior appeal of a universal creed with a universal message, offering spiritual outlets and spiritual consolations lacking in superstitious polytheism. This was the case in barbarian Europe, later in Spanish America, later still in Africa. In its confrontations with great world religions, on the other hand, with Buddhism and Hinduism, with Islam and with the ethical system of Confucianism, Christianity has made little headway. There is an active Christian community in Japan; but Japan is best regarded as the exception that proves the rule, for Japanese Shintoism, in essence an animistic religion of ancestor worship, was never much of a challenge, either to Buddhism or to Christianity. Elsewhere its successes have been sporadic, localized, and with little discernible influence over society as a whole. There may have been Christian impulses of some sort intermingled in the great T'ai-p'ing rebellion in 19th-century China; but, if so, they were soon lost to sight.

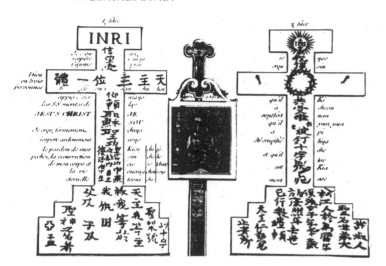

Christianity has always been marked by a missionary spirit. In each continent, however, it assimilated something of the cultures it was trying to convert.

China (left): an 18th-century Jesuit diagram showing both sides of a cross inscribed in Chinese characters, and their French translations.

Japan (right): Christ and the cross, made by a Japanese convert shortly before the suppression of Christianity there in 1614.

India (below): the miraculous cross of St Thomas, the Apostle of India, from a 17th-century Dutch work.

Mexico: a 17th-century Indian cross carved with the face of Christ, the crown of thorns and the instruments of the Passion.

Crux miraculosa S. Thomæ Apostoli Meliaporæ in India.

Ethiopia: a processional cross of the 17th century, remote from any European prototype.

Congo: a 19th-century crucifix in the African tradition with two praying figures on the arms.

The queen-empress presents a Bible to one of her distant subjects, a perfect image of Victorian England's confidence in its mission to Christianize the earth. By contrast, Christianity today is enlisted to justify liberation and self-determination in the Third World (below).

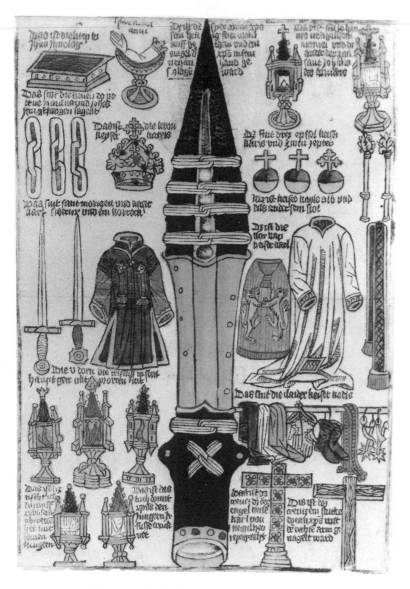

The history of the Holy Roman Empire demonstrates how western states have sought to underline their authority by religious sanctions. This woodcut of its insignia dates from the late 15th century; besides crowns, robes, orbs, etc., it includes the Holy Lance and a number of other venerated relics.

What all this implies is a shrinkage of the Christian world. Of course, its losses in Asia have been compensated for by gains in Africa and America. Nevertheless, ever since it was shut in and thrown back upon itself by the great advance of Islam in the 8th century, it has been, in effect, a European religion. Even its missionary activities have been conducted almost exclusively by Europeans or North Americans, inculcating European standards, European dress, the methods and content of European education, sometimes with ludicrous results, as when children in mission schools in the Congo learned Belgian history and Nigerian children lisped the dates of the kings of England, or little girls in Uganda were drilled in gymsmocks and black stockings. This has, perhaps, nothing to do with Christianity as such, in absolute terms, but it has certainly something to do with the association

between Christianity and Europe. It brings us to the final question – and, in the perspective of the present-day world, a world in which the relations between the different continents, peoples and races, are visibly in a state of rapid flux, it is indisputably an important question.

For historical reasons, which I have tried very briefly to indicate, Christianity has been closely associated, for upward of a thousand years, with Europe and with European society and European civilization. What we have to ask ourselves, at the end of the account, is whether its close, historically conditioned association with Europe, particularly with western Europe, has been an advantage or a disadvantage to the Christian religion? Has it not, perhaps, narrowed its compass, linked it too closely with one civilization at the expense of others? Is the identification of Christian values with Western values, which is so frequently made today, a valid equation? It must be admitted, straight away, that these are questions to which no positive answer can be given, if only because the interplay over the centuries between Christianity and the Western peoples has been so continuous that it is impossible to say with assurance which, at any given time, has been the recipient and which the donor. The extent of Christian influence over Western society and culture emerges in all clarity from this book; no one would question it. But what we have now to ask ourselves is whether it is not also possible that Western culture and Western values influenced the Christian churches, wherever they came into contact with them. What the historical record seems to show is a two-way process; and what we have to ask is whether, in the longer run – which is, after all, the perspective of the Christian churches – Christianity has gained more than it has lost.

These are questions about which we can never expect agreement, because there are too many imponderables; but there are certain facts which no one seriously considering the place of Christianity in the world today can afford to ignore. The foremost, unhappily, is that many people in the so-called Third World – indeed, an overwhelming majority – regard Christianity as little more than the ideological superstructure of Western civilization, a spurious religious cover for the aggresive, conquering force of Western capitalism, and a pretext for European or North American dominance. This may be a partisan view, and it is certainly unfair to some, though by no means all, of the missionaries who propagated the Christian faith in Africa and elsewhere. But it is a fact it would be foolish to ignore, and it springs from the association of Christian civilization with Western civilization. For people outside or on the fringe, Christianity is a Western religion and tainted with what, in their eyes, are the faults and sins of the

West. It is a means, subtle and indirect, perhaps, but no less insidious for that, of propagating Western values – the values, for example, of individualism, dynamism, self-advancement and liberalism – among peoples with different, and not necessarily inferior, ethical codes.

In a historical context this reaction is not surprising. For over a thousand years the leadership of Christianity has been in European hands – all the popes since the year AD 752 have been Europeans – and they would have been more than human if they had not, almost without exception, interpreted their Christian duties in terms of their inherited culture. It was not necessary, however. The Jesuit missionaries to China in the 17th century, far from attempting to impose a European pattern of Christianity, did all they could to assimilate Christianity to Chinese patterns of civilization. They were careful to dress in the robes of Chinese mandarins, and their object was to show that Christian doctrine and Confucianism were compatible and supplemented each other. Unfortunately, their efforts, after some initial success, were brought to nothing, not by Chinese hostility, but by the opposition of Christians in Europe. Their missionary example does, however, show that the equation between Christianity and Europe and the identification of Christian with European values is no more than incidental. We should beware of regarding it as part of the divine dispensation, or of supposing that it will continue in perpetuity. It was, as I have indicated, a historical accident, and accidents can, and no doubt will, be repaired.

In Europe itself the association between Christian values and Western values was also the result of a long and to some degree fortuitous chain of historical circumstances. Primitive Christianity, perhaps for its first thousand years, was an otherworldly religion, always aware that the kingdom of God is not, and never can be, of this world, and looking forward to the imminent advent of the Second Coming and the Last Judgment. This spiritual otherworldliness remained a characteristic of the Greek and later of the Russian church; it is their great contribution to the Christian heritage, as Sir Steven Runciman shows in a later chapter of this book. In the west, the course of development was different – though never, of course, completely so. It led, by steps that historians have fairly convincingly traced, from withdrawal from the world to the conquest of the world, and to the attempt – vain, perhaps, but irresistible – to shape the world in accordance with what it believed to be God's design.

The historian can put his finger almost exactly on the moment when this great transformation occurred. It was in the year 1049, when the influence of the new Europe rising north of the Alps first made its impact felt, and almost immediately – only five years later –

The image of the Christian warrior defeating the forces of unbelief has a long history, and has perhaps done Christianity more harm than good. In this 16th-century woodcut the Franks under Clovis battle with the heathen Alemanni (shown anachronistically fighting under the double-headed eagle). Clovis had sworn to become a Christian if victorious. At the top, his wife, already converted, leads him away from pagan idols towards a crucifix while an angel presents a banner bearing the fleur-de-lis.

came the breach, which proved to be a permanent breach, between western and eastern Christianity. Its causes, narrowly defined, were dogmatic and liturgical; but in reality it expressed two different visions of Christianity and of Christ's message. After 1054 the western church became a militant church, the outward expression of which was the First Crusade in 1099. It was, from a historical point of view, the triumphal entry of the warrior spirit of northern Germanic Europe into Christianity, and it has left its mark ever since. Not for nothing was St Michael, the angel who drove Satan from heaven, one of the most popular saints of the 11th century. His shrines range from Mont St Michel in Brittany to S. Michele di Monte Gargano in Italy, and characteristically he is depicted everywhere as a fighting warrior. But he was only one of the warrior saints popular at the time, sharing priority with St George and St Maurice. The result was that, from that moment, Christianity was identified, in the eyes of non-Christians, with the thrusting, dynamic expansion of Western civilization, usually to its detriment.

In the centuries that followed, the consequences were compounded. The fact that the Spanish pillage of Mexico and Peru was carried out under the banner of Christianity did not help its reputation, as the famous Dominican missionary Las Casas was well aware. The much discussed 'Protestant ethic', as it took shape in the 17th century, seemed to provide a justification for European exploitation of backward peoples. These are part of the history of Christianity and of its permeation by impulses which are, at best, only partly Christian. They lead to the final question, which this book makes no attempt to answer directly. The existence of a 'Christian world' is beyond doubt. With all its differences – and they are more fundamental than is often assumed – it is clearly distinct from the world of

Islam, or from the Hindu or Chinese or Japanese worlds. But can Christians in the world today afford to identify themselves, as they have too easily done in the past, with the West and with Western values? This may have been the tendency in earlier times, for historical reasons which have been briefly indicated; and it may still be the easiest way out. But is the historical record any guide to the future? Can the vision of man which Christianity conveys be confined within the Eurocentric dimensions of traditional Christianity? The Western world is a 'Christian world' of sorts, without doubt; but does it reflect more than a stunted and defective vision of the Christian message? There are, as we have seen, other versions of Christianity, other responses with (I would venture to think) a deeper spiritual content. Is it not time, as the apocalypse draws nigh, to give them greater attention? The time is short, and the need is great.

For Christians at least – perhaps for all of us – this is one of the great overriding questions of our day. No one is going to deny that Christianity has contributed to the formation of Western civilization, though it is possible to debate how far its consequences have been beneficial or detrimental. But the question today is whether that is enough. Rather, what we have to ask is whether it can transcend its European background and assert its universal message, without fear or favour to any people, race or colour. Is it to constitute one of the competing 'worlds', which will turn the real world in which we are all condemned to live into a holocaust of chaos and dissension, or is it to provide a message of hope and conciliation for the future? This book does not attempt to answer this question – can anyone honestly pretend to answer it? But it will, I hope, provide some of the evidence upon which any answer must depend.

St Michael overcoming Satan: the archetypical warrior saint. From a printer's tailpiece, Paris, c. 1640.

THE ANCIENT WORLD

DURING THE THREE CENTURIES between the death of Jesus and the official recognition of the church by Constantine, Christianity acquired all the main elements that characterize it today. Our knowledge of this crucial period is patchy, with some parts known in considerable detail, others barely guessed at. After 330, on the other hand, both written and material evidence is plentiful and the historian's account becomes relatively assured.

It was the heroic age of Christianity. Beginning as a series of cells within the Jewish communities of the Diaspora, the church developed into an organization that eventually paralleled that of the state itself. Its structure, with a hierarchy of officers from deacon to archbishop attached to specific territories, did to some extent follow that of the Roman state. As so often in history, sporadic persecution had the opposite effect from the one intended and acted only as a spur and an inspiration. 'The blood of the martyrs', Tertullian wrote truly, 'was the seed of the church.' Naturally legends accumulated round these early struggles. But the sheer administrative achievement of the church is not in doubt. It is another of those facts which are so familiar to us that they have ceased to be amazing. From St Paul onwards, the church was blessed with organizers of genius, men who could not only inspire and motivate their communities but also provide the machinery for them to continue.

Equally vital, and much more fully documented, is the development of Christian doctrine. This evolved through a sequence of controversies and compromises. Confronted with the demands of practical life on the one hand and the probing analysis of Greek philosophy on the other, questions that had not occurred to the first Christians had to be solved. Through the administrative structure, councils were held which could officially endorse or condemn the various solutions, and their decisions, incorporated into an evolving liturgy, became a sophisticated system of beliefs (dogma) that could hold its own against any attacks. As later chapters will show, virtually every Christian movement from now on, including many heresies, could appeal for support to the opinions first enunciated by these thinkers, the so called 'Fathers of the Church'. How far these developments were intended or foreseen by the founder of Christianity is not a question that the historian can answer.

The intellectual life of the church at this time is still vivid and exciting. Much less clear is the social life of ordinary Christians. The pastoral letters of churchmen, reports by the secular authorities, incidental details in the stories of saints – all these can tell us something. But perhaps we come closest to them in the works of art and material objects that have survived. Here we can trace the creation of a new iconography by Christians seeking to express their faith in visual terms, and drawing for that purpose upon the imagery available to them from the classical culture within which they lived their lives.

As a state religion
Christianity could realize opportunities on a scale hardly contemplated before (the programme of church building under Constantine is only one obvious indication). It also faced challenges to which it had not been exposed in its days of persecution. While the character of its hierarchy remained broadly constant, that of its lay community was inevitably transformed. Where membership of the church had previously been an act of spiritual dedication attended with danger or even death, it was now the road to worldly success. And as the church as an institution became 'official' so did its art. A work such as this mosaic in S. Apollinare in Classe at Ravenna (*opposite*) is as much a political as a religious monument. The Emperor Constantius IV is granting privileges to the church of Ravenna. He and Bishop Reparatus are both haloed, to indicate superior status. On the left stands Constantius's brother Tiberius, while the scroll is received by a priest, his hand draped in token of respect. (1)

Underground Christianity

The earliest works made by Christians are such pictures as these painted on the walls and ceilings of catacombs, burial places outside the walls of Rome. Here the images that were to constitute Christian art find their beginning.

Themes of redemption, drawn from both Old and New Testaments, figure prominently in the catacomb paintings, often combined with conventional classical motifs. *Left:* a view down one of the passages in the Catacomb of the Jordani. On the wall in the foreground are Daniel between lions and Abraham sacrificing the ram. *Below:* baptismal scene from the Catacomb of S. Callisto. Baptism was established as one of the essential sacraments; originally it meant total immersion. (2, 3)

The three youths in the fiery furnace is one of the favourite themes of catacomb painting (*left*), along with Noah and Daniel. All three themes symbolize redemption and are grouped together in the liturgy – here one sees art and liturgy evolving together. (4)

Bread and fish are an allusion to the miracle performed by Christ, with other meanings superimposed – the Eucharist, the bread of life, the fish as an acronym of 'Jesus Christ Son of God Saviour' in Greek. (6)

The sacrifice of Isaac, the loving father prepared to sacrifice his son, prefigured the sacrifice of Christ for man's redemption. *Above:* from the Catacomb of Via Latina. (7)

The first attitude of prayer among Christians was standing with arms raised – the classical pose known as orant. One of the best-known instances is that called the 'Donna Velata' – from the cloth over her head – in the Catacomb of St Priscilla, Rome. (5)

The heavenly banquet is another image with multiple layers of meaning. As a funerary rite it has parallels in pre-Christian religion; as the 'love feast' of the Early Christians it straight-forwardly represents a real scene; as the Eucharist it symbolizes eating the body and blood of Christ. (8)

From hermit to monk

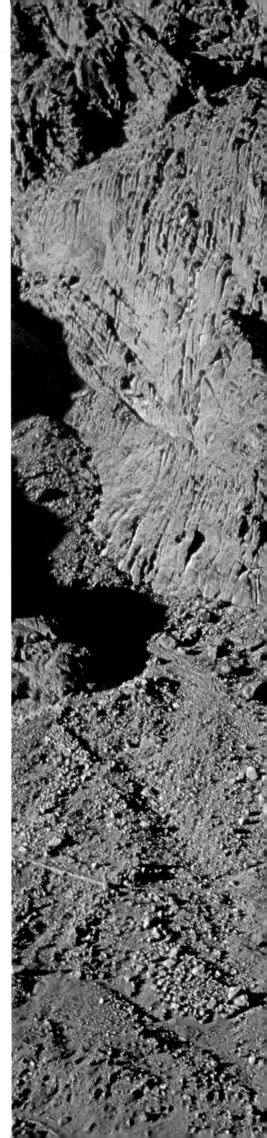

The quest for perfection led many ascetics to a life of
fasting and prayer in the desert. *Above:* 15th-century Tuscan
view of the desert fathers, the *Thebaide*. *Below:* landscape in
Cappadocia, formerly inhabited by monks living in caves, a
late survival of the same tradition. This solitary ideal soon
led to loosely organized 'families' and then to a more formal
monastic structure. *Opposite:* the monastery of St Catherine
in Sinai, beside its oasis. Though given a more monumental
look by its 19th-century library building, it is still essentially
a fortified village. (9–11)

A continuity of images

It was natural that Christian artists should use the visual language that they already knew from Roman art. But from this starting-point they evolved a new and highly expressive language of their own.

Disparate symbols may rub shoulders on late classical sarcophagi, and it can even be doubtful whether the occupant is Christian or pagan. In this instance (*left*): Jonah cast up by the whale, a prefiguration of Christ rising from the dead; an orant figure, prayer; and a seated philosopher, a symbol of wisdom taken over from Roman funerary art. (12)

The lamb of God stands for sacrifice; behind it the Chi-Rho and the cross; perched on an arm of the cross, the dove of peace bringing a wreath of victory. Here is a symbolic language that speaks more succinctly than words. (14)

Peacocks were symbols of eternity because their flesh was supposed to be incorruptible; the vine, too, occurs on Roman tombs and mausolea; but the Chi-Rho sign (the first letters of Christ's name), incorporating the cross, stamp this relief plaque as Christian. (13)

Baptism – itself a symbol – acquired a richly symbolic decoration. Here, at Kelibia in North Africa, the deeper levels harbour the Chi-Rho, the letters alpha and omega, and (doubly appropriate beneath the water of life) the Christian fish. (15)

Christ as emperor sits enthroned in the New Jerusalem; beneath him the apostles, with Peter and Paul crowned by personifications of the churches of the Jews and the Gentiles. In the sky above hover the animals of the evangelists beside a jewelled cross. The 5th-century mosaic in the apse of S. Pudenziana in Rome is the end-product of a long process of iconographic evolution, of which three of the stages are represented by the details at the top of the page. *Left:* Christ riding the chariot of Sol, the sun-god, from the cemetery below St Peter's, Rome. *Centre:* head of Christ from Hinton St Mary, Dorset, the centrepiece of a floor mosaic which includes Bellerephon slaying the Chimaera. *Right:* Christ as the Good Shepherd, from the mausoleum of Galla Placidia, Ravenna. (16–19)

The triumphant Gospel

After the official endorsement of Christianity by Constantine, religious art virtually took over from civic art. But the change from imperial to Christian values dictated a change in style away from naturalism and towards a more schematic and emotive approach.

A picture of world history now took shape that was to remain the norm until the end of the Middle Ages. *Left:* mosaic in S. Maria Maggiore, Rome. At the top Joseph makes his offering at the Temple, and the angel explains Mary's pregnancy to him; next, Christ is recognized by a pagan ruler during the flight into Egypt; at the bottom the three Magi stand before Herod. (20)

Pharaoh's daughter, who saved Moses, is represented as a Roman empress with jewel box on one of the nave panels of the 5th-century mosaics of S. Maria Maggiore. (21)

In manuscripts a similar conversion of the classical style was taking place. *Below:* Christ's entry into Jerusalem, from the Rossano Gospels. The four prophets underneath draw attention to texts which foretell or comment on the event. (23)

Rebecca gives Eliezer water to drink – a miniature from the Vienna Genesis, a manuscript full of classical echoes. (22)

40

Another world of pure spirituality takes the place of the natural world in some of the Ravenna mosaics. In the apse of S. Apollinare in Classe (*above*) the transfiguration is represented in purely symbolic terms as a jewelled cross floating in the sky. The three apostles who were present have become three lambs in a schematic landscape. Only St Apollinaris himself, hands raised in the orant position, keeps contact with the world of appearances. (24)

At Mount Sinai Christ of the transfiguration (*right*) is given human form but is placed in an abstract context that expresses the timelessness of the event. (25)

The Roman heritage

Until the 5th century a citizen of Rome or Constantinople would not have seen his adoption of Christianity as a break with the past. The flying angels of a child's sarcophagus (*above*) are the 'victories' of pagan iconography. The tomb of Christ, in an ivory of about 400 (*below*), is a pagan mausoleum, and the three Marys typical Roman matrons. Even Christ, rising from the dead to grasp his Father's hand, might be a hero in Vergil. (26, 27)

When Rome fell, Ravenna, in marshland near the Adriatic coast, became the seat of the emperor, and after a period of occupation by the Ostrogoths under Theodoric was again reconquered by Justinian. The mausoleum of Galla Placidia (*left*) belongs to the first of these periods. The far lunette shows St Lawrence and a bookcase containing the Gospels. In Theodoric's church of S. Apollinare Nuovo (*below*) the Virgin and Child flanked by angels remain from the original decoration but the procession of Virgins and the three Magi belong to the alterations of the Justinian period. (28, 29)

From Constantinople came the inspiration, the design, the artists and probably many of the materials of Justinian's church of S. Vitale at Ravenna. Octagonal in plan, surrounded by an ambulatory glimpsed through double arcades (*right*), it culminates in a richly decorated presbytery whose mosaics expound the theme of the Eucharist. This lunette (*above*) shows the sacrifices of Abel and Melchisedek. (31, 32)

Justinian removed the Ostrogothic court portraits that formerly stood between the columns of the 'Palatium' on the nave wall of S. Apollinare Nuovo (*left*), replacing them by curtains (one hand alone survives, third column from the left). The apostles above were left intact. (30)

43

Two baptisteries at Ravenna reflect an important schism in the early church between orthodox and Arians. The dispute concerned the nature of Christ, the orthodox party maintaining that he was 'of the same substance as the Father', i.e. divine, the Arians believing him to be part of the created order and therefore inferior to the Father. In the dome of the Orthodox Baptistery (*above*), the baptism of Christ occupies the centre, the apostles bearing crowns the next circle and beyond these a series of thrones and altars displaying the Gospels. When the Arian Ostrogoths took over Ravenna, Theodoric built another baptistery (*right*). The central medallion is similar to the earlier work but the apostles now converge on a throne and the ring of thrones and altars is omitted. (33, 34)

I
Christianity in the Roman Empire

WILLIAM H.C. FREND

T HE RELIGIOUS REVOLUTION that took place in the Mediterranean world in Constantine's reign (306–37) had been long in preparation. Christianity was not only a religion but a social and cultural movement, and while the values of classical civilization retained their vigour it made little progress. Down to the end of the 2nd century, it was an urban cult established in the environment of the Jewish Dispersion and mirroring many of the attitudes of the latter towards pagan society. Only as that century drew to a close could its adherents make good their claim to be a 'third race', independent of both Judaism and paganism. It was another century before it gained an appreciable following in the countryside and began to spread beyond the borders of the empire. When, however, late in 302, Diocletian and his colleagues decided that they had to face the issue of whether the traditional gods of Rome or the Christian God were to be recognized as guardian of the Roman Empire, and committed themselves to a policy of persecution, they failed to break the Christians. Constantine drew his own conclusions from that failure, and within a dozen years, between 313 and 325, brought about the transition from a pagan to a Christian empire whose effects remain with us today. This chapter traces the stages in that transition and looks forward into the period when Christianity absorbed much of the pagan–classical heritage, thus laying the foundations on which the civilizations of the west and also of the Slavonic world have been built.

Christianity within Judaism

We begin with Judaism, for Christianity began in Palestine as a renewal movement within rural Judaism. The outlook of the Early Christians had much in common with that of their contemporaries, the Covenanters of Qumran, but, in contrast to the men of Qumran, the Christians were from the outset missionaries. They were not content to await the coming deliverance 'in the wilderness', and were determined to proclaim their message in Jerusalem and thence to the remainder of the Jewish community, however scattered.

The Jews whom the first Christian missionaries sought to persuade were by no means a uniform

community. There was in Israel the unresolved tension between the prophetic and the priestly traditions, which would re-emerge in Christianity. More important, even, were the cultural differences between the Jews of Palestine and those who either had remained in fairly prosperous circumstances in Babylonia or who had taken advantage of the opening up of the eastern Mediterranean world, through the conquests of Alexander the Great, to trade and colonize in the successor-states of Alexander's empire. All the way from the Crimea to Volubilis in Morocco, the Jews have left their mark. These communities provided a vehicle for the spread of Christianity.

In these Dispersion communities the majority of the Jews adopted Greek, for daily life and for their Scriptures. Despite contact with their Gentile neighbours, they remained separate. The Jews in the Dispersion had their own synagogues, schools, courts of law and cemeteries, and refused to participate in any act that they considered idolatrous. Near the end of the 1st century AD, the Jewish historian Josephus explained to his pagan opponents 'that one ought not to wonder at us if we are more courageous in dying than other men are'. The Christian martyr tradition was the heir to that of Judaism.

Josephus had not spoken lightly. Both in Palestine and in the Dispersion, relations between Jew and Greek at the time of Christ were bad. Communal hatreds were never far below the surface. The pogrom of Jews in Alexandria in AD 38 was only the worst example. Jewish relations with Rome were originally rather better. During most of the 1st century BC, Rome had needed the good will of the Jews in Asia Minor to counterbalance the grumbling hostility of the Greek cities there. But two developments changed this situation. First, the enthusiasm with which the Greeks throughout the eastern Mediterranean greeted the institution of the cult of the emperor and the rule of Augustus (30 BC–AD 14) began the transformation of Roman hegemony into a Greco-Roman world. In this new-found harmony between the Greeks and their Roman masters, the latter no longer needed the Jews as allies; and so more fundamental religious and cultural differences surfaced. Second, in Palestine, Rome failed to find a satisfactory successor to Herod, who had ruled as a cruel but efficient client-king from 37 BC to 4 BC. In AD 6, Augustus imposed direct rule on the Jewish territories through a Roman Procurator. An order immediately afterwards, that the Jews should pay tribute, provoked a ferocious rebellion led by Galilean nationalists. No tribute, they claimed, was to be paid to any but God. The revolt was crushed with equal ferocity. One of those who may have witnessed both the uprising and its suppression was a boy of 12 or 13, Jesus of Nazareth.

The New Testament, however, indicates that in no sense was Jesus's teaching directed against the Romans. Relations between individual members of the forces of occupation and Jews could still be good. Indeed, the Gospels stress Jesus's rejection of the temptation either to seize earthly messianic power, or to aspire to be king of a restored Israel. The reversal of values that he preached, and the end of the age that he proclaimed as imminent, posed no threat to the Romans in Palestine. His enemies were among the religious and political leaders of his own people. Both feared that popular acceptance of Jesus as 'the prophet' would undermine their own positions. Self-preservation and fear of Roman power provided the incentives for the accusation that Jesus was making a treasonable claim to be 'king of the Jews', and to engineer his death at the hands of the Roman governor, Pontius Pilate, probably in April of AD 30.

For the authorities, Jesus's burial in Joseph of Arimathea's rock-cut tomb marked the end of the story. Eighty years later, the historian Tacitus (*c.* AD 115) explained to his readers that 'one of our procurators, Pontius Pilate,' had had Jesus executed. However, the plans of the high-priesthood and of the Roman authorities miscarried. Quite apart from the memory of Jesus's life and works that inspired the writing of the Gospels, *c.* AD 70–90, the belief that Jesus really had risen from the dead, supported by his appearances in Galilee, revived the disciples' faith in him. They returned to Jerusalem and confronted the high-priests with the news that Jesus was indeed the Messiah, of David's line, but greater than David. A final chance for repentance was being offered before the end of the age and Jesus's return, this time as Judge.

Automatically, the disciples became missionaries, and in so doing transformed their master's ministry. Jesus had concentrated on the people of rural Galilee and Jerusalem, but had left the Greek-speaking towns of Palestine alone. Almost at once, the Greek synagogues in Jerusalem were attracted to the disciples' message, and Jesus was being preached as far afield as Damascus and Antioch. The conversion of Barnabas, a Levite from Cyprus, and Paul, a Pharisee from Tarsus, gave the movement further impetus towards converting the Jews of the Dispersion. The baptism of the

centurion, Cornelius, showed that the new sect would have a place for Gentiles. By AD 45 the foundations of the Christian mission and the future composition of the church had been laid.

The next thirteen years, 45–58, were decisive in the history of Christianity. Paul provided the church with drive and vision fuelled by a sense of urgency, derived from his conviction that the Last Days and the return of Jesus as Messiah were approaching. With Barnabas, he opened up horizons unimaginable to the disciples, now led by Jesus's brother James at Jerusalem. The message he and Barnabas preached during the first great missionary journey of 46–48, to Cyprus and thence through the southern provinces of Asia Minor, was what very many Jews and Gentiles who worshipped in synagogues wanted to hear. On their return from Asia Minor in 48, Paul and Barnabas confronted an assembly of the brethren at Jerusalem, and convinced them that Christianity must be open at least to the outer circle of synagogue worshippers, the uncircumcised God-fearers who were so prominent in the life of the synagogues in Asia Minor. James's pronouncement that such Christians need keep only the requirements of the Noachian covenant enabled Christianity to emerge from the status of a reform movement within Judaism to that of a potential world religion.

In the next decade, Paul accomplished a revolution in the Dispersion in the eastern Mediterranean. His proclamation that, through Jesus Christ, God had revealed the mystery of salvation which had been hid from previous ages brought an immediate response from his hearers. Paul preached to audiences who read their Septuagint, were aware of the recent prophetic upsurge inspired by John the Baptist in Palestine and lived the life of the synagogue. For such Gentile God-fearers his message spelled freedom. 'We are kings', was the reaction of his Corinthian converts. It was not, however, a message for the masses. Paul, himself a Roman citizen, associated easily with the provincial upper classes. He chose the provincial capitals Corinth and Ephesus as his missionary bases. He established his communities in households, i.e. well-to-do families with their slaves, and some of his closest supporters were those who, like Prisca and Aquila, travelled widely and probably possessed property in Rome as well as Ephesus. It was their association with Christianity that divided the Dispersion communities, and Paul's establishment of Christian synagogues, with their ministries staffed by permanent officers (presbyters and deacons), made schism permanent. The anger aroused among the Jews who remained loyal to Judaism is vividly demonstrated by the speech of the advocate Tertullus, when, in 58, Paul's enemies had at last brought him to book in Jerusalem (Acts

XXIV:1–6). He escaped their clutches by exercising his right to appeal to Caesar, made his long epic voyage to Rome and spent the last two years of his recorded existence (60–62) preaching and making converts including some from among the imperial freedmen in the city.

Up to this point relations with the authorities had been good; Paul's quarrel with his fellow Jews meant nothing to them, while his social and political ideas were conservative. 'The powers that be' were of God: slaves were to obey their masters, the approaching end of the age did not mean the immediate end of work. Everyone must remain in the same state to which they were called. There was no appeal to the latent discontent of the native rural populations of the countryside. Except for the riot of Ephesus, the Roman authorities had no cause to complain. Throughout Acts, Luke consistently portrays them as well disposed towards Paul and his companions.

Two unconnected events were to change this, and to involve the Christians in an opposition to the empire that would last until Constantine's conversion. The first was accidental, resulting from the great fire in Rome on 19 July 64. The second, the capture of Jerusalem by Titus in August 70, was also only indirectly the concern of the Christians. For two years – up until the spring of 62 at least – Paul had been free to preach the Gospel. Then on 19 July 64 a conflagration devastated two entire quarters of Rome. Suspicion fell on the Emperor Nero himself, suspected of wanting to rid the city of some slum areas in order to extend his palace. The obvious answer was to find a scapegoat. To put an end to the rumours, the historian Tacitus tells us, 'Nero fastened the guilt and inflicted the most exquisite tortures on a class hated for their abominations, called Christians by the populace.' Henceforth, the Christians had precedent against them; they were on the wrong side of the law.

The fall of Jerusalem had even more serious consequences. Nero's persecution had not extended either to the Jews of the Dispersion or to Palestine. In 65, however, Rome sent out a governor who had even less than normal sympathy for the Jews. Next year the Jews of Palestine rose in revolt. While the heroic defence of Jerusalem and Masada passed into Jewish folklore, the Christians stood aside. For this they received no thanks from either the victors or the vanquished. Their position in Palestine was ruined. Henceforward, except for expansion north-eastward to Aramaic-speaking Edessa, Christianity became a 'western' religion with Greek as its main language. The Christians became an urban sect. They found themselves out on a limb, repudiated by the Jews and themselves rejecting the worship of the gods of their cities. They could be

Gnostic engraved gem with a serpent and the mysterious name Chnoubis. Gnostic doctrine is still obscure, but the gem was no doubt an amulet against evil powers.

regarded as 'atheists' and, as the first century drew to a close, suspected also for black magic and noxious rites. Their existence was illegal.

In the next generation, between 100 and 135, missionary zeal seems to have flagged. The church settled down as a sort of federation of communities with a resident ministry of bishops, presbyters (or presbyter-bishops) and deacons, able to communicate with each other over considerable distances and intent on keeping pure the tradition received from their apostolic predecessors. They were already potentially formidable as an organization but were of relatively little concern to the authorities. There survive only three imperial rescripts (letters) in the whole of the 2nd century that apply to Christians. In 113, in reply to questions by his special commissioner in Bithynia, Pliny, the Emperor Trajan affirmed the illegality of Christianity, but conceded that Christians 'should not be sought out', and, if they recanted, they should be pardoned. A decade later, his successor Hadrian allowed Christians virtual freedom from denunciation, the accuser having to prove that his victim had 'offended against the laws'. If he failed, the charge would rebound on him. For nearly half a century the ordinary Christian enjoyed a real if legally precarious peace.

During the 2nd century the membership of the church was changing, from followers exclusively in the Dispersion to adherents gained directly from paganism, such as Justin Martyr (c. 100–65), and even from the literate Gentile population of the eastern Mediterranean. Greeks became increasingly attracted to Christianity. This development contributed to the first major effort to harmonize the Christian message contained in the New Testament with current Platonist-dominated philosophy.

In the last twenty years a great deal has become

known about the Gnostic movement, following the discovery in 1945 of a library of fifty-two Gnostic texts in a Christian cemetery at Nag Hammadi near Luxor. The documents reveal a joyous, creative religion, self-consciously Christian, whose leaders sought to integrate all available religious experience, from whatever source, into a quest of self-discovery through Christ. Gnosticism loosed Christianity from its historical links with Judaism, dissolved the unity between the Old and New Testaments and denied the historical character of Jesus's earthly ministry. Scriptural revelation had neither more nor less validity than the books of Plato or Homer. Mission, let alone challenge to the Greco-Roman world, was far from the thoughts of the Gnostics. The world was to escape from, not to convert and reform.

The scapegoats

Their opponents in the 170s, now termed 'the Great Church', were moving along radically different paths. If the Gnostics were sects, the orthodox were well organized communities ruled by clergy. As such they were becoming feared by the rest of the provincials. Since the middle of the century the Christian church had been seen increasingly as an enemy of Greco-Roman society. Christians had replaced Jews as the scapegoats for natural disaster. By refusing to worship the Roman and territorial gods, Christians were regarded as responsible for every manner of ill. In addition, they were said to be guilty of evil practices, and were charged with being 'atheists'. Thus, to quote the North African writer, Tertullian (*c.* 197): 'If the Tiber reaches the walls, if the Nile does not rise to the fields, if the sky does not move or the earth does, if there is famine, if there is plague, the cry is at once "Christians to the lion."'

In the reign of Marcus Aurelius (161–80) popular opinion boiled over against the Christians. In Smyrna, Polycarp was martyred by burning, 'the Jews who were extremely zealous, as is their custom,' assisting the pagan mob. In 177 there was a terrible incident at Lyons, where Christians, mainly immigrant merchants from Asia Minor, were condemned to death in the amphitheatre. Eventually, forty-eight perished, including the heroic martyr, the slave Blandina, who emerged as their natural leader. The account of their sufferings in the form of a letter sent by a survivor and preserved by the church historian Eusebius is interesting. It shows not only the intense conviction among the confessors that their sufferings would hasten the Last Times, but also the outlook of ordinary Gallic provincials towards what they regarded as a new and outlandish sect; and, on the other hand, it shows the contempt that the 'wild and barbarous' Gauls aroused

among the articulate Christian colony. After describing how, from top to bottom of society, all were glad to see the victims done to death and their bones left unburied, the writer continued: 'Others again, of a more forebearing nature and seeming to extend to them a measure of fellow-feeling, uttered many reproaches, saying, "Where is their god?", and "What profit has their religion brought them that they have preferred it to their own life?"' The mutual incomprehension was total.

The methods of Christian proselytizers are described by Celsus in *c.* 178, writing probably in Syria:

We see them in our homes, wool dressers, cobblers, and fullers, the most uneducated and common individuals not daring to say a word in the presence of their masters who are older and wiser, but when they get hold of the children in private and silly women with them, they are wonderfully eloquent, to the effect that the children must not listen to their father but believe them and be taught by them. (Origen, *Contra Celsum* III: 55)

Progress, therefore, was being made largely among the artisan class, but whoever he may have been, the Christian missionary was quite indifferent to the rules and customs of Greco-Roman society.

Finally, goaded by its Gnostic and pagan opponents, the church was building up its intellectual defences and its organization. The Apologists, Justin, Melito of Sardis, Athenagoras, Theophilus of Antioch and Tertullian, who flourished in the second half of the 2nd century, denounced current paganism as 'idol worship' and the gods as so many promoted mortals. They also began to elaborate a defence of orthodoxy based on monotheism, the validity of both Testaments proving that Christ did fulfil the prophecies made concerning the Messiah, and asserting the moral superiority of Christianity over paganism and Gnostic heresy. In addition, the orthodox leaders were evolving a simple scriptural defence of their faith. The Rule of Faith was founded on tradition. It spelled out the oneness of God, the reality of Christ's ministry, the work of the Spirit and the coming resurrection and judgment of each individual. This deposit of truth was safeguarded by the presbyters, to whom, Irenaeus of Lyons (*c.* 185) urged, obedience was due, as standing in succession from the apostles, and on whom the charisma of the Spirit had descended. By the end of the 2nd century, the church had developed its own organization, its Scriptures and liturgy and its standard of orthodox belief. Its leaders were in contact with each other from one end of the Mediterranean to the other. Apart from the religion of the immortal gods of Rome, Christianity was already by far the best organized religion in the empire, though its adherents were still fewer in number than, for instance, the worshippers of Mithras and Isis. If the empire and its prosperity were to falter, Christianity would be the gainer.

A self-confident community

From *c.* 190 onwards, the church entered an entirely new phase of its history. With the spread of Christianity to Carthage, Greek and Aramaic were no longer the sole languages of the faith and liturgy, but were joined by Latin. Suddenly one becomes aware of the existence of major Christian communities in Rome and Carthage in the west and Alexandria, Antioch and Ephesus in the east, led by bishops who wielded undisputed authority over congregations scattered over considerable areas. With the postponement of the Coming it was now reckoned that several hundred years had to elapse before the six thousand years marking the end of man's stay on earth would be filled. In the meantime, how was Christ to be worshipped 'as God' and how were his relations with the other Persons of the Trinity to be understood? Each of the major Christian centres would have its own view. Both the archbishoprics and the patriarchates, whose rivalries dominate the 4th and 5th centuries of church history, and the doctrinal elements in their disputes, began to emerge at this time.

All the while, the church was gathering strength. The age of the Severi (193–235) witnessed widespread individual conversions in towns of the Mediterranean provinces. Except for sporadic but savage outbreaks of persecution, especially between 202 and 212, Christians were left alone. In the west, Tertullian could speak of the world passing from paganism to Christianity, and in 212 he taunted the proconsul, Scapula, that, even if he wanted to, he could never get rid of the Christians, so numerous had they become. Apocalyptic hopes and defiant martyrdom were their hallmarks in North Africa.

In Rome, too, there was a strong puritanical tradition, but this was modified by a more pragmatic attitude towards the empire on the part of the Roman bishops. Rome was already a wealthy see. In the last years of the 2nd century the papacy became the owner of a catacomb, the S. Callisto. In this and other Christian catacombs of the early 3rd century, one finds a brilliant naturalistic Christian art, the art of a self-confident community, not of a persecuted sect.

In some of the eastern provinces the progress of Christianity was even more rapid. Symbolic of this was the building of churches. One such was the house-church at Dura-Europos, a garrison town on the Euphrates frontier, located near the city wall not far from the synagogue. The assembly hall would have held a congregation of about seventy. Graffiti suggest that adherents came from many of the communities within the city, and the striking wall-frescoes show that, while Old Testament themes tended to predominate, the artists chose incidents that prefigured events in the New Testament.

The symbol of this era of advance was the Alexandrian Christian teacher Origen (185–254). Born of Greek-Egyptian Christian parents, Origen showed signs of genius at an early age, and at eighteen was appointed by Bishop Demetrius as head of the Christian school of Alexandria. A teacher and missionary for his cause, he sensed that the church was winning against all that 'the senate and the Roman people could do' to prevent the spread of Christianity. Unlike his contemporaries at Carthage, who gloried in the church as a 'sect' or 'school', Origen foresaw the possibility of Christianity becoming the religion of all mankind, a time when church and empire would be working in harmony. He noted also the changing status of the church in Greco-Roman society. He pointed out that, far from Christians being simpletons and yokels, as Celsus has described them in the 170s, they included zealous men and women of every class in the community. 'I admit', he wrote, 'that at the present time [*c.* 248], when, perhaps on account of the multitude of people coming into the faith, even rich men and persons of position and honour and ladies of refinement and high birth favourably regard the adherents of the faith, one might venture to say that some become leaders of the Christian teachers for the sake of a little prestige.'

Origen himself was one of those 'favourably regarded'. In about 214 he had been consulted by the governor of Arabia – the first recorded instance of an official contact since Paul discussed the new religion with Sergius Paullus, the governor of Cyprus, in 46. Later, probably in 232, Origen had an audience with the empress mother, Julia Mammaea, and praised her as 'a most religious woman'. In the reign of Philip (244–49) he also corresponded with the emperor and his wife. Christianity could no longer be ignored.

Origen represented a new and ultimately triumphant method, harmonizing, as far as possible, Christianity with current pagan philosophy, under the banner of orthodoxy. In this, his influence in the Greek Christian world was to be far reaching. Starting from a fundamentally Christian position, Origen nevertheless interpreted the books of the Bible from the standpoint of a Platonist philosopher, in such a way that an individual brought up in the philosophic schools of the day could recognize Christianity as a philosophical religion, and, if he accepted it, as a step towards achieving a rational understanding of the universe, involving both divine revelation and the moral qualities innate in man. All men could find peace and harmony as Christians. Many educated Greeks, such as

Gold medallion of Diocletian, emperor from 284 to 305, who began the last great persecution of Christians.

Origen's faithful Gregory 'the wonder-worker', were finding that Christianity answered the problems left unanswered by philosophers, and was indeed a revealed faith that was also a rational one.

With Origen one senses a turning point in the fortunes of Christianity and paganism. Henceforth, the latter would be on the defensive and Christianity on the advance. The succession of episcopal councils that Cyprian held at Carthage between 251 and 256 indicates a degree of organization that outdid anything else in the empire. Moreover, in an age of increasing economic stress, the churches remained wealthy. Pagan cults and Gnostic sects without a hierarchy and dependent on intermittent donations began to decline in face of the financial strains resulting from the empire's military disasters. The church, however, continued to gain ground. The key would seem to be organization financed by regular tithes from the faithful. In Rome, at the time of Pope Cornelius (251–53), the church had already become a state within a state with its own civil service, property and funds. No wonder the Emperor Decius declared in 250 that he would rather have a usurper to contend with than another bishop of Rome.

Decius had instituted the first world-wide repression of Christianity. In 257, however, the authorities struck again, this time, partly at the wealth of the church and partly at its leadership. Both Dionysius, bishop of Alexandria, and Cyprian, bishop of Carthage, were arrested and exiled. On 13 September 258, Cyprian was brought back to Carthage to face a proconsul, Galerius Maximus, and, having refused to conform to the 'Roman rites' was condemned to death. Eighty years earlier Celsus defined the church as 'an illegal organization'. Still illegal, it now had the strength to challenge the immortal gods of Rome, and when Cyprian was martyred, on 14 September 258, his body was escorted in triumph for burial by the faithful.

Another long period of relative obscurity followed, but where evidence exists it shows dramatic developments at work. First, Christianity at last began to take root among the nine-tenths of the population of the empire living on the land. The number of bishoprics in rural Numidia in North Africa appears to have doubled. In the Nile valley the same period saw the beginning of the monastic movement among the native Copts of upper Egypt. St Anthony withdrew from his village to the neighbouring desert about the year 270, and in Syria a similar ascetic movement was also finding support.

More important even than the extension of the church beyond the city walls were the differences of interpretation of the faith that began to prevail in town and countryside. In the towns the church was well established. Christian communities gained unofficial recognition as having their own laws and organization, but were subject to the authorities' surveillance. They accepted the social system of the day. The Council of Elvira in Spain, *c.* 309, proclaimed worse penalties for adultery than for killing a slave. Slaves were taken for granted and so, too, were their masters' rights to inflict arbitrary punishment. In the countryside, however, Christianity was an ideal. For the first time since the early missions of the disciples, Jesus's sayings were taken literally. 'Go, sell all that thou hast': such were the words that inspired Anthony. With idealism revived the spirit of opposition to the empire as representing the powers of idolatry.

The final trial of strength came in 303. Why Diocletian decided on a show-down may never be known. During nineteen years of rule he had worked towards creating a vast military state in which provincial organization, buildings, coinage and prices of every type of goods and services would be on a uniform basis inspired by the virtues of the Roman past. Rome now could not brook the Christian rival. The chosen day on which persecution was to start was 23 February 303, the Feast of Terminalia. It would mark the end of the Christian church. Diocletian had intended the persecution to be bloodless, and at first it was. Churches were destroyed; their Scriptures and valuables were ordered to be handed over. Efforts were made to force clergy to sacrifice. Then, early in 304, Diocletian became ill. Power fell to his deputy, Galerius, a convinced anti-Christian. The persecution was extended to the laity and a general sacrifice was ordered. Martyrdoms mounted, not least among the peasants of Egypt and North Africa. Diocletian survived but not to take up the reins of government again. On 1 May 305, he abdicated.

A new dawn

In the struggle for the leadership that followed, it is interesting to see how Christianity had now become an element to be reckoned with in politics. Already in 286 Diocletian had divided the empire administratively into

'The martyrs Simplicius and Faustinus who suffered death in the river Tiber and have been laid to rest in the cemetery of Generosa above Philippi: a grave slab dating from the early 4th century. At the top is the symbol of Christ, the Chi-Rho.

east and west. In the east his successor was Galerius, who between 306 and 311 made every effort to reduce the Christians to conformity.

In the spring of 311, however, Galerius fell ill, and in desperation he looked to the Christian God for aid. On 30 April, six days before he died, he signed an edict that effectively ended the persecution; but he still accepted the superiority of the Roman gods. However, it was better that those who had refused to conform to traditional worship should worship their own God than no god at all. Hence: 'Christians may exist again, and may establish their meeting-houses, provided they do nothing contrary to good order.'

In the west, the empire was disputed between Constantine, based in the north (he was proclaimed emperor at York), and Maxentius, in Rome, both of whom called off the persecution. For Constantine, this was not a decision of great moment, because there were few Christians north of the Alps. Maxentius's policy was more positive. One author tells us that he 'restored liberty' to the churches in North Africa. In Rome the church was restored to its position before Diocletian's persecution. A new papal election was allowed. Constantine, however, proclaimed the sun-god his patron. In 310, a vision of Apollo at a temple at Autun strengthened his belief that he would be ruler of the Roman world for thirty years. He still showed no inclination towards Christianity.

In the spring of 312, Constantine crossed from Gaul into Italy. A hard campaign followed. It was 26 October before he was in striking distance of Rome. That night he had a second vision, this time susceptible to a Christian interpretation. According to the Christian author Lactantius, he 'was directed to mark the heavenly sign of God on the shields of his soldiers and thus join battle' and 'did as he was ordered'. Against the odds, he defeated and slew Maxentius at the Milvian Bridge just north of Rome on 28 October. Next day he entered the city in triumph. The embers of the persecution were extinguished. In February 313, he met Licinius, the ruler of the Balkan provinces, and agreed the religious policy enshrined in the Edict of Milan.

Nominally, the Edict of Milan guaranteed religious freedom for all. Authority was granted to 'both Christians and all others to follow whatever worship each man desired, so that whatsoever Divinity dwells in heaven may be benevolent and propitious to us and all who are placed under our authority'. There is, however, a significant change in tone from Galerius's edict of two years before. The Christians were now the positive force. The pagans were 'the others'. There was no reference to the immortal gods of Rome but only to the Supreme Deity. Both Constantine and Licinius, therefore, declared themselves monotheists bound to the service of the Deity so that his favour, 'which we have experienced in so many affairs shall continue for all time to give us prosperity and success, together with the happiness of the State'. The transition had been made, for there could not be two rival guardians over the fortunes of the empire. But there was still room for differences as to who the divine guardian was. For Licinius, it was to be Jupiter; for Constantine, with equal certainty, it was Christ.

For ten years, between 313 and 323, Constantine havered. His copper coinage, minted in massive quantities throughout his dominions, continued to bear an inscription to the 'Unconquered Sun'. At the same time, his benefactions to the Christian church, especially the church of Rome, were magnificent, and on the site of the shrine dedicated to the memory of Peter a great basilica began to take shape, c. 320. 'Kindness' and favour to the Christians, accepted by officials as the imperial policy, gradually changed to the conviction that Christianity must be the religion of the empire. By 314 Constantine was declaring himself a 'servant of God', and when the inevitable conflict with Licinius broke out in 324 Constantine fought as Christian champion against an enemy who put his trust in the pagan gods. At Chrysopolis, on the east shores of the Bosphorus, 18 September 324, he triumphed and became the sole ruler of the Roman world. In a manifesto issued shortly afterwards, he proclaimed himself a Christian.

The Donatists: the first schism

Yet the wreckage of the persecutions remained. Constantine soon found that in the west the 'ministers of the Supreme Deity' were far from united. North Africa had fallen to him without a blow, but when he ordered all lands and goods confiscated in the persecution to be handed back to the church, he became aware of trouble. He had heard, he said, of the 'attempts of some irresponsible individuals to corrupt the congregation of the holy and catholic church with vain and base falsifications'.

What were the motives of these 'irresponsible individuals'? Here, as in so much of the history of the early church, personal quarrels reflected theological and cultural differences. The quarrel went back to an incident in a small township near Carthage, in 303, when the local bishop had surrendered the Scriptures to the authorities. His congregation promptly disowned him and formed a group of their own, condemning him and the Carthaginian hierarchy as 'betrayers'. Support came from Christian leaders in neighbouring Numidia, and Donatus, bishop of a settlement on the edge of the Sahara, became their leader. When in 311/12 a new bishop of Carthage was elected, the Numidians refused to acknowledge him. The North African church was split into two hostile camps.

Constantine remitted the case first to Pope Miltiades in Rome (313), then to a council assembled at Arles (314) and finally gave his own judgment. All three decisions were against the Donatists, but they refused to submit. In North Africa, the conversion of Constantine made little difference to a basic Christian hostility towards the state and its representatives.

Arianism: the rise of Athanasius

In the east the emperor was luckier. Here, too, he was confronted with a division among Christians, but primarily over doctrinal rather than disciplinary issues. At the centre of the dispute was an Alexandrian priest named Arius. He was accused, in 318, by his bishop Alexander of holding unorthodox opinions about the relationship between God and Christ. He had declared that the Son was less than the Father, that Jesus belonged to the created order, and hence could not be part of the Godhead.

Behind the dispute lay a century of disagreement between the sees of Antioch and Alexandria, and within the Alexandrian church itself. Whether Christ was to be regarded as the most exalted of the prophets or as a Being of the same essential nature as the Father, or as the divine agent of creation, might not have led to schism had the subject remained on the level of learned debate. With the rise of the monastic movement at the end of the 3rd century, all this changed. The monks were fighting demons. They wanted to be assured that they were putting their trust in a Saviour who was wholly divine and needed no redemption himself. Arius's theories would not guarantee this.

Constantine did not jump to conclusions as he had with the Donatists. Failing to reconcile the parties, he summoned a council of bishops to meet at Nicaea on 20 May 325, the largest Christian assembly ever gathered together. Some 250 bishops attended, mainly from the eastern Greek-speaking provinces, but with a scattering of westerners. Constantine acted as *de facto* president. After long debates, Arius and his supporters were condemned. Out of their deliberations emerged four clear results. First, the Son must be recognized as 'of the same substance as the Father', i.e. as part of the divine order. Second, the ecumenical council was the sovereign means of settling disputes and ordering the discipline of the church. Third, the three leading bishoprics, Rome, Antioch and Alexandria, were accorded direct responsibility over bishops within a defined territorial radius; and fourth, the emperor was acknowledged as having the right to summon the councils of the church and to guide their decisions. The church was never to be for clerics alone.

Constantine had aimed at unity within the church. He reckoned, however, without Athanasius, who succeeded as bishop of Alexandria in June 328. Athanasius had already made his mark at Nicaea as a strong opponent of Arius, and now he was hailed as 'an upright man and virtuous, a good Christian and an ascetic'. The last term is important, for it associated him with the monks at the outset, and in the forty-five stormy years of his episcopate (328–73) his alliance with them was unbreakable. Support of the monks, however, required undeviating acceptance of the Creed of Nicaea, and this brought Athanasius into conflict with the great majority of the eastern episcopate. They feared that the creed as it stood played down both the biblical account of Christ and the reality of his ministry. It was too near Judaism. They joined Athanasius's opponents, the followers of Meletius of Lycopolis, as well as supporters of Arius. In 335, Athanasius's enemies had him arraigned, for indiscipline and uncanonical election, before a council at Tyre presided over by an imperial official. His role was a key factor, for it shows how in the east the growing integration of church and empire was resulting in increasing lay control over the church. Athanasius was condemned and exiled by Constantine to Trier (7 November 335).

Constantine, meanwhile, had celebrated his thirty years' rule at Jerusalem and laid the foundations of the church of the Holy Sepulchre there. At Easter, 337, he was baptized by Eusebius of Nicomedia, and died a few weeks later on 22 May 337. Since Nicaea his views had developed in a Christian direction. His capital on the Bosphorus, Constantinople (Constantine's city), dedicated on 11 May 330, was to be an exclusively Christian city. Major temples were ransacked for objects with which to embellish it, and to provide gold and silver for the new currency. Constantine was, by then, thinking in terms of Christianity as a world religion. Alliances with border kingdoms were made on the basis of common faith, opposing heathen enemies.

The church he had championed had 'come up from below'. While never an organization of slaves and outcasts it had been an opposition movement, drawing its support from artisan and non-official classes in the towns, with all the prejudices of provincial townsmen. The Jewish background was never lost, and influenced the divisions that emerged as triumph approached. When Constantine died the social and religious problems of Donatism remained in North Africa. In the east there was no reconciliation between Athanasius and his opponents. Nonetheless, Constantine, the first Christian emperor, had achieved the union between religion and empire that had eluded his pagan predecessors. This was the legacy he bequeathed to his sons.

The Christian empire

With the reign of Constantine's son and successor, Constantius II (337–61), as ruler of the eastern provinces of the empire, begins a new era in the history of Christianity. It became the most important religion of the empire, if not that of the majority of its inhabitants, except in the north-western provinces, including Britain. Paganism became associated irrevocably with the past. Temples were replaced by magnificent churches, such as that of the Golden Dome at Antioch, whose dedication in 341 was presided over by the Emperor Constantius himself. Extensive Christian quarters grew up outside the city boundaries – Salona on the Dalmatian coast, for example, and Djemila (Cuicul) in North Africa. Bishops became the emperors' advisers and were prominent at all levels of civic and political life. The names of no less than 1,100 clergy, from pope to deacon, have survived in contemporary records, mainly Christian.

In much of the empire, however, the spirit of Christianity had changed. With the North African provinces rent by the Donatist schism, some of the militancy of the previous age had gone. The tendency, in the period 337–61, was for Christianity to absorb what it could of the pagan heritage; and, as multitudes streamed into the church, the process went on smoothly and rapidly. The most fruitful synthesis was in cultural life. The new faith could now be combined with a

A Roman calendar of about 354 shows the Christian Emperor Constantius II with the attributes of the god Sol, an example of cultural overlap between paganism and Christianity.

respect for the classical past. A cultured Christian would still be represented on his sarcophagus gazing quietly at an open scroll. The Christian wife of a pagan prefect of Rome would write a Vergilian canto 'to celebrate Christ's holy gifts announced in Vergil'. Mosaics in the country houses of the rich, not least in Britain, illustrate a similar absorption and assimilation of pagan ideas. Constantius's ideal of 'the restoration of prosperous times', proclaimed on his coinage, was a combination of old and new with the new predominating.

In its triumph, however, the church was not to be united. The age of the Fathers was to be an age of controversies, first Trinitarian and then Christological, which often masked cultural and even political differences. The western clergy accepted the Creed of Nicaea, seeing all three Persons of the Trinity as sharing a single nature. Most the eastern bishops believed that the creed failed to make sufficient distinction between Father and Son. During his exile, therefore, Athanasius found more support in the west; and, in 340, Pope Julius (337–52) wrote to the eastern bishops demanding his restoration. The easterners at first refused, but in 346 he did return to Alexandria in triumph, an event that demonstrated the triumph of Christianity in Egypt.

In the 350s, east and west clashed again, this time over the nature of the emperor's authority in the church. The aged Hosius of Cordoba, who had accompanied Constantine to victory over Maxentius in 312, spoke for the western bishops, drawing on the analogy of the Two Swords to point to the distinction between royal and ecclesiastical rule. The emperor's authority was restricted to the former. In the east, however, church and empire were already becoming integrated around the sacred person of the emperor. In North Africa, the Donatists' insistence of the irreconcilable distinction between church and state led to a strange, part religious, part social, revolution known as the Circumcellion Movement, based on the Gospels and the Book of Revelation. Creditors could no longer claim payment of debts, masters were forced to change places with their slaves, and run in front of their own chariots. 'By the judgment and command of these outlaws', wrote a hostile Catholic writer, 'the condition of masters and slaves was completely reversed.'

Debt and inequitable taxation had stirred the Circumcellions into action. In the east, similar conditions helped to produce the Monastic Movement. St Anthony died in 356, at the age of 105; he and his followers had taken on themselves 'the whole yoke of the Lord', offering a refuge to the outcasts of society. These monks were individualists, dedicated by their feats of asceticism (a substitute for martyrdom) to defeating the demonic forces they believed to inhabit the desert. They were regarded, in Egypt and Syria, as men in touch with angelic powers, and hence their word and judgment were those of God himself. The foundations of monastic influence in affairs of state were being laid.

In upper Egypt, however, monasticism was taking on a different form. Pachomius (*c.* 290–346), an ex-soldier who failed as a solitary hermit, decided to establish monasteries on communal lines as self-sufficient villages. The idea took on amazingly. At the end of the century, Jerome described how 'brethren of the same trades were lodged together in one house under its own superior. Manual work was encouraged. Excesses of fasting discouraged.' Discipline was strict. A monk wore a uniform consisting of a sleeveless tunic covered by a brown habit and hood, and drawn together by a leather girdle. He was part of a purposeful religious community. In contrast to the Circumcellions, the monks were loyal to the empire and respectful of the emperor's authority, which ensured the power and influence of the church of Alexandria for the next century.

All these developments foreshadowing the future were taking place in the reign of Constantius II. The pagan reaction that followed under his successor, Julian, showed that Christianity was unshakeable. In the east Athanasius dismissed the disturbance: 'It is but a little cloud and it will soon pass.' In the west, its consequences were perhaps more lasting. In Britain it may have contributed to the revival of the power of the Romano-Celtic deities, exemplified by the temple of Nodens at Lydney, built *c.* 364, and delayed decisively the Christianization of the countryside. During the Roman occupation, Christianity was never to be the religion of the mass of the people in Britain. In North Africa, Julian's reign saw the return of the Donatists to almost unrestricted power. African Catholicism remained in the doldrums until its revival by St Augustine of Hippo at the end of the century.

Earthly power, spiritual compromise

Nevertheless, the generation that succeeded Julian's death was the most productive in the history of the early church. It is impossible to speak in terms of the 'decline of the Roman Empire' when confronted with men such as the Cappadocian Fathers: Basil of Caesarea (d. 379), his brother Gregory of Nyssa (d. *c.* 385) and Gregory of Nazianzus (d. *c.* 390) in the east, and Priscillian, Jerome, Ambrose and Augustine in the west. Divergent though their views were, they shared a common heritage of a classical education in literature, rhetoric and philosophy, to which Christianity had been grafted. The result was the great formative age of Christian thought and teaching, accompanied by the establishment of orthodox Christianity as the religion of the state.

First, Basil of Caesarea established monasticism in an urban setting under episcopal control. The emphasis in his Rule was on practical works of charity and education; eastern monasticism has retained the pattern set by Basil to this day. Second, the Cappadocian Fathers constructed a bridge between the Trinitarian theology of Athanasius and that of his opponents. Surely, they asked, for Father and Son to be 'like in all respects' and the Son to be 'an exact image of the Father', was the same as asserting that he was 'of the essence'? A Christian world weary of these controversies agreed. At least it was preferable to denying the true community between Father and Son, as the Arians appeared to do. At the second ecumenical council, of 150 bishops, held at Constantinople in May 381, Arianism in all its forms was condemned, the role of the Holy Spirit defined and the creed embodying the resultant truths has come down to posterity as the 'Nicene Creed'.

Arianism had gradually become discredited, and with the defeat and death of its last patron, the Emperor Valens, at the battle of Adrianople, on 9 August 378, its fate was sealed. What now took place was an attempt by Valens's successor, Theodosius I (379–95), to establish Catholic orthodoxy as the sole religion of the Roman Empire. In eleven years (381–92), a series of harsh and vigorous laws prohibited, under the severest penalties, the practice of every known heresy and paganism. The Altar of Victory was removed from the Senate House in Rome in 382. The last significant bastion of the old religion, the Roman senatorial aristocracy, capitulated after the disastrous failure of the revolt of Eugenius (392–94) against Theodosius, which many of them had supported. In the next generation, the noble families became as bountiful patrons of the papacy as they had previously been of the temples, and thus retained their power and privileges in the Rome of the early Middle Ages.

Theodosius's policy had social and economic as well as religious effects. First, it consolidated the position of the church as a wealthy, if not the wealthiest, landowner in the empire, and second, it offered an alternative avenue of success for the talents of the ablest members of the provincial middle classes.

The church's wealth had been accumulating since the 3rd century. Constantine bestowed magnificent gifts on the churches in Rome, but, even more important, he gave the church the unrestricted right to receive bequests (in 321). Nominally, this merely put the church on the same level as the pagan priesthood. But there was a difference. For the church, contributions through alms had been habitual. During the 4th century, almsgiving was supplemented by a steady stream of legacies, together with the surrender of the property of those who became presbyters to the church of their ordination. Statistics of church property are difficult to come by, but in North Africa Augustine administered church lands at Hippo worth twenty times his father's estates, together with five churches in the town. In the east, Basil of Caesarea stated that each landowner should reckon on leaving to the church the equivalent of the portion of an eldest son.

Much of Augustine's time as bishop was spent in administration, and the skills required to look after the material possessions of the church attracted to it an ever increasing number of recruits from the provincial middle classes, who would otherwise have been obliged to take on expensive duties as city councillors. The church was providing one essential avenue of social mobility in both east and west.

This, however, had its disadvantages. Not only were slaves and labourers to all intents and purposes ineligible for ordination, but the glut of worldly possessions the church enjoyed blunted the edge of reforming zeal among its members. The chance of a radical reform of society, or something approaching Christian ideals, was lost. True, some churchmen, such as Ambrose of Milan, inveighed against the evils of the time – 'Naboth's vineyard was a daily story', he said – but oppressive institutions were left untouched. These, such as slavery, were regarded as among the consequences of the Fall and original sin. The last half of the 4th century saw the Catholic church in the west committed irrevocably to the possessing, landowning interests. Reform tended to become identified with schismatic and heretical movements, such as the Donatists and to a lesser extent the Pelagians. It was a fateful legacy to the European Middle Ages.

Theodosius I was the last emperor to rule both the eastern and the western parts of the empire, and on his death in 395 his empire was divided between his sons, Arcadius (d. 408) and Honorius (d. 423). The two parts

Basalt stele, probably the tombstone of an abbot, 6th or 7th century, from Egypt. He holds a wreath in one hand and a staff with a cross in the other.

of the empire became to all intents and purposes separate states, each moving towards its own destiny: for the west the barbarian states of medieval Europe, for the east, the Byzantine Empire.

Nevertheless, in AD 400, on the very eve of the great Barbarian inroads, the position still looked secure. In south-western Gaul, for instance, the biographer of Martin of Tours was describing the churches he had built for his tenants on his estates. In Nola (southern Italy), Paulinus, another former senior official turned ascetic, was filling his poems with small talk, reporting miraculous events for the benefit of the peasant worshippers at the shrine of the martyr Felix. The blows that befell the western provinces of the empire between 406, when a vast horde of Vandal and Alan tribesmen crossed the frozen Rhine into Gaul, and the fall of Rome to Alaric the Visigoth (24 August 410) were sudden and devastating. 'All Gaul burned on one pyre' was the verdict of one Gallic contemporary. The fall of Rome seemed like the end of the world. 'Happy were those who were no longer alive to see that day', wrote Jerome from his cell near Bethlehem.

Behind these disasters, however, lay factors in the internal life of the empire, and equally in that of the church. From about 360 onwards, when the former Illyrian soldier Martin (c. 330–97) established himself as a hermit, the Christian ideal in the west developed in a strongly ascetic and world-renouncing direction. On a popular level this was marked by the increase of pilgrimages, such as Etheria's to the Holy Land in 385, growing devotion to the cult of saints and martyrs and rising traffic in their relics. Symptomatic of the new mood was Ambrose of Milan's establishment of convents for women in towns in his diocese, in 374–76. Less than a decade later, Jerome (c. 347–420) began a three-year stay in Rome (382–85). Though this ended in personal disaster it gave a tremendous impetus among the aristocracy towards both asceticism and renunciation of the world as the ideal service to Christ.

Jerome and Augustine

Jerome himself was a man of contradictions, a deeply patriotic and even soldierly strain in his character conflicting at every turn with his world-renouncing and ascetic zeal. He represented the new generation of Christians that was repelled by the complacent formal Christianity now dominating the west. 'The Church after it had arrived [at the existence] of Christian princes became greater in power [as measured by its wealth], but less in virtue', he commented sourly. Jerome sought perfection through solitude, but was frustrated; he came to loathe the Syrian anchorites among whom he settled (375–77). He failed to rid himself of a love of classics, the product of his education. The famous dream, in which he saw himself standing before the Judgment of Christ and being challenged to confess whether he was 'a Ciceronian' or a 'Christian', happened in these years. Vivid fears of the Judgment and damnation contributed to his belief that secular service of any sort was incompatible with service to Christ. This was the message he preached at Rome to the noble Christian house of the Anicii. A scholar, one of the few westerners who understood both Greek and Hebrew, Jerome was chosen by Pope Damasus (366–84) to make a new authoritative Latin version of the Scriptures, translating directly from the Hebrew. His salon, on the Aventine, graced by the rich matron Paula and her daughter Eustochium, became the centre of Christian learning in Rome. But Jerome was not content. Irascible and arrogant by nature, he pushed matters to extremes. One of his protégées expired due to her excessive fasting. The scandal was too much even for his reputation. Jerome left for a well appointed cave at Bethlehem, accompanied by his women friends; his teaching still continued to influence religious life in the capital.

Jerome lived to see the sack of Rome by Alaric and shed bitter tears at the collapse of the empire in the west. A contemporary, who also watched the catastrophe from afar but regarded it dispassionately as the will of God, summed up in himself many of the contradictions of the age. This was Augustine of Hippo.

Augustine was born on 13 November 354, at Thagaste (Souk Ahras) in Numidia, the son of a pagan father, Patritius, and Monica, who was a Christian. For the first thirty-two years of his life he reflected the attitudes of the Christianized though still strongly traditional urban middle class of Roman North Africa. He accepted his father's Roman and local patriotisms and developed a love for the Latin classics, but he placed himself firmly on the Christian side of the pagan–Christian divide. Even his disillusion with his mother's literal Old Testament-based religion and his

enthusiasm for Cicero did not lead him back to paganism. Quest for truth, however, which Cicero defined as the supreme happiness of life, opened Augustine to an acceptance of a system that proclaimed itself to be the Christianity for the alert and inquiring mind. This was the radical dualism of the Manichees. At the age of nineteen, as a student in Carthage at the university, Augustine became a Manichaean 'Hearer' and remained such for nine years at least, the most formative years of his life.

Throughout these years Augustine's ambitions were political. 'I thirsted for honours, position, marriage and power', was his summary of his hopes as he set them down in his *Confessions* in 397. He became a professor of rhetoric in Carthage, then in Rome and finally Milan, where he was also public orator. He would probably have become a provincial governor and eventually, perhaps, the Pretorian Prefect of the west.

But Augustine threw it all away. Why? The short answer was given in his *Soliloquia*: 'I want to know God and my own soul. Anything else? Nothing whatever.' The *Confessions* do not tell the whole story, but one can see how, beneath the ambitious and worldly politician with his mistress and their brilliant young son, was an unquiet spirit obsessed with the problem of evil, and fearful of the results he might suffer hereafter for his moral failings. The famous, 'Give me chastity, but not yet', comes in this period of his life.

Manichaeism failed to answer his questions. Neoplatonism, teaching that evil, if it existed, must be considered in negative terms only as a progressive deprivation of good, destroyed Manichaean arguments in favour of dualism; and the allegorical interpretation of Scripture that he heard from Ambrose in his sermons in Milan Cathedral rekindled his faith in the Bible. His inability to find a suitable north Italian wife together with his mother's arrival in Milan proved decisive. He was ready to listen to the stories of the conversion of brilliant young civil servants (like himself) to the ascetic way of life. Finally, at Easter in 387, he was baptized and resigned all his secular appointments. Next year, after his mother's death, he returned to his native Thagaste to establish a monastery for himself and a few friends, leaving the cares of the world far behind him.

In Augustine's renunciation of the world, the empire had lost a potentially brilliant administrator. With other similar renunciations it lost a great deal more. *Alienatio*, estrangement from the world in order to dedicate oneself wholly to Christ, involved the deliberate abandonment of responsibilities as well as the quest for moral perfection; two from the ruling aristocracy who did both are Paulinus of Nola, and Melania, the Romano-Spanish heiress. Religious escapism brought disastrous consequences. As a friend warned Paulinus, the disposal of his 'kingdom' would mean simply that fragments would be bought up by greedy and uncaring bailiffs. The traditional links between landowner and farmer would be broken, and the result could be disaster for the tenant. Such acts of charity by the very wealthy on the scale practised in the last decades of the 4th century upset the economic equilibrium of the western provinces. Many dispossessed and disgruntled tenant-farmers were ready to welcome the Germanic barbarians when they came.

Moreover, *alienatio* as an ideal hardly buttressed the morale of citizens who wanted to resist the barbarians. One may sympathize with the local civic leaders at Turin, who, when trying in 401 to put their town in a state of defence to meet the threat of attack, were exhorted by their bishop to look to their souls that were eternal rather than the temporary safety of their city.

Such was the spirit that enabled Augustine to regard the fall of Rome dispassionately. *The City of God* was begun in 411, in the white heat of controversy against the pagans. 'When we used to sacrifice to the gods', they said, 'Rome was flourishing. Now our sacrifices are forbidden and see what is happening to Rome everywhere.' Augustine replied that the old gods had not helped Rome in the past. They would not do so now. The lives of individuals and empires alike lay in the hands of God. Things which he had made would pass away: how much more that which Romulus had founded? The individual should think only of his salvation. Pagan Rome was the type of the 'earthly city' and was doomed to disappear. The barbarians were the instruments of Providence. It was not a message to inspire resistance to the end.

Augustine had become bishop of Hippo in 395. Though Manichaeism was seldom far from his mind, his immediate task had been to combat the Donatists. The combination of Augustinian argument and imperial pressure eventually proved too much for them, and after a three-day confrontation with the Catholics, in May 411, they were proscribed by law (30 January 412). In the course of the 15-year debate Augustine had evolved a justification for religious persecution based on an interpretation of Luke XIV: 23 ('Compel them to come in'), which was to serve the Inquisition well.

A new Christendom

Augustine's victories in fact brought neither social justice nor social peace. Nor did the Catholics seek to convert the African tribes. In 427, these tribes struck, spreading terror among the settled Romanized population. Two years later a new enemy arrived. In 429, the Vandals, having moved through Gaul and Spain, were led by their king, Gaiseric, across the Straits of Gibraltar into North Africa. Resistance collapsed. Augustine himself died in August 430, during the siege of Hippo. In a few years, Possidius, Augustine's biographer, records that little was left of Catholic Africa. Churches were destroyed, congregations scattered, clergy put to the sword. All over the west, the old order dominated by Catholic Christianity seemed on the brink of destruction. Not even Aetius's victory over the Huns at Chalons, in 451, could alter the basic situation.

The eastern provinces, meanwhile, had been enjoying long spells of peace. In contrast to the west, the provincials rallied to the empire's defence. Integration of church and empire meant that 'the race of Christians' defended their heritage successfully against all comers. Internal peace was threatened, however, by the rival views of Alexandria and Antioch regarding the Person of Christ. Within a few months of Aetius's victory over Attila, the Emperor Marcian (450–57) convoked the greatest council of bishops that the church had ever assembled. They met at Chalcedon, in October 451.

The *Definition of Faith*, as it has remained down to our own day, was agreed upon. Christ was recognized as 'consubstantial with the Father according to the Godhead', and 'consubstantial with us according to the manhood, like us in all things, sin apart ... Son and Lord, only-begotten made known to us in Two Natures ... the difference of the Natures in no way removed because of the Union, but rather the properties of each nature being preserved and concurring in one Person'.

It was a neat compromise between two rival systems of theology, but religious compromises seldom command unanimous assent. Temporarily, doctrinal agreement might be reached but not agreement on matters of jurisdiction and precedence. The twenty-eighth canon of the council reaffirmed the precedence of Constantinople over all other bishoprics except Rome, to whom primacy of honour was conceded. This, Pope Leo refused to accept, and after months of argument the emperor promulgated the results of the council as binding on all his subjects, without his agreement.

Apart from the attendance of the papal legates, Chalcedon had been another purely eastern council. From now on, east and west confronted their own problems, with scant concern for those of the other. In the west, the period following Chalcedon saw the slow but progressive recovery of Catholicism from the depredations of the Arian Germanic rulers. Demoralization reached its low point around 450. At that date, Arian Germanic kingdoms were established in North Africa, Spain, southern and eastern Gaul and modern Switzerland. Britain, divided roughly down the line of the Pennines – between pagan and Jutes, and

Anglo-Saxons on the east, and leaving the west to the Celtic tribes – was lost to organized episcopal Christianity. Only in Ireland, thanks to the Romano-Celtic missionary, Patrick, was there evidence of new growth. A generation later, western Catholicism received a further blow when, in 476, Italy fell to the Herul, Odovacar; in 493 he was replaced by another and far abler Arian monarch, the Ostrogoth Theodoric, who was to rule the peninsula until his death in 526.

Why was Germanic Arianism eventually unsuccessful? The most obvious reason was that the Romanized provincials in the west, having accepted Catholic teaching, cult and organization, were not prepared to exchange these for the Arianism of their masters. After the fall of Rome in 410, the Spanish Catholic political thinker and friend of Augustine, Orosius, set down his belief that a Romano-Gothic commonwealth might succeed the Roman Empire. For a century this hope influenced the ideas and acts of some of the Germanic rulers and of members of the provincial aristocracies. It came nearest to success in Theodoric's Italy. Even then, however, there was little blending between Goth and Roman. The Goths were Arian, the Romans Catholic; and the mass of the people remained loyal to their by now traditional Catholicism.

Moreover, within the newly established barbarian kingdoms, the church produced leaders of uncommon ability. In Gaul, in particular, the cult of flight from the world had been replaced by that of service to the church. The monastic settlement of Lerins, off the French Mediterranean coast, established as a refuge for aristocratic 'drop-outs' in the first years of the 5th century, developed by the 440s into a training ground for skilled and theologically equipped bishops, men like Lupus of Tours and Remigius of Remi (Rheims), who found their way into positions of trust at the barbarian courts. Remigius was instrumental in bringing about a decisive stroke in favour of Catholicism, namely the conversion of Clovis, king of the Franks, from paganism to Catholicism (*c*. 499). Some fifteen years later, Avitus, bishop of Vienne, played a similar part in converting the Burgundian court. The fact was that the barbarians were neither numerous enough nor administratively sufficiently well equipped in North Africa, Gaul, Italy and Spain to do without the Romanized provincials. Within two generations they were being absorbed into the surroundings, dominated by the religion and language of their subjects. And all the time, the aura of Rome and the papacy survived. The Catholic clergy of the west looked to Rome for leadership and were not disappointed. By the time Justinian became sole ruler of the eastern Roman empire in 527 and planned the reconquest of the western, the Arian kingdoms of the Vandals, the

Ostrogoths and even Visigothic Spain were losing their capacity to resist.

That the reconquest was so long delayed was due partly to the long and angry dispute between Rome and Constantinople known as the Acacian Schism (484–519). In the eastern Roman provinces, particularly Egypt and Palestine, the Chalcedonian definition of the faith had been ill received, and in both Jerusalem and Alexandria troops had to be used to suppress anti-Chalcedonian mobs. Nevertheless, the anti-Chalcedonians, the forerunners of the Monophysites, were in no sense political or even religious rebels. Their aim was to persuade the emperor of the rightness of their views, namely that the Incarnate Christ should be confessed 'in one nature' and not two. In the thirty years following Chalcedon, and in particular after the end of the western empire in 476, the eastern Roman emperors had to reckon with this powerful current of anti-Chalcedonian sentiment. At length, on 28 July 482, on the advice of Acacius, the patriarch of Constantinople, the emperor sent a formal letter to the bishops, monks and laymen of Alexandria, Egypt and Cyrenaica conceding that religious orthodoxy should be based on the one nature of Christ, saving only that the Council of Chalcedon itself should not lose its canonical status (i.e. Constantinople retained its rights over other sees). Almost at the same time the School of Antioch (i.e. the Nestorian end of the Nestorian–Monophysite spectrum) moved across the frontier into Persia to set up a new headquarters at Nisibis, in 489, and to prepare thence the great missionary drive that during the next century would take the Nestorian church into Central Asia and in 635 to China itself.

The attempt to placate the Christians of Egypt and Cyrenaica alienated the pope in Rome, who saw it as an abuse of authority by the see of Constantinople and the emperor. The result was the Acacian Schism, which lasted through much of the reign of Zeno and all that of Anastasius (491–518). While the churches in east and west continued to move apart, popes Felix III (483–92) and Gelasius (492–96) underlined the differences between the eastern and western attitudes towards the emperor's relations with the church. Pope Leo I had conceded to the emperor a priestly role, but Gelasius emphasized the utter inferiority of imperial 'power' when compared to papal 'authority'. Bishops not kings would be called upon to give an account of their congregations at Judgment Day. Of the Two Swords indicating royal and ecclesiastical power, the latter was by far the sharper. To other correspondents, Gelasius wrote of the Byzantines as 'Greeks' and people 'among whom heresies abounded'. With such sentiments, the idea of a united Christendom could hardly be achieved.

Rebuffed by the papacy, the Emperor Anastasius

followed his own religious inclinations and sought to maintain close relations among Constantinople, Alexandria and Antioch. He was moving with the tide, for in the last quarter of the 5th century much of Syria, with Antioch itself, swung decisively towards Monophysitism. But the slide towards Monophysitism was halted by Anastasius's death on 9 July 518. His successor was Justin, an elderly soldier from the Latin provinces of the empire, whose sympathies were strongly pro-Chalcedonian and Roman. Within a year he had summoned papal legates to Constantinople and ended the schism (March 519). Unity between the two Romes was restored, with the primacy of the elder city safeguarded. Ostensibly, the east was humiliated, but, *de facto*, Rome had to acknowledge that the initiative in ecclesiastical matters lay with the emperor.

The reign of Justinian (527–65) witnessed the slow working out of this situation. In the west the emperor's generals reconquered North Africa, Sicily and Italy for the empire. The pope became once more the emperor's subject. In the east the emergence of a separate identity for the Monophysite church was hastened by the establishment in 530/31 of an independent Monophysite hierarchy, and in the 540s by successful Monophysite missions throughout the Middle East and down the Nile valley.

The hero of the one was James Bar' adai (d. 578), the virtual founder of a separate Syriac-speaking Monophysite church, and of the latter the presbyter Julian and his colleagues, who converted the Nubian kingdoms beyond the Roman frontier in Egypt to Monophysite Christianity. The brilliant frescoes found at Faras and the fine liturgical manuscripts from Q'asr Ibrim were the products of this Christian civilization, which lasted from the 540s to *c.* 1400.

In the last decades of the 6th century, Christendom divided in sentiment, language and cult. The Monophysites dominated a huge area extending from Armenia in the north to Ethiopia in the south and including much of Syria, Mesopotamia, on the Persian frontier, and the Nile valley. Chalcedonian orthodoxy prevailed in Palestine, Asia Minor and the Balkan provinces of the Byzantine Empire, with a foothold in Alexandria. Rome dominated the Christian west. Under Pope Gregory I (590–604) the future outlines of western Christianity could be discerned. Gregory was personally loyal to the emperor in Constantinople, but circumstances were directing otherwise. Much of Italy was occupied by new invaders, the Lombards. The pope was forced to act as civil administrator, responsible for supplying necessities and making such agreements as were possible with the invaders.

Italians were becoming used to looking to the pope as their secular as well as their ecclesiastical leader. With Gregory, the papacy became the centre of an intricate and efficient administration staffed by clerics, responsible for the conduct of diplomacy, the organization of charity, the administration of the vast estates of the papacy in Italy, Sicily and North Africa, and the despatch of missions to the still barbarian world. In this last activity Gregory was only partially successful. Augustine landed in Kent in 597 and converted King Ethelbert but failed either to establish a hierarchy based on Canterbury, London and York as he hoped, or to conciliate the Celtic Christians in the north and west of Britain. The lion's share of the work of converting the Anglo-Saxons in the next century fell to the Celtic missionaries. Similarly, Gregory's successors in the papacy did not continue the monastic-dominated administration introduced by him. Nonetheless, it was to be the Rule of St Benedict of Nursia (*c.* 480–*c.* 547), whose life and miracles Gregory had recorded, that was destined gradually to dominate the ascetic vocation in the west. This lay in the future, but Gregory had given a direction to western Christian civilization that was to survive the Dark Ages while witnessing the slow but irreversible separation of eastern and western Christendom.

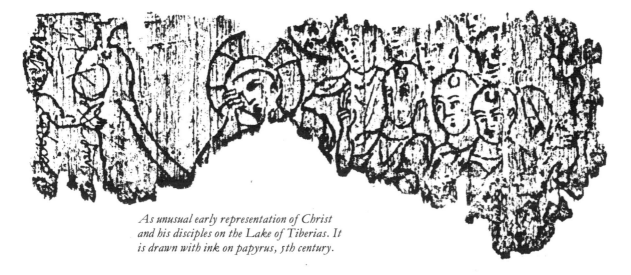

As unusual early representation of Christ and his disciples on the Lake of Tiberias. It is drawn with ink on papyrus, 5th century.

The first two centuries of official Christianity saw a campaign of church building that was not to be equalled until the cathedrals of the Middle Ages. Old St Peter's was replaced by the designs of Bramante and Michelangelo in the 16th century; others have been substantially rebuilt; Hagia Sophia (dating into the 6th century) remains intact.

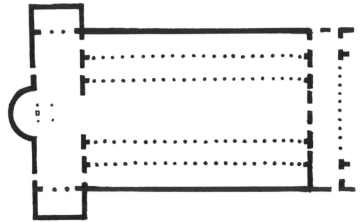

Old St Peter's, Rome: section and perspective (above left), isometric view (left) and plan (above).

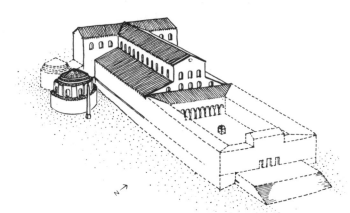

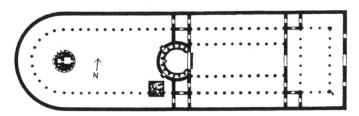

Church of the Holy Sepulchre, Jerusalem.

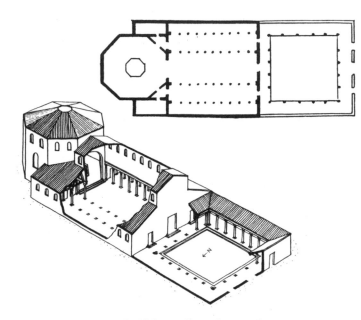

Church of the Nativity, Bethlehem: plan and isometric reconstruction.

Hagia Sophia, Constantinople: longitudinal section and plan.

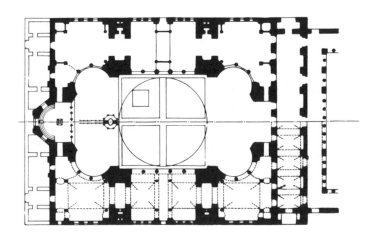

2

The rise of Christian art

JOACHIM GAEHDE

FOR NEARLY TWO CENTURIES after its birth, Christianity had no part in the artistic culture of the Roman Empire. While temples, sculpture, painting and ritual objects served the cults of the state and smaller but sometimes lavishly appointed sanctuaries provided for the rites of the mystery religions, the Christians, members of a proscribed sect and of low social standing, initially had no need for special buildings. As indicated in the Acts of the Apostles, they gathered in private houses or in apartments of urban tenements for the *agape* meal, prayers, hymns and sermons. Religious art was conspicuously absent, a fact noted by the police searching for evidence of subversive activities. The Early Christians avoided the visual arts as being contrary to their spiritual faith. 'Graven images', already prohibited by Mosaic Law, were seen as manifestations of pagan luxury and as lending themselves to idolatrous abuse.

By the end of the 2nd century, the Christian communities had grown considerably and had become organized; membership now included educated men of wealth and rank. With a change of position came a change of outlook. Christians began to come to terms with imagery, although Tertullian, for instance, still demanded that artists not be admitted to the church unless they gave up their art for more humble occupations. Tertullian's ire was also directed against actual practices such as the use of chalices with representations of the Good Shepherd.

The oldest surviving imagery with Christian content appears in the early 3rd century in the mural paintings of burial chambers, *cubicula*, owned by well-to-do Christians in subterranean cemeteries, particularly the catacombs of Rome, and, slightly later, on sarcophagi from Rome and southern Gaul. There is, however, sufficient evidence to assume that Christian tombs in open-air cemeteries were also decorated; and paintings with analogous themes, discovered in the baptistery of the Christian meeting-house of about 230 at Dura-Europos, in northern Syria, suggest that community houses elsewhere had also been provided with images by that time.

Old languages, new images

The earliest decorative schemes, for example those in the so called 'Chapel of the Sacraments' in the catacombs of S. Callisto or the *'cubiculum* of the Good Shepherd' in the catacombs of Domitilla, are entirely in the tradition of wall-paintings in contemporary Roman houses or pagan mausolea. The walls and vaulted ceilings are divided into a variety of geometric fields by a loose grid of thin frames, a characteristic late antique simplification of the simulated architecture in Roman interiors of the late 2nd century and earlier. Within these frames, small insubstantial figures were painted on the white ground in a volatile, sketchy style no different from that of pagan wall decorations of the same period. Also borrowed from pagan contexts are symbols of nature in its benevolent aspects: floral motifs, birds, harvesting cupids and personifications of the seasons.

Other images, however, are clearly Christian in content: the orant figure with arms raised in prayer, the Good Shepherd, Adam and Eve, the adoration of the Magi, scenes of baptism, Christ as the fisher of men, fish and bread, and communal banquets, the last two alluding to the Eucharist. Most subjects are based on the Old Testament and, to a lesser degree, on the New. Nearly all show instances of the deliverance of the faithful from death or want, for example Jonah cast to the whale and delivered, Moses striking the rock for water, Daniel in the lions' den, Noah saved from the flood, Susannah and the Elders, the three Hebrews in the fiery furnace, Isaac saved from sacrifice, Christ drawing water for the woman of Samaria, healing the paralytic and the woman with issue of blood, the raising of Lazarus and the miracle of Cana. Many of these themes, selected from a far greater number of saving miracles in Scripture, have a parallel in prayers for the dead, the *commendatio animae*: 'Save the soul of thy servant as you have saved Noah from the flood, Daniel from the lions' den,' and so forth. Derived from Jewish prayers, the earliest Latin version of this liturgy dates from the 5th century but must have been known as early as the 3rd.

The painters, routine artisans at best, did not create these images on their own, solely inspired by Scripture or liturgy. They extracted and adapted their figures, with stereotyped gestures and conventional classical garments, from the vast visual repertory of paganism. This was not difficult, because pagan models often carried similar connotations of piety or salvation. The orant figures, for example, had their pagan counterparts in personifications of piety on coins and public statuary and on tombstones, as images of private devotion. The Good Shepherd of the parables of the Gospels of Luke and John had various precedents: the bucolic imagery cherished by pagan city dwellers; the figure of Hermes Criophorus; a symbol of *Humanitas*, philanthropy; and, in some versions, the figure of Orpheus, focus of a mystery cult. Likewise, Jonah delivered and reclining nude under the gourd vine is cast in the shape of Endymion, who, as told in the myth and depicted on numerous Roman sarcophagi, had been given eternal life and fertility in a perpetual slumber. These and many more pagan types associated with afterlife or divinity were adapted to Christian contexts because they did not directly refer to pagan gods and were familiar to the new converts.

Jewish pictorial sources are also likely to have been used, although evidence is here more fragmentary and circumstantial. It is certainly no coincidence that the Jews renounced their taboo against images at about the same time as the Christians, if not somewhat earlier. As seen in the mid-3rd-century paintings of the synagogue at Dura-Europos, which presuppose earlier Jewish models, they also adapted current pictorial forms to affirm the reality of redemption by reference to their past history.

There is however, a significant difference between the murals of the synagogue and Christian paintings in the catacombs, as well as those of the baptistery at Dura-Europos. Many of the panels in the synagogue preserve some narrative continuity and present themselves as paradigmatic tales in the manner common to late antiquity in general. The Christian images, on the other hand, are, for the most part, pared down to the fewest figures and furnishings necessary to convey but one message: deliverance through divine intervention and through the sacraments of baptism and the Eucharist. It is this message that justified imagery to the Christians, but reluctance to express spiritual truths in material form is still discernible. Until about the middle of the 3rd century, the paintings are generally so abridged and their style so dematerialized that they are signs rather than representations. The figure of the Good Shepherd, for instance, was not intended to be a portrait or even a symbol of Christ. Like the Old Testament types of Daniel, Jonah and others, it was meant to remind the viewer of the workings of the Godhead, its power to save.

Visualization of religious concepts by means of 'sign images' had been part of the pictorial programmes of some pagan mystery cults; the earliest Christian painters, however, used this pictographic language to the exclusion of all others. As commonplace as the paintings are in type and style of execution so are they overcharged with content. A small still-life showing a fish and a basket of bread would have brought to mind the entire mystery of the Eucharist. Noah saved from the flood or Jonah delivered from the whale not only evoked the idea of salvation but, because they went 'through water', also alluded to the sacrament of baptism, without which salvation was not possible. Adam and Eve stood for original sin but also pointed to the Garden of Eden to be recovered, and the adoration of the Magi was seen as proof of Christ's incarnation and his entire work on earth, upon which the church was founded.

From the mid-3rd century onwards, the style of catacomb painting began to change. In the '*cubiculum* of the "Velatio"' in the Catacomb of Priscilla, for instance, the figures are large, individualized and more carefully painted. They begin to be presences as well as signs. These and later paintings, for example in the Coemeterium Majus, bear witness to the developing tastes of affluent Christian patrons and to their ability to engage skilled artists trained in the classicizing styles current in contemporary pagan art. Even such costly materials as mosaics were employed. A small, late 2nd-century mausoleum discovered under St Peter's in Rome was redecorated during the third quarter of the 3rd century with wall-mosaics depicting subjects familiar in catacomb painting. On the yellow mosaic ground of the ceiling vault, encircled by vines, Christ also appears, in the guise of the sun-god, Sol Invictus, triumphantly carried to heaven in a chariot drawn by white horses.

The use of pagan themes, styles and techniques is especially marked in Christian marble sarcophagi, a fact not too surprising when one considers that many workshops served pagan as well as Christian clients. The more or less overtly Christian subjects of the reliefs are the same as in painting: the orant figure, the Good Shepherd, Daniel, Jonah and other paradigms of salvation. Frequently added, however, were figures of sages or philosophers in the act of reading or teaching, a subject taken from pagan sarcophagi, where the philosopher figure was often given the features of the deceased. He is represented as a *homo spiritualis* anxious to complete his intellectual quest for truth in the beyond. On Christian sarcophagi, for instance on a sarcophagus at S. Maria Antiqua in Rome, made about 260, the philosopher – his head and that of the orant figure to his right unfinished and ready to receive the portraits of future occupants – now shows that the deceased had been initiated into the 'true wisdom', the teachings of Christ, which vouchsafc salvation to thc baptized as alluded to in the reliefs on each side: Jonah delivered and the Good Shepherd, followed by the baptism of Christ and two fishermen. The spaciously deployed figures are carved in a style dependent on the attenuated classicism seen in many contemporary pagan works. Other 3rd-century Christian sarcophagi exhibit different modes but all make use of various pagan motifs and reflect the stylistic currents of late Roman art in general.

The lengths to which wealthy Christians could go in emulating pagan culture is strikingly documented by small-scale free-standing sculptures, such as five lively statuettes from Asia Minor recently acquired by the Cleveland Museum of Art. Dated to between 270 and 280, by comparison to portrait busts of the same provenance and workmanship, one statuette represents the Good Shepherd, whose facial features recall idealized portraits of Alexander the Great, and the other four present Jonah: swallowed, cast up, praying and reclining under the gourd vine. Whether intended for a funerary context or for decoration of a private fountain, these works belong to the genre of small sculptures of mythological subjects enjoyed by pagans and displayed in villas or gardens.

We do not know whether church authorities directed or even encouraged religious imagery but, by the end of the 3rd century, it was irrevocably established as an integral part of Christian life. Many pagan motifs and forms, particularly those with a general or neutral meaning, had ceased to be viewed with aversion because they could be, and had been, filled with new content.

Despite the empire-wide persecutions and confiscations of Christian property in 250 and 257–60, the congregations had prospered and had become organized into administrative hierarchies responsible as much for the spiritual and social welfare of the living as for the care of the cemeteries. The church enjoyed complete tolerance between 260 and 303, but the milieu of worship still remained private and inconspicuous. The Christian cemeteries above ground were indistinguishable from others in form, and the catacombs answered purely practical needs arising from the high cost of available land. Romantic notions notwithstanding, the dank, narrow corridors and small *cubicula* of the catacombs were patently not large enough to be 'secret' meeting or hiding places for even a fraction of the about fifty thousand Christians living in Rome by the middle of the 3rd century.

Singled out for communal worship, however, were graves of Christian martyrs or other sites linked to

Remains of a martyrium, here reconstructed, probably built about 160 in what was then a cemetery, have been found beneath the altar of St Peter's in Rome.

martyrdom or manifestations of divinity. This practice was again entirely in the tradition of pagan antiquity which, for centuries, had distinguished places associated with the memory or the graves of its major or minor, mythical or historical, heroes with so called *heroa*, more or less elaborate structures combining the function of mausoleum and sanctuary. The earliest known Christian *martyrium* or *memoria* was found below the high altar of St Peter's in Rome in a once open-air cemetery dating from between 120 and 160 and mostly occupied by mausolea belonging to adherents of Oriental mystery cults but also by a few modest Christian graves. About 160, one of these, believed to be that of St Peter, was closed off by a wall and given emphasis by a small *aedicula*, a niche framed by two columns carrying a projecting slab designed to receive offerings and, above it, two columns supporting a gable. Nothing distinguishes such modest architectural decoration from other graves found around Rome and elsewhere.

The remains of numerous *memoriae* dating after the mid-3rd century testify to the growing popularity of martyr cults throughout the empire. Many were open-air precincts with various layouts, which could include covered spaces for funerary banquets as was also pagan custom. By 300 and later, however, small elaborate two-storeyed vaulted structures were introduced. Their plans, rectangular, cruciform, hexagonal or triconchal, were taken from pagan mausolea and *heroa*, which, the Christians felt, were not as much permeated with idolatric connotations as were the public temples and sanctuaries.

Indeed, the Christian community houses, the *domus ecclesiae*, where congregations met for regular services, had no resemblance to public architecture whatsoever. They still belonged to the domestic realm. They were apartment houses or other private buildings donated or purchased and remodelled to serve as a place for worship, baptism, instruction, administration and as living quarters for the clergy. In Rome, these properties were identified by the name of the original holder of the legal title which was affixed to the building, for instance the 'titulus Clementis', the house of Clement. This title and others survive to this day with the prefix 'Saint' in later churches erected on the site: S. Clemente, S. Pudenziana, S. Sabina and more.

The church enthroned

The political and social circumstances of Christianity changed radically with its legitimization by the Emperor Constantine's Edict of Milan in 313. Although Constantine's own religious convictions remained ambiguous – he was baptized only on his deathbed – he gave Christian communities, first in Rome and then elsewhere, the land and funds to build churches of immense scale and splendid enough to demonstrate the religion's newly powerful position. Because the classical architectural forms employed for pagan temples containing pagan cult images were unacceptable to the Christians, the architects adapted a more neutral class of building, the basilica, which, for centuries, had served numerous civic functions, as law court, for example, or as covered market, military drill hall, reception hall and throne room.

While public basilicas had been built in various designs, the Christians preferred the longitudinal kind, which consisted of a high, timber roofed nave amply lit by clerestory windows. The nave was preceded by a vestibule, or *narthex*, terminated by an apse, and accompanied by two or four windowless side aisles separated from the nave and each other by regularly spaced columns. This design allowed for all the necessities and movements of the Christian liturgy, which had begun to take on many of the hieratic aspects of imperial ceremonial. In a stately procession, the clergy, like members of a court, took their places in the raised sanctuary extending from the apse to the nave and separated from it by a screen. It contained the priest bench dominated by the bishop's seat, which imitated the seat of a high magistrate, and the altar, the 'throne' of the new King of Kings, Christ. The atrium, an open forecourt preceding the *narthex*, was accessible to non-believers and postulants. Penitents and catechumens, converts not yet baptized, could enter the church proper for the mass devoted to them, which ended with the rite of oblation, a solemn procession of the congregation bringing their offerings to the altar or a nearby table. During the following mass of the faithful, the penitents and catechumens were required to withdraw to the aisles or the *narthex*.

The basic design of Christian basilicas of the Constantinian age was subject to variations, according to specific functions as well as to local building traditions and liturgical customs. Endowed by the emperor perhaps as early as 313, the Lateran basilica of the bishop of Rome – its foundations survive in the present S. Giovanni in Laterano – was laid out as a large but simple elongated hall with a nave flanked by two aisles on each side and terminated by an apse. On the other hand, Old St Peter's, built between 320 and 329, was not only a congregational church but also the apostle's memorial shrine and it served as a funerary basilica for those wishing to rest close to the martyr. These two functions determined the plan. A transept intervening between the apse and the nave, accompanied by four aisles, contained the altar set exactly over St Peter's tomb. This transverse space was the focus of the saint's veneration while the services for the dead had their place in the basilica proper.

The church of the Holy Sepulchre in Jerusalem also combined several religious functions within one complex. Commissioned by Constantine in 325/6 and designed by the Syrian or Palestinian architect, Zenobius, and the presbyter Eusthatius from Constantinople, it consisted of an atrium and a basilica with galleries over its four side aisles. Behind it was a porticoed courtyard, with the site of the cross of Golgatha in the southern corner, alongside of which was the small church of Golgatha, whose atrium connected with a baptistery. This hieratic sequence of open and closed spaces culminated in the tomb of Christ, the Anastasis, which was surrounded by a terminating courtyard and, by the middle of the 4th century, was enclosed by a rotunda capped by a wooden dome. A more compact layout was chosen for Constantine's church of the Nativity in Bethlehem. A large octagonal structure was set over the grotto of Christ's birth and axially fused with a basilica. Other ground-plans were used elsewhere. The cathedrals of Aquileia and Trier, for instance, consist of two interconnected parallel basilicas with rectangular ends instead of apses, while in North Africa, at Orleansville, the nave had an apse on each end.

The exteriors of all these buildings were plain, as was common to late antique architecture in general. Their abundantly lit interiors, however, were sheathed in shining coloured marbles, gold mosaic and other costly materials. Nothing survives; however, the descriptions of Bishop Eusebius of Caesarea of the church of the Holy Sepulchre and the cathedral at Tyre as well as the list of Constantine's donations to the Lateran basilica and St Peter's in the *Liber Pontificalis*, the Book of the Popes, give a vivid picture of the amount and wealth of the furnishings.

This imperial munificence, especially solid silver statues of Christ and the apostles set up in the Lateran, may have raised some apprehension among more purist

Sarcophagus of Junius Bassus, city prefect of Rome, died 359. Scenes from the Old and New Testaments, described in the text below, *express the theme of redemption through Christ's Passion, but there are also elements of classical imperial allegory.*

Christians. In fact, the imperial intervention that so drastically changed the forms of Christian architecture had, at this time, no similar effect on the styles of Christian imagery. A series of sarcophagi turned out by Roman workshops just before and during the first decades after the Peace of the Church suggests that the issue of the graven image was particularly acute at that moment. Instead of continuing in the traditional vein of pagan funerary sculpture transplanted to Christian context, the sculptors employed a vulgarized style that, for centuries, had been current in the lower strata of Roman society and in the provinces, and had also appeared on Roman state monuments between about 300 and 315. The figures and scenes are so tightly compressed into a continuous frieze and they are arranged in such a seemingly arbitrary fashion that it takes effort and familiarity with Christian topics to read their meaning. The crowding of as many figures into the frieze as it can possibly hold stresses the importance of content over form, which was made deliberately tenuous by indifference to its aesthetic values. The content, reiterated by each scene, holds the same message of salvation through divine intervention that was signalled in 3rd-century catacomb painting.

Use of this style lasted for about one generation. Sculptors of Roman sarcophagi produced during the second quarter of the 4th century gradually returned to a classicizing manner. This trend reached a high point in the sarcophagus of Junius Bassus, city prefect of Rome, who died in 359. The front of the sarcophagus is divided into two registers. The central scene of the upper register shows the *traditio legis*, that is, Christ enthroned between St Peter and St Paul, whom he entrusts with their missions. His feet rest on a veil held by Coelus representing heaven and taken from the context of imperial allegory. The *traditio legis* is flanked by the arrest of St Paul and the sacrifice of Isaac on the left, and, extending over two niches on the right, Christ brought before Pilate. The lower register depicts Christ's entry into Jerusalem in the centre – it is the beginning of his Passion as well as the advent of the 'New Emperor'. To the left are Adam and Eve and the affliction of Job and to the right Daniel in the lions' den and St Paul led to his martyrdom. Six Old and New Testament scenes are performed by lambs instead of human figures in the spandrels of the lower colonnade. On the short sides, executed in lower relief, are generalized allusions to paradise and the cycles of eternity: harvesting cupids above and cupids representing the seasons below.

Instead of the uniformly repetitive invocations of deliverance shown on the earlier frieze sarcophagi, the general content of redemption through the Passion is here presented by differentiated scenes that introduce categories of content beyond the general message of salvation. The *traditio legis* refers to doctrine, and Christ before Pilate and the scenes from the life of St Paul are 'historical' representations. The observer is now invited to look at events before pondering what these events stand for.

'Christ of Psammatia', a fragment from a columnar sarcophagus. Christ is flanked by two apostles, represented in a slightly smaller scale.

Byzantium: art for the Christian elite

In 330 Constantine had moved the capital of the empire to the city named after him, Constantinople. It was there, during the reign of Theodosius the Great from 379 to 395, that Christian art ceased to be foremost an expression of individual piety and became a vehicle of the state. Christian art became imperial and imperial art became Christian. Even before all pagan cults were banned in 391, imperial largesse had turned to the task of glorifying the Christian state by monuments of art, and the style sponsored by the court set the example for the private domain. A large silver plate, now in Madrid, commemorating the tenth anniversary of Theodosius's accession to the throne, and reliefs on the base of an obelisk erected about 390 in the hippodrome of Constantinople are characteristic examples of the official court style. The single figures betray a conscious effort to revive classical form. Their relationship to each other and the whole is, however, based on symmetry and hieratic scaling, which restrict inessential movement and eliminate natural space. Furthermore, the figures do not communicate among themselves but address the beholder in strict frontality. This feature, destined to become one of the hallmarks of Byzantine art, had long been associated with the depiction of imperial or divine presences or funerary portraits referring to the beyond.

Purely Christian subjects were cast in the same Hellenizing 'aristocratic' mode, for instance the so

called Christ of Psammatia, in Berlin, showing Christ flanked by two smaller apostles; and an unfinished child's sarcophagus in Istanbul, which depicts on its front two flying victories or angels bearing a wreath encircling the triumphal *chrismon*, and on one side, a cross flanked by two apostles.

A parallel trend towards classicism appeared in the west at about the same time. Here, however, the impetus came from pagan quarters, namely a last attempt by a senatorial party in Rome to preserve and revive the ancient cults of state. Short-lived as it was, the pagan revival movement had a strong impact on contemporary Christian art. However, the finest works of a group of Christian ivories made in Italy during the years around 400 transcend the self-conscious coolness of the pagan examples by infusing them with religious emotion. A plaque in Munich representing the three Marys at the tomb of Christ and the ascension of Christ narrates these events with eloquence. The hushed wonder of the women receiving the message of Christ's resurrection from the angel seated before the tomb is movingly conveyed by the rhythm of their gestures, while the ascent of the vigorously upward striding Christ draws awestruck reactions from two kneeling apostles. But more than narrative was intended. There are deeper levels of meaning. The artist composed the ivory not only from pagan elements, such as the tomb which recalls pagan mausolea set into sacred groves, but also from figures with analogous Christian connotations. It has recently been suggested that the posture of Christ holding a scroll is modelled after depictions of Moses receiving the Law from the hand of God, thus indicating that Christ, returning to heaven fulfils the mission of Moses. Likewise, the two kneeling apostles, unique in ascension inconography, are taken from the context of the transfiguration, where, according to Matthew, 'the disciples fell on their faces in terror'. The artist thus linked two epiphanies which prefigure the Second Coming of Christ.

Members of the Christian elite also acquired luxury editions of the Scriptures. The earliest extant illustrations in biblical manuscripts are four leaves surviving from a Book of Kings, the so called Quedlinburg *Itala*, now in Berlin. Each page of the text in this manuscript seems to have been faced by a picture page containing two or four framed miniatures with several scenes. It has been calculated that the complete codex contained between 200 and 300 episodes. The intent was obviously to provide the text with a dense sequence of narrative illustrations in the same manner as the famous Vergil manuscript of the *Georgics* and the *Aeneid* in the Vatican Library. Indeed, the pseudo-illusionistic style of the miniatures in both manuscripts is so closely related that they may have been made in the same atelier. On the Quedlinburg miniatures, however, written instructions to the painters have come to light under flaked-off paint. They provide a summary of the story and tell what elements were to be included in the painting. This seems to indicate that the illuminators were not very familiar with the text and that they had no earlier Bible illustrations at their disposal for copying.

Only a few illustrated Christian manuscripts from the 4th to the 6th century have survived, but extensive pictorial cycles for the Book of Genesis, for example, must have existed in several picture recensions. One is preserved in the charred fragments of the so called Cotton Genesis from the 5th or 6th century, in London, and another in the miniatures from a 6th-century manuscript written with silver ink in Greek uncials on purple-stained parchment, in the Vienna Library. The Vienna Genesis was made for someone who delighted in pictures at the expense of the text, which was shortened to allow more space for the illustrations. Scene often follows upon scene without break, in a lively narration which emphasizes the episodal. Some anecdotal scenes extraneous to Scripture may have been derived from stories told in the Hebrew Midrashim. The style, on the other hand, reflects the impressionistic modes of Hellenistic painting.

Two 6th-century Greek Gospel-Books, also written in metallic ink on purple parchment, are related to the Vienna Genesis in style. The earlier, the fragment from Sinope, now in Paris, illustrates New Testament episodes on the purple ground of the lower margin on each page. These episodes are flanked by two Old Testament prophets holding unfurled scrolls upon which their predictions relevant to the Gospel events are inscribed. Such typological concordance is also found in the Gospels preserved in the cathedral treasure at Rossano. Here, all remaining miniatures are placed on full pages at the beginning of the book. Nine pages show four prophets pointing upward, from panels containing quotations from their writings, to the New Testament deeds by which their words are fulfilled. The selection and sequence of these images prove that their purpose was not to narrate but to offer visual counterparts to readings of the Greek liturgy. Another page depicts St Mark directed by a female figure to put his pen to a scroll. This evangelist portrait, the earliest one surviving from the Greek east, still betrays its ancestry in representations of poets or philosophers inspired by a Muse, now a personification of Wisdom. Two more miniatures, finally, are scenic renderings of the trial of Christ, complete with the appurtenances of imperial judicial procedure. One has Christ before Pilate above and the repentance and death of Judas below, while the other depicts the Jews' choice between Christ and Barrabas.

S. Constanza, Rome, was begun as the mausoleum of Constantine's daughter. Its decoration combined syncretic themes, such as the vine harvest shown here, with biblical subjects, now lost.

The ideal medium: mosaic

The first known mosaic ensembles with Christian themes are found in mausolea: the already mentioned tomb structure under St Peter's in Rome, a mid-4th-century domed building at Centcelles in Spain and the mausoleum built about 350 in Rome for Constantine's daughter, Constantia, now known as S. Constanza. The remains at Centcelles enable reconstruction of the dome mosaic, arranged in three concentric rings: the lower one had hunting scenes, the next, Christian subjects of the kind found in the catacombs and the last, images alluding to paradise and eternity. At S. Constanza, only the mosaics in the ambulatory vaults have survived. Their geometric patterns, floral motifs and cupids harvesting grapes are not overtly Christian, but 16th-century drawings of the lost mosaics in the central dome indicate the presence of Old Testament scenes framed by caryatids with Bacchic panthers at their feet.

Ample evidence of paintings and mosaics in churches appears in literary sources and surviving monuments around the year 400. There is the letter of St Nilus of Sinai advising the prefect Olympiodorus in Constantinople to abandon the idea of decorating a church with hunting and fishing scenes in favour of a single cross in the sanctuary and 'to fill the holy church on both sides with pictures from the Old and New Testaments, executed by an excellent painter, so that the illiterate who are unable to read the Holy Scriptures, may, by gazing at the pictures, . . . be roused to emulate these glories and celebrated feats'. The didactic function of church decoration is stressed again by Paulinus of Nola. In a poem, written in the first years of the 5th century, he describes a cycle of Old Testament scenes along the walls of the new basilica he had built at the martyrium complex of St Felix at Nola, and episodes from the New Testament in the older church he had restored there. By the middle of the century, such fresco cycles also covered the nave walls of St Peter's and the large basilica built between 386 and 440 over the tomb of St Paul outside the walls of Rome. The paintings in St Paul's were repeatedly restored and in 1823 were destroyed by a fire. They are known only from 17th-century drawings.

As the nave walls of Christian basilicas were given to biblical scenes relating to the history of salvation, the apses received eschatological images. Paulinus of Nola composed inscriptions explaining the symbolical imagery of mosaics in two apses, one at Nola and the other at Fundi. At Nola, the advent of the Trinity was represented by the hand of God, the cross surrounded by a wreath of doves and the Holy Ghost. Below, *Christus in agno*, the lamb, the rock of the church, stood elevated on a mound from which flowed four streams, the rivers of paradise, which Paulinus likened to the four evangelists. Palms and purple (a veil above the cross?) signify triumph and kingdom. The similar composition at Fundi placed the cross on a throne and connected the Trinitarian theme with the Last Judgment of sheep and goats by the lamb.

The designers of the earliest preserved apse mosaics did not avoid the depiction of Christ by using emblematic symbolism. In the chapel of S. Aquilino in the church of S. Lorenzo at Milan, Christ is seated amidst the apostles as a teacher. Ultimately derived from renderings of assembled philosophers, this composition provided a celestial mirror to the actual seating arrangements of bishop and clergy below. In the apse of S. Pudenziana in Rome, probably executed between 402 and 417, reflections of reality were given imperial connotations and were interwoven with the eschatological imagery of the Book of Revelation to present the faithful with a vision of the kingdom to come. Repeated restorations have left little trace of the original style but the general outlines of the composition are intact. Christ is enthroned in imperial splendour among the apostles within a semicircular court. Female personifications of the church of the Jews and the church of the Gentiles raise triumphal wreaths, either as offerings to Christ or as crowns for Peter and Paul. Behind the court rises a huge jewelled cross on the hill of Golgatha. Still further back appears a vista of

buildings whose forms suggest the church of the Holy Sepulchre and the church of the Nativity. They represent the New Jerusalem, the heavenly city of the Book of Revelation. From the multicoloured clouds of the sky emerge the four apocalyptic symbols of Christ's Second Coming: the winged man, lion, ox and eagle, which, since St Irenaeus in the 2nd century, were also identified with the four evangelists.

In 431, the Council of Ephesus had declared the Virgin Mary to be the Mother of God. A year later, Pope Sixtus III dedicated to her a large basilica in Rome, S. Maria Maggiore. It has been shown that the architectural details of this church make deliberate reference to the classical past in order to reassert Rome's importance at a time when the imperial court of the east resided in Constantinople and that of the west in Ravenna. S. Maria Maggiore is the oldest church preserving a sizable portion of its original mosaic decoration. Still to be seen are the mosaics on the arch separating the nave from the apse. They represent, in three tiers, apocryphal episodes of Christ's infancy phrased in the formal terms of imperial ceremonial. Also visible are more than half the original number of framed mosaic panels below the clerestory windows of the nave, depicting episodes from the lives of Abraham, Isaac and Jacob on the left wall and scenes from the stories of Moses and Joshua on the right. While the narrative often goes into considerable detail, the scenes concentrate on those Old Testament heroes who most advanced the quest for the Promised Land, a quest fulfilled by the triumphal advent of Christ as the universal ruler, seen on the apsidal arch. Reversing the historical sequence and thereby emphasizing the pre-existence of divinity, the Old Testament scenes are to be read from the sanctuary to the entrance.

There is little doubt about the connection of the nave panels with miniatures in illuminated manuscripts. Indeed, the mosaics' pseudo-illusionistic style is closely related to that of the miniatures in the Vatican Vergil and the Quedlinburg *Itala* fragments. Individual motifs, too, take up formulae of Roman triumphal art; this, as has recently been argued with persuasion, was an intentional response to the pagans' claim to be the sole guardians of a venerated past, such as the deeds of Aeneas celebrated by Vergil. The 'true' history of salvation was pitted against pagan mythology and legend.

It is significant in this respect that the style of the mosaics on the apsidal arch is different from that of most of the Old Testament panels. It recalls some aspects of Theodosian court art by its reduction of spatial effects, by the ceremonial movements and gestures of more weighty and taller figures and by the tendency to present them frontally wherever possible.

Part of the dome mosaic of the church of St George, Salonica, described in detail below.

Form was attuned to content. The style of the arch underlines its Christological import whereas the lively style of late Roman narrative illumination was deemed suitable for the depiction of biblical history. Even there, however, one notices a change of pace as the arch is approached. In the last panels – to the left, Melchisedek offering bread and wine to Abraham and to the right, in two tiers, Moses adopted by the daughter of Pharaoh and Moses among the wise men of Egypt – the narrative style has given way to the ceremonial one of the arch. Moreover, these scenes have a typological meaning. Moses among the wise men related to young Jesus among the doctors while the Melchisedek episode, placed out of the usual chronological sequence, prefigures the Eucharist. These panels thus link the timeless message of the arch to Old Testament history.

The Christian aim to reveal transcendental truths through imagery had found its ideal medium in mosaic. Solid walls or vaults are dissolved into multicoloured or golden surfaces irradiated by light. This effect is well caught by mosaic inscriptions in the archiepiscopal chapel at Revenna: 'The light is either born here or, imprisoned, reigns here in freedom'; and, in the church of SS Cosmas and Damian in Rome: 'The house of God shines with the brilliance of purest metals, and the light of the faith glows here more preciously.

At S. Maria Maggiore, it is only the mosaics on the arch that render this effect and meaning. The nave panels, framed and separated by pilasters, offer just glimpses of scenes, observed as it were, through small windows. A 5th-century visitor to the church of St George at Salonica, however, must have been overwhelmed by the radiance of the mosaics in its vast dome. The great rotunda was originally part of the palace of the Emperor Galerius but had been converted into a church, probably in the second quarter of the 5th century. Little of the original decoration remains but it is enough to indicate the main elements of the composition and enable one to savour the quality of the details. The summit of the dome may have held an image of the Second Coming of Christ encircled by a – still existing – ring of stars, elaborate floral wreath and rainbow pattern, the whole carried by four huge angels, whose heads and wings are still visible. The broad ring below is lost but some traces show that many figures in various poses once acclaimed the apparition above. Best preserved is the longest ring. It consists of a golden band, over eight metres high, which is divided into eight sections. Each section displays a splendidly

69

elaborate architectural complex and before it stand either two or three saints in the orant pose. The airy structures recall the architectural fantasies of Roman wall-painting or the show façades of Roman public architecture in Asia Minor as well as the *scenae frons*, the stage set, of Roman theatres. In the mosaics, however, the buildings have become impalpable and other-worldly because they are largely rendered in gold on a golden ground.

Ravenna: Byzantine outpost in the west

The threat of invasion by the Visigoths, under King Alarich, had compelled Honorius, emperor of the west to transfer his capital from Milan to Ravenna in 402, that city on the Adriatic Sea, which a mid-5th-century visitor, Apollinarius Sidonius, described as being 'no more than a swamp where all the forms of life show themselves as the inverse of what they should be; ... where the walls fall and the waters stand, ... where eunuchs study the art of war and the barbarian mercenaries the art of poetry'. This city of paradox was to be, in turn, the last outpost of the moribund empire of the west, which ended with the death of Romulus Augustulus in 476; the capital of the Ostrogoth conquerors of Italy under Theodoric, from 493 to 526; and, seized in 540 by the Emperor Justinian's general, Belisarius, the seat of the Byzantine governors of Italy until the Longobards conquered the city in 751. The inextricably interwoven cultural cross-currents of this turbulent history are embodied in the art of Ravenna. Nowhere else do as many buildings and mosaics from the 5th and 6th centuries survive and nowhere else do the monuments speak with such fulness of the concerns of the times.

The first phase of the art of Ravenna belongs to Galla Placidia, who, after the death of her brother Honorius in 423, ruled the western empire until her death in 450. About 424/5 she began to build the churches of S. Giovanni Evangelista and S. Croce. The first was dedicated to St John the Evangelist, in gratitude for her rescue from a tempest at sea. The original layout of the church, a spacious basilica with two aisles, has survived several rebuildings but has lost its mosaic decoration. We know, however, that, besides images of Christ and St John, the apse and the apse wall contained numerous portraits of Christian emperors and their families, a fusion of piety and propaganda characteristic of imperial patronage. The basilica of S. Croce has largely disappeared but a small cruciform structure, added to one side of the basilica's entrance porch, is well preserved. Although Galla Placidia was eventually buried in Rome, this annex was intended to be her mausoleum as well as a martyr's chapel dedicated to St Lawrence.

The lower walls inside the building are covered with yellow marble while everything else is overlaid with mosaics. The visitor experiences the interior as a kind of splendid pergola held aloft by rich ornamental bands on the faces and soffits of the arches, which frame each segment of the surface, and he feels sheltered by the dense and glowing star patterns on the night-blue ground of the vaults. The dome surmounting the crossing, with the symbols of the four evangelists in the pendentives, is held in suspension by hundreds of golden stars on blue, which seem to rotate in concentric circles around a golden cross. The two lunettes terminating the barrel vaults of the lateral cross arms are filled by a veritable acanthus forest with two stags approaching a pool of water, an allusion to Psalm XLII: 'as the hart panteth after the waterbrooks, so panteth my soul after thee, O God'.

The other lunettes, however, which are given to figural representations, offer visions of intangible realms beyond the limits imposed by solid structure, thus expanding actual space into domains of grace. Each of the four arched walls below the dome seems to open into an indefinite depth in which, beneath a shell-like canopy, stands a pair of apostles acclaiming the star-centred cross above. The lunette at the end of the longitudinal cross arm, faced upon entering, also draws the eye beyond its surface to behold St Lawrence shouldering a triumphal cross and about to stride past the fiery grill of his martyrdom towards a bookcase displaying the Gospels for which he had given his life. Opposite, above the entrance, is an image of Christ as the Good Shepherd seated within a rocky landscape amidst six sheep, caressing one. Christ's golden tunic and purple cloak, however, and the cross staff he holds like an imperial insignia, bring the bucolic theme of earlier Christianity into the courtly ambience.

An even more sumptuously appointed building is the so called Orthodox Baptistery. It belonged to a cathedral built in the first quarter of the 5th century by Bishop Ursus. The cathedral no longer exists, but the octagonal baptistery, remodelled by Bishop Neon between 450 and 460, still contains most of its interior decor of stucco and mosaics circumscribing the mystery of baptism in which the 'old Adam' dies in the font and is resurrected as a neophite free from sin.

Because the number eight was often associated with regeneration and resurrection in the writings of the early church Fathers, the octagonal ground-plan – with four projecting niches in alternating sides – may here have signified spiritual rebirth. The interior elevation consists of two zones and the dome. The lower zone, now partly sunk underground because of the marshy terrain, is articulated by eight blind arches, the spandrels of which are decorated with tendrils enveloping male figures, presumably prophets. The second zone holds eight arched windows, which are framed by triple stucco arcades with the two flanking ones containing painted stucco figures, again of prophets. The windows and arcades are in turn surmounted by wide arches, the spandrels of which form the pendentives of the dome. The mosaics of the dome are arranged in three consecutive rings. The lowest one is divided into eight sections by floral candelabra rising from the pendentives. They contain celestial structures in which thrones bearing the imperial insignia of Christ alternate with altars on which the four Gospels are displayed. The next and broader ring shows crown-bearing apostles, again divided by floral candelabra. They advance, clockwise and counter-clockwise, in two processional groups, one led by St Peter, the other by St Paul. The dome's apex holds a medallion depicting the baptism of Christ, at once a celestial vision and an example for the neophite standing in the font below.

After his conquest of Ravenna, Theodoric initiated his own building campaign. The Ostrogoths, adherents of the Arian doctrine which denied the consubstantiality of the three Persons of the Trinity, required their own churches. A cathedral, now Spirito Santo, was built first. The basilica still stands but deprived of its mosaic decoration. The nearby baptistery, however, does retain its dome mosaics. Like the structure itself, they were based on the design of the Orthodox Baptistery, but profound changes in style and concept were introduced. The ring of thrones and altars was omitted. What remains is the central medallion with the baptism of Christ and an outer ring of apostles. They are again arranged in two files but their procession now has a goal: a splendid throne surmounted by a jewelled cross. The floral candelabra, which, in the Orthodox Baptistery, divided the ring of apostles into sections, have been replaced by palm trees no higher than the figures themselves. Corporeality has been reduced, the draped folds of the apostles' white garments have been simplified and flattened, movement has been stilled, and most of the faces have lost individuality but have gained in expression by virtue of the intense gaze of large eyes.

A very similar trend towards abstraction and restrained movement characterizes the mosaics remaining in the archiepiscopal chapel, built at the turn of the century, as well as those in the contemporary palace church of Theodoric, now known as S. Apollinare Nuovo. Except for S. Maria Maggiore in Rome, S. Apollinare Nuovo is the only Early Christian basilica in which the mosaic decoration of the nave walls survives. Not all of it, however, is of the period of Theodoric. When, some twenty years after the defeat of the Ostrogoths, the Arian church was turned over to Catholic use, Archbishop Agnellus removed images celebrating the rule of Theodoric and replaced them with the solemn processions of female and male martyrs now to be seen on the broad continuous friezes below the clerestory of the left and right walls, respectively. The older mosaics at each end of the processions were left intact. Near the apse are depicted the Virgin and Child, on the left wall, and Christ, on the right, both enthroned and flanked by angels, while near the entrance are pictures of the harbour suburb of Classe to the left and to the right the palace and city of Ravenna, from which, however, images of Theodoric and his courtiers were expunged.

Also of Theodoric's time is the sequence of panels above. Those over the standing figures contain shell-shaped canopies whose proper function of providing a spatial niche for the figure below was no longer of concern. Separated from these figures by a frame, they have become symbolic ornament, alternating with the panels over the windows which represent episodes of the miracles and parables of Christ, on the left wall, and his Passion and resurrection on the right. This is the earliest extant example of a New Testament cycle on the walls of a church. As the scenes are not given in chronological order, particularly on the left wall, their meaning is evidently not narrative but liturgical, similar to the juxtaposition of prophets and Gospel scenes in the Rossano Gospels.

The age of Justinian

During the early reign of Justinian I, emperor since 527, a new style made its appearance, which revived the Hellenistic elements of Theodosian court art without surrendering the trend towards essentially two-dimensional form. This powerful synthesis of classical traditions and a striving for incorporeal, timeless evocation is most splendidly manifest in the mosaics of the presbytery of S. Vitale at Ravenna. The church was founded in the late 520s by Bishop Ecclesius but it was not before 538 that building proceeded in earnest. The mosaics in the chancel and apse were completed under Bishop Maximian, between 546 and 548.

The central theme of the programme relates to the Eucharist celebrated by the officiating priest on the altar below. The side walls represent Old Testament antetypes of sacrifice, prophecy and theophany. One side shows the sacrifice of Abel and Melchisedek and, above it, Isaiah foretelling Christ's incarnation and Moses as a Good Shepherd herding the sheep of Jethro and, again, Moses addressed by the hand of God on Mount Horeb. The other side depicts Abraham entertaining the three angels under the oak of Mamre and his sacrifice of Isaac. The space above is occupied by Jeremiah, who foresaw the Passion of Christ, and

Moses receiving the Law on Mount Sinai. Between the prophets and Moses scenes on each wall are pairs of flying angels bearing a cross medallion. Still further up are portraits of the four evangelists with their symbols. The superposed Old and New Testament images are encompassed by the *Agnus Dei*, the sacrificial lamb. It is placed in the centre of the vault directly over the altar and is framed by a floral wreath held by four angels and four floral bands, which rise at the springing of the vault from peacocks, old symbols of eternity. All other surfaces are filled with paradisical vines and lush acanthus foliage populated by all kinds of pleasant creatures. Christ himself appears in the golden conch of the apse seated on a cosmic globe before a paradisical landscape. Flanked by angels, he holds the seven-sealed scroll of revelation on his right knee and extends with his left hand the martyr's crown to St Vitalis; from the right, Bishop Ecclesius offers him a model of the church. On the lower wall of the apse, finally, are the two famous panels depicting Justinian and Theodora with their retinue and bearing gifts for the church, a paten and chalice for the Eucharistic rite.

The architectural form of S. Vitale is surely derived from the east, even if the architect was a westerner. We have proof that the marble revetments and drilled capitals, which hide and dematerialize solid structure, were imported from the eastern capital. The complex but harmonious layout and elevation of S. Vitale has its closest parallel in Justinian's palace church of SS Sergius and Bacchus in Constantinople. Both churches share basic features: an octagonal core surmounted by a dome resting on eight tall piers and arches, which frame screened niches opening into the enveloping ring of the ambulatory and the galleries above. This design is ultimately based on the tradition of imperial architecture harking as far back as the period of Hadrian.

Thanks to Procopius, Justinian's – not always friendly – chronicler, we know of the emperor's far-flung and ambitious building enterprises, which pioneered bold innovations in church architecture. While the basilical type remained the favoured form throughout the Middle Ages in the west, Justinian's builders based their variant designs on a domed central plan, a scheme that guided Byzantine church architecture to the end.

The Hagia Sophia in Constantinople is the most grandiose monument dependent on this concept. Replacing a Theodosian basilica destroyed in the Nika riot of 532, the huge edifice was completed in 537, a remarkably short time of five years and ten months. The architects were Anthemios of Tralles and Isidorus of Miletus, both theoreticians and university professors rather than the usual master builders. The plan and elevation are deceptively simple, giving no indication

of the enormous structural problems that had to be overcome to cover such immense space with vaults. Basically, the church is a basilica with a wide nave flanked by broad side aisles and galleries. The longitudinal plan, however, is countered by the effect of the central dome, on pendentives, carried by four arches on piers rising at the corners of the nave's central square. Half domes, supported on secondary piers, abut the central dome towards the east and the west. They, in turn, encompass three arched niches, the central one to the east holds the sanctuary, that of the west leads into the inner *narthex*.

The breathtaking effect of the vast interior is one of weightlessness because all major supporting elements are concealed, just as materiality was disclaimed in the mosaics of S. Vitale. Procopius described it well: 'the huge spherical dome . . . seems not to rest upon solid masonry but to cover the space with its golden sphere suspended from heaven. All these elements, marvellously adjusted to one another, poised in mid-air one above the other and supported only by those adjacent to them, produce a total and most extraordinary harmony: they do not allow the beholder to dwell long over any one of them, but each, in turn, attracts his gaze and leads it on without effort to itself.' Procopius also wrote of the effect of light streaming through the windows: 'Indeed one might say that its interior is not illuminated from outside by the sun, but that radiance comes into being without it, such an abundance of light bathes this shrine.' This 'radiance', of course, is owed to the decoration, to the reflecting gleam of polished coloured marbles and porphyry, intricately carved and partly gilded revetments and capitals, and, above all, to the gold mosaic covering all vaulted surfaces.

Hagia Sophia has remained unique. No church of similar size and structural daring was ever attempted again in the east. Subsequent builders chose more sober designs and more conventional means of constructing domed churches. It seems that the momentum for the creation of bold and rich syntheses of the material and the immaterial was slowing by the middle of the century. This is also borne out by surviving mosaics in the church of the monastery of St Catherine on Mount Sinai, built at the order of Justinian between 548 and 565, and in the Ravennate church S. Apollinare in Classe, consecrated by Bishop Maximian in 549. They no longer display that powerful fusion of revived classical forms and abstract concerns possessed by the mosaics of S. Vitale but, in their own way, return to the more 'abstract' principles favoured around 500.

The mosaics at St Catherine's depict the transfiguration, in the apse, and, on the wall above, Moses at the burning bush and Moses receiving the Law. Gold mosaic neutralizes the ground, and landscape formations are reduced to mere props. The figures, while retaining a good deal of corporeality and, where needed, mobility, are silhouetted against the gold ground as neatly isolated patterns, thus forming a static and balanced composition which affirms the timelessness of the event.

The apse mosaic in the basilica of S. Apollinare in Classe also shows the transfiguration but it does so in a largely symbolic manner. Instead of the figure of Christ at Sinai, the composition is dominated by a large jewelled cross amidst ninety-nine stars on the blue ground of a framed medallion. Moses and Elias emerge among clouds from the golden ground above, while three lambs on the expanse of a green meadow below symbolize the apostles, witnesses of Christ's transfiguration, who were portrayed in person at Sinai. Exactly under the cross stands St Apollinaris facing the beholder and raising his arms in the orant gesture. Six lambs approach him from each side. The complex ideological content of the mosaic is conveyed by simplified and flattened forms, a trend that was to dominate mosaic decoration in the subsequent century.

The face of holiness

Commemorative portraits of holy personages had become popular already by the 4th century. To a society accustomed to official, private and funerary portraiture it seemed only natural to extend this practice into the Christian environment. In his *Historia Ecclesiastica*, Eusebius wrote: 'It is not surprising that pagans who a long time ago received a benefit from our Saviour should have done this, considering that I have examined images of the apostles Paul and Peter and indeed of Christ himself preserved in painting: presumably men of olden times were heedlessly wont to honour them thus in their houses, as the pagan custom is with regard to saviours.' Eusebius did not approve. When Constantina, sister of Constantine, requested him to send her a painted portrait of Christ, he answered that Christ, being God, could not be portrayed accurately in human form. From St Augustine, about a hundred years later, we hear first of Christians actually worshipping images of martyrs displayed in their tombs and, in another context, he argued against images on the grounds that they must, necessarily, contain an element of illusion, a contradiction of that higher truth 'which is not self-contradictory and two-faced'. The issue of idolatric abuse was most succinctly stated by St Augustine's contemporary, Epiphanius of Salamis on Cyprus: 'When images are put up, the custom of the pagans do the rest.'

The eastern church Fathers of the 4th and 5th centuries, on the other hand, regarded images favourably. St Basil, for instance, considered images to be

The first use of Christ's face on coinage occurs with the gold solidus of Justinian II (685–95). It coincides with a turning away from symbolism and a return to the representation of Christ as a man.

equal to the written word as didactic and hortatory devices. Whatever the theological arguments, individual images of Christ, the Virgin and saints became increasingly popular, and their commemorative or didactic function became overshadowed by a growing belief in their miraculous powers. The portrait tended to be confused with the portrayed.

Miracle stories connected with icons begin to proliferate in hagiographic and other writings after the middle of the 6th century. Images are reported to have bled when attacked, to have moved and spoken, to have cured disease, to have granted some material favour and to have brought help in times of danger. A group of mid-7th-century votive mosaics in S. Demetrius at Salonica belong to this class of imagery, insofar as some of their inscriptions give thanks to the saint for his succour. One, for example, refers to a recent naval attack by the Avars and Slavs: 'You see the founders of this famous house on each side of St Demetrius, who averts the barbarians' terrible naval might and saves the city.' However, the reality of the concerns that caused the dignitaries of Salonica to dedicate these ex votos to their patron saint had no reflection in the abstracted style of the mosaics. A deliberate avoidance of nearly all pictorial devices of illusionism preserved in other 7th-century works of art was here part of the mosaics' function as objects of individual piety.

The cautions that can be sensed in the Salonican mosaics had elsewhere and earlier been worn down by the increasingly important role of icons in private and public worship. This is confirmed by portable icons painted in the encaustic technique on wooden panels, which are preserved in the monastery of St Catherine on Mount Sinai. The most beautiful Sinai icon is an almost life-size portrait of Christ, which has been dated to the later 6th century by some scholars, and to the late 7th by others. Numismatic evidence places the icon's origin in Constantinople. Gold coins struck during the first reign of Justinian II, between 685 and 695, bear the same type of Christ on their obverses. Significantly, this was the first appearance of an image of Christ on coinage, a fact that has a parallel in the eighty-second canon of the so called Quinisext council of 691/2, which required that Christ be represented as a man and not as a lamb in order to emphasize 'His Life in the Flesh, His Passion,

His saving Death, and the Ransom for the world that was won thereby'.

This ordinance must have resulted in a great increase of portraits of Christ but, except for the coins, only the Sinai icon has survived. The calm authority and deep humanity of the majestic image recalls Greek classical art to such a degree that the ultimate inspiration for this particular figuration of a bearded Christ with flowing hair has been sought in images of Zeus. Indeed, the icon is a compelling witness to the power and longevity of the Greek humanist vision in a changed world. Faced with the haunting immediacy of this image of Christ, the modern observer has little difficulty in imagining the impact it must have had on early medieval believers inclined to accord a veneration to icons which, properly, only belonged to their prototypes. By the same token, one might, perhaps, understand the hostility of those to whom such life-like icons were proof of a relapse into idolatry.

This view had gained strength in the provinces of Asia Minor and it was shared by the Emperor Leo III. All ill fortunes of the empire, particularly the threat posed by the iconophobic Arabs, were blamed on the superstitious veneration of icons which had sullied the Christian religion and had drawn the wrath of the Almighty. The issue came to a bloody head when, in 726, imperial officers attempted to remove an especially popular icon over the entrance of the imperial palace but encountered the murderous fury of the populace. In 730, Leo decreed the destruction of all holy images and from then on, save for a period under the Empress Irene from 780 to 802, iconoclasm prevailed in the east until the final restitution of images and the triumph of orthodoxy in 843, during the regency of the Empress Theodora.

Iconoclasm deflected the course of Byzantine religious art for more than a century but from the arguments between iconoclasts and orthodox emerged a clear definition of holy images, particularly in the writings of John of Damascus and Theodore the Studite and the declarations of the seventh ecumenical council at Nicaea in 787. Against the iconoclasts' contention that divine nature is uncircumscribable and cannot, therefore, be circumscribed by 'the illicit craft of the painter', it was reasoned that the image must not be confused with its subject. The icon is only an imitation of the person depicted just as man was made in the image of God. It is, however, related to its prototype in a Neoplatonic manner. It reflects the invisible as a shadow is cast by a material object and as the Father produced the Son in the incarnation of Christ. The image, although differing from the prototype in its essence, is nevertheless identical with it according to its meaning, and the honour – not worship

– accorded it is passed on through the image to its prototype.

The west had rejected iconoclasm. In 731, Pope Gregory III called a synod to Rome where all iconoclasts were excommunicated, and in 738 he appealed to the Frank, Charles Martel, for help against the Byzantines. This break between Rome and Constantinople had far-reaching consequences for the history of the west, where the Franks were soon to forge their own version of the Roman Empire under Charlemagne, who, in 800, was crowned Imperator Augustus in St Peter's in Rome. Earlier, Charlemagne had embarked on an all-embracing reconstruction of cultural life, which began as a reform of clerical literacy and liturgical practice along the lines prescribed by Rome and was soon to include the visual arts.

Charlemagne and his advisors had little taste or understanding for the subtleties of either the iconodule or iconoclast arguments. When he received the minutes of the orthodox Nicaean council of 787, he immediately charged one of his theologians – probably Theodulph of Orleans – to compose the so called *Libri Carolini*, which appeared between 790 and 792 and condemned the iconodule position. The 'Caroline Books' are important not only as a rejection of Byzantine authority over the affairs of the universal church but also as a statement on art, which goes beyond its ecclesiastical functions. The most constantly reiterated criticism of the Byzantine view is that all things that are rightly to be adored are instituted by God and inspired by the Holy Spirit, while images are no more than the mundane products of an artisan's skill. Art has no intrinsic piety and the artist, in order to advance in his craft, must seek out good models and masters; he may attain piety in his person but not in the products of his art.

Insistence on the didactic and aesthetic functions of art released the Carolingians from the obligation to destroy or prohibit images. Hence their indifference to the iconoclast point of view. Artists were free to find models or masters wherever possible and suitable. The entire heritage of the past was at their disposal, Christian as well as pagan, Italian as well as Irish and Anglo-Saxon. We even know that Byzantine or Byzantine-trained painters were called to Charlemagne's court at Aachen, where they produced the Gospel-Book on which later German emperors swore their coronation oaths and which is now kept in the Imperial Treasury at Vienna. Within less than two generations, the Carolingian *renovatio* secured many of the achievements of the past and transformed them into a new and specifically western artistic language that was to provide the basis for European art into the 12th century.

A CONQUERING MISSION

3
The conversion of the barbarian peoples

WITH THE BREAK-UP of the Roman Empire in the 5th century, Christianity entered a new and momentous phase. In the eastern empire the situation remained basically unchanged, as we shall see in Chapter 4. In Italy the barbarian invaders, the Goths, were already Christian – though of the unorthodox, Arian persuasion – so that the existence of the church was not directly threatened. But in the north the Christians were faced with the alternative of either converting the Germanic tribes who were overrunning their countries, or being obliterated. It was a second age of persecution, of martyrdom, of heroism – and ultimately a second victory.

Why was the success of Christianity so complete? There are several answers. The church was well organized and highly motivated. In the monastic system it had found a method of surviving social and cultural upheaval, and in its missionary fervour it had a determination that had no echo among the heathens. It also shared the status of Latin civilization which the tribes were anxious to acquire. When a Frank or a Vandal learned to read, he read Christian literature. The old polytheistic religions, whose ethical content was unsuited to a more advanced society, had no means of resisting this multiple attack, except the force of tradition and the fear of change. Slowly but inevitably, the old gods lost their hold.

This is not to say that the process was an easy one. Missionary activity was dangerous, the results uncertain. Much depended on diplomacy. Political and material advantages normally weighed more heavily than spiritual ones, though a narrative such as Bede's *Ecclesiastical History of the English People* makes it clear that the spiritual dimension was important too. If a king were converted, his people followed as a matter of course.

Parts of Gaul were able to preserve continuity with Roman Christianity. Irish monasticism, which had developed in isolation despite its Mediterranean origins, spread to northern England in the 6th century. In 597 Augustine arrived at Canterbury from Rome. During the 7th and 8th centuries missionaries penetrated Germany from France, England and Ireland, preparing the way for the establishment of Charlemagne's Christian empire in 800. Pressing east, they had converted the Scandinavians by about 1100. In spite of sufferings and setbacks there was now a firmly knit network of bishoprics and parishes with its centre in papal Rome.

The most important result of this disturbed history was to make the church greater than any individual country, a fact that was to be crucial for the whole of the European Middle Ages. For five hundred years it functioned as a universal, independent state within the state, challenging secular authority and claiming an allegiance above that of king or emperor. Familiarity makes us accept this as something natural, but it is hard to parallel in other times and cultures.

Two Frankish noblemen
raise their hands in token of abjuring paganism and
accepting Christianity. Between them stands John the Baptist, holding a disc
with the lamb of God. The sandstone relief is in the parish church of
Grosskirbach in Upper Franconia, whose dedication to the Baptist suggests that
it was a baptismal centre. Traditionally the scene is thought to commemorate an
otherwise unrecorded conversion. The inscription at the top, 'Wolfherus Abbas',
refers to Wolfher, abbot of Munster-Schwarzach from about 1034 to 1046. By
this date, Christianity was the official religion of all parts of Germany, but the age
of conversion had marked a turning point in the history of the northern peoples.
Indeed, history, in a sense, began with Christianity, since before that there were
no written records. (1)

WOLFHERVS ABBAS

IOHAN
NES
BABTIS
TA

Signs and wonders

Many of the stories concerning the conversion of northern barbarians are the stuff of legend. There are few documents and we must normally rely on chroniclers who were ready to see the hand of God where a modern historian might prefer other explanations.

Harold Bluetooth, king of the Danes, is converted by a missionary named Poppo. The gold plaques of the Tamdrup altar, made about 1200, tell the story in expressive detail. *Left:* a bishop preaches to Harold, who is unwilling to receive the new faith. *Below left:* in order to bear witness to Christ, Poppo consents to wear an iron gauntlet while it is heated red-hot over a fire. *Below right:* Poppo approaches the king holding the gauntlet, his hand unharmed. *Right:* Harold, convinced of the truth of Christianity, consents to be baptized. One fact is certain: King Harold Bluetooth did become a Christian about 980, and with him the whole nation of the Danes. (2–5)

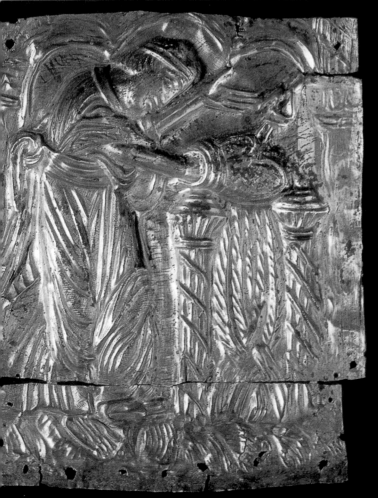

Between two faiths

For ordinary people conversion was not a sudden revelation but the gradual giving up of one set of practices for another. During the transition period it was quite normal to believe in both Christ and the pagan gods. The works on this page are evidence of this strange ambivalence.

Christian, Gnostic, Mithraic . . . symbols from a variety of backgrounds mingle in an early 6th-century floor mosaic from Teurnia, in Carinthia. The only definitely Christian elements are the chalice and paten in the centre (with the dove over them). The serpents may be Gnostic symbols of dark powers; the bull belongs to Mithras; the tree is probably the Germanic Tree of Life. (6)

Christs of the north: Christ on the cross is incorporated into a German stele (*top*), 7th century, from the Rhineland. *Above:* the transfigured Christ equated with a Frankish warrior of the same date and provenance. *Below:* detail from the Jelling stone erected by Harold Bluetooth, with a Viking Christ amid serpentine lines. (7–9)

White magic: just as a Viking of the pagan era carried an amulet of Thor to ward off evil powers, a Christian carried one of the crucifixion; the decorative techniques are identical. (10)

Jesus the warrior: a crucifix at Tirstrup, Denmark, *c.* 1150, shows Christ wearing the crown of a Danish king, triumphant over death. (11)

The three Magi bringing gifts to Bethlehem (*right*) make one scene of the 8th-century Franks casket; others include Wayland the smith, Romulus and Remus and the death of Sigurd. (13)

A Germanic Trinity: according to the Icelandic chronicler Snorri Sturluson, King Gylfi of Sweden met the gods face to face. Clearly influenced by Snorri's own knowledge of the Trinity, they are represented as three gods called 'High One, Just-as-High and Third'. (12)

The power of writing

The barbarian tribes had no written script. Literacy and Christianity arrived together, and books were long regarded with superstitious awe. Knowledge of writing, the virtual preserve of the monasteries, became identified with authority, both religious and secular.

Pen in hand, the evangelist St Matthew waits for divine inspiration. Portraits of the evangelists are often included in Carolingian and Ottonian Gospels, even when there are no other illustrations. (14)

Books were like reliquaries, bound in gold and silver and often encrusted with jewels. This psalter of the 11th century bears a portrait in silver gilt that may be of Charlemagne's grandson Lothair. (15)

St Jerome distributes copies of the Vulgate to monks who carry it through the world; a 10th-century miniature. His translation of the Bible into Latin was itself regarded as divinely inspired and its interpretation mandatory. (16)

The Book of Judgment was an idea that to an illiterate ▷ populace must have carried religious overtones. Christ the Judge is commonly shown holding a bejewelled book, source of the Commandments and of God's Law. (17)

HOC MEMBRA POSTVL

THEODLECHELDIS INT FME

3
The conversion of the barbarian peoples

IAN N. WOOD

THE CONVERSION OF THE Emperor Constantine in 312 was expected by many to mark the beginning of a golden age for Christians, and, indeed, tolerance and wealth rapidly altered the position of the church. But riches compromised ideals, and greater opportunities for doctrinal debate brought heresy and schism, especially over the question of the nature of the Godhead, where the Arians saw the Trinity as a hierarchy – in which the Son was not equal and co-eternal with the Father – while the orthodox emphasized the single unified nature of the Father, Son and Spirit. Moreover, the Christianization of the empire was far from complete; as late as the 380s it was still unclear whether the majority of the Roman senate was pagan or Christian, and Christianity had scarcely touched the rural populace of western Europe. Nevertheless, there was plenty of optimism; the empire was seen as the agent by which the whole world would be Christianized, and the fact that the birth of Christ coincided with the reign of the first Roman emperor was thought to substantiate these expectations.

This confidence was suddenly broken when the Visigoths sacked Rome in 410. Not that the event was unheralded. In 378 the Visigoths had defeated and killed an emperor in battle at Adrianople, within the empire; in 406 an Ostrogothic army threatened Italy and in the winter of that year other barbarian tribes, Vandals, Alans and Sueves, crossed the Rhine. But it was the sack of Rome that dispelled the unrealistic optimism of the late empire. Pagan Romans claimed that the disaster would not have happened if the old gods had not been deserted, and Christians in their turn had to reconsider their position. In Africa, Augustine of Hippo embarked on the monumental intellectual task of disentangling the association of Christianity and empire by writing *The City of God*.

Agilbert, bishop of Wessex, one of the spokesmen for the 'Roman' party at the Synod of Whitby (664), is buried at Jouarre, in France, where his sarcophagus still exists (*opposite above*). The praying figures have an intensity that conveys something of the fervour of missionary Christianity. In the same crypt lies the sarcophagus of his sister Theodechilde, first abbess of Jouarre (*below*), decorated with the scallop-shell. (18, 19)

In the west, worse was to come. It was only in the decades after 410 and above all after 455 that the barbarians began to dismantle the western empire, creating kingdoms of their own within the old imperial frontiers, rendering the existence of an emperor superfluous by 476. The establishment of new kingdoms in Spain, France, Italy and along the rivers Rhine and Danube was only a temporary set-back in the work of conversion, however, because, just as Christianity had made little headway in rural areas before 410, it had scarcely touched the homelands of the barbarians. On the other hand, except in the case of the Franks and Anglo-Saxons, the barbarian kings who founded new kingdoms in the territory of the empire and some, at least, of their followers were already Christian, albeit heretical. Even Alaric I, the captor of Rome, was an Arian. It was under the barbarians, and not under Rome, that western Europe was converted.

Missions to the north

The Christianization of the Goths had, in fact, begun as early as the 3rd century. There were already bishops and, seemingly, a Christian king in the Gothic Crimea by the time of Constantine; and the Visigoths, the most influential of the early invaders, were converted at about the time of their entry into the empire in 376. There had been Christian prisoners within the Visigothic kingdom, however, ever since the mid-3rd-century raids on the Roman province of Cappadocia, although probably these Christians made little attempt to convert their masters. Even when one of their descendants, Ulfilas, was consecrated by Eusebius of Nicomedia in 341 he became bishop not for the Visigoths, but only for the Christians living among them. Nor did his ministry last long, for in 348 persecution drove him across the imperial frontier to Nicopolis. Ulfilas's greatest achievement was not his early episcopal ministry, but his translation of the Bible into Gothic; for the first time, it seems, the language was set down in writing. There were later Visigothic persecutions in the course of which Christians of various sects were martyred, but when the Huns drove the Visigoths, with the agreement of the emperor, to cross the Danube, Ulfilas's pupils, armed with the Bible in Gothic, were well placed to carry out

Bishop Ulfilas, working among the tribes of Bulgaria and Serbia, undertook the stupendous task of translating the Bible into Gothic. Fragments of his version still exist – the only surviving example of the Gothic language – written in silver ink on purple-stained parchment.

the task of evangelization. The conversion was thus closely associated with the entry of the Visigoths into the Roman Empire.

The doctrine that was regarded as orthodox by the court of Constantinople, however, both at the time of Ulfilas's consecration and at the moment of the settlement of the Visigoths in the Balkans, was soon to be anathematized as heresy at the Council of Constantinople in 381. It is from this date that the split between orthodox – or Catholics – and the Arians becomes definite. Although Arianism was condemned, it continued to be the religion of the Visigoths and, because they played a significant role in the evangeli-

zation of the other barbarians who entered the empire before 476, Arianism came to be a doctrine associated primarily with the Germanic tribes. The history of these Gothic missions is unfortunately obscure; the Ostrogoths appear to have been converted in the 5th century by Visigoths from Constantinople, or at least they used a church calendar that passed through that milieu. As the Visigoths themselves moved westwards they seem to have influenced other peoples: the Rugi on the Danube, the Burgundians on the Rhône, perhaps as a result of a marriage alliance, and possibly the Vandals in Spain. There were others also involved in this missionary activity, including Arian Romans, who had been hounded as heretics by the imperial church, and at least one man with a Greek name, Ajax, who Christianized the Sueves. The complexity and uncertainty of this period is shown most clearly in the case of the Lombards who entered the old territories of the Roman Empire only in the 6th century. They are described as Catholics early in the century and as pagans in the middle years, and themselves claimed to have been converted to Arianism in the territory of the Rugi; they were certainly predominantly Arian by 590, but there were also pagans and Catholics among them. The only tribe to be converted directly and finally to Catholicism was that of the Franks, whose king, Clovis, was baptized around the year 500, partly because he was in close contact with the Catholic episcopate of Gaul, but also because his great rival was the Arian Visigoth, Alaric II, while his greatest ally, the Emperor Anastasius, he wrongly assumed to be Catholic.

Unlike the Arians, the Catholics made little attempt to Christianize the pagan tribes; Clovis's conversion did not result from any episcopal initiative. The Catholics were active in the conversion of Arian monarchs to orthodoxy, though, and some of their bishops took great pains to combat the rather sterile biblical fundamentalism, which seems to have characterized the Arian theology of the Germans, with their own Catholic doctrine, which owed much to the philosophical traditions of the Mediterranean. In the event, the conversions of the ruling dynasties of the Burgundians, Visigoths and Lombards to Catholicism were not dependent solely on doctrinal debate, athough this should not be underestimated, but they were also associated with the growing social and cultural integration of barbarian and Roman populations, which played into the hands of the well established Catholic episcopate.

These early conversions had not acquainted the Catholics with the northern world; theirs was a Mediterranean church both in its philosophy and, being dependent on the presence of towns, in its organization. Indeed, the papacy was long to remain ignorant of the difficulties posed by the lands north of the Alps. In 601, Gregory the Great assumed that England could be rapidly divided into twenty-four dioceses. At the opposite extreme, in 743, Pope Zacharias doubted whether Boniface should have founded bishoprics at Würzburg, Buraburg and Erfurt, because he thought that they might be places of insufficient size, paying no attention to the vastness of the region and the lack of any centres that a Roman would have identified as a town. Later, in 864, Pope Nicholas I did realize the need for compromise over ecclesiastical organization when he acquiesced in the union of the dioceses of Hamburg and Bremen.

Although the creation of a northern church was one of the greatest achievements of the Dark Ages, in the beginning missionary activity was rare, despite the Gospel injunction: 'Go ye therefore and teach all nations, baptizing them in the name of the Father and of the Son and of the Holy Ghost.' Pope Celestine, it is true, sent Palladius to Ireland in 431, but, as with Ulfilas in 341, the injunction was to care for those who were already Christian. Moreover, Palladius's mission seems to have achieved little, and the real apostle of Ireland, Patrick, whose mission began after Palladius had faded from the scene, was inspired not by papal directive, but by the saint's own experience of living as a captive among the pagan Irish. The ecclesiastical organization that emerged in Ireland during the 6th and 7th centuries, however, was not the work of Patrick but of numerous monastic saints influenced by their Welsh contemporaries, and it was in the Irish monastic church of the 6th century that missionary activity came to be seen as a natural development of the ascetic life. Thus, Columba, a member of the royal dynasty of the Ui Neill, having been compelled to leave Ireland, founded the monastery of Iona in 563. From it he began the Christianization of the Picts, and his successors became involved in the Christianization of the English.

Although the Britons of Wales had been willing to help the nascent Irish church in the 6th century, they resolutely refused to involve themselves in the Christianization of their English enemies, whose conversion was instigated by a second papal initiative: Augustine of Canterbury arrived in England in 597, sent by Pope Gregory the Great. He was received by Aethelbert, king of Kent, and his Christian Frankish wife, Bertha. The early success of the mission in Kent, Essex and East Anglia was associated with Aethelbert's prestige, and on his death the enterprise nearly foundered, until the conversion of his son Eadbald. This Canterbury-based mission is often contrasted with the Christianization of Northumbria, which was achieved, at King Oswald's request, largely by monks from Iona, the most notable of whom was Aidan. Historians have

Constantine burning the books of the 'damned Arian heretics', an illustration to a 'Compendium of Canon Law' made in the 9th century. All the barbarian tribes except the Franks and the Anglo-Saxons had been converted by Arian missionaries. This doctrine, which denied the Trinity and held that Christ was created by and not co-eternal with God, divided Christendom for centuries.

tended to emphasize the divergent national origins and some specific differences of religious practice which were resolved at a synod held at Whitby in 664, but the two sides were not totally opposed. Augustine, like Aidan, was a monk. Wilfrid, later bishop of York and missionary in his own right to Frisia and Sussex, was spokesman for the 'Roman' party at Whitby, although his training had been with the Irish monks of Lindisfarne, where he was later, briefly, abbot. There was a third influence on Wilfrid, and on England, that of the Frankish church, from which came Agilbert, bishop of Wessex, and Felix, missionary in East Anglia. The Christianization of the English was inevitably the work of individual preachers under the protection of particular kings, but the missionaries rapidly reduced paganism to little more than superstitious custom, and their work was soon given coherent shape by Theodore, a monk from Asia Minor, who was appointed archbishop of Canterbury by Pope Vitalian, in 666.

Frankish, Irish and, later, English influences were also at work on the continent. The barbarian migrations of the 5th century had interrupted church organization in various cities of the Rhineland and what is now north-eastern France and Belgium, while the countryside in these regions had probably never been evangelized. From the early 6th century the Frankish kings set about re-establishing sees, for instance at Maastricht, Cologne and Mainz, and notable bishops, such as Vedast of Arras, were also involved in the evangelization of the rural areas. This work was given additional impetus by the arrival of an Irish monk, Columbanus, *c.* 590. Like his Frankish contemporaries, Columbanus worked in regions that had once been Christian: north Burgundy and then Bregenz, where his pupil Gallus carried on his mission. His greatest contributions to the work of conversion, however, were his monastic foundations, especially that at Luxeuil, though his Italian monastery of Bobbio was important in combating Arianism among the Lombards. Luxeuil's importance lay above all in the impression it made on the courtiers of Chlothar I and Dagobert I, to whom it became a model for other monastic foundations, which in their turn became centres for the evangelization of the countryside of northern France and Belgium. Dagobert also showed an interest in Christianity in such frontier areas as Utrecht, Augsburg and Konstanz and, although no later Merovingian king offered comparable support, missionary work continued, culminating in the foundations of the sees of Regensburg, Freising, Salzburg and Passau.

The evangelization carried out by Columbanus and his successors was, however, not an orderly affair. Order was much more apparent in the work of two other missionaries, Willibrord and Boniface, both of whom had the support of the papacy and the powerful Carolingian family. Boniface, a native of Devon who began his mission to the Germans in 718, was frequently critical of the work of the Irish and Frankish missionaries of his day; nevertheless, it should be remembered in their defence that their work provided a foundation for the more dramatic successes of the English. Wilfrid had already spent a year preaching in Frisia, where he was followed by Willibrord, a fellow Northumbrian, who spent most of the period between 690 and 739 working there. In 716 Boniface joined

Willibrord for a year, and he was to return to Frisia and his martyrdom at Dokkum in 754; the majority of his work lay to the south, however: in Hesse, where conversions followed dramatically after his destruction of the sacred oak at Geismar in 724, and in Thuringia. In both areas the work of Christianization went hand in hand with the foundation of monasteries (especially at Fulda) and of bishoprics. In addition, he initiated reform in the churches of Bavaria and the Frankish kingdom.

Many of Boniface's helpers were Englishmen who developed a responsibility towards their continental kinsmen, the Saxons, but the continuation of his work was supervised above all by a Frank, Gregory abbot of Utrecht. The next generation of missionaries was well aware that it was carrying on the work of Boniface and his pupil Gregory. At the same time the evangelization of Saxony marked a dramatic change from peaceful to forcible methods of Christianization. Charlemagne not only destroyed a great religious totem known as the Irminsul, but he also converted the Saxons by the sword, leaving the churchmen to organize the church and make it palatable. Royal influence also lay behind the first major attempt to evangelize Denmark, for, although Willibrord had embarked on the task, it was not until the reign of Louis the Pious (814–40) that anything was achieved. In 831, Anskar, a monk from Picardy, was created bishop of Hamburg to supervise missions to Denmark and Sweden with papal and imperial backing. He had some successes and was able to found churches at Schleswig, Birka and Ribe, but the emergence of the Vikings destroyed his work. The greatest missionary period, which had begun with Wilfrid and Willibrord and which thought of itself as a unity, had come to an end.

Christianity and politics

During the 9th century some headway was made against the pagans of central Europe. The church of Salzburg showed a steady concern with the Slavs to the east, but its hostile reaction to the missionary activities of Methodius provided the first indication of jealous competition which was to affect the rival Catholic and orthodox missions. Much of the early work of Cyril and Methodius, however, was swept away when the Magyars destroyed the Moravian Empire, and in the late 9th century Bohemia came into the orbit of the Carolingian church. In the mid-10th century Christianity was accepted into Poland from Bohemia, through a royal marriage, thus forestalling any aggressive policy of Christianization in the region by the German Ottonian emperors, who had already forcibly evangelized the Slav lands on their eastern

Map of northern Europe showing the sites and regions mentioned in this chapter.

Burgundian bronze belt-buckle with a series of symbols that seem to combine pagan and Christian motifs. The human figures stand in the orant position originally adopted for prayer by the Early Christians.

frontier, creating a new archdiocese at Magdeburg in 962. The Baltic coast, however, remained defiantly pagan, providing Poland with a martyr, St Adalbert (buried at Gniezno), until the military conquests of the Teutonic knights in the High Middle Ages.

The military and political emergence of the Ottonians as heirs to the Carolingian Empire also played a part in the Christianization of Denmark because of the threat posed by Henry and Otto I to the Danish kings, Gorm and Harold Bluetooth. In addition, the archdiocese of Hamburg-Bremen, backed by the empire and later aided by the kings of Denmark as well, revived its interests in the Scandinavian world. The Vikings, also, when they travelled beyond the Baltic, were exposed increasingly to Christianity. Swedish and Norse kings converted in England brought Anglo-Saxon missionaries back with them, thus opening up a final opportunity for missionary work to the English and depriving the archbishops of Hamburg of a Christian monopoly.

Denmark was constantly open to Christian influence because of its geographical position and accessible markets, but, after the failure of the work of Anskar and Rimbert, little headway was made until Henry I defeated Gorm, leaving the country open to Unni, archbishop of Hamburg. Even so, it was not until Harold, Gorm's son, was converted, perhaps by the missionary Poppo, who miraculously undertook the ordeal of wearing a red-hot metal glove without harm, that Christianity was given full support by the king. Although Harold was later killed in battle, the church in Denmark was never again seriously undermined. Harold also promoted the activities of missionaries in the Danish islands and in Norway and Sweden; Hakon the Good, king of Norway, whom he is said to have persuaded to accept Christianity, may in fact have been baptized already in England at the court of Athelstan,

reputedly his godfather. Similarly, of the two kings who did most to promote Christianity in Norway, one, Olaf Tryggvason, was baptized in England, the other, Olaf Haroldson, probably at Rouen. Even these two men met with difficulty when enforcing Christianity in the face of pagan tradition and magic. The death of Olaf Haroldson in battle, in 1030, provided the Christians with a martyr whose cult created a focus for national devotion, even though the war in which he died was anything but religious.

It is sometimes alleged that Olaf Tryggvason was also influential in the Christianization of Iceland, because he threatened to invade unless the Icelanders converted. Since he was scarcely able to overcome paganism at home, it is doubtful whether he would have had more success abroad. Nevertheless, he did exert pressure by seizing Icelandic travellers after the failure of his missionary Thangbrand. On the other hand, Christianity was not new to Iceland, many of whose first settlers had been Christians at least in name; and, although subsequent generations had lapsed into a paganism based on the family and the common interests of the island, outside contacts must have ensured a continuing awareness of the Christian religion. However, when Icelanders were converted on their travels and returned to Christianize their homeland, they threatened the fragile harmony on which their kingless island depended. And when Tryggvason compelled Hjalti Skeggison and Gizur the Wise to return home as missionaries, in 1000, the Icelanders were faced with a choice between Christianity and civil war; the inspired solution (by a pagan, Thorgeir) was to enforce Christianity in public but to allow some pagan practices to continue, particularly in the privacy of the home.

By comparison with Iceland, the Christianization of Sweden was an untidy affair. Kings and their councils

After Olaf Haroldson, king of Norway, had received Christian baptism (probably at Rouen) about the year 1000, he committed himself to imposing the new faith upon his subjects, often in the face of stubborn resistance. This drawing from a manuscript of some four hundred years later shows him holding the royal axe and orb and trampling beneath his feet a deformed figure representing paganism.

had sometimes allowed a church to function in the trading centre of Birka, from as early as the days of Anskar, or permitted preachers to evangelize. When the kings of Denmark were powerful, the missionaries they supported achieved some success. But even when the kings of Sweden themselves had been converted they were powerless against the paganism of their subjects, and they refused to condone the desecration of the famous pagan sanctuary at Uppsala. The destruction of this temple and the foundation of a church on the site marks the triumph of Christianity in Swedish Uppland, but that was not to happen much before 1090.

Old and new gods

Many incidents in the Christianization of northern Europe were not recorded and even the documents that do survive cannot always be taken at face value. The majority of the sources were written by clerics who had little wish to understand the beliefs of the pagans, and they wrote in Latin, a language not always well equipped to describe alien societies. Moreover, since many authors delighted in displaying their learning by borrowing a phrase or an image from a classical author, the pagan north often appears in a Mediterranean light. As early as Tacitus, Wodan was equated with Mercury, rightly or wrongly, while as late as the 10th century Widukind could identify a Slav idol as Saturn. In addition, some sources show very specific bias; Adam of Bremen, for instance, associated the baptism of Olaf Tryggvason with the see of Hamburg, although the event took place in England. Furthermore, because biographies of saints were written primarily for the moral edification of the clergy, especially monks, most passages in a saint's life were carefully constructed to illustrate a virtue or vice. What interested the author and his audience was an abstract religious truth, not strict historical accuracy. There was no need to record the confrontation between pagan and Christian exactly.

Nor does the vernacular evidence necessarily provide a more authentic view of the pagans, since all of it was written by Christians, usually clerics, and much of it is not strictly contemporary. The great Icelandic sagas of the 12th century are the works of Christians and the accuracy of their view of the pagan gods and heroes may be doubted. The tale of Baldr – an innocent victim laid low by the powers of evil – was certainly influenced by Christianity, and the tale of the destruction of the gods, which gives Scandinavian mythology so much of its melancholy, might have been developed by clerics in order to emphasize the end of the pagan world. Such a bias is obviously not present in many finds of the archaeologist, but even grave-goods rarely allow the beliefs of the dead to be adequately reconstructed. Nevertheless, certain general aspects of

authentic pagan thought are clear, although there must have been much variation and divergence in the beliefs of different peoples. Moreover, some of these beliefs seem almost to have been contradictory. This is not impossible; few religions are entirely systematic and paganism seems not to have offered an orderly explanation of the universe.

Adam of Bremen claimed that the gods of the Saxons were too immense to be confined within temple walls, and that instead their existence was contemplated in sacred groves. Presumably he envisaged some sort of nature religion which might have included the cult of trees, like the sacred oak at Geismar, stones and springs, all of which are mentioned in literary texts and supported by archaeological finds. In addition, there were the beliefs surrounding the sacred totem of the Saxons, the Irminsul, the pillar of the universe. Perhaps quite separate in origin were the gods that could be depicted or confined to shrines; some of them were associated with particular places, like Fosite on Helgoland or Redigost at Rethra, while others, like Wodan, Thor, Frey and Saxnot, were widely worshipped. Together, the gods formed a pantheon; on one occasion a man claimed to have come from their council. This pantheon, moreover, was evolving during the historical period; the cult of Wodan seems to have been losing ground to that of Thor. When faced with the arrival of the God of the Christians, the pagan deities of Birka were reported to have opposed this cult, offering instead to accept the hero Eric as one of their number. The fact that leading families claimed to be descended from particular gods may suggest that the line between heroes and members of the pantheon had always been blurred. Further, Adam recounted that the trees on which sacrifices were hung in the grove of Uppsala had been infused with divinity by their charges.

From their gods the pagans expected present help and they associated different deities with particular spheres of influence: Wodan, who had been the god of war for the early Germans, was approached by Scandinavians during famine; Thor was the god of battles; and Frey of fertility. In addition the pagan could fortify himself with charms, amulets and phylacteries, which might well accompany him into the grave. Protection of this sort was important for any major undertaking, and further security could be sought by consulting sorcerers before embarking on any project. Divination by casting lots, observing the flights of birds, particularly of storks, and by inspecting entrails was common. Boniface and his contemporaries inveighed against phylacteries and augurers, and the truth behind their complaints is confirmed by the presence of the bones of birds in graves. Norway was still notable for its sorcerers in the 11th century. For the pagan and, indeed, for the semi-Christian, these practices provided assurance; it was necessary to have access to the unseen in order to ensure survival in an eminently unstable world.

As well as providing personal security, the pagan cults played a public role in barbarian society. In Scandinavia and in England the temples had their priests, there were sacrifices, sometimes human, and there was ritual consumption of horseflesh in Germany, England and Scandinavian Iceland. Archaeology has also revealed traces of funerary banquets in cemeteries. In Iceland and probably elsewhere there were family cults, presided over by the paterfamilias, as among the pagan aristocracy of the later Roman Empire, where the head of the family was often the last to be converted to Christianity. Ritual occasions were a formal display of concord among the basic units of society, the nation or tribe and the family. Conformity was required, because not to conform was regarded as a challenge to the general security. All this left the Christian in a quandary; his attachment to a single God was not intended to challenge the peace of the community, but refusal to sacrifice to the gods of imperial Rome or, as in the case of the Christian, Sabas (who was martyred for his non-conformity), to the idols of the Visigoths was construed as just such a challenge. Because good Christians could not conform to the public cults of pagan society, converts were a problem to kings and their councils and, not unnaturally, missionaries found it expedient to act with official approval; in Denmark and Sweden, kings are specifically said to have allowed men to be baptized. Moreover, by recognizing that his pagan ancestors were condemned to hell the Christian was striking at the family itself. Avitus of Vienne specially commended Clovis for a perspicacity greater than that of his forebears; and, although the story is apocryphal, the alleged refusal of the Frisian, Radbod, to convert because by so doing he would damn his predecessors illustrates a genuine issue. One solution to this was followed by Harold, who disinterred his parents, Gorm and Thyri, and had them reburied in a fine church next to their original burial mound at Jelling.

The experience of conversion

Because paganism was closely associated with the tribe and the family, it was weakest when those institutions were either irrelevant or in decay. A merchant on a trading voyage could not rely on the protection of his family, the chief security that any barbarian was likely to have; his family gods, therefore, were not a good guarantee of security. The Icelander, Helgi the Lean, expected that Thor would bring a prosperous voyage, although he also believed in Christ; those who sailed along the Frisian coast offered gifts to the patron of the region, Fosite. The majority must also have resorted to charms and amulets. If a pagan's destination was one of the great markets of Scandinavia he might well have found a shrine to a god he recognized, but in the towns of the Christian Franks or English his own gods had no sanctuary and their God had no rival. Dependent on the peace provided by a Christian monarch, deprived of the gods of his family, many a merchant received baptism in France, the Low Countries or England, while others underwent *prima signatio*, a less binding form of Christian initiation. Back home, such a man might still live a good pagan life, but the fact remained that his gods lacked influence in a Christian milieu. The Christians, on the other hand, claimed that their God was omnipotent, while in the cults of saints and in relics they could offer reassurance for the individual equal to anything the pagans possessed.

The merchant's experience was repeated on a much larger scale for many of the barbarian peoples; every member of the migrating hordes of the 4th and 5th centuries witnessed the failure of the social system to which he had been accustomed. A nomadic existence forced men to leave behind cult sites associated with springs, trees and ancestral groves; and the elevation of the survival of the tribe above the life of the family must have exaggerated the social upheaval and contributed to the disruption of traditional beliefs. At the same time, because of the need for effective leadership, migration facilitated the emergence of kings, who rapidly came into contact with the political and cultural ideals of the emperor and were well placed to promote the new religion among their own subjects. Not surprisingly, almost every barbarian people was Christianized within a generation of entering the Roman Empire; the exceptions were to be found in the north, notably Britain.

For various reasons this pattern was not repeated in the second age of migration, the Viking period. In the 4th and 5th centuries, whole tribes had been set on the move to ensure their survival in the face of the Huns; in the 8th, 9th and 10th centuries the pressures were smaller and the migrants were individual chieftains with their warrior followings. The Christian kingdoms of this period were not equal to the Roman Empire in status or cultural achievement, but they did respond to the threats posed by the Vikings, and, especially when there was no immediate danger, they furthered the work of Christianization. Having defeated the invading forces of Guthrum at Edington, Alfred insisted that the Dane accept baptism. Other Christian courts whose prestige was unchallenged could go further; when

Identity of purpose between secular and religious powers, initiated during the missionary era, remained an ideal until the end of the Middle Ages. An optimistic image of pope and emperor embracing comes from the 13th-century 'Sachsenspiegel'.

Harold Klak, the exiled king of Denmark, appealed to Charlemagne's son Louis the Pious for help, Louis kept him in his entourage until he was baptized; and the fame of Athelstan of England was such that, according to Icelandic tradition, the half-brothers Hakon of Norway and Eric Bloodaxe were baptized at his instigation.

Already in the 7th century the Christianization of Anglo-Saxon England had been advanced by the greatest of the kings as they strove to assert their hegemony over their neighbours. Oswald, king of Northumbria, for instance, stood godfather at the baptism of Cynegisl of Wessex; and Oswiu, Oswald's successor, insisted on the conversion of Peada, king of the Middle Angles, when the latter asked for the hand of his daughter in marriage. Similarly, in Scandinavia, powerful kings, such as Horic I and Swein Estridson, used their influence to ensure a favourable reception for the missionaries. This association between missionary activity and political hegemony was even more marked in the kingdom of the Franks, along the frontiers of which there were many peoples sometimes regarded as tributary. Willibrord's work in Frisia was supported, in word if not in deed, by Pippin II, and Boniface had the backing of Charles Martel and Pippin III. As the Carolingians became more powerful and their policies more aggressive, so their support for missionary work became more forceful. The God of the Old Testament was the God of battles and as such appealed directly to the Germans, who had once dedicated themselves to Wodan for the duration of military campaigns, and to the Scandinavians, who revered Thor. Ulfilas had been aware that the warlike Israelites of the Old Testament

would bring out the worst in the Goths and so had omitted the Book of Kings from his translation of the Bible. Nevertheless, it was impossible to dissociate the Christian God from battle; Constantine had been converted in battle, an unexpected victory won Clovis for Christ and a party of Swedes were convinced in similar circumstances during a campaign against the Slavs. At a less elevated level, in the 5th and 6th centuries, barbarians began to adorn their armour with crosses, as can be seen on a helmet from Vezeronce; they took the image of the breastplate of faith literally. Success in battle led the Carolingians to place great emphasis on their special relationship with the true God. One missionary, Lebuin, ironically turned this argument upside-down when he told the Saxons that they should become Christians in order to overcome the Frankish threat. They ignored his advice and Christianity was forced on them.

The idea that men should be forcibly brought to the true faith was not new. Christ, in a parable, had stated that the recalcitrant would be compelled to enter the banquet, and Augustine had insisted on the relevance of this text when dealing with heretics. In the early 7th century, Amandus is said to have asked Dagobert I to force the unwilling to undergo baptism. This was nothing compared with the enormities of Charlemagne's Christianization of Saxony, where the newly conquered were forcibly baptized, despite the protests of so eminent a cleric as Alcuin. When the Saxons rebelled and returned to their pagan gods, their treason and apostasy only increased the determination of the emperor, and 4,500 rebels were massacred at Verden in 782. Despite the work of a small group of notable missionaries, Saxony was Christianized by the sword and by the application of a ferocious law-code. Later monarchs used force, Otto I, in the Slav lands round Magdeburg, and Olaf Tryggvason, in Norway, but their brutality did not equal Charlemagne's.

A policy that depended on military superiority had its disadvantages. To associate God with the success of one nation naturally put its opponents on their guard; the Frisian king, Radbod, was much more inclined to welcome missionaries before they became associated with the aggressive policies of Charles Martel. In the 9th and 10th centuries the cult of Thor seems to have become more vigorous, perhaps in response to militant Christianity. There were further aggravations; as well as lamenting the means by which Saxony was Christianized, Alcuin attacked the ruthless exaction of tithes, not only in Saxony, but also in the diocese of Salzburg. During the 11th century, the Danish king, Swein Estridson, commented that the Saxons would probably have converted the northern Slavs had they not been so avaricious.

Christianity, however, was not dependent on military success. According to his biographer, the missionary Rimbert, when Anskar saw his achievements destroyed he found solace in the story of Job. Many missionaries were killed, as was the Englishman, Wulfred, who had mutilated a statue of Thor. Onlookers might have regarded his death as divine vengeance, but for Christians martyrdom was one of the finest achievements, and some, like Bruno of Querfurt, longed for it with a morbid intensity. Apparent failure may have disturbed the missionaries, but it could be comprehended within their philosophy. Moreover, the virtues of almsgiving and care for the poor and bereaved meant that the church was well prepared to alleviate disasters and that it could fulfil certain social duties that would once have fallen to relatives in the family-oriented society of the northern barbarians.

Although the Carolingian monarchs and the papacy offered protection and support to Willibrord and Boniface and others like them, the work of evangelization could be dissociated from politics. Certainly, the missionaries usually approached the local king, chieftain or assembly for permission to preach. If they were lucky, they were provided with a church or a site for one, as at Canterbury, Schleswig, Birka and elsewhere. From then on their duty was to confound paganism and to spread the Gospel. The first of these tasks might involve breaking up a temple or cult object to prove that the gods were no more than stones and pieces of wood. The Northumbrian high-priest, Coifi, dramatically abandoned his old beliefs by mounting a stallion and throwing a spear into the sanctuary of the temple – an act of ritual profanation. Pagan deities were not always overcome in this manner. Boniface was advised to argue with the pagans, showing that because their gods had a beginning they could not have created the world. That is not to say that they did not exist – many Christians accepted that they did – but that they were demons.

More important than the attack on paganism was the preaching of the Gospel, which was the central factor in the work of Christianization. For the believer, the Old Testament offered a complete explanation of the origin of the world, while the New Testament offered a different (and imperfectly understood) system of ethics as well as a promise of salvation. According to Bede, one of Edwin's followers compared earthly existence with the flight of a sparrow through a lighted hall, and suggested that if Christianity could dispel some of the darkness that came before or after, it was worthy to be considered; although the story may be fictitious, it illustrates something of the impact that the Gospel might have had. But the Bible was in Latin and the barbarians spoke in various vernaculars. The Gothic

The rite of baptism was a turning point in the lives of the barbarian peoples and is frequently represented in iconography. A portable altar or reliquary of about 1100 contained this relief of St Peter baptizing.

translation of Ulfilas seems not to have remained in circulation after the 6th century and while in eastern Europe his achievement was surpassed by Cyril and Methodius, who produced a Slavonic translation and a whole script in which to write it down, in the west the church of Salzburg was hostile to the use of Slavonic. Bede, admittedly, began to translate the Gospel of St John into Old English, but Boniface regarded the vernacular as the language of paganism. The result was that the Gospel and the liturgy remained in Latin and that they had to be explained to men who understood not a word of it. The missionaries were not even always competent in the language of the people they were addressing; in Northumbria, Oswald interpreted for Aidan, while later, in the Slav lands subject to the see of Hamburg, Prince Gottschalk translated the words of the clergy into plain Slavonic. In Wessex, Bishop Agilbert had his see reduced because he remained unintelligible to the king.

This problem of understanding was approached in two different ways. A number of missionaries bought and trained enslaved members of the nation which they intended to evangelize. Of the indigenous clergy thus created we hear practically nothing, which may imply that they did their job well, as labourers in the field, and it may be that it was such men as these who translated the baptismal vows into various Old German dialects, thus leaving converts in no doubt about their renunciation of paganism. The other approach was concerned rather with making Latin intelligible. At first the Irish were the great masters of this; they were the earliest western converts to whom Latin was totally alien, and to make up for this they filled their services with ritual so that they could follow them even if the language remained incomprehensible. They did learn Latin, however, and became great teachers, and their successors, the English, followed them in this. Before embarking on his missionary career, Boniface had already taught Latin grammar, as had the Frank, Anskar, while much of the influence of the Anglo-Saxon missionary Willehad lay in his school where he taught the children of the Frisian nobility. For the missionaries it was vital that they understood the scriptures, as Boniface impressed on his disciple Gregory, when he asked him to explain (probably still in Latin) what he had just read. To misunderstand could lead to heresy, which Boniface thought prevalent; when he met a priest who had baptized ungrammatically he insisted on rebaptism. The papacy was rather less dogmatic on such points of detail.

The monasteries:
power-houses of the missions

Because missionary activity was necessarily associated with learning, the power-houses of the Dark Age missions were the monasteries; Britain, the Low Countries and Germany were all Christianized from monastic centres and many of the leading missionaries in Scandinavia and Poland were monks and ascetics. The monastery provided a refuge and a place of rest, but above all it provided a scriptorium and a library. Gospels, liturgical books and works of theology were all accessible and they contained all the philosophy, culture and science which the early medieval church had taken from classical antiquity. By the standards of what had been and what was to come this may not have been much, but to the northern barbarians it was new and was a mark of the superiority of Christianity over other religions. Even to the illiterate, books were significant. Although after the martyrdom of Boniface his killers threw away his books in disgust, having expected more valuable treasure, the Scandinavians in later centuries kept manuscripts as booty. Boniface specially commissioned a copy of the Epistles of St Peter in gold lettering, as an inspiration for himself and to impress his audience; runes were thought at times to be magic, and a German might well have assumed that golden letters had similar properties.

Monastic culture was intended to be useful; once educated, a monk could play his part in the Christianization of the surrounding countryside or further afield. Not surprisingly, within the monasteries the two missionary traditions of teaching Latin and creating a vernacular clergy coalesced, especially in the greatest of Boniface's foundations, Fulda. There, at the centre of the German mission, as elsewhere, vernacular glosses began to be written in the margins of the manuscripts. Steadily, the barbarians were provided with an ecclesiastical vocabulary, and they were also being given a written language. The contents of the earliest known vernacular works are almost all religious, ranging from glosses, baptismal vows and the hymn of the English poet Caedmon to the Old Saxon epic on the Saviour, the *Heliand*, commissioned, it seems, for missionary purposes by Louis the Pious. Even the Old English laws and charters show signs of ecclesiastical influence. These Christian authors did not create a completely new literature – they drew on classical, Mediterranean models and an northern oral tradition; but for the first time the vernacular languages of the north were written down.

The progress of Christianity was inevitably uneven; in the rural areas pagan worship continued long after the aristocracy had been converted, and the work of evangelizing the countryside often continued for centuries after a kingdom was regarded as Christian. The cult of idols continued in France throughout the 6th century; in Wessex, King Ine legislated against idolatry in *c.* 694, but in 786 a legatine mission to England regarded paganism as consisting merely of tattooing, docking horses' tails and eating horseflesh. While the peasants were least thoroughly affected by Christianity, not every member of the aristocracy made a clean break with his old beliefs. Redwald, king of East Anglia, worshipped Christ in the company of other gods, and in Germany, too, there were rulers who continued to worship idols while claiming to be Christian. The Lombards of Benevento may have taken over an ancient Abruzzian cult of snake worship, but the evidence is untrustworthy. Among the early Icelanders and the Swedish merchants of the 9th and 10th centuries, there were those who believed in Christ *and* the old gods. Pagan heroes were also remembered in the company of the Gospel, and on the Franks casket the adoration of the Magi appears next to the story of Wayland the smith; similarly, there is a carving of Sigurd on the Andreas cross. The exploits of pagan heroes, to Alcuin's disgust, even delighted Northumbrian monks, who, he said, preferred the legendary Ingeld to Christ.

In some cases pagan tradition was deliberately Christianized. Gregory the Great recommended that pagan temples be cleansed and converted into churches and that pagan festivals be transformed into feasts in honour of the saints. The church also had to take trial by ordeal under its aegis. Presumably a pagan custom, it was certainly Christianized by the Arian clergy of the Burgundians and thence passed into the Catholic church. As early as the 8th century the Lombard king, Liutprand, doubted its efficacy but did not stamp it out; in the 10th century, by contrast, a Christian cleric was willing to undergo the judgment of God to demonstrate the truth of his faith, if the story of Poppo's ordeal is not a legend. The custom finally fell from favour only in the 12th century.

The northern church

The values of the barbarians also affected Christianity. The image of the God of battles blended well with a delight in military prowess and this connection was strengthened by Germanic vocabulary, which tended to associate lordship with war-leadership. Christ, therefore, was transformed into a warrior; he appears as such on a plaque from Grésin, on which he is also given the attributes of a fertility god. Virility, however, was less easily accepted as a virtue by the church; as a result there was some conflict between Christian ethics and barbarian custom, despite the fact that the Germans had long been regarded as a moral people. This latter view is apparent as early as Tacitus, who, like Salvian in the 5th century, used the barbarians as a stick with which to beat his own society. But it was more than a platitude; Boniface pointed out that the marital behaviour of the Christian king Aethelbald of Mercia compared unfavourably with that of the pagans of central Germany, who insisted on the death penalty for adultery, and the law-codes corroborate his account. On the other hand, some, if not all, barbarian peoples practised concubinage and they (or their kings at least) continued to do so long after they had been Christianized. The rulers of the Franks still had concubines in the 8th century, and Adam of Bremen, writing in the 11th, commended the Danes for their virtues, but commented that they were still intemperate with regard to women and drink. The Christian ideal of marriage was only accepted gradually among the northern peoples. As in so much else, the 12th century marked the victory of ecclesiastical law, although the southern barbarians responded earlier, having been Christianized long before their northern counterparts and having settled nearer the ancient centres of Christian culture.

Christianity, however, was only one factor influencing the development of barbarian society. As a result of the migrations of the 4th and 5th centuries, kingship had become stronger and more permanent, and as the successor states of the Roman Empire came into being, so their rulers turned for assistance in government to their subject populations: in the south to secular administrators, but in the north, as often as not, to the clergy. In those regions where the art of written administration had been forgotten, as in Britain, or had never been known, the church introduced forms of documentation, the written law-code and the charter, both of which helped place further power in the hands

One of the rare documents bearing witness to the conversion of the Germanic tribes is this copy of a baptismal oath administered about 820, preserved in the library of Fulda. The manuscript employs two languages; the catechism on this page being in Saxon and the charge in Latin.

of the king. Order had once been kept largely by the family; the danger of initiating a blood-feud between families was a powerful incentive against murder. Perhaps influenced by the church, kings, such as the Lombard, Rothari, discouraged the feud, promoting instead the, admittedly old, idea of paid compensation, the administration of which might involve royal officials. Charters also changed the position of the family since family land seems largely to have been inalienable in the pre-literate period. For their churches and monasteries, the missionaries and their ecclesiastical successors needed property; land was granted to them and the charter helped to make this alienation possible.

For such reasons Christianization seems often to be associated with the growth of royal authority. Sometimes the church gained directly from a recent increase in an individual's power, as happened with Clovis and, more graphically, with Harold Bluetooth, who directly juxtaposed the Christianization of Denmark and his conquest of Denmark and Norway in an inscribed stone set up at Jelling. The great fortresses at Trelleborg and Fyrkat demonstrate his hold over the country. Not surprisingly, therefore, ecclesiastics turned their attention to the question of kingship, a subject on which the Old Testament had much to offer, if only in providing analogies for current developments. Gaiseric, an Arian king of the Vandals, in the 5th century, seems to have been the first barbarian to attribute his rule to the grace of God, perhaps to compete with the emperor; while another Arian, the Visigoth, Leovigild, claimed similar divine support a century and a half later. But it was the Catholic clergy who developed the ceremony of unction, for which there is a possible 6th-century reference in Britain and certain 7th-century evidence in Visigothic Spain. The church began to elevate the king, infusing his office with moral responsibilities while enhancing his authority, nowhere more so than for the Carolingian and Ottonian emperors of the 9th and 10th centuries. The resulting confusion between church and state would only be resolved during the conflict between papacy and empire in the High Middle Ages.

Rulers were not the only secular beneficiaries of the new Christian society, however. The nobility had also supported the missionaries, granting estates and founding monasteries, and the church repaid them. The alienation of land in favour of the church was not always detrimental to the owner; the family became associated with the foundation it had endowed and many churches and monasteries came to be regarded as family property. Pious founders might be remembered as saints, as happened to several members of the Frankish aristocracy, who were influenced by the example of Columbanus at Luxeuil, most notably Gertrude of Nivelles and Arnulf of Metz, ancestors of the Carolingian dynasty. Their monasteries naturally helped to propagate their cults. Occasionally the development of a saintly aristocracy has been interpreted as a replacement for a charisma said to have been possessed by the pagan nobility; although the paterfamilias of a noble family is likely to have performed priestly functions in heathen times, this hardly provides a direct parallel, and it seems less fanciful to regard the two religious traditions as being quite separate.

The emergence of a proprietary church is one major indication of a transformation within Christianity itself; another is the appearance in the 8th century of warrior bishops. The kings and aristocrats of the Dark Ages created an institution in accordance with their own view of society, which was a military one. Nevertheless, there were men who carried a different ideal with them and the great ecclesiastical reforms of the 11th and 12th centuries were built on their work. Not only was Boniface a missionary, he was also a stern upholder of ecclesiastical standards; so, too, were many members of the Carolingian episcopate. The Benedictine Rule was diffused precisely by the men who Christianized Europe: those influenced by Luxeuil, the English of Northumbria and, above all, Boniface. Legislation on church matters, by the 12th century, was essentially the codification of judgments, given especially in the 5th and 6th centuries and handed down by the bishops of the Carolingian age. By the standards of the canonists, Dark Age Christianity was a bizarre affair, but in reality the churchmen had undertaken a heroic task in Christianizing the north, and in doing so not only had they created a northern church, they had also preserved enough Christian and classical culture to provide the foundation for a more intellectual age.

THE EASTERN CHURCH

4
The Greek church and the peoples
of eastern Europe

A DIVISION BETWEEN EAST AND WEST existed in the Roman Empire long before Christianity was officially sanctioned; it was inevitable, therefore, that the churches in the two halves should evolve in different ways. During the so called 'Dark Ages' in the west, as we saw in the previous chapter, the church became the most stable institution in the state, the refuge of literacy, administrative skill and culture. In the east the secular power remained intact and the church was never its rival. The duality of powers, which will become so characteristic in the western Middle Ages, never arose here. The church remained distinctly the lesser partner, but on the other hand, the emperor acquired a more priestly function. While western Christianity looked to two leaders, pope and emperor, the east had only one, at once royal pope and sacred monarch.

The Orthodox church survived the long years of Ottoman supremacy, but in a pale and diminished form. Cast off from its imperial stem it could only wither, though it continued to produce able and interesting men. The monasteries of Mount Athos and the Meteora preserved – and still preserve – a way of life that made no concessions to change. And in the 20th century, the Greek church proved sufficiently resilient to take on a new role in the eastern Mediterranean, with centres in many separate and often mutually hostile countries – Istanbul, Athens, Cairo and Jerusalem. As an alternative form of Christianity to the Catholic and Protestant churches (both tainted with Western imperialist associations) it offers considerable appeal to the Third World.

The story of the Orthodox church in Russia is a saga in its own right. Founded on similar lines to that of Byzantium, it never enjoyed the same understanding with the state. From the beginning, the tsars exercised a tyrannical control over ecclesiastical affairs. By the 19th century it was virtually a department of the civil service, and since the Bolshevik Revolution its very existence has been under threat. Yet its hold over the people of Russia seems never to have relaxed, and it has nourished the imagination of many of her most profound thinkers and poets.

Life is a ladder
reaching from the earth to heaven, but at every rung the forces of hell are ready to drag the sinner to damnation. This 12th-century icon from St Catherine's, Sinai, shirks none of the implications. It was inspired by a treatise by John Climacus, an abbot of Mount Sinai about five hundred years earlier, in which the ladder served as a metaphor for moral aspiration, each rung corresponding to a chapter in the book. At the bottom, a band of monks still on earth pray for the salvation of their brethren. At the top, Christ and his angels wait to receive them. In between, an army of black devils wielding pikes, ropes and bows and arrows wage eternal war on humanity. To the Middle Ages this was no fantasy or figure of speech. It was the literal and terrible truth. (1)

The monastic family

There were no equivalents to monastic orders in the Greek church. Each monastery had its own rules and was headed by its own abbot. Monks often led secluded lives but were close to the common people.

Isolated from the world by high walls, the typical Orthodox monastery looks in upon a courtyard containing the cells and enclosing the community's church. Rila, in Bulgaria (*above* and *above right*), was founded in the 10th century and became one of the most famous spiritual centres of the Balkans. Many times destroyed and rebuilt, the present complex dates from 1816–47. (2, 3)

Zagorsk, the monastery of the Holy Trinity and St Sergius (*below*), not far from Moscow, is like a small town. It includes six churches, a palace for the metropolitan and numerous buildings for pilgrims. Here, from left to right, we can see St Sergius and its refectory, the tall bell-tower, the five-domed Cathedral of the Assumption and the octagonal Pyatnitsa tower. (4)

The holy mountain of Mount Athos rises at the end of a narrow finger of land pointing south-east from the northern coast of Greece. From the 10th century onwards monks have come here to seek solitude. There are now twenty monasteries with a total population of something over 1,000. Edward Lear's picturesque oil painting (*above*) shows one overlooking the sea. (5)

The Meteora (*below*) is a strange region of precipitous mountains upon whose crags the early monks built their refuges, some of them accessible only by a basket lifted from above. They flourished between the 14th and 17th centuries, under Turkish occupation, when their remoteness was an advantage, but are now no longer functioning as monasteries. (7)

The Grand Lavra at the foot of Mount Athos is the largest and finest of the monasteries. Its refectory (*above*), where the 150 monks take their meals, was built in 1512 and decorated with frescoes by Theophanes the Cretan. (6)

Attendant saints

Most Orthodox churches are small in scale. Congregations preferred an intimate liturgy to the grander ceremonial of the west. The tall screens, which became popular at a fairly late stage, served to display more icons and bring the protecting saints closer.

A glowing iconostasis, carved, gilded and hung with sacred icons, separates the sanctuary from the body of the church. The central doors, through which the priest appears and disappears, add mystery and drama to the rite. This sumptuous interior at Rila incorporates dozens of icons. (8)

The figure of Christ could be, by comparison with the west, remote and forbidding, the Judge rather than the Victim. *Above:* Christ Pantocrater ('Ruler of the Universe') from Hosios Loukas, Greece. *Below:* the Anastasis (the Harrowing of Hell, see p. 9), a later icon from Cyprus, dated 1563. (9, 10)

A sacred monarchy

In Byzantium, church and state were not merely linked, they were integral parts of one another.

The emperor was God's viceroy, sharing something of his sanctity. *Left:* Constantine being crowned by the hand of God, a gold medal of the 4th century. *Below:* in a later (10th century) mosaic above the entrance to Hagia Sophia, Justinian presents his church and Constantine his city to the Virgin and Child. (11, 12)

Constantine VII Porphyrogenitus is crowned by Christ, an ivory of the mid-10th century. The emperor, robed and jewelled, stands only a little lower than Christ. (13)

Russia inherited the Byzantine concept of the sacred monarchy but interpreted it in cruder terms. *Right:* an elaborate allegorial engraving of 1683. While Christ blesses the young co-emperors Peter (later the Great) and his half-brother Ivan, their enemies are defeated by angels. (15)

At religious councils the emperor presided as God's representative, though he was not a priest. Here John Cantacuzenus (reigned 1341–54) opens a session surrounded by patriarchs and metropolitans. (14)

The unchanging image

The Byzantine icon tradition is to western eyes depressingly uninventive; but this is partly due to the role of the icon itself, which is a semi-holy object in which novelty would be out of place.

Our Lady of Vladimir, the earliest, the most famous and the most copied of extant icons, was commissioned by a prince of Kiev from a Constantinopolitan artist about 1130 (*above*). The tenderness and pity left unexpressed in representations of Christ, shine through in those of the Virgin. A 19th-century version, painted on glass (*below*) shows the same theme transposed into Romanian folk-art. (17, 18)

St Demetrius of Salonica defeats the Roman Emperor Diocletian: a 19th-century icon still following Byzantine convention. Demetrius was a half-legendary figure from the last persecution, around 300, and became one of the most popular Orthodox saints. (16)

4
The Greek church and the peoples of eastern Europe

STEVEN RUNCIMAN

I N 1648 the Greek-born Catholic scholar, Leo Allatius, published a work which he entitled 'On the Perpetual Consension between the Western and Eastern Churches', in which he sought to prove that there were no fundamental differences between the two churches and that unity could easily be restored were the east to submit to the authority of Rome. Two generations later, another Greek scholar, Dositheus, Orthodox patriarch of Jerusalem, answered him in his great history of his patriarchate, which was in fact a history of the whole Orthodox church, in which he showed that from the earliest centuries of Christendom, Greek and Latin thinkers had begun to drift apart, in both their philosophical and their ecclesiastical points of view.

From its inception, long before the Triumph of the Cross, the Roman Empire had been divided into two halves, the Latin and the Greek. No one can tell us exactly how far language reflects the thought of those that speak it and how far it dictates their thought. The Latin language is both sonorous and precise, language admirably suited for rhetoric and for ceremony and for clear definitions, a language for lawyers rather than for subtle thinkers. Greek is a far more flexible tongue, capable of delicate shades of meaning, even of ambiguities, a language of ideas rather than of facts, better suited for philosophy than for law. The difference of outlook began to show in the works of the Early Christian Fathers. It is clearly visible in the great councils of the church, held to deal with the heresies of the 4th, 5th and 6th centuries, where Rome tried to insist on a simple statement of doctrinal fact, while the east inserted delicate qualifications that at times amounted to ambiguity. As a consequence, the Greek and Latin Acts of the councils were often somewhat at variance. This gave the east a certain contempt for the west. After all, the first Christian theologians had written in Greek, to express the new faith in terms acceptable to Greek philosophy. If the Latins had to simplify it all to fit the needs of their language and mentality, they had no right to impose their simplifications on the east.

A sacred monarchy

This difference was enhanced by the barbarian invasions, which resulted in the west in the disappearance of the former lay lawyers, teachers and adminis-trators. Only the ecclesiastics remained at their posts; and they, therefore, had to provide the barbarian rulers with not only the necessary lawyers and schoolmasters, but even the clerks. This could not but increase the legalistic outlook of the Roman church. In the east the barbarians never penetrated into the great imperial metropolis of Constantinople; and lay life continued undisturbed. The lawyers were laymen. Canon law was restricted to matters of purely ecclesiastical concern. It was not till after the controversy over the Emperor Leo VI's fourth marriage in the early 10th century that the church acquired legal control over marriage. The church had its schools. The Patriarchal Academy was founded early in the 7th century, and is still in existence; but it seems to have concentrated on the education of future clerics. In the provinces the church often ran elementary schools. But in the cities the best schools were run by monks unattached to any monastery, or by laymen; and most of the finest scholars, and many of the best theologians, were laymen, or only took holy orders late in life. In such a society the ecclesiastical organization was not required to play the dominant role that it had to play in the west. In general its role in the running of the state was confined to its moral influence.

The failure of the barbarians to disrupt the eastern empire also worked against the growth of an over-powerful church by enabling the empire to maintain the doctrine of imperial sovereignty that Constantine the Great's devoted friend Eusebius of Caesarea had promulgated. Pagan philosophers, particularly in Hellenistic times, had put forward the idea that the king was the earthly representative and imitation of God. Eusebius adapted the notion to the Christian empire. The emperor was the viceroy of God, who, in his words, will 'frame his earthly government according to the pattern of the divine original, finding strength in its conformity with the monarchy of God'.

This remained the basic theory of the empire so long as the Christian empire lasted in Constantinople; and it was inherited by the Russian tsars. But it left a fundamental ambiguity unresolved. The eastern empire, Byzantium, had inherited the Roman respect for 'the law'. The Roman emperors were under the law. They had been officially elected by the Senate, the army and the people of Rome, acting in conjunction, and, should they seem not to be ruling according to the law, whether deliberately or through incompetence, the electors could depose them. There was the legal right of revolution. The Byzantines retained this theory. The Eusebian doctrine made the monarch the source of law, but he was not the creator of laws but the interpreter of the law, who could perhaps issue new interpretations or amend old ones, but he remained subject to the law, and as God's viceroy it was his special duty to rule according to it. Should he fail to do so he must go; he was unworthy of the role. The Eusebian conception was thus modified. It was the office, not the person, of the emperor that was sacrosanct.

The Byzantines believed firmly in this sacrosanctity. The emperor's palace was the Sacred Palace. Its ceremonies were religious ceremonies, following an ordered symbolic ritual. It was proper to prostrate oneself before him, not because he was an earthly despot but because he was the image of God. It was for him to see that the church elected suitable bishops and a suitable patriarch of Constantinople and deposed those that were unsuitable. It was for him to summon and preside over a council of bishops when the true doctrine had to be defined. But he was not a bishop. He lacked that special charisma. He was not even a priest, though the coronation ceremony, from the late 5th century onwards, gave him certain priestly powers. To some extent the patriarchate was his Ministry of Religion, over which he exercised practical control. But, just as he was bound by Roman law, so he was bound by the Laws of God, of which the priesthood was the guardian. He might control the church organization; but it was at his peril that he flouted its moral commands. Public opinion soon found him unworthy of his office. Equally, church leaders, such as the patriarchs Nicholas Mysticus in the early 10th and Michael Cerularius in the mid-11th century, who tried to follow up a moral victory by interfering in secular politics, quickly lost popularity and respect. Byzantines strongly disapproved of ecclesiastics who meddled in secular affairs.

The Byzantine hierarchy

On the whole, the Byzantine hierarchy was orderly, hard-working and devout. It was theoretically democratic. The village recommended to the bishop the man whom they desired as parish priest. The priests elected the bishop, the bishops the metropolitan, or archbishop, the metropolitans the patriarch. In fact the elections were controlled from above; and imperial approval was needed for all the higher appointments. By the mid-Byzantine period it came to be established that the parish priest should be a local man, already married, though a monk might occasionally be appointed to an important parish. He was supervised by

the bishop's exarch, who made regular visits round the diocese. The bishop was a far humbler figure than his fellows in the contemporary west. His diocese was much smaller, as were his revenues. But he enjoyed a high local standing and was consulted by the local lay officials. He had his own law-court, where cases involving clerics in the diocese were heard and from which appeals could be made to the patriarchal law-court. His income came from the estates of the bishopric and the rents of the local monasteries that were not under the special jurisdiction of the patriarch or the emperor. He also received a fee whenever a priest was ordained and a fee for registering a betrothal. The metropolitan sees were richer and their endowments larger; but expenses were greater as the metropolitan had to supervise the bishops of the province. The patriarch's revenues, in the days of the empire's prosperity, were enormous. He owned estates all over the empire, including valuable town property in Constantinople. He received rents from the monasteries which were of patriarchal foundation, as well as a large annual grant from the imperial exchequer. But his income barely covered his expenses. He had to run the supreme ecclesiastical law-court, as well as the Patriarchal Academy and the Patriarchal Library. He had to finance synods. His officials included the Grand Economus, who was chief treasurer, the Grand Sacellarius, in charge of the patriarchal monasteries, the Grand Skevophylax, in charge of liturgical matters and of relics, the Grand Chartophylax, librarian and keeper of the records, and the Syncellus, who was his secretary of state and his liaison with the lay government. These high officials ranked above the metropolitans and till the mid-11th century were appointed by the emperor. The patriarch himself received in the late 6th century the epithet of 'Oecumenical', to the fury of the pope; but in fact it only signified that he was the patriarch of the capital city of the empire, which in Byzantine Greek was known as the 'Oecumene'.

The bishops were drawn from the monastic order; but it was advisable, in view of their duties, that they should be men of the world. Laymen were often appointed, especially to the patriarchate. Only former civil servants and tax-collectors were barred, unless the Holy Synod gave a special dispensation. If he were married, his wife must retire into a nunnery. He was then hurried through the ecclesiastical orders, though three months should elapse before he could be invested. This rule was not always obeyed, as in the case of the Patriarch Photius, whose elevation his enemies therefore considered invalid. The system provided the empire with many of its most efficient and most learned patriarchs.

In the earlier centuries the emperors continually

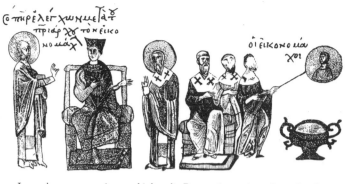

Iconoclasm was an issue which split Byzantine society along clearly defined lines, the emperors being hostile to images, the monks strongly in favour. This miniature from a post-iconoclast manuscript (11th century) shows a fresco being whitewashed.

interfered in church affairs, in attempts to settle doctrinal issues that were causing schism, summoning and often directing oecumenical councils, and arbitrating between the rival patriarchates. The rivalry ended when the Arabs conquered Syria and Egypt, and the Orthodox patriarchs there became the heads of a second-class people in an infidel land, and when Rome moved out of imperial control. The patriarch of Constantinople was left the one great hierarch within the empire; and his power and prestige thereby grew.

The turning point in Byzantine religious and artistic life came with the iconoclastic controversy, when the emperor attempted to impose on his subjects a religious reform which was supported by powerful forces in the state, in particular the army, but which was resented by the greater part of the populace. The iconoclastic emperors were able to enforce their policy through the control of the hierarchy that earlier emperors had established; but it was defeated in the end by a power that they could not dominate: the power of the monasteries.

Monks and inconoclasts

East Christian monasticism differed greatly from that of the west. There was no fixed Rule nor were there monastic orders. Each monastery had its own constitution, laid down by its founder, whether he were the local bishop, a rich layman or laywoman, or the patriarch or the emperor himself. A *brevion* was issued, listing the endowments and the liturgical duties desired by the founder, and a *typicon*, which regulated the rights and tasks of the monks. The earliest type of eastern monastery, the *lavra*, followed the traditions of the desert fathers, being composed of groups of ascetics who came together for mutual protection and to share in the liturgy and in acts of charity. But in the 5th century, St Basil of Caesarea introduced reforms to make monastic life more orderly, ordaining that monks should always live communal lives, in communities under an elected head who should command perfect obedience, and that they should work as well as pray.

Justinian I passed laws to make every monastic establishment follow the Basilian pattern and to see that the monks should own no personal property. He also ordered the terms under which a man or a woman might enter monastic life and the length of the noviciate. A monk need not take priestly vows, but there were ordained monks in each monastery to perform the church services, and it was customary for the abbot to be ordained. For female establishments the bishop provided chaplains. The abbot, the 'higoumen' or the 'archimandrite', was elected by a majority vote of the monks but received his pastoral staff from the bishop. He had absolute power over his monks, as did the abbess, similarly elected, over her nuns.

The regulations were strict; but they were not always obeyed. *Lavras* continued to exist, especially in the remoter eastern provinces. There were individual hermits living in caves or, like St Simeon, on pillars, all greatly respected in their localities. Many monks were very loosely attached to monasteries, pursuing professional careers in separate establishments. The monasteries themselves were varied. Some were very well endowed, often with large estates all over the empire, acquired through pious donations or bequests. Others, especially in the country districts, were poor, with the monks having to work as labourers in order to subsist. Some were centres of intellectual and artistic activities, where manuscripts were copied and illuminated and studied, and where painting was encouraged; others concentrated on farming and forestry, others on good works. Altogether, they played an enormous part in Byzantine life. The state ran a number of orphanages, hospitals and hostels, but the monasteries provided most of such institutions. They were homes for the elderly. Most men and women who reached old age liked to retire to them, so as not to burden their families. Married couples would separate and hand on their possessions to their children, to end their days in godly peace. Fallen princes and politicians were relegated to them. At the same time, the family confessor for rich and poor alike was usually a monk from a neighbouring monastery; and it was usually a monk who provided elementary education for the children.

The patriarch and the bishops were respected but remote figures. The monks moved among the people. They were in touch with public opinion and in a position to influence it. The monks in general were opposed to iconoclasm. They disliked its theology, which seemed to deny the Incarnation; and they held that a portrait was not a graven image but, as a symbol, acquired some of the grace of the original and so was worthy of special respect. They resented the attempt of a lay emperor to force a religious doctrine on the church; and they were aware that the bulk of their congregations were unhappy at his interference with religious practices to which they had become used. The iconoclastic emperors recognized the monks as their chief enemies; their persecution of them, however, though probably less severe than monkish propaganda claimed, merely produced popular martyrs and strengthened the monks' opposition. The army continued to support iconoclasm, but it was powerless against public opinion organized by the monks. The Empress Irene, with the aid of her tactful Patriarch Tarasius, was able to reintroduce image worship without openly damaging imperial prestige. But the whole episode showed the limits of imperial control over religious matters. When, a little later, Leo V sought to revive iconoclasm, the formidable abbot, Theodore of Studion, told him to his face that it was the emperor's business to look after the political government and the army and to leave the church to the care of its pastors. Such a scene would have been unthinkable in the days of Justinian. Theodore was exiled and iconoclasm was reintroduced, but in a muted form. Within half a century it was finally abandoned.

Henceforward, the emperors, though they still kept control of appointments to the hierarchy, were cautious about religious affairs. Many of them were, like most educated Byzantines, deeply interested in theology but did not try to press their views if there were ecclesiatical opposition to them. And henceforward, there was what might loosely be called a monastic party, ready to protest should the emperor seem to overstep his limits and to block any policy of which it disapproved. It was the monks, with the support of the common people, who sabotaged imperial attempts to achieve ecclesiastical union with Rome, even though the upper hierarchs might be willing to carry out the emperor's wishes. On the whole, the monks were suspicious of the hierarchy, considering it the tool of the emperor; even if one of their party were appointed to the patriarchate they were apt to turn against him. They also tended to disapprove of the splendour of the patriarchate and to resent any hierarch who seemed over-interested in intellectual affairs. But it would be wrong to regard Byzantine monasticism as an obscurantist force. Many monasteries followed the tradition laid down by Theodore of Studion, who wished them to be intellectual centres; and many leading scholars were monks, such as Manuel Planudes in the late 13th century, the most learned and enterprising scholar of his generation.

Learning and liturgy

Despite the monks' efforts, the Eusebian conception of the Christian empire as the earthly copy of the Kingdom of Heaven, with the emperor as the viceroy of God, lasted on till Constantinople fell to the infidel in 1453.

Every Byzantine genuinely believed in it, and believed, however unscrupulously he behaved in this life, that this life was but a prelude to the everlasting life to come. He was very superstitious, but no more so than his contemporaries in the western or the Islamic world. He greatly respected scholarship; but secular learning was to him the Lower Learning. The Higher Learning was the study of God; and in that he was always conscious of the limits of the human intellect. He disliked precise theological statements such as the western scholastics enjoyed. He preferred mystery, believing that true knowledge was only attained by the mystic, who, by the grace of God, could free himself from the world and penetrate into the divine. When fundamental doctrines were called into question, he approved that the Fathers of the Church should meet together and be inspired by the Holy Spirit to find a formula that would express the faith. But he was content to let many doctrines remain undefined. The Orthodox church has never, for instance, made an official pronouncement on transubstantiation. Its catechisms merely say that what happens at the consecration of the elements in the Eucharist remains a mystery. They take a similar line on the doctrine of Purgatory.

What meant most to the Byzantine in his religion was the liturgy. The regular liturgy, attributed to St John Chrysostom, was established by the end of the 7th century. Ten times a year the liturgy of St Basil the Great, which only differed in the length of certain prayers, was used, and for Wednesdays and Fridays in Lent and the first three days of Holy Week, the liturgy of the Presanctified, when communion is given from elements consecrated on the previous Sunday. These remain the liturgies of the Orthodox church. Though the divine drama is enacted by the priests, the Orthodox congregation feels itself to be taking part in the service; and the images of Christ and the saints depicted in mosaic or fresco round the church building show that they too are present. It is not surprising that the iconoclasts' attempt to remove them was so bitterly resented. The great cathedrals of Hagia Sophia and the Holy Apostles were needed for the sacred ceremonies of the empire; but the Byzantines tended increasingly to prefer smaller churches, where the services were more intimate and the saints were closer. The iconostasis, the high screen, usually of richly carved and gilded wood and hung with panel icons, which today separates the sanctuary from the body of an Orthodox church, only came into use late in the Byzantine period. The Early Christian altar-rail was low, though there might be pillars or poles along its length to enable curtains to be hung to veil the sanctuary. The silver screen in Hagia Sophia, destroyed by the Crusaders in 1204, was in no sense an iconostasis. But the taste for higher screens developed, partly because they emphasized the drama of the mass and partly because of the growing liking for panel icons, which could now be hung where they were more accessible for intimate worship than the figures on the walls.

Greeks and Latins

It was his devotion to his liturgy that made the Greek Christian so hostile to the Latin church. The Byzantines in general could not accept the conception of papal supremacy, which seemed to them alien to the traditions of the church. They saw that when southern Italy, with its largely Greek population, fell under the domination of rulers belonging to the Roman faith, the Greek churches were forced to adopt the Latin liturgy. Earlier disputes between Rome and Constantinople had mainly concerned the rivalries of hierarchs and attacks on each other's theology. When the Patriarch Photius in the 9th century discovered that the Roman church was adopting the doctrine of the dual procession of the Holy Ghost, which involved the addition of the word *filioque* (and from the Son) to the creed as laid down by the oecumenical councils, he provided Byzantine theologians with a weapon that they could use for the centuries to come; but he did not arouse much feeling among the Byzantine populace. Two centuries later, when the Byzantine public was aware of Norman political and religious aggression in southern Italy and the Patriarch Michael Cerularius raised a ritual issue, complaining of the Latin use of unleavened bread in the sacrament – when to the Orthodox the leaven symbolized the New Dispensation – he won such instant popular support that the emperor, who was planning an alliance with Rome, had to abandon his scheme. There followed the ugly scene in 1054, when a papal legate, Cardinal Humbert, who had actually lost his legatine powers because the pope who appointed him was dead, and the patriarch angrily excommunicated each other. This did not cause the final schism, as was later supposed. The excommunications were purely personal and specifically did not involve the congregations. But the episode caused lasting ill-will; and the problem of relations with Rome has remained a bitter issue among the Orthodox ever since.

It was unfortunate that the closer political and social contacts between eastern and western Christendom should have coincided with the period when the Roman papacy was claiming plentitude of power. The established Orthodox theory was that, doctrinally, the only authority was a council of the universal church, represented by its bishops, which would be inspired by the Holy Spirit, as were the disciples at Pentecost: administrative and disciplinary authority was in the hands of the Pentarchy of Patriarchs, Rome, Con-stantinople, Alexandria, Antioch and Jerusalem, Rome holding the primacy of honour and so deserving special respect. But Rome now seemed to be sponsoring heresy, making uncanonical claims of authority and following incorrect ritual. She was forfeiting her place in the Pentarchy.

The Crusading movement, which Pope Urban II had hoped would reunite Christendom, proved disastrously divisive. The Byzantines and the Crusaders mistrusted each other; and in the territories that they occupied the Crusaders ejected Orthodox bishops and replaced them by Latins. Growing enmity led at last to the Fourth Crusade in 1204, when a western army captured and sacked Constantinople and set up a Latin emperor there, and a Latin patriarch; and in all the lands conquered by Crusader princes, a Latin hierarchy was superimposed, and the Byzantine liturgy was firmly discouraged. This was never forgiven. The memory of 1204 is still the main barrier against the union of the churches. The Greeks recovered Constantinople in 1261; but the restored empire was no longer a great power. It needed allies, especially against the growing menace of the Ottoman Turks. Several emperors and statesmen now strove for union. Michael VIII accepted the union terms decided at the Council of Lyons in 1274, and John VIII signed a union decree at Florence in 1439; this union decree was read out in Constantinople a few months before the city's fall. But though there were scholars who, impressed by the works of Thomas Aquinas, were prepared to unite with the west, on its terms, other scholars clung to older Byzantine traditions; and, though many bishops, on the emperor's orders, subscribed to the decree, the bulk of the clergy and all the monkish communities rejected it; and the public followed their lead. To most of them, valiantly though they fought to defend their city when the final onslaught came, the sultan's turban was preferable to the cardinal's hat. The Turks would not interfere with their doctrine or their liturgy.

The Byzantine mystics

Apart from the schisms that arose when the monkish party considered that the hierarchs were condoning the emperor's misdemeanours, the one great controversy that disturbed the later Byzantine church concerned mysticism. While the western church has always tended to discourage its mystics, being suspicious of anyone who takes a short-cut through to God, mystics have always held an honourable place in the eastern church. In the late Byzantine world there were scholars to whom both the theory of mysticism and the practices of the mystics seemed wrong and even ridiculous. The great 13th-century theologian, Gregory Palamas, sprang to the defence of the Hesychasts, the 'quiet

A *19th-century engraving of the Grand Lavra, largest and richest of the monasteries on Mount Athos. Here, Orthodox monasticism continued through the long years of Turkish rule, and lives on today as a uniquely unchanged survival of that tradition.*

ones', as the Byzantine mystics were called, explaining that there was nothing wrong in physical exercises intended to induce concentration, and putting forward the doctrine that what the mystic saw at the end of his path was the uncreated Light, the Light of Tabor, which was part of the energies of God, the divine emanations that were visible to humans who had freed themselves from all worldliness. The doctrine had been inherent in east Christian theology since the days of St Cyril of Alexandria. But it was only after bitter controversy that it was admitted as a definite dogma of the Orthodox church. The western churches have never accepted it.

Palamas approved of an eremitical life, so long as the hermit had been trained by a spiritual mentor and so long as he was attached to a monastery and regularly attended the liturgy. The most distinguished of the Palamists, Nicholas Cabasilas, thought the eremitical life too egocentric. The true Christocentric life was to be found by staying in the world, not by fleeing from it. He was a scholar who combined his mysticism with the humanism of his time. There was, however, at the same time a revival of strict eremitism, led by Gregory of Sinai (1255–1346), an Anatolian who spent many years

at Sinai, then moved to Mount Athos. He harked back to the desert fathers, advocating complete solitude and regarding attendance at the liturgy as irrelevant, even harmful. This was too much even for the Athonites, and he moved to Bulgaria, where he found pupils who carried his doctrines to Russia. He was the ancestor of the Russian *staretz*, the solitary holy man unattached to any monastery, who wandered about alone; though Gregory would have disapproved of the political influence that the later *staretzi* would often obtain.

Mount Athos was now emerging as the chief monastic centre of the Orthodox. Hermits had long ago settled there; the oldest monastery, the Grand Lavra, had been founded in 963, and many others were founded during the next hundred years. They formed a community with a constitution that was revised in 1052, which made it self-governing, owing allegiance to the emperor alone. As the Turks began to overrun the older monastic communities in Cappadocia, on Mount Talmos, on the Aegean coast of Anatolia and Bithynian Olympus, its importance grew, as well as its wealth. Rich patrons endowed each monastery with estates on the mainland. On Athos itself the monks exploited the forests and exported timber. Life was firmly disciplined and austere. No female creature was allowed on the mountain; the Mother of God, its patroness, was to have no rivals: though the rule could not be enforced on lesser mammals, the birds of the air or reptiles. Liturgical duties were heavy; hermits had to come from their caves to share in them. But there were good libraries, and theological studies were encouraged. By the 14th century, Athos had become the chief centre of monastic activity and thought in the Orthodox world. Serbian, Russian and Georgian establishments were to be found alongside the Greek.

Under the rule of the sultan

With the territorial losses of the Byzantine Empire in the last two centuries of its existence, more and more of the faithful fell under alien domination. The fall of Constantinople to the Turks, terrible though it was, had the result of uniting practically the whole Greek world under the rule of the sultan. But the Greeks were now second-class citizens, living among a master-race that despised them as infidels. Their legal rights had no physical sanction behind them. It was not safe for them to offend a Muslim; and they had to suffer such indignities and sorrows as seeing their sons snatched from them and converted to Islam, to form the sultan's corps of Janissaries.

At first things did not go badly. The conquering sultan, Mehmet II, though pitiless and truculent, was a just man. He admired Greek learning and saw himself as the heir of the Christian emperors; and he personally liked the new patriarch, the scholar George Scholarius Gennadius, whom, like a Byzantine emperor, he ordered the Holy Synod to elect. Together he and Gennadius worked out a constitution. There was no likelihood of anyone coming to rescue the Greeks from their bondage; so the patriarch had to make the best terms that he could.

The new dispensation entirely altered the functions of the patriarchal office. It had now to provide law-courts where civil as well as religious cases could be heard. Its financial bureau had to cope with the collection of taxes and their transference to the sultan's treasury. The bishops had to be organized as local adminstrators, with their own local courts; and they had to keep order without the help of any police of their own. The taxes were actually collected and the local registers kept by the head-man of the village or the local community; but the bishop had to see that part of the money raised went to the provincial Turkish governor and part to the patriarch to be handed on to the central government. The Orthodox clergy were untrained for such functions. It was necessary to employ laymen, who began to exercise an increasing influence on the patriarchate. Money was a constant problem. With the decline of the empire and the final Turkish conquest, the church had lost most of its endowments, and the Turks disapproved of Christians acquiring landed estates. With the exception of Mount Athos, which had made its own treaty with the sultan, allowing its houses to keep their estates, the monasteries were particularly hard-hit. They could no longer afford to keep up their libraries and to be cultural centres. The monks existed by farming such properties as they were allowed to retain. The bishops and the patriarch had to depend on what money they could raise from the faithful, who for the most part were very poor, and on such gifts as they could obtain from Orthodox princes abroad, who were few. And soon there was an additional expense. Even in Mehmet II's reign an ambitious cleric, Symeon of Trebizond, who coveted the patriarchate, offered the sultan's ministers 2,000 pieces of gold if they would order the Holy Synod to depose the reigning patriarch and elect him. The one Christian whom the sultan regarded with deference, his stepmother, the Serbian princess, Mara, widow of Murad II, hastened to his court to cancel the transaction; but she had to pay him a similar sum out of her own pocket.

Henceforward, no patriarch could be elected without a gift in money to the sultan and his ministers. This gift, known as the *peshtesh*, grew in size as unscrupulous candidates bid against each other to secure the throne; and it was naturally to the advantage of the sultan that new appointments should be made as frequently as possible. The earlier sultans were temperate in their demands. But after the death of Suleiman the Magnificent in 1566 there was a rapid decline in Ottoman standards. Corruption and intrigue were rife, and enforced change in the patriarchate was an easy way of raising money. The synod would be ordered to depose a patriarch on some flimsy excuse, though he might later be allowed to buy his way back to the throne. In the century from 1595 to 1695 there were sixty-one changes on the patriarchal throne, though only thirty-one individual patriarchs. Matthew II reigned for twenty days in 1595, then four years, from 1598 to 1602, then seventeen days in 1603. Cyril I Lucaris enjoyed seven different spells on the throne. The *peshtesh* rose all the while. Calixtus III paid some 5,600 gold pounds in 1726, and died of joy, from a heart attack, the day following his election. Meanwhile, from the beginning of the 17th century, the sultan demanded a yearly tax of 20,000 piastres; and the patriarchate paid various minor taxes, including the sum required to provide mutton daily for the palace guard. Unless rich friends offered help, all these sums had to be recouped from the Orthodox congregations.

In addition to its financial difficulties the church was handicapped by its lack of educational facilities. The Turks discouraged Greek schools. The Patriarchal Academy was allowed to continue; and the patriarchate valiantly tried to maintain its standards. There were, at various times, schools at Janina, at Nanplia and in several of the islands. But the teaching that they provided was fairly elementary, and all were liable to arbitrary closure. Until the mid-18th century, a boy who wanted a decent education would go to Venice, where there was a rich Greek colony that ran a school and was generous with scholarships; and he could go on to the University of Padua, the one Italian university that did not insist on its pupils being Catholic. Alternatively, he could apply to the Jesuits, who ran the College of St Athanasius for Greek boys in Rome. But there the pressure on him to become a Roman convert was very strong, though not invariably successful.

In the mid-18th century the princes of Wallachia and Moldavia, who were now drawn from the rich Greek families of Constantinople, each founded academies at their capitals, Bucharest and Jassy. But these were to be centres of up-to-date secular learning; no one there was interested in educating future clergy. However, each possessed a printing-press, which was ready to produce religious as well as secular works. Hitherto, Greek books had to be printed in the west, mainly at Vienna or Venice. The Patriarch Cyril Lucaris had, with the help of the English ambassador, set up a press in Constantinople in 1627, but the Turks destroyed it almost at once. Books were thus hard to obtain and were very expensive.

Even on Mount Athos there was a lowering of standards. In the 16th century several monasteries had come together to buy the remarkable library of Michael Cantacuzenus, the first Greek millionaire of Ottoman times, whom the Turks had put to death; and in the 17th century the Athonite houses were still adding secular as well as theological books to their collections. This ended in the following century, and the monks sank into the obscurantist ignorance noted by travellers in the early 19th century. This was mainly in reaction against Constantinople, where the patriarchate seemed to be controlled by laymen, the Phanariots, the rich Greeks who lived clustered round the patriarchal buildings in the Phanar quarter of the city. Their younger fold had discovered contemporary western philosophy. When the learned Patriarch Cyril V sought to re-educate the Athonites by founding an academy on the mountain, the professor whom he sent, Evgenios Vulgaris, lectured to the monks on German metaphysics. They soon forced him to leave. If such godlessness was learning, they preferred to remain ignorant.

Achievements of a subject church

In the 16th century, when on the whole the Turks treated their Christian subjects fairly, apart from such pricks as annexing churches and transforming them into mosques, the best life for a bright Greek boy had been in holy orders. There were many eminent churchmen, administrators such as the patriarchs Jeremias I and II, who both enjoyed comparatively long reigns, as they were respected by the sultans of the time, and scholars such as Maximus Margunius or Gabriel Severus, whose reputations were known in the west in their day. The church still produced distinguished men in the 17th century, in spite of more unstable conditions. These uncertainties caused many ambitious young Greeks to prefer the profession of medicine, as an able doctor could rely on the support of his Turkish clients; and already many Greeks were making fortunes as merchants and bankers. But the controversy roused by the remarkable Patriarch Cyril Lucaris, a Cretan by birth, showed that there were still subtle and profound theologians among the Greeks, though the greatest Greek scholar of the time, the Chiot Leo Allatius, was a convert to Rome and spent his career in Italy. At the end of the century came the Peloponnesian Dositheus Notaras, patriarch of Jerusalem, who enjoyed international fame. But in the 18th century the church produced very few men of eminence.

In the 16th and 17th centuries the Protestant churches took an interest in the Orthodox, largely hoping to find in them an ally against Rome. Luther's disciples included men like Melanchthon, who were good Greek scholars; and they wrote to Constantinople in the hope of establishing intercommunion. Their hopes were eventually dashed when the Patriarch Jeremias II sent them a courteously worded statement listing the Lutheran tenets and practices that his church could not condone. In England, Cranmer took an interest in the Byzantine liturgy, basing parts of his prayerbook on it. In the next century the Patriarch Cyril Lucaris was in close touch with the higher Calvinists of Geneva and the Netherlands; and he was a close friend of two successive English ambassadors in Constantinople, Sir Thomas Roe and Sir Peter Wych. In 1630 he published his own Confession of Faith, which included some definitely Calvinist beliefs. It was eventually denounced by his own church as being unorthodox. A little later in the century there began a long flirtation by the Anglican church with the Orthodox, which resulted in the visits of several Orthodox divines to England and the foundation of a short-lived Greek college at Oxford. But the Anglicans could not persuade the Orthodox divines to give the desired answers on controversial issues of belief, while the Orthodox were far more greatly interested in financial subsidies than in ecclesiastical union. The English Non-jurors and the Scottish Episcopalians carried on negotiations till well into the 18th century, but to no effect. But as the 18th century progressed, the west with its new rationalism regarded the Orthodox as superstitious and out-of-date. Only the Jesuits, who had been working in Greek lands since the end of the 16th century, continued to take an interest in them. But their aim was the complete submission of the Greeks to Rome. In spite of the amenities offered by the College of St Athanasius, they achieved very little. Meanwhile the Orthodox had found a new and powerful protector who was of their faith, the Russian tsar.

The movement towards Greek independence at the end of the century put the patriarchate into a quandary. Each patriarch on his appointment swore an oath of personal allegiance to the sultan and swore to keep his flock loyal to Turkish rule. Could he break his oath, and should he encourage his flock to take a path that might well lead to disaster? The Turkish army was still powerful, and every previous Christian attempt to revolt had been suppressed with pitiless efficiency. The patriarchate preached caution, to the contempt of Greek intellectuals such as Adamentios Korais, who urged rebellion from the safety of residence in western Europe and who, reared on Montesquieu, Voltaire and Gibbon, despised the Byzantine tradition, and to the disappointment of the Greeks in Greece itself, where the brigand Klephts were conducting a vigorous guerrilla war against the Turkish authorities, with the support of the local population, including the monks and some of the bishops. When the moment for rising came, in 1821, it was the archbishop of Patras who raised the standard of independence in the Peloponnese. Throughout the long war that followed, the church in Greece gave valiant assistance to the cause.

The patriarchates today

When the news of the rebellion reached Constantinople the patriarch, Gregory V, could not bring himself to denounce it, as the Turks demanded. To them he was a traitor; and they hanged him and his leading bishops at the gate of the patriarchate. The patriarchate was shorn of many of its judicial and financial powers, but it survived. Till the Balkan Wars early this century, the majority of Greeks still lived under Ottoman rule and needed their pastors. The increase of Greek territory after the Balkan Wars, and then the exchange of populations that followed the Treaty of Lausanne, which emptied the Turkish dominions of all Greeks except for those living in or around Constantinople, or Istanbul, as the Turks preferred to call it, left the patriarchate with a tiny direct congregation. But the patriarch of Constantinople exercises a nominal authority over northern Greece and a more real authority over Crete and the Dodecannese; and he is the canonical head of all the Greek churches in western Europe, in the Americas and in Australasia. Athenagoras I, a great man whom even the Turks learned grudgingly to respect, showed, in his reign from 1948 to 1972, that the patriarch still could be a figure of world importance, all the stronger because he lived *in partibus infidelium*, free from the pressure of some national Orthodox government. But the Turks would like to get rid of the patriarchate; and its outlook is far from bright.

The other three ancient patriarchates have played a small part in history since the Arab invasions of the 7th century, except for the period of the Crusades, when the Latins took over Jerusalem and Antioch, to the chagrin of the Orthodox. The expansion of the Ottoman Empire brought the three patriarchs in closer contact with their brother of Constantinople, who acted as their spokesman before the sultan but who in return insisted on exercising authority over them. The most venerable of the three sees, Alexandria, had the smallest following, as nearly all the Egyptian Christians belonged to the separated Coptic church. But the Ottoman conquest resulted in numbers of Greek merchants settling in Egypt, bringing new wealth to the church there. But many of the patriarchs preferred to live in Constantinople rather than in Cairo, whither the see had been moved soon after 1600; and they often acted as unofficial seconds-in-command to their brother of

Medal commemorating the Greek War of Independence, 1821. Conspicuously in the centre between the patriots stands the figure of the church, in the person of the archbishop of Patras.

Constantinople. The Greeks have left Egypt now; but the patriarchate still commands the allegiance of Greek settlers all over Africa; and its role may be changing. Some of the emergent African countries, seeking for a branch of Christianity that is venerable but untainted by Western imperialism, are taking an interest in a historic church whose headquarters are in Africa.

The patriarchate of Antioch, which moved to Damascus in the later Middle Ages, has a larger congregation, all of Arabic-speaking Christians in Syria and Lebanon. Its patriarchs have been native Syrians for some centuries, and, though in permanent financial difficulties, it has a certain influence in the politics of that disturbed area.

The patriarchate of Jerusalem, though with the smallest congregation, was in Ottoman times the richest of the three, with estates in Wallachia and Moldavia and in Russia. All have been lost, from revolution or land reform; and the present situation in the Holy Land adds to its difficulties. Though its followers are all the Christian Arabs in Israel and Jordan, it has always been dominated by a Greek hierarchy; and it is only recently that the native Christians have had any say in its affairs. They hope eventually to be in complete control.

There are two autonomous Orthodox archbishops in the Levant. The archbishop of Sinai is abbot of the monastery of St Catherine on Mount Sinai and its fourteen tiny daughter-houses; and that is the whole extent of his diocese. The church of Cyprus was given complete independence at the Council of Ephesus in 431, as the Church of the Apostle Barnabas. Its rights were in abeyance when the Latins were in control of the island, from 1191 to 1570; but with the Ottoman conquest the archbishop became ethnarch of the Christians on the island. The British, when they took over the administration in 1878, paid no attention to the ethnarchy. It was not surprising that the movement to oust them was led by the archbishop, Macarius, who became first president of independent Cyprus. But the old ethnarchy has been effectively abolished by the democratic constitution that he introduced.

The ancient Orthodox church of Georgia, with its vernacular liturgy, was granted autocephaly under its catholicus in the 11th century. This was withdrawn when the Russians conquered the Caucasus, the church being put under an exarch whom they appointed. Autocephaly was restored in 1917; but the Soviet authorities have since then done their best to impoverish and discredit it. It still carries on, half underground, as an expression of Georgian nationalism.

When the independent kingdom of Greece was established, its church was declared to be autonomous, under the archbishop of Athens. This autonomy was only recognized by the patriarchate in 1852, largely because King Otho's German minister tried to treat the church as a department of state. The patriarchate insisted on the freedom of the church from state control. Thenceforward, Greek politicians took very little interest in church affairs, until the seizure of power by the Junta in 1967. The government then tried to use the church to back its authority, making appointments which produced chaos and scandal among the episcopate; and the troubles have survived the Junta's fall. Land reforms and modern fashions have impoverished and emptied the monasteries. Few survive; but there are still some convents whose nuns perform useful social works. There was a revival of interest in the church earlier this century and a real attempt to improve ecclesiastical education, mainly based on the University of Thessalonica. On Mount Athos, which is still under the patriarchate spiritually but politically under the Greek Foreign Ministry, where standards had fallen very low, there are now faint signs of spiritual regeneration. Though they may not concern themselves much about its welfare, the Greeks remain passionately loyal to their church.

Missions to the north: Bulgarians and Serbs

The Orthodox church has never been very active in the missionary field except when urged on for political reasons. In the mid-9th century, the Byzantine government decided that it would be advantageous to bring the Slavs of central Europe into the Byzantine sphere of influence by converting them to Christianity. In 863, at the request of Rostislav, the pagan king of Moravia, two brothers from Thessalonica, Constantine (better known by his later name of Cyril) and Methodius, set out for the central Danube, armed with a liturgy in the Slavonic language spoken in Macedonia and an alphabet invented by Cyril in which it could be written. The Moravian mission was unsuccessful, chiefly owing to the hostility of the neighbouring German church. Cyril's disciples were ejected, and found their way to the Balkans. The peninsula was dominated by the Bulgarians – a Turkic tribe. The

Byzantines had long wanted to convert them; and in 864 their khan, Boris, was induced to receive baptism, not unwillingly, as he wished his country to enter into the civilized family of nations, and he hoped that as a crowned Christian king he would be elevated high above the clan chieftains who tried to limit his monarchy. He was cautious. He negotiated with Rome to see if a Latin church would allow him more freedom than a Greek church before he chose the latter. The arrival of the Slav missionaries gave him a better solution. He settled them in Macedonia, which the Bulgarians had recently occupied; and from there they gradually Slavized the whole Bulgarian church. Constantinople, which had never objected to daughter-churches having a liturgy in their own tongues, as long as they paid deference to the patriarch, made no objection. It was less happy when later Bulgarian and Serbian monarchs unilaterally gave their chief bishop a patriarchal title.

With the Ottoman conquest, the Balkan churches were placed under the authority of the patriarch of Constantinople, as the ethnarch of all the Orthodox. They kept their Slavonic liturgy and native lower clergy; but the hierarchy was now all Greek, under the archbishops of Ochrid and of Péc, who were nominally autonomous but in fact subservient to the patriarch. This was resented by both Bulgarians and Serbs. In 1557, a vizier of Bosnian origin, Mehmet Sököllü, to please his Christian kinsfolk insisted on the revival of the patriarchate of Péc; and it was only in 1755 that the Greeks of Constantinople managed to suppress it; and in 1766 and 1767 they abolished the nominal autonomy of the two Balkan churches. The Serbs won political autonomy from the Turks in 1817; and their religious autonomy was recognized in 1831, and complete religious independence in 1879. In 1920 the archbishop of Belgrade assumed the title of patriarch, with the consent of the Constantinopolitan patriarch; but it was made clear that he ranked below the patriarchs of the historic Pentarchy. Montenegro, that small wild country that the Turks never conquered, was ruled from 1697 to 1815 by a prince-bishop of the family of Petrović, each being succeeded by a nephew. This ended when Prince Danilo refused to take holy orders and married. He was childless, and was succeeded in 1860 by his nephew, another layman, Nicholas I, who fifty years later proclaimed himself king, but was forced to abdicate after the First World War, in which his sons had played an inglorious part. The state and the church were then merged into Serbia.

The Bulgarians had to wait longer for religious freedom. In 1870, with the consent of the sultan, they declared their autonomy, dismissing the Greek hierarchy. For this they were excommunicated by the patriarch and denounced as schismatics. The breach was not healed till 1945, when Constantinople recognized Bulgarian autonomy. Soon afterwards, the archbishop of Sofia, the exarch of Bulgaria, took the title of patriarch; but only the Russian church has so far endorsed it.

The Romanian principalities, Wallachia and Moldavia, received Christianity through Bulgaria, together with the Slavonic liturgy, unintelligible to the people. It was only under the Greek princes of the 18th century that a liturgy in Romanian came into general use in the smaller churches, with the hierarchy using Greek in the major centres. The Greek influence was removed in the early 19th century; and the autocephaly of the church was acknowledged by Constantinople in 1885. The annexation of Transylvania, with its largely Orthodox population, after the First World War made the Romanian church the largest Orthodox church after the Russian. Constantinople bestowed the title of patriarch on its chief bishop in 1925.

The conversion of Russia

The great achievement of Byzantine missionary work was the conversion of Russia. In 989, the Great Prince Vladimir of Kiev accepted baptism and was rewarded with the hand of a purple-born princess of Byzantium. His motives were similar to those of Boris of Bulgaria. He wished his people to enter into the Christian family of nations, and he hoped for divine sanction for his autocracy that would give him authority over his troublesome kinsfolk and rival princes. The Russians were unwilling converts at first; but the introduction of the Slavonic liturgy, written in a language near enough to their own to be intelligible, made things easier. Many of their first priests and all their first religious books came from Bulgaria. But Constantinople insisted on appointing the head of the Russian church. Indeed, the establishment and expansion of the ecclesiastical organization needed the help of an experienced and educated prelate such as Byzantium alone in the Orthodox world could provide. But the appointment had to be ratified by the Russian ruler. It was not inconvenient to have a foreigner in charge of the church. He could keep it in touch with Byzantium; and when, in the 12th century, Kiev lost the hegemony, which passed round various rival local princes, it was as well to have a hierarch who could keep himself detached from their quarrels.

When the schism developed between eastern and western Christendom, the Russians whole-heartedly sided with Byzantium, showing early their lasting phobia of the west, which seemed justified in the later Middle Ages, when campaigns by the Scandinavian kings against them ranked as Crusades. They were

The Russian tradition of picture Bibles goes back to German models, but in many scenes the Russian view was an individual one. Here, in a 17th-century woodcut, a benevolent angel hands clothes to Adam and Eve before they are expelled from Eden.

horrified when the Crusaders sacked Constantinople in 1204, considering the pope to be the villain of the story. They opposed any attempt to reunite the churches; and when their Greek-born archbishop, Isidore, signed the union decree of Florence, he was promptly dismissed. The fall of Constantinople to the Turks, shocking though it was, seemed to them the just punishment for its acceptance of the Latin heresy.

The Russian ruler, the Great Prince of Moscow, could not wholly regret the fall of Constantinople. While Byzantium had been declining Russia was freeing herself from vassalage to the Golden Horde, under the leadership of the Muscovite princes. But, so long as Byzantium lasted, its emperor, however powerless, still commanded a mystical prestige among the Orthodox. After 1453 the Russian monarch was the undoubted chief potentate in the Orthodox world. In 1470, Ivan III declared the Russian church to be independent of the captive church of Constantinople, though every archbishop, now entitled 'Metropolitan of Moscow and All the Russias', liked to have patriarchal approval of his appointment. In 1473 Ivan, who had recently married the niece of the last Byzantine emperor, took the title of tsar, the word used by old Slavonic chroniclers for the emperor.

Rome and Constantinople had fallen. There arose in Russia the notion that the Third Rome, destined to last forever, was Moscow, the unsullied capital of the true faith. Russia was Holy Russia, the true Christian empire, the unswervingly Orthodox heir of Byzantium.

But it was Byzantium with a difference. In Byzantium

the autocracy of the viceroy of God was tempered by two elements. In Byzantium there had always been a well educated and vocal laity which manned the civil service and produced the most articulate intellectuals. In Russia, literacy was confined to the clergy and to the tsar and his family and a few high officials. Except in the merchant cities of the west, such as Novgorod, whose power was soon to be crushed, there was no active bourgeoisie. The merchants of Moscow were almost as illiterate as the nobles and landowners. There was no one in Russia outside the church who would protest against misgovernment and injustice, and arrange, as the Byzantine civil service had often done, that an unworthy ruler should be removed. And injustice was rife, as the Russians never understood the concept of the rule of law. They had never belonged to the old Roman world, with its innate respect for the law. The Byzantine clerics who came to civilize them only brought with them their limited canon law. To the Russians, as to many other Orientals, the law is little more than the means by which the government justifies its actions.

Tsars and patriarchs, 1500–1700

During the 16th century there were two parties in the Russian church, usually called the Possessors and the Non-Possessors. The latter, whose teaching stemmed from a Bulgarian-born metropolitan of Moscow, Cyprian of Tirnovo, himself a disciple of Gregory of Sinai, demanded that the church, bishoprics and monasteries alike, should have as few possessions and as little organization as possible and should be entirely divorced from the state. The tsars preferred the views of the Possessors, or Josephians, as they were sometimes called, from their leader, Joseph, abbot of Volokolamsk; though, in fact, he had wished for the church to be efficiently organized and wealthy so that it could influence and dominate the state. The tsars' ideal metropolitan was the 16th-century Macarius, who reformed the monastic system, closing the small monasteries, in which Non-Possessors were plentiful, or merging them with the larger houses, all of which were placed under the tight control of the hierarchy; and he brought the hierarchy into close co-operation with the tsar. The Non-Possessors were defeated; but their tradition lasted on, to appear a century later with the Old Believers, and to recur throughout Russian history with the hermits and the *staretsi*, intinerant monks with no possessions, some saints, some charlatans; the last and most famous was Gregory Rasputin.

The Possessors buttressed up the tsars' autocracy more than they had intended. The Tsar expected his hierarchs to be subservient, as Ivan IV, the Terrible, showed when he had the metropolitan Philip tortured to death in 1569 for daring to reprove his cruelty and immorality. They also did harm in encouraging nationalism, largely to show their independence of the ancient patriarchates. In 1551, a synod summoned by Ivan IV issued decrees known as the *Stoglav*, the Hundred Chapters, which legitimized all the ritual usages that had grown up in Russia, many of them unknown to Orthodox usage elsewhere. This was greatly resented by other Orthodox churches, as well as by many Russians. Russia and the ancient patriarchates, however, needed each other, and in 1589 Jeremias II agreed to come from Constantinople to confer the title of patriarch upon the metropolitan of Moscow.

The old dynasty died out in 1596 and a disturbed period ensued until the election of Michael, the first of the Romanovs, with his father Philaret as patriarch. Till he died in 1633, Russia enjoyed the edifying spectacle of father and son as patriarch and tsar; and as the father had the stronger character and better brain, it was the church that ruled Russia. Philaret was an able ruler. He re-established contact with the eastern patriarchates and interested himself in the efforts of Peter Mogila, metropolitan of Kiev, to reform the church. Mogila was resisting the attempts of his Polish overlords to impose the Latin church on the Ukraine. His theological seminary at Kiev was the most up-to-date in the Orthodox world. Michael's successor, Tsar Alexis, invited clerics from Kiev to come to his dominions, but under the influence of a learned and charming Greek visitor, Paisius, patriarch of Jerusalem, he reverted to Greek traditions.

It was Paisius who brought to his notice Nikon, a priest of peasant origin, who, after being a hermit, then abbot of a far north monastery, came to Moscow in 1646. He impressed everyone by his abilities; and in 1649 Alexis appointed him metropolitan of Novgorod, the second see in the empire. There he reformed the monasteries, insisting on better discipline and education, and recovered for them lands that the boyars had annexed during the time of troubles, and he raised the standards of parish priests. He persuaded the tsar to revoke a law intended to tighten state control over the church and limit its acquisition of lands. The church must be wholly independent under the patriarch, though it should defer to the tsar as the supreme authority. In 1652, Nikon, who had already forced the tsar to do penance for the murder of Archbishop Philip by his predecessor, Ivan IV, was made patriarch. As patriarch he continued the reforms that he had started at Novgorod. He imported books that the clerics were told to read; and he kept in close contact with Constantinople and its theologians, and revised the liturgy to make it conform with the proper liturgy of St John Chrysostom.

These reforms were not all popular. Clerics disliked having to read books that were inevitably printed in the west, there being as yet no printing-press in the Orthodox world. The congregations resented the tampering with the liturgy that they knew. The Old Believers, as they were called, under such leaders as the saintly Arch-priest Avvakum, refused to obey the hierarchy. They had much popular backing. Their suppression was only achieved by long-drawn-out and brutal persecution. Many of them preferred to burn themselves to death rather than submit.

The tsar approved of the reforms; but when Nikon published a book proclaiming the superiority of the sacerdotium over the state and assumed titles to which he had no right, Alexis began to snub him, refusing to invite him to state banquets and shunning services at which he officiated. Nikon resigned, expecting to be recalled. When the tsar happily accepted the resignation, Nikon fought for eight years in law-courts and church councils to recover his position. At last the tsar summoned a council at which all the eastern patriarchs were represented. It confirmed his reforms but formally deposed him.

The next two patriarchs were unambitious men; but in 1674, some eighteen months before he died, Alexis appointed a more formidable cleric, Joachim. Alexis's eldest son, Feodor, was a sickly youth, easily dominated by the patriarch. When he died in 1682, leaving the throne jointly to his brother Ivan, who was feeble-minded, and his half-brother, Peter, who was aged ten, Joachim assumed the regency. His pretensions were not liked. He was soon ousted by Ivan's sister, Sophia, till she in her turn was ousted in 1689 by Peter, aged seventeen.

From reform to revolution

Peter, known to history as Peter the Great, had little feeling for religion. He knew of his father's experience with Nikon, and he had disliked Joachim. He soon quarrelled with the church authorities when they tried to forbid him from divorcing his innocent young wife. But he moved prudently. In 1690, when Joachim died, he agreed grudgingly to appoint the candidate proposed by the synod of bishops and supported by his mother. But when this patriarch, Adrian, died in 1700, Peter, who had been abroad and had noted how the Lutheran monarchs ran their churches, forbade the election of a new patriarch. Instead, he appointed an exarch of the patriarchal throne, Stephen Yavorsky, who had been brought up in the Ukrainian school and was hostile to the old ecclesiastical establishment. Even he was driven to protest at Peter's reforming edicts, which were summarized in 1721 in a code that put the whole church under strict state control. The patriar-

chate was abolished. The church was put under a Ministry of Religion, the Clerical College or the Holy Governing Synod, composed of twelve clerics, three of them bishops, all directly appointed by the tsar. Over the Clerical College was a lay official, the Ecclesiastical Procurator or Chief Inquisitor, whose inspectors went round the provinces to see that the Clerical College's directives were obeyed. All church properties were transferred to the Ministry of State Lands, and the salaries of all ecclesiastics were to be paid by the state. The ecclesiastical courts could hear only cases concerning church discipline and practice. All other cases, including prosecutions for heresy, were to go to the civil courts.

No church can keep its spiritual force if it is run as a department of state. The civil servants, eager to show their admiration for western thought, despised the humble Russian worshipper as superstitious and ignorant, and took no steps to educate the village clergy, while the higher clergy were trained in seminaries where Latin was the dominant language, and German philosophy, which few understood, was taught. The members of the hierarchy, though they appeared in splendour at the great religious festivals, were patronized by the court as part of the imperial mystique. The Grand Inquisitors were often appointed because they were known to have no sympathy with Orthodoxy. Nicholas I appointed a retired cavalry officer, General Protasov, who tried to rule the church as though it were his regiment. During the 18th and 19th centuries there were only two distinguished metropolitans of Moscow. The first was Philaret Drozdov, who held the see from 1821 to 1867. He was ready to oppose Nicholas I and General Protasov on religious issues, and was too highly respected for them to dethrone him. With the accession of the liberal Tsar Alexander II he was able to direct the church towards social work; and his proudest moment came when the tsar asked him to draft the decree freeing the serfs. His successor, Innocent, had been bishop of Kamshchatka and a notable missionary. He carried on Philaret's tradition. Had Alexander II not been assassinated, the church might have been freed. Alexander III reverted to Nicholas I's policies.

The decline in Russian spiritual life can be illustrated by the decline in religious art. Till the 18th century it was still a great art, sincere and intense. Later it became either sentimentalized in a slick western style or else a lifeless copy of the past. But the Russians are basically devout; and when the hierarchy could not give them comfort they turned to the hermits and the *staretsi*. The first teacher to revive the Orthodox spirit was the monk Tikhon of Zadonsk (1724–82); but the greatest influence in the revival was Seraphim of Sarov

(1759–1833) to whose cell in the forests of central Russia pilgrims came in their thousands to hear the old Orthodox teaching. Paisi Velichkovsky, who set about the revival of monasticism (1722–94), had to retire to Moldavia, but his work was carried on in Russia by the monastery of Optino Pustina, near Tula, administered by a succession of highly educated *staretsi* who had no connection with and were disliked by the hierarchy. It was to Optino that the great 19th-century Russian thinkers came for refreshment, such as Gogol, Dostoievsky, Tolstoy and Soloviev. It flourished from 1829 till it was closed in 1923. More questionably helpful were the evangelical revivalists, of whom the most eminent was Father John of Kronstadt (1829–1908), a great preacher, devoted to the care of the poor and the sick, a healer himself, but somewhat hysterical, an advocate of such practices as public confession. His best known pupil was Rasputin.

By the 20th century many thoughtful elements in the Russian church disliked the tsarist regime. The peasants might still call the tsar their Little Father, but they had little respect for the hierarchy. They belonged, rather, to the tradition of the Non-Possessors and the Old Believers.

The Revolution of 1917 was thus not wholly unwelcome. Few Orthodox wished to see the monarchy abolished, as it was part of Orthodox tradition. But the Kerensky government appointed a sympathetic procurator, Prince Lvov, who at once set about summoning a council of the church; and his successor, Professor Kartashev, dropped the hated title, becoming Minister for Religion. The council met in August, 1917, and in October it voted to restore the patriarchate. On 5 November, Tikhon, metropolitan of Moscow, was elected patriarch. But in the meantime there had been the October Revolution, and Lenin and his friends were in power. Tikhon hoped that the church could survive by keeping clear of politics. But the government was determined to destroy it. In January 1918, the church was disestablished and all its possessions, its buildings and their contents and its properties, were confiscated. Many ecclesiastics were killed for protesting, as well as many laymen and laywomen who tried to preserve icons and relics from destruction. It was the beginning of a deliberate attempt to crush the Christian religion in Russia.

The attempt has not been successful. Until 1923 the persecution was severe. Some 7,000 priests, monks and nuns were put to death. Then it eased a little, with the formation of a pro-Communist church, known as the 'living church' or, later, the 'renewed church'. It soon faded out. When Tikhon, who had spent some time in prison, died in 1925 – and 300,000 people marched in his funeral procession – no new patriarch was appointed. The *locum tenens*, Sergius, had to govern the church from his see of Nijni Novgorod, till, in 1927, he announced his full support of the Soviet regime. Many bishops protested, preferring exile and even death to acceptance; and the Russian church in exile broke off connections with Moscow. From 1929 to 1934 there was renewed persecution. Then things improved, and improved further when the war with Germany began. Stalin realized how valuable was the support of the church. The improvement lasted till 1959, with churches reopening and Russian prelates encouraged to travel abroad. A new patriarch, Alexis of Leningrad, was elected in 1945. Since 1959 the liberty given to the church has been reduced. Many monasteries have been closed and priests forbidden to function. The hierarchy is in a difficult position. How far can it compromise its integrity in order to prevent further persecution? The Patriarch Alexis likened the position to that of the Early Christians under the pagan emperors. The Christian must render to Caesar that which is Caesar's. He must hope that in the end Caesar will see the light.

Among the intellectual classes, and among the young, there is a revived interest in Orthodoxy. But it is the Orthodoxy of the Non-Possessors and of Optino, rather than that of the official hierarchy.

In the three Balkan countries that found themselves under Communist rule after the last war, the national Orthodox churches survive. In Bulgaria the church is tolerated, but discouraged and kept under strict control. A seminary for priests is permitted, and religious books suitable for children are published. The church services are well attended. The hierarchy is careful to emphasize its loyalty to the regime, and will no doubt survive. In Yugoslavia, after a period of persecution when Tito first came into power, the church is allowed to manage its own affairs, as long as it remains loyal to the state. But it is poor. It has neither the money nor the personnel to maintain all its parishes, though the churches that remain are well attended. It too will survive. The Romanian church is the most prosperous of the three. Though controlled by the state it is generously supported by the state. The monasteries operate. There are several active seminaries. The patriarch is treated as a figure of national importance. Of all the Orthodox churches in Europe it is probably the most efficiently run, with its future assured.

But it is in the lands of the Diaspora that Orthodoxy is now most lively, in western Europe, in America and in Australia. There the Orthodox are showing that they still have a contribution to make to religious thought.

THE AGE OF
FAITH

5
Medieval Christendom

DURING THE MIDDLE AGES institutional Christianity, that is, the Catholic church, dominated the intellectual and social life of Europe to a greater extent than at any time before or since. Whatever area one chooses to study – history, philosophy, social organization, art or literature – everything is securely placed within a framework set by Christian dogma.

Two of the most obvious signs of this Christian culture are the churches and monasteries which rose all over Europe in numbers – and on a scale – that were never surpassed. Almost every village had a church; larger towns had a more ambitious structure which – depending on their prosperity – would be enlarged and rebuilt more magnificently; in the cities the cathedrals dominated the skyline, representing a sizable proportion of the resources of their region. In the countryside the traveller would come frequently upon large monastic estates, often miniature towns in themselves, their churches rivalling the cathedrals in size and splendour.

Outwardly, the picture of a total Christian society was impressive. How far did it correspond with reality? The answer must vary according to the kind of society being discussed. Monks and canons lived lives that were in intention genuinely apostolic; ordinary parish priests offered an ethic that was somewhat lower on the scale of perfection; and laymen concerned with secular affairs could be indifferent or even hostile to ecclesiastical interests altogether. Chapter 6 will show that at the humblest level the sway of the church was by no means absolute. It was nevertheless not without reason that later centuries looked back at the Middle Ages as 'the Age of Faith'. Never again would the universal church be so secure, so powerful and so creative.

Charity

was a social obligation. It was also, more cogently, a Christian ideal. In St Matthew's Gospel, Jesus enumerates those acts that will help to win salvation in heaven, which later came to be known as the Acts of Mercy: 'As long as you did it for one of these, the least of my brethren, you did it for me.' The series was among the most popular subjects of medieval art, and can be found in manuscripts, relief sculpture and stained glass. This example is a 12th-century book cover, made for the psalter of Queen Melisende of the Latin Kingdom of Jerusalem. In each scene the protagonist seems to be a king, perhaps Melisende's husband Fulk. From left to right, it shows: feeding the hungry; giving drink to the thirsty; welcoming the stranger; clothing the naked; comforting the sick; and visiting the prisoner. Between the roundels are fabulous beasts, some of them ferociously attacking each other. The heron at the top is given its bestiary title Herodius. In the foliage borders are bright blue turquoises and dark red garnets.

Many of the details in the little scenes repay close examination: the counter with various shapes of loaf, the pantiled house into which the stranger is being received, the bed on which the sick person rests (is his pulse being felt?) and the hand- and foot-shackles of the prisoner. (1)

'A white robe of churches'

Every medieval town and village was dominated by its church, visible symbol of a universal faith.

The king of Sicily, William II, presents his church of S. Maria at Monreale to the Virgin – a carving on one of the capitals of the cloister. (2)

Ortonovo (*below*): a typical Italian hill village near La Spezia. The church, at the focal point, was rebuilt in the 18th century, but its medieval round tower survives. (3)

Durham (*right*): founded in the 11th century and completed in the 15th, the cathedral rises above the city, which in this photograph was largely Victorian. Castle and cathedral confront each other within a few hundred metres, physical symbols of the secular and the spiritual powers. (5)

Venançon (*above*), in the Alpes Maritimes: here the ancient church, occupying the site of a stronghold on an impregnable rock, is conspicuous from one end of the valley to the other. (4)

Zamora: the squat Romanesque cathedral, with its ornate polygonal crossing tower and unfinished campanile, is still the main accent in a Spanish city at one time ruled by the Moors. (6)

Quedlinburg: an important collegiate establishment. The church, consecrated in the 12th century, was a royal foundation and contains the body of the Emperor Henry I. (7)

The problem of poverty

It was assumed that 'the poor are always with you', and although they were to be aided by alms-giving, there was no thought that poverty could be permanently abolished. Relief measures, even when initiated by the secular powers, were administered by the church.

Poverty could also be holy – something not just to be endured but to be deliberately embraced. St Francis's mendicant order of friars, given official approval only after much hesitation, provided a needed link between the hierarchy of the church and the mass of the people. *Right:* St Francis marries the Lady Poverty, an allegorical painting in the lower church of S. Francesco at Assisi. (10)

The saintly King Edmund distributes alms, from a manuscript of about 1130. Edmund had been murdered by the Danes in 869; venerated as a martyr, he quickly became credited with all the virtues necessary for sanctity, including generosity to the poor. This miniature gives a lively impression of medieval beggars: all are barefoot and one carries a crutch. (8)

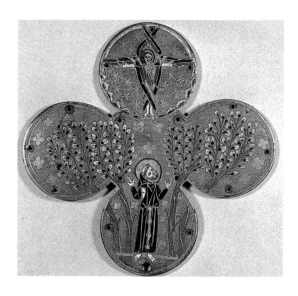

The cult of St Francis spread rapidly over Europe, borne by the Franciscan order. This Limoges enamel from a reliquary, showing the saint receiving the stigmata, was made about 1230, only four years after his death. (11)

The church as the source of charity. *Left*: altarpiece of the Confraternity of the Annunciation, founded by Cardinal Torrecremata to provide dowries for poor girls. The cardinal and three girls kneel between the angel and the Virgin, who personally presents the money. *Above*: the hospital of St Matthew, Florence; all medieval hospitals were religious foundations. (9, 12)

129

The soldiers of Christ

Warrior saints and warrior monks were the church's
answer to the violence that pervaded medieval society.
The image of life as an endless struggle, a war against
the armies of darkness, took deep root in men's minds.

Michael the Archangel, the conqueror of Satan, embodied
the warrior ideal, here seen on a German tapestry of the
13th century, with the devil represented as a dragon. *Left:*
9th-century wall-painting at Malles, commemorating a
member of the nobility. The sword held by the blade came
to be a form of cross and was often included on tomb
monuments. (13, 14)

The battle of the soul – *psychomachia* – was traditionally
represented as a physical fight between Virtues (tall
handsome knights) and Vices (deformed and terrifying
demons). At a time when Christians were fighting Muslims
in Spain and the Holy Land, this easily acquired racist
overtones. (15)

Christian chivalry brought together secular and religious values. The knight was a crusader for the faith, the priest and monk were soldiers in the war against evil. The Emperor Charlemagne (*above* from a Spanish manuscript, *c.* 1130) became an archetype of heroic virtue and relics of him were treasured like those of a saint. (16)

Priest and knight were both central to medieval society, both capable of realizing the highest Christian ideals and brought into unity in the three military orders of the Templars, the Hospitallers and the Teutonic knights. *Far left:* two figures from the late 12th-century cloister of Jerpoint Abbey, Ireland. *Left:* the priest Conrad and the nobleman Tosti, two benefactors of Kirkeby church, Denmark, *c.* 1200. *Below:* effigy of a Templar, from the Temple Church, London. (17–19)

5
Medieval Christendom

COLIN MORRIS

B Y THE 11th century Europe had become almost completely Christian in its profession. The frontiers of Christendom had been pushed forward until they included the whole continent except some regions around the Baltic and (to the south) Sicily and most of Spain, which were under Muslim rule. Within these wide boundaries there were few alternatives to Christian worship. In a few regions Viking settlers had reintroduced pagan rituals, but these had virtually been abolished again by 1050; in the greater cities there were Jewish communities, rich and cultured at first, which continued to exist in an atmosphere of growing intolerance. With these exceptions, every western European was in a sense born a Christian and could expect to live his life without ever meeting the adherent of another religion.

An expanding society

It is often supposed that medieval society was fixed and unchanging in its structures, and it is indeed true that it was not subject to the huge technological developments which have so profoundly altered Europe in the 20th century. Yet the changes that were taking place between 1000 and 1200, if less dramatic, were important and were creating a form of society in which we would readily recognize the Europe our grandparents knew. Throughout these two centuries the population was increasing steadily, and people were moving on a large scale into the forests and wastes which still covered such a large part of the countryside. It has been called the age of the great clearances. New villages were planted, marshes drained and forests cut down; quite literally, the wolf was being driven from the door. The movement affected almost every part of Europe. In the marshes of Flanders we hear that Count Baldwin V (1035–67) had 'made fertile by his care and industry land which was uncultivated until recently'. On the

river Elbe settlers were invited in 1108 to move into territories occupied by the pagan Wends: 'here you can save your souls and, if you wish, acquire the best of land to inhabit'. When Urban II preached the First Crusade in 1095 he told his audience, at least according to one of the reports, that the cause of the prevalent violence in French society was overcrowding, and that more *Lebensraum* had to be found. Under the impetus of this population pressure there was a movement to settle new lands on the frontiers, in Germany and Spain, and a still larger internal colonization of the unoccupied spaces within western Europe.

There was also a rapid development in the cities. In the year 1000 urban culture was almost non-existent, and a writer in northern Italy, the most urbanized region of all, expressed his astonishment that the inhabitants of Venice existed without tilling the ground. From 1050 onwards people were moving into the cities in great numbers. We have little information about their precise population, but it is likely that by the late 13th century Milan and Venice, Genoa and Palermo each contained approaching 100,000 people. There were fewer large cities north of the Alps, but Paris and Cologne were big, and it must be remembered that even a community of a few thousand people presented all sorts of opportunities and problems that did not exist in a village of two hundred. The cities were sustained by large trading areas. The cloth industry of Flanders drew wool from England and Spain, wine from Gascony and corn from the Île-de-France, and exported its products as far afield as Italy. The vessels of Venice, Pisa and Genoa traded with Egypt, Syria, and Constantinople. The cities all required not only the use of money on a large scale but also techniques of banking and credit, which had been extensively developed by the 13th century, and they were governed by an urban patriciate whose fortunes rested ultimately on trade and more immediately upon the ownership of urban property.

The aristocracy, too, although it enjoyed traditional stories and ancient values, was caught up in the pattern of change. Its basis for social control now became the castles. These were private fortresses, which first became important in France in the 11th century, and which were brought to England by the Norman Conquest of 1066 and to Germany shortly afterwards.

The two extremes of medieval Christianity – contemplation, in the person of St Anthony Abbot, action, in the person of St George – are represented in this altarpiece by Pisanello. St Anthony was revered as the father of monasticism. St George, a less historical figure, had reputedly killed a dragon and became the embodiment of knightly prowess. (20)

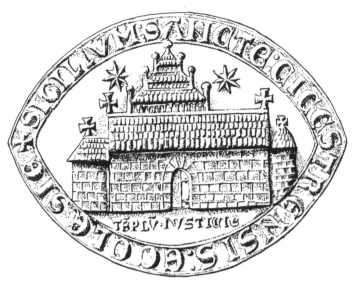

Seal of Chichester Cathedral, made from a silver die of the 12th century. Around the edge, the motto (translated) reads: 'Seal of the holy church of Chichester', and underneath the relief, 'Temple of Justice'.

The castle gave to noble families a hereditary identity, a local habitation and a name, which they had previously lacked, and they were often called after their main centre, Clare or Montfort or Hohenstaufen. Their military force came no longer from the freeholders of the countryside, as it had under the Carolingians, but from their own household warriors and tenants, the *milites* or knights, a force of heavy cavalrymen noted for their courage on the field of battle and their violence in the ordinary affairs of life. The rise of the cities and increasing economic activity in the countryside did not mean the end of the dominance of the aristocracy. On the contrary, the period from about 1050 to 1250 was something of a golden age for the nobility.

Social and economic change was accompanied by a great increase in educational opportunity. Until about the middle of the 11th century it was difficult to obtain even elementary instruction. Monasteries accepted recruits as small boys, to train them in the complex round of Latin offices, and the best parish priests often came from the families of clergy, with sons being taught by their fathers. This situation changed with the growth of the towns. The grammar schools improved, and by 1100 it was possible to obtain more advanced education, not only in Italian cities but in French centres such as Laon and Reims, Tournai, Chartres and Paris. By the later 12th century Paris and Bologna had a population of students and a large number of masters, having become universities in all but name. The growth of education introduced two new forces into the social history of the church: civil servants and intellectuals. For the first time the governments of the medieval west

had administrators, *officiales*, trained as secretaries or as lawyers, and the papacy led the way in the employment of these experts in the conduct of government. At the same time the schools were developing skills in argument, which they applied in the fields of canon law and theology. There were men who were capable of evaluating the conduct of popes and bishops, criticizing the state of the church, and proposing new solutions.

'A white robe of churches'

The circumstances of the 11th century meant that within Europe there was no call to proclaim the faith to the unbeliever, and the most urgent task was to make real the practice of Christianity by a society which already professed belief in it. Medieval assumptions about religion were different from ours. In our eyes it is a matter of personal commitment that fashions the way we behave to other people. The men of the 11th century placed far more stress on the duty of maintaining the worship of God with the dignity which was his due. The welfare of kingdom and countryside, of harvest and family, depended on paying due respect to God and to the local saint. The liturgy must be performed with proper solemnity, and the relics of the saint must be suitably enshrined in gold and silver and his memory honoured in a splendid building. To do this was the general aspiration of medieval society at all

A drawing from the late 12th century shows the building of a chapel by the 8th-century hermit-saint Guthlac. He appears in the foreground, with tonsure, and is assisted by other monks in cowled robes.

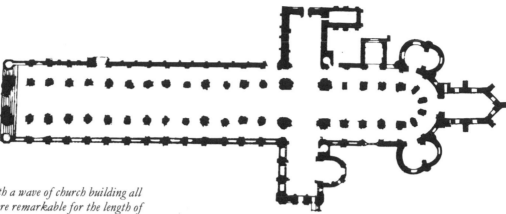

The Norman conquest coincided with a wave of church building all over Europe. English cathedrals were remarkable for the length of their naves. Norwich, built from the late 11th century onwards, had one of the longest, 75 metres, and still preserves its original plan.

levels. Royal houses built themselves shrines of great magnificence, such as Westminster Abbey, the Capella Palatina at Palermo, or the Ste-Chapelle at Paris. The desire to build was equally apparent in the countryside. Already in the Carolingian period bishops and nobles had been active in founding local churches, which at first were usually made of wood; indeed, as late as 1160 the archbishop of Canterbury had to hear a complaint that the church of Ranworth (Norfolk) had been stolen by a neighbouring lord, who had dismantled and removed it. Soon after 1000, however, we hear that the land was being covered by a 'white robe of churches', and between then and 1200 a church of stone was provided in very many villages. This was a formidable undertaking, and to it was added the need to provide facilities for worship in the growing cities. Often the citizens were eager to provide themselves with churches, and particularly with a great shrine for their patron saint. The emblem of Venice was the lion of St Mark, and his church there, originally the chapel of the Doges, became one of the most splendid buildings in western Europe. Milan rejoiced in the protection of St Ambrose, and the merchants of Bari (Apulia) celebrated the growth of their city in 1087 by stealing the body of St Nicholas of Myra and making it the centre of a major pilgrimage. On the whole, Carolingian buildings had been of fairly modest size, and the huge cathedrals, many of which still survive, were mostly built from the late 11th century onwards. The Normans in England had a liking for inordinately long cathedrals, as at Winchester and Norwich, while in the late 12th century the French builders were beginning to create Gothic churches of dizzying height. Most cities had at least one vast central church, and in some parts of Europe, most notably in England, many smaller street-corner churches were built. London had over a hundred of them by 1200.

The churches had, therefore, come to the people. People were also, without needing much encouragement, flocking to the great churches. By its very nature the growth of popular pilgrimage is difficult to date, but its great extension seems to belong to the 11th century. The most important new centres tended to be those which had relics of the apostles, of other New Testament figures, or of Christ himself. The head of John the Baptist had been found at Angéli (western France) in 1010 – a discovery which embarrassed a few scholars, who knew there was already a head at Constantinople. Vézelay acquired the body of Mary Magdalene shortly after 1037. In Spain, the body of St James had been discovered at Compostella long before, but the international popularity of this pilgrimage grew rapidly in the later 11th century. In Italy the body of St Matthew was found at Salerno in 1080; another major centre was Lucca, where there was a statue which exactly preserved the holy countenance (*Santo Volto*) of Christ. The most esteemed of all the pilgrimages was to Jerusalem, to the scene of the Passion and death of the Lord. Apart from these international shrines there were many of more local importance. The celebration of the feast of the patron saint, with its accompaniment of ceremonial, preaching and recital of legends and sometimes of miraculous healing, brought the ordinary visitor into touch with the power of Christian worship in a way that the modest services of a village church could not achieve.

The search for the apostolic life

The worship conducted in these splendid buildings must be offered by devout ministers. Once again there is a difference of assumption between medieval thinkers and the prevalent religion of the modern world. The mission of the church was to be holy, and any impact it had upon society was an extension, or a by-product, of this vocation to holiness. The reformers of the 11th century gave this renewal of the church a clear ideological formulation: it was the intention to bring back the perfection of the apostolic life. The *vita apostolica* was the objective of important groups in many parts of the church in the 11th century. From 1045 onwards the popes were choosing names for themselves which recalled the days of primitive purity: Clement, Damasus, and Stephen, Leo and Gregory. Under Leo IX (1049–54) a party of reformers secured control within the Roman church and were able to obtain the election of like-minded popes. The most powerful personality among this party, Hildebrand, was pope himself as Gregory VII from 1073 to 1085.

The Benedictine Rule was established at Mont St Michel in the 10th century. In this 12th-century Cartulary of the abbey, Richard I of Normandy, who made over the monastery to the monks, is seated beside the new abbot, Maynard; below, the assembled monks receive the Rule, which is symbolically handed down to them.

The accepted definition of the *vita apostolica* came from the description of the church at Jerusalem in the Acts of the Apostles: 'the company of those who believed was of one heart and soul, and no one said that any of the things he possessed was his own, but they had everything in common'.

These words were the starting-point for a series of experiments in communal living, which were one of the most striking features of the 11th and 12th centuries. Conservatives were disturbed at what was happening, and inclined to ask (so we are told by Anselm of Havelberg, himself a member of one of the new orders): 'Why are there so many innovations in God's church? Why are so many new orders appearing inside it?'

Experiment began with the monks, who believed that the monastic life, if it were truly followed, faithfully reproduced that of the apostles at Jerusalem. Legend asserted that the first monasteries had been founded by men who wanted to preserve the charity of the apostolic days, which was being threatened by the influx of lukewarm converts. Apologists argued that 'all the apostles were truly monks', and the prestige of monasticism was such that the claim did not seem exaggerated. The first attempt to embody the apostolic ideal in a new organization was made by the Cluniacs. Cluny was a Burgundian abbey, founded in 910, and under Abbot Hugh (1049–1109) it underwent a spectacular expansion, establishing houses in Spain, Italy, southern Germany and England. It was protected by privileges from interference by lay or ecclesiastical authorities and to maintain its coherence it adopted an original structure, with the abbot of Cluny exercising a sort of monarchical authority over the affiliated houses. This was not to everyone's taste, and Hugh's critics described him as an 'arch-abbot'. The order was thus by design insulated from the society around, but in practice Cluny's influence was widespread. The aristocracy accepted the principle that the monks should lead a holy life on their behalf, thus bringing them the grace of God by proxy. They endowed Cluniac monasteries handsomely, sought to be linked with them in a brotherhood of prayer, and sometimes retired to Cluny to die there. Hugh was a friend of popes and godfather of Henry IV, and the influence of the order contributed to a unique period in papal history: from 1073 to 1119 every pope was a monk. Cluny's contribution to economic change was also great. It drew revenues from as far afield as England and Spain and used them to feed great numbers of poor and to build one of the largest churches that has ever been constructed. A large abbey of this kind could make as great an impression upon its region as a substantial city.

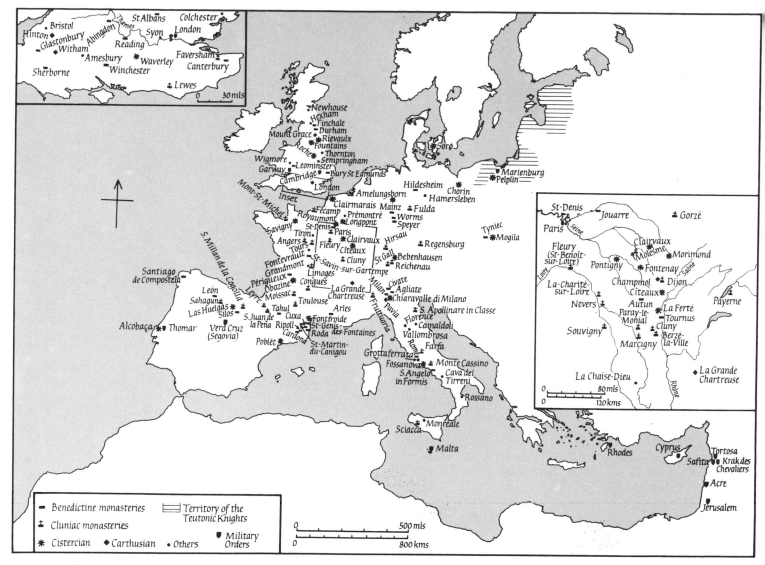

From the 10th to the 14th century, the monasteries expanded on a massive scale, as indicated on this map of important medieval monastic sites. By the 12th century the monasteries provided a framework of administration, education and social service, while the military orders sent their missionaries into new territories to secure them for Christianity.

For all the renown of Cluny, it was challenged in the early 12th century by another and more critical type of monasticism. The Cistercians agreed with Cluny that the Rule of St Benedict was the embodiment of apostolic perfection, but insisted that it should be followed literally, shorn of the customs and accretions which had been introduced in recent centuries. They aimed at a decisive separation from society and would accept as endowments only gifts of land in full ownership, declining tithes, rents and churches, which would entangle them in the affairs of society around. The mother-house of Cîteaux was founded about 1098. It began to establish daughter-houses during the second decade of the 12th century, and for a generation after that expansion continued at a staggering rate. By 1150 there were 328 Cistercian monasteries, extending from Norway to Portugal. This expansion was due in part to the brilliant propagandist work of Abbot Bernard of Clairvaux (1115–53), who was one of the most influential men of his age, but more profoundly it was the consequence of the Cistercians' appeal to the aspirations of a more educated class. The spirituality was that of a fellowship of converts who had chosen as adults to join the order. No children were accepted; the liturgy was simplified and thus adapted to the needs of men who had not spent a life-time mastering it; the life of the order was governed by a written constitution and legislation; and an attempt was made to restore original Benedictine practice along critical, almost along archaistic, lines. Cistercian economy was also well devised to take advantage of new developments, and an order based on the principle of withdrawal from the world paradoxically found itself making an important contribution to the development of the European economy by bringing into use regions which in the past had been little exploited. The Yorkshire abbeys such as Fountains and Reivaulx helped to establish the wool production of northern England; Les Dunes developed the sandy and low-lying regions of the Flemish coastline; and Poblet and Alcobaça took the lead in

Ludwug IV of Bavaria endowing Dietrich von Altenburg, Grand Master of the Teutonic Order, with Lithuanian land, 1337. Founded as a crusading order of warrior monks in 1198, the knights conquered Prussia and became a ruling aristocracy in eastern Germany and northern Poland.

settling depopulated areas recovered from the Moors in Spain and Portugal. In monastic terms the 11th century belonged to Cluny and the 12th to the Cistercians.

It was not only the monastic world that was transformed by the apostolic ideal. Since the apostles had lived in a sort of primitive communism, it was asserted that all clergy should do so. As early as 1059 Hildebrand spoke strongly at a synod at Rome in favour of groups of clergy who wished to live in communities without personal property, and it became the policy of the reformers at Rome to encourage the creation of houses of regular canons. Whereas the clergy at most cathedrals and collegiate churches now had a personal income and did not always eat and sleep in the common refectory and dormitory, the reformed canons lived together and held all their property in common. It was thought by many to be the true form of the clerical life. Enthusiastic bishops tried to force it upon their cathedral chapters, and although no one seriously undertook the replacement of the country clergy, with their individual benefices, the principle was accepted by reformers that the apostolic communal ministry should be extended as far as possible. There were those who argued that canons, not monks, were the true successors of the apostles, because they followed them in the ministry of Word and sacrament, and in 1092 Urban II recognized that monks and

regular canons both followed versions of the apostolic life, leaving the laity and, by implication, the secular clergy in a sort of sub-Christian limbo. Most of the orders of monks followed the Rule of St Benedict as their basic discipline but there was no single clear Rule for canons. By the late 11th century it was accepted that they were following the pattern of life prescribed by St Augustine for his clergy, but there were several quite different texts which set this out, and families of canons adapted them freely. The Augustinians or regular canons fulfilled many different functions. In a few regions of Germany they virtually replaced the secular clergy in the administration of the dioceses, and reformers such as Archbishop Conrad of Salzburg (1105–47) came close to creating a situation in which all except the village priests were 'apostolic', either as monks or canons. Other Augustinian communities were to all intents and purposes monks – this was true in particular of the large and influential Premonstratensian order. In yet other cases the Augustinian Rule was adapted to form the basis of such specialist ministries as running hospitals or forming military orders to fight the heathen in Spain, Syria or Prussia.

The impact of regular canons upon the structure of the church was great, because their ideals, like those of the Cistercians, were in tune with other social changes. Until recently, a hereditary clergy had been the only practicable arrangement, however little it fitted with the opposition of canon law to married priests, because the one way of obtaining training in a profession was within the family. Now, with the growth of schools, the regular canons offered an alternative: the recruitment of educated men into communities of clerks living under Rule. They were trained to think about the pastoral structure of the church, and some of the scholars who contributed most in this field were themselves regular canons: Bishop Ivo of Chartres (author of three great collections of canon law), Hugh of St Victor, Gerhoh of Reichersberg and Anselm of Havelberg. In its central objective, however, the canonical reform was not successful. The clergy of cathedrals and greater churches were in most cases successful in retaining their privileges and in resisting the attempts of reforming bishops to compel them to live a communal life without personal property. By the middle of the 12th century it was becoming apparent that there was no way of realizing the hope of Gregory VII and his supporters, that the pastoral affairs of the church would be directed by 'apostolic' communities of monks and canons. The programme would have created a church very different from the one that emerged in the later Middle Ages, but it was already clear that it could not be fulfilled in its true revolutionary potential.

Hierarchy or poverty (1150–1250)

The check to the canonical reform movement was part of a wider change which was taking place in ecclesiastical government in the middle of the 12th century. Although the prestige and influence of the monks remained great, the programme of apostolic reform, as expressed by Cluny, Cîteaux and the Augustinians, was losing its general appeal. From 1200, or even somewhat earlier, the recruitment of monks and canons and the foundation and endowment of new houses slowed very markedly. At the same time, the administration of the church was being transformed by the emergence of a new class, the *officiales*, professionals whose training in literary skills and legal knowledge was made available to the government in both church and state. Already under Urban II (1089–99) a beginning was being made with the establishment of a papal household, which was separate from the Lateran palace staff and travelled with the pope, called, in imitation of lay usage, his Court or Curia. Meanwhile, progress was being made with the codification of canon law in a form in which it could effectively be applied in the courts, and about 1140 Gratian at Bologna completed his *Decretum*, which was to be accepted as the authoritative summary of the old law. This was, however, only the preparation for change. The new system emerged primarily under Alexander III (1159–81), with the hearing of many cases either by lawyers under papal authority in the Curia or in the provinces by judges with delegated powers. The law of the church was henceforth to be changed by papal decretals, letters issued in response to inquiries from the ecclesiastical courts. The papal fulness of power was being applied to the detailed regulation of the affairs of the western church in a way that in the past would have been inconceivable, but it was a rather peculiar sort of headship. Papal authority was manifested less in pastoral or doctrinal questions than in hearing judicial business, much of which was essentially matters of dispute about property rights, based on litigation over tithes or marriages or benefices.

There were many critics of the legalistic character of the hierarchy. The satirists complained about it: 'Now the pastor's seat is turned/Into a tribunal.' There were protests from the ranks of the monks and regular canons. Bernard of Clairvaux remarked that at Rome more was heard of the laws of Justinian than the Law of Christ, and Gerhoh of Reichersberg disliked the use of the term 'papal Curia', which equated the government of the pope with that of any secular prince. The most important challenge came from a different branch of the movement for the apostolic life. Although some of the orders which have been considered so far did admit

Brother John of Wallingford, an intriguing vignette by the 12th-century chronicler Matthew of Paris. Matthew was a Benedictine monk of St Albans, and his 'Chronica maiora' gives us a first-hand account of Henry III and his times.

laymen into association as lay brethren or *conversi*, they were in essence elitist. The apostolic life was for those with the training and education to participate in the round of liturgical prayer. There was already a range of opinion of another kind. The hermit, Stephen of Muret, who died in 1124, insisted that he wanted 'no Rule except the Gospel of Christ'. On this interpretation, the apostolic life could be opened to ordinary people, either by accepting them directly into communities or by creating communities of preachers and ministers who would live simply in their midst. A 'poverty and preaching' tradition arose, most notably in France, and in the later 12th century, as the hierarchy assumed steadily a more distant character as a bureaucratic organization, popular interest grew in a simpler form of religion. The relations between the hierarchy and the preachers were difficult, because the hierarchy was concerned to suppress unauthorized preaching and in particular was suspicious of the activity of the unlearned. Waldo, a Lyons merchant, adopted a ministry of poverty and preaching about 1174, but he was forbidden to continue and his followers, the Waldensians, were treated as heretics, although their faith at first was thoroughly orthodox. There was by this time a great deal of heresy in Lombardy and southern France, and an increasing tendency for the hierarchy to resort to force to suppress it.

Complete alienation between the authorities and the mass of the population was averted primarily by the work of two outstanding men. From the point of view of the hierarchy, the easier to digest was Dominic de Guzmán. Dominic, a Spaniard by birth, had preached among the heretics in the south of France, and it was his ambition to found an order that would witness to the Catholic faith, not only by word, but by holiness and poverty. Francis of Assisi was an even more striking personality, whose calling was to live the life of the apostles, in total poverty, with a group of companions. He was not an easy man to absorb within any organization, and had little idea of founding a society or formulating a Rule, but the potential of both movements was discerned by Pope Innocent III (1198–1216), and Rules were approved for both the Dominicans and Franciscans. Like the Cluniacs and Cistercians before them, the friars now experienced a great expansion. The structure of their life was quite different from that of monks, for they were committed to the work of preaching and witnessing. Their houses were at first modest affairs in the larger cities, and as their popularity increased they built hall-churches, designed for preaching to big congregations. Some aspects of their impact on medieval society were unexpected. Although they were by intention simple in their mode of living, they came to exercise a major artistic influence through such churches as the basilica of St Francis at Assisi and S. Maria Novella and S. Croce at Florence. They attracted highly educated recruits, and their ranks included some of the most distinguished scholars of the 13th and the early 14th century: Albertus Magnus, Thomas Aquinas, Roger Bacon and Duns Scotus, to mention only a few. Their main importance, nevertheless, was in bringing the faith to the people. Their ministry was popular, and in the face of tensions with the local clergy the papacy upheld the friars' right to preach and to hear confessions. Several of the practices which they introduced were later to become standard elements in Catholic devotion, including for example the Christmas crib and the Rosary. In the friars, there had been created an influential channel of communication between the hierarchy and the people.

The order of the laity

Liberal critics of the medieval church have accused it of having little interest in the structure of lay society and in the way ordinary people lived. It will be evident already that there is some substance in this criticism. The primary duty of Christians was to live the apostolic life, and in its perfect form this was open to clergy and to those laymen who would withdraw from the world into some sort of religious community. There was even a marked tendency to think of powerful and influential laity, not as the church's natural allies, but as enemies, and Gratian's collection of canon law included a good deal of material which expressed this 'state of siege' mentality. He stressed that laymen had no status (*nulla facultas*) to make decisions in ecclesiastical affairs, and included a remarkable text, quite often quoted at the time, which stated that 'laity are altogether hostile to clergy'. One of the key principles of the Gregorian reform in the 11th century was to remove from laymen the right to appoint and invest bishops or to possess tithes and other ecclesiastical revenues, and the suspicion in which the lay power was held had a particularly destructive effect on the relations of pope and emperor. The imperial office was originally the model of the co-operation of church and state, or more exactly of *regnum* and *sacerdotium*, for the emperor was the protector of the Roman church, from which he in turn received his dignity. The close connection between these two powers made bitter disputes the more certain when an atmosphere of suspicion arose. The first long struggle between papacy and empire, the Investiture Contest, as it is often termed, lasted from 1076 to 1122, and in 1159 the conflict was renewed between the popes and the Hohenstaufen emperors, and continued in various forms for more than a century. These conflicts were fought with all the propaganda resources, and the political and military means, which the two sides could command. A deep chasm had opened within the Christian community, with clergy and laity discerned as different, and even hostile, societies. About 1160 the canonist Stephen of Tournai wrote: 'there are two peoples, two orders in the church, clergy and laity; two lives, spiritual and carnal; two authorities, the *sacerdotium* and *regnum*; a twofold jurisdiction of divine and human law'. One curious consequence of this dualism was that the lay power was almost compelled to base its authority on foundations quite distinct from, and even contrary to, those of the church. This reaction can be seen already in the interest of Frederick Barbarossa (1152–90) in the Roman law as the basis for imperial rights, and it was later taken further by the national monarchies, notably by Philip IV of France (1285–1314). The idea of the secular state was a natural

St Martin of Tours was a young officer in the Roman army. Even before he was baptized as a Christian he displayed exemplary generosity by cutting his cloak in half to share it with a beggar, an act that was pictured over and over again in Christian iconography. This drawing comes from a manuscript of about 1200.

reaction to the separation of the 'two peoples and two orders' in canon law.

Nevertheless, this dualism was never intended to imply that the Gospel had no relevance to the daily affairs of ordinary people. The laity were recognized by Stephen of Tournai as constituting an order. By this was understood a way of life approved by God, and as social organization became more complex there was a tendency to sanctify each emerging social group by recognizing it as an *ordo*. In the late Carolingian period there was the famous trio of those who prayed, those who fought and those who worked. Now, other groups were inserted into the scheme. People were conceived of, not as equal individuals, but as members of one of the orders within society, and sermon collections quite often included addresses designed specially for a particular *ordo*, for clergy or knights or merchants or married men. With all these groups, thinkers and preachers sought to define their duties and to find a place for them within the economy of salvation. The discussion of social responsibility in this period was wide ranging, and can best be illustrated by taking as examples the attempt to deal with a growing problem (poverty), the attitude to an emerging group (the knights) and the refashioning of an existing institution (marriage).

Poor relief

To understand the problem of poverty, one has to define it first. In an economy with a poor technology the standard of living of most people was low by comparison with modern Europe. There was, however, no awareness of a need to improve the general prosperity of the population as a whole, an objective which would have been impracticable and would have been hard even to imagine. In medieval eyes the poor were not those who lived at the normal level, but those who fell below it and were temporarily or permanently without means of support. There are good reasons to think that the number of destitute was increasing rapidly from the 11th century onwards. It was a more mobile society, and men were leaving their villages to look for employment in the growing cities, or for land to cultivate in the forests, or were taking to the pilgrimage roads. When they left the village, they abandoned also the traditional network of support. As contemporary documents put it, they 'had left their land and kindred'. In this sense there was a problem of poverty on a scale that had not existed before. It was clear in canon law that the relief of the poor was a charge upon the resources of the church. Most of the texts made the bishop responsible, but they reflected a much earlier structure in which the revenues were under his control, and in practice the first institutions to take action were the great monasteries. At abbeys such as Cluny, the care of the poor was incorporated into the liturgical round of worship. A small group of bedesmen was in permanent residence, and on fast days the food which was not required by the monks was given to the crowds of poor who assembled there. The arrangement may displease the modern reader because of its ceremonial character, but it possessed the virtue of incorporating poor relief into the structure of monastic life. It was not an optional extra, but a component part of the monk's devotions, and the seriousness with which this was taken is shown by the emergence of the special office of almoner in many abbeys in the course of the 11th century.

The monasteries however could not provide a sufficient answer to the problem of poverty. In particular, many of the new poor were gathered in the cities, and even in a small town there could be an aggregation of sickness or deprivation on a scale unknown to the rural world of the past. The principal way of providing poor relief in the cities was through the foundation of hospitals. The modern use of the word may mislead us: a hospital catered, at the preference of its founder, for the sick, the aged and destitute, or travellers, and frequently for all at the same time. It was a refuge or a group home rather than a medical establishment. Such institutions had existed in the classical past, but hospitals were now founded on quite a new scale. It is likely that substantial foundations began about 1100, and that they were most frequent between about 1175 and 1225. Even by 1150, considerable progress had been made, so that there were at least twenty-five foundations in one area of northern France corresponding to three modern départements. Many of the larger hospitals were run by communities under the Rule of St Augustine; in 1226 we hear of 'congregations without any estimate or definite number in all the regions of the west, who humbly and devoutly minister to the poor and sick'.

Alongside the hospitals were institutions of another kind; leper-houses or *ladreries*. Leprosy was giving rise to serious concern at this time. It used to be suggested that it had been brought back from the east by returning Crusaders, but it is more likely that the problem had become more acute with the gathering of larger populations into cities. The contagious nature of the disease was already understood, and so was the importance of isolating the sufferers. Leper-houses might be provided by an abbey, a lay benefactor, or a leper in a spirit of self-help. Typically, the house would be a short way outside the city, but close to a main road where one of the occupants could beg for alms.

We do not have statistics that would enable us to

estimate how far the scale of the relief being made available was adequate for the needs of sufferers, but it is at least clear that canon law accepted a responsibility for the poor, and that charity was directed to the support of quite specific groups who had lost their place within society. There are hints, at least, that the poor were treated in a way designed to safeguard their dignity, as when monasteries were required to find for the post of almoner a man of burning charity, and when the brothers serving a hospital were themselves enjoined to be poorly dressed. There seems to have been no trace of the modern assumption that the poor were responsible for their own destitution and needed a lecture on self-help. It is clear, too, that the provision for relief went far beyond a simple series of appeals for money, and that it had issued in the foundation of new institutions and communities on a massive scale. The evidence suggests that the church's action had been both rapid and well directed.

Chivalry

A second major problem was the level of violence endemic within society, and this was associated with the emergence of the knights, or *milites*. Disorder was particularly acute in France from the 10th century onwards, for there royal power had broken down and even the great princes were no longer in effective control of their territories. The countryside was dominated by local lords and their bodyguards of knights. The Christian tradition had come to terms with kings and princes, who had a God-given duty to maintain peace and to protect the church, but the knights were essentially men of violence who lived by oppression and whose character was inimical to the Gospel. They represented something evil in principle: *militia–malitia*, as the slogan expressed it. One of the most remarkable developments of the period was the achievement of a symbiosis between the ideals of the clergy and the knights.

The first stage was the Peace of God Movement. In co-operation with some sympathetic princes, the French bishops from the late 10th century put the weight of their spiritual authority behind the maintenance of peace. A series of councils prohibited violence on holy days and in protected places. By accepting responsibility for the repression of violence, the clergy necessarily began to distinguish between bad knights and good knights, between those who broke the prescribed limits and those who helped to uphold them. A further change took place when, especially in Italy, the papal reformers showed themselves ready to resort to war against their enemies. Leo IX led an army to its defeat at Civitate in 1053 against the Normans of southern Italy; a decade later Erlembald was tyranniz-

The idea of knighthood as a Christian vocation grew up only in the late 11th century. Before that, the knight had been regarded as a man of violence. With the preaching of the First Crusade, knighthood became accepted as a way of life that could be dedicated to Christ. The military orders – the Templars, the Hospitallers, the Teutonic knights – were a logical extension of this theory. Right: Crusader from an English psalter of the 13th century.

ing over the clergy at Milan in the name of reform; and from 1080 onwards, Gregory VII was urging his supporters to do battle with the Emperor Henry IV. These warriors were soldiers of St Peter, *milites sancti Petri*. Admittedly, within the frontiers of the empire, the knights had not become a distinctive social group as they had in France, but the principle had been clearly established that the papacy could legitimately conduct warfare against its enemies, and ask for volunteers to take the field. The most important step of all was taken in 1095, when Pope Urban II appealed to the knights of France to go to the help of the persecuted brethren in the east and to join the First Crusade. It was designed as an opportunity for repentance and was accompanied by the remission of all sins; those who enlisted would become, in New Testament terms, *milites Christi*, soldiers of Christ. Even this did not mean that knighthood had been accepted as a normal Christian vocation, because Urban's assumption was that French knights were evil persecutors of their brethren who stood in danger of damnation. Yet the Crusade did establish that, to be saved, a knight did not necessarily have to give up the practice of arms, but that on the contrary the Christian warrior might fulfil a noble part in the purposes of God; and it is about 1100 that we find knighthood being described as an order. In 1098, in fact, the young prince Louis of France was 'ordained' a knight. Writers began to formulate the duties of the

Marriage existed as a civil institution before the Middle Ages, and has come to be one again in modern times. It was Pope Alexander III (1159–81) who fully defined it as an ecclesiastical institution. Here, in a drawing of about 1420, this attitude is projected back into the Old Testament.

tried with some success to reduce the level of violence in French society, but it had done so not so much by abolishing the use of force as by redirecting it into warfare against enemies of the papacy and the unbelievers on the frontiers of Christendom. Warfare was now authorized by the pope and proclaimed by the church. One is not sure whether to speak of the conversion of the knights or the militarization of the Gospel.

Marriage

The clergy were not only concerned to find answers to new problems and to provide teaching for new social groups. They also were intent upon regulating existing social institutions. Of this, marriage is an outstanding example. In early medieval society it was essentially a family treaty. It was often initiated by the betrothal of two small children. The marriage ceremonies proper varied from one region to another, but they were almost always a combination of family and ecclesiastical rituals, and might include a nuptial mass with the blessing of the couple under a veil, the handing-over of the bride and payment to her of a marriage portion, and a solemn procession to the new family home with the blessing of the nuptial bed by the priest. Lay opinion seems to have had no objection to divorce and the taking of a second wife, provided that the family interests of the first wife were duly respected, and the attitude of the clergy to such remarriages was ambiguous. In some royal houses, notably the Capetian kings of France, matrimonial scandal and divorce were almost a family tradition. Marriage, however, was the sacrament which specially distinguished the lay order, and it was the church's business to see that it was held in due honour. By the 11th century it was generally recognized that decisions about marriage fell under ecclesiastical authority, but there remained a tangle of customs and discordant views. When an English expert was consulted just before 1100, he began his answer with a quotation from St Augustine: 'I am aware that no cases are more obscure or perplexing than matrimonial ones.' It was the objective of the canonists of Bologna and the theologians of Paris to introduce consistency, and the principles they had formulated were applied in the field of legal decisions by Alexander III (1159–81).

The first principle was the indissolubility of marriage. This was certainly not a new element in Christian thinking, but it had not previously been applied so rigorously, to exclude all possible exceptions such as insanity, sterility and misrepresentation of social status. It was rooted in the character of marriage as a sacrament which 'means Christ and the church' (Ephesians v:32). This inner significance of marriage

Christian warrior, beginning with the Italian writer Bonizo of Sutri about 1090. In France, Bernard of Clairvaux formulated the theory of crusading knighthood about 1128 in a pamphlet he wrote to defend the ideals of the Templars, *In Praise of the New Militia*, and in 1159 John of Salisbury described in detail the religious rituals involved in making a man a knight. Whether it was a factual account or a programme that John was advocating is not clear, but it is evident that in his mind the knight was following a Christian vocation. The ideal of chivalry had been fully formulated, and from that time onwards it was common for preachers, moralists and the writers of romances to set out the duties of the knightly office.

One of the newly emerging social groups, the knights, had thus been given a hope of salvation and an ethic by which to live. This had been achieved by a change in traditional Christian values. The church had would become a mockery if the relationship were disavowed and restarted with someone else. The implications of this doctrine were particularly great because it was not a simple recommendation of life-long marriage, but a legal principle enforced in the church courts, which had a monopoly of matrimonial cases. From this time on, divorce and remarriage were abolished as social institutions, and they have only been reintroduced in most western countries within relatively recent years. The second principle was that of consent: 'the effective cause of marriage is consent'. The immediate source of this idea was Roman law, but Alexander III took it further than the Roman lawyers wished, and treated it as an absolute principle. No one could be married against his or her will, nor could they be married under the age of consent. The wish of the families was irrelevant. Most remarkably of all, the performance of formal ceremonies was of secondary importance. Provided that the man and woman accepted each other in marriage, they needed neither witnesses nor blessing by the priest. In theory this was a head-on attack on marriage as a family institution. In practice it was less extreme, because it was in no way opposed to the negotiation of family settlements with the consent of the parties. It did establish that marriage was entered, as a life-long commitment, by an act of free will, and the power of the family to coerce was significantly reduced. Perhaps more influential even than legal decisions was the introduction of a new rite. In the course of the 12th century there appeared in England and France a wedding ceremony which is the direct ancestor of our modern one, including some elements of family ritual (the giving away of the bride and the gift of a gold ring) but centred on the marriage vow: 'I take thee to my wedded wife.' The theologians of the 12th century had weakened the grip of the kin-group and given marriage a more human face.

Triumphalism or social concern?

A serious attempt was therefore being made to apply to social problems the teaching of the Gospels and of the early church, to meet the challenge of new circumstances and to provide a way of life relevant to new groups within a developing culture. We must end by asking how successful this attempt was. The answer cannot be a simple one, because the extent and intensity of Christianity cannot be measured by any directly applicable test; but it is fair to pose the question. To what extent did the work of preachers and pastors create a genuinely Christian society?

The first part of the answer is that they were not even trying. The *vita apostolica*, the truly Christian way, was followed by only a minority, by monks and hermits, regular canons and clergy. True, it was a large minority,

but the majority of the population was not regarded as following unambiguously the path of Christ. In a Marxist society, it is recognized that true communism cannot at once be introduced, but that there must be an intervening phase of socialism; in a rather similar way, medieval thinkers accepted the impossibility of reorganizing society on a thoroughly Christian basis. Most people lived under the Gospel but did not live by the Gospel. This situation explains why so much emphasis was placed upon what has been called 'triumphalism'. The splendour of God's glory, and his triumph over the forces of evil, were to be splendidly celebrated; hence the vast programme of building, the rich treasures and elaborate ceremonial. It was the task of the laity to provide for the clergy, initially by paying tithes and then by endowments and alms. Heresy must be suppressed. The laity must obey. This triumphalist programme always had its critics. It was an inherent part of the medieval scheme of things that the monks should witness to a perfect way and, therefore, to the inadequacy of the religion that was offered to the laity. Sometimes, as in the Franciscan Movement, the apostolic life was brought out of the cloister and made accessible to larger areas of society, but fundamentally the concept remained a two-level one. It was a natural expression of Christianity in a society which was founded on ideas of lordship and deference and divided into distinct ranks and estates.

We have also seen that the judgment of lay responsibility was not wholly negative. The laity formed an order (or alternatively a series of orders) with its own duties and its own place in the economy of salvation, even if the way was a less perfect one. The definition of these social responsibilities engaged some of the best minds of the period. It fell within the task of the theologians, among them Peter Abelard, Peter Lombard and Thomas Aquinas, and also within the sphere of canon law. Outside the universities the ideas were disseminated by preachers, in manuals for confessors, and in some spheres such as marriage by the judgments of ecclesiastical courts. University men rose to high rank and incorporated what they had previously learned in the formulation of policy. Innocent III (1198–1216) was in close touch with Peter the Chanter's circle at Paris, which had some interesting theories of social reform, and he promoted members of the group and implemented some of its suggestions. There was nothing amateurish about the work of such thinkers, or about the briefing of confessors and formulation of legal practice. It rested on a solid intention to apply the teaching of the Scriptures and the Fathers to medieval social conditions. The detailed programmes for social action inevitably incorporated elements of biblical ideas side by side with contemporary assumptions, and sometimes the one, sometimes the other emerged as dominant. In a developing commercial system, school-men and preachers remained hostile for a long time to the payment of interest on loans because of the Old Testament teaching about usury. On the other hand, they could be ready to absorb contemporary assumptions and clothe them in biblical dress; the justification of crusading as an act of charity would have startled St Paul. The fact remains that there was a sustained attempt to formulate the duties of the various ranks in society, and that it compares favourably with a good deal of modern social thinking.

The most difficult class to associate with responsibilities of this kind was the peasantry, but even here some progress was made in educating them in the principles of the Gospel. Christian worship was the only available religious system. We can trace a few survivals from heathenism in charms and spells, and possibly also in beliefs such as the attitude to fate, but they are only fragments which have become embedded within a new religion. The peasantry were provided with plenty of stories to fortify their faith, although it must be said that the legendary element was large, not only in the stories of the saints, but in the tales which had been added to the central Gospel events of Christmas and Easter. There are also signs that it was felt that the peasantry should have more than a purely external commitment to the Gospel. It was required by the Fourth Lateran Council in 1215 that every member of the church should make an annual confession. At this point, at least, the attempt was being made to bring an interior religion and the practice of self-examination into every cottage in western Europe.

In the final resort there was a self-contradiction in the character of the medieval church. Its main structure was a triumphalist one, with great cathedrals, huge endowments and a privileged elite who alone were thought to be living the truly Christian life. There could have been no other way of establishing the position of the church within a society founded on aristocratic dominance, with poor technology and communications and an illiterate populace. What is striking is the extent to which the church went beyond this. There was a real attempt to define the duties of the Christian laity and their social responsibility, and a desire to evoke, from all the subjects of Christendom, commitment rather than external obedience. The character of Christian society in the Middle Ages was determined by this uneasy coexistence between authority and participation.

The most enduring legacy of the Middle Ages is likely to be its architecture. In this detail from a stained glass window at Chartres, we see a master mason checking a wall with a plumb-line, while workmen prepare stones for building. In the background hang plans and templates.

THE RELIGION OF THE PEOPLE

6

*Popular religious movements in
the Middle Ages*

THE RELIGIOUS LIFE of ordinary people during the Middle Ages has until recently received scant attention from historians. It was natural that the fullest records should be those dealing with questions that interested the literate classes – theological controversy, disputes between church and state, ecclesiastical administration and the lives of popes and prelates. To understand the thoughts and beliefs of the illiterate masses needs a certain detective talent, for the evidence tends to be scattered or disguised or biased. Yet without this 'silent majority' of humble Christians there could have been no Christendom.

Between high and low there was always tension. As popular enthusiasm outgrew official control it ran an increasing risk of being condemned as heretical. Sometimes these movements were suppressed and left little record; sometimes they were finally accepted by the church and became themselves part of official teaching. The line between heresy and sanctity could be surprisingly thin.

Popular piety showed itself in a variety of ways: veneration of relics, pilgrimages to a famous shrine, attendance at the sermons of a powerful preacher, prayers for the dead or joining one of the brotherhoods through which salvation could be made more certain. One of the sources of friction between the hierarchy and the people was money. The church exalted poverty but was itself blatantly rich. Resentment against the church's wealth is a constant motif in the late Middle Ages, and heretical movements, from the Cathars to the Lollards, drew much of their support from it. By contrast, the mendicant orders of friars presented an officially approved poverty in the service of the church. This was a development on which it may be argued that lay feeling affected ecclesiastical thinking, in that interplay of forces that made up medieval Christianity.

In remote parish churches,
far from the great centres of patronage,
one can still find vivid reminders of popular piety. A particularly
rewarding group remains on the Danish island of Møn, where
throughout the Middle Ages local painters decorated the walls and
vaults with scenes from the Bible, historical episodes and pictures
illustrating a moral. The detail shown here is the vault of the church
of Keldby. Two men are at prayer, one rich, one poor, and the
supplications of each are indicated by the red lines emerging from
their mouths. The poor man beseeches Christ crucified and his
wounds. The rich man asks God for possessions – clothes, treasures
in a chest, a cask of wine, a horse and (at the bottom) a servant with a
cooking pot. The date of these paintings is about 1480. (1)

Pilgrimage

In the Middle Ages holiness was localized. To visit the very spot where a miracle had occurred or a martyr been killed was to come closer to a saint's supernatural power. A long journey to a distant shrine stored up merit for the pilgrim and strengthened his faith.

Canterbury and Compostela were among the most visited holy places in Europe and both grew immensely rich on offerings. At Canterbury (*above*, a pilgrim's badge of the 13th century) lay the saintly archbishop Thomas Becket, murdered in his cathedral in 1170. Compostela held the body of St James (Santiago), patron saint of the war against the Moors. *Right*: figure of St James at Zamora, northern Spain, showing his emblem, the scallop-shell. (2, 3)

Many came in search of a cure for disease; others, like Chaucer's pilgrims, at least partly for fun. *Above*: a countryside pilgrimage, the open-air shrine of S. Giustino, 15th century. *Right*: the shrine of St Thomas Cantilupe in Hereford Cathedral. Cantilupe was a bishop of Hereford who died in 1282. In 1287 his remains were moved to this new shrine and immediately miraculous cures were reported which marked the beginning of a new popular cult. The saint was honoured here until 1349, when his bones were translated to a still more splendid shrine. (4, 6)

The abbey of Vézelay in Burgundy became one of the most visited holy places of France, thanks to its claim, published in the mid-11th century, to possess the body of St Mary Magdalene. Its Romanesque church, built in the early 12th, is entered through a portal (*right*) decorated with the theme of Christianity's mission to convert the world. Round the border are exotic races, including men with animal heads. (7)

Jerusalem was the ultimate pilgrimage, but one which a surprising number of people in the Middle Ages contrived to make. Here (*above*) in a French fresco of the 14th century, a group reaches the holy city at last. (5)

Raymond Lull's pilgrimage (*right*) was the result of a vision that he experienced while writing an amorous poem. Suddenly, he saw five crosses, which he describes as increasing in size. Shaken by the experience, he made a pilgrimage to the Holy Virgin of Montserrat, and then to the shrine of St James at Compostela. Lull, a strange, mystical character, who lived *c.* 1233 to 1316, was to dedicate his life as missionary and scholar to the conversion of Islam. This miniature is from a series made during his lifetime. (8)

The power of relics

The relic was a tangible link with the saint and through him with God himself. The vast majority of miracles associated with relics are medical, and there is no reason to doubt that a large number of cures did in fact take place.

To be as close to the saint's body as possible, worshippers would squeeze through niches in the shrine to touch the tomb. *Left:* a manuscript life of Edward the Confessor, showing his shrine in Westminster Abbey in the 13th century. (9)

The shrine of St Ursula at Bruges (*opposite*). According to ▷ the legend (only dimly historical), Ursula had been murdered by Huns at Cologne, together with 11,000 virgin companions. She is depicted above the altar spreading her cloak to shelter them. On a bracket behind are tokens of thanksgiving for cures – a foot, a hand, an arm – and a ship for safe return after voyages. (12).

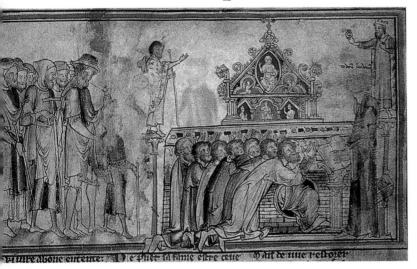

Flagellation began as an imitation of Christ and grew into a movement of extreme penitents who hoped by suffering to redeem their sins. *Above:* a procession of Flagellants depicted in Flanders, about 1500. *Right:* pilgrims at the tomb of a saint in Italy, 16th century. By this time, a form of spiritual 'inflation' was taking over. Relics, shrines, and prayers multiplied to the extent that their real meaning was becoming devalued. (10, 11)

The limits of orthodoxy

The untutored enthusiasm of the masses could easily clash with orthodox dogma and practice. Where possible, it was officially endorsed and its heroes canonized; where not, it was branded as heresy and suppressed.

The Dominicans and Franciscans could speak for the poor, exercising an influence that was as much social as spiritual. Both cultivated the spoken word, attracting huge audiences often resented by local priests, who saw their own congregations dwindling. Here St Dominic preaches from an open-air pulpit to a crowd that includes both rich and poor. The painting is by Lorenzo Lotto. (13)

Confraternities were voluntary associations of lay people, existing in parishes of every kind. Founded for mutual aid and charity, they dedicated themselves to the service of God and his saints. *Right*: the Confraternity of S. Giovanni Evangelista, Venice. (14)

The Crusade of the Pastoureux was one of those popular movements of which few records remain. In 1251 news reached France that King Louis IX (St Louis) had been captured by the Muslims in Egypt. A fanatical preacher known as 'the Master of Hungary' gathered an army of poor people in northern France with the object of rescuing him. In this miniature (*right*) they are met by the clergy of Paris. In fact the movement turned to attacking priests, was suppressed and disintegrated before it ever left France. (17)

Not everyone passively accepted orthodox teaching; evidence of medieval scepticism is sparse but interesting. *Above:* a heretic puts his tongue out at a priest, from a Bible Moralisée of the 1230s. (15)

'When women preach people learn ill': the message of a tiny painted window from Limoges, about 1564. One of the questions that the Lollards were alleged to have asked was: 'Why should not women be priested and enabled to celebrate and preach like men?' (16)

Heresy was the result of popular enthusiasm combined with independence of thought – hence official distrust of both. *Right:* the Hussites of Bohemia, who questioned the church's teaching on the sacraments, found a leader in Jan Žižka. In this miniature he still leads his army, though blind, following a priest with a monstrance. (18)

6

Popular religious movements in the Middle Ages

MARGARET ASTON

THE RELIGION OF THE PEOPLE belongs to the unscripted history of the church. It is true of Christianity in all periods that, as well as the church forming the people, the people also form the church. If an institution is to remain alive there has to be a continuous process of interaction (what one might call a dialectical relationship) between its forms and formulas and the beliefs of its members. They must contribute to each other's existence. This dialectical process was particularly evident in the late medieval church, which, having reached a high point of doctrinal and institutional definition in the 13th century, was confronted by a rising tide of devotional activity among believers. It represented a challenge that tested the limits of the organized church. While Christianity tended to become more and more clerical, lay society, in becoming more religious, generated an increasing number of spiritual initiatives. The religion of the people always amounted to a great deal more than a vulgarized reflection of the clerical elite, and the fact that some of these initiatives were declared heretical tells more of weakened church structures that it does of the nature of popular piety.

There was a tension, latent or explicit, between the church defined as ecclesiastical hierarchy and the church defined as community of faithful believers. Or, to put it differently, there was potential alienation, or at least divergence, between the knowing and the unknowing. The religion of the learned and the religion of the people were expressed in different ways of thinking and doing, each with its own momentum, though it would be quite wrong to think of them as belonging to separate worlds.

Christ's continuing Passion is symbolized in popular religion by this strange variant of the Man of Sorrows. Christ stands surrounded by workmen's tools – knives, hatchets, rakes, sickles, trowels, hammers. Wherever they touch him, they draw blood. To his body he clasps a giant sheep-shears. Bobbins from a loom pierce his hands. What is its meaning? At a general level, that the sins of ordinary men in their everyday lives (represented by the tools of their trades) wound Christ as cruelly as the spear and the nails. More specifically, that those who labour on Sunday are sinning by the very act of work. (19)

In the strictest sense, the religion of the people is impenetrable. It remains a forever closed book by virtue of the fact that it was so largely remote from books. Deprived of the oral communications of the past, we can only see the beliefs of the illiterate refracted through the writings of the literate, whose religious understanding was professedly of a different order. Since so much popular religion existed in the life of the spoken word, vanished passages of pulpit oratory and the transient flight of speech constitute a very large loss. Nor can the visual arts, for all their importance, bridge this gap. Not only is their survival and coverage at best patchy; as reporters they belong in the main to the same world as literary sources. We are, therefore, distanced by the nature of the records, as well as by the passage of time, from direct knowledge of the religion of the people, and all that we can say of the religious mentality of the humblest believers amounts, in effect, to deduction.

While the hierarchy mobilized the people, the people could mobilize the hierarchy. The church, which in one sense undeniably was the people, also had to beware of the people. Since those who were capable of guiding and instructing the mass of believers were always a tiny minority, and clerical education in fact always lagged far behind theory, the more actively the laity concerned themselves with doctrine, the greater the danger. Wherever and whenever there was a quickening of the intellectual tempo, a stirring of thought in the shape of new ideas and more people coming into contact with learning (not necessarily through direct contact with books, but through hearing about the world of books), there was the greater likelihood that error would arise. The devotions of the illiterate posed almost insuperable problems of control, and there was almost no spiritual activity that was not open to misinterpretation and misuse. The veneration of images could turn back into something resembling pagan idolatry, and the perverse inversion of image-worship was the manipulation of images for magical purposes. Mass pilgrimages might result in anticlerical demonstrations, like that which attended the apocalyptic preaching of the shepherd, Hans Böhm, at Niklashausen in 1476. Self-imposed penance could give way to displays that seemed to suggest an alternative to the ministry of the church. The

The relics of St Alban being moved to a new chapel (from a 14th-century manuscript). Preceded by the cross and a vessel of holy water, the relics themselves are housed in a costly shrine. As they pass, two cripples by the side of the road invoke the saint's intervention.

ideals of holy poverty and chastity, withdrawn from clerical supervision and imitated by the laity, were capable of building what seemed like heretical counter-churches in the hands of Cathars and Waldensians.

The religious movements of the later Middle Ages reflect the interactions of two worlds: the literate clerical and the illiterate secular. Some took their beginnings from an inspired leader in the literate world, whose ideas were translated from academic hall to street corner, thereby undergoing a sea-change. Others started with leadership that was itself of the people, or else arose at the prompting not of an individual but of catastrophic events. What we might call the folkways of devotional piety included various forms of traditional group activity that could spring into larger life under the stress of circumstance without any guiding hand. Penitential pilgrimage and corporate associations for the service of the dead lent themselves to spontaneous demonstrations of fervour at times of common need. Individuals were mutually bonded in more ways and groups than are dreamt of in our cellular society.

Piety on the move: saints and salvation

A great part of popular piety amounted to an endeavour to live with the inexplicable and intolerable. God and the saints (specially the latter) bore the consequences of the general incomprehension of natural phenomena. The religion of the people was deeply impregnated by ancient peasant fears of natural forces. Those who had no inkling of scientific laws, who suffered many mortal and crippling diseases, found their own laws of explanation in healing and punishing saints. Surrounded by mysterious powers and unaccountable events, people sought aid in formulaic expressions of word or deed. God dwelt in some places more than others and the habitations of saints were geographically dispersed. Holiness in this age was very much located. Through chosen people, particular places and special

objects one found access to spiritual controls. It was on the move, in pursuit of these mediatory powers, that the people's religion was most in evidence – whether the movement was that of groups of laymen taking to the roads and leaving home, or gatherings of large numbers mobilized in their own locality by some religious visitor.

The habit of pilgrimage has suffered from the jibes of critics, but it was among the oldest devotional practices of the church and its popularity in the 13th, 14th and 15th centuries shows that it answered widely felt needs. Whether or not the pilgrim could say his paternoster or the creed, he believed that the appropriate prayer or offering rendered to his saint might secure the desired material or spiritual benefit. Though the most famous pilgrimage centres were the most distant – Jerusalem, Rome and Santiago de Compostela – and pilgrims travelled singly and in groups to all these places, it is a mistake to think only, or even first, of them. For every well-placed pilgrim, like the 15th-century travellers Felix Fabri (a Dominican of Ulm who went twice to the Holy Land), or Margery Kempe (wife of a Norfolk burgess who went to Rome, Jerusalem, Compostela, Canterbury and Wilsnack), both of whom wrote up their experiences, there were countless others whose similar, less distant journeyings, went unrecorded. The great bulk of the pilgrim traffic was formed by cults that remained as they started, relatively local. For most people a journey of any kind was a luxury; a journey to Jerusalem or Rome almost as unthinkable as a trip to the moon still is today. But that did not mean that the spiritual hopes that fastened on a pilgrim road were closed to those peasants and labourers and lesser mortals who formed perhaps eighty per cent of the population. On the contrary, as time went on the probability increased that a holy man, or a miraculous event would present itself within the walking range and work round of such people. When these workers and wives downed tools and left their hearths for several days' journey to a local shrine, it was irrelevant to them whether or not the holy place or saintly person had received an official stamp of approval. They had their own understanding of the holy, which had nothing to do with canonists and records and the proprieties of Rome.

Popular belief attached itself to the concrete and the seen, not because the faith of the people was materialistic, but because for them matter was an expression of spiritual forces. Holiness was real because one could see its effects. A peasant of Sabarthès believed that the harvests had been less good since the Cathar 'perfect' had left the area. Likewise it seemed that the arrival in Hereford of the bones of Thomas Cantilupe had brought more abundant crops. One looked to divine powers for prodigious physical results. Such attitudes – orthodox or otherwise – sometimes seemed shocking, even at the time. 'Don't you see how stupid, foolish and senseless are these people who wish to see me?' complained Dauphine de Signe (1284–1360) in 1353, when a crowd of blind, epileptic and other diseased people gathered from a wide area to wait outside her house in hopes of a miraculous cure. 'Why do they come to me, who am neither Christ nor Peter nor Paul, but a stinking body, food for worms and heap of iniquities? They ask for signs, they want prodigies, miracles!' She stressed the need to place trust in God above hope in creatures. One should confess and do penance for one's sins before taking requests to the saints.

Too often the priorities were reversed. The saints were cultivated at the expense of the sacraments. And suppliants frequently appeared to invoke saints for specific remedies in a manner suggestive of a contract: 'If I . . . may it please you to . . . .' People endangered by shipwreck would vow an offering to the Virgin (*stella maris*, patroness of the sea) if they were spared. Those threatened by plague made promises to St Roch. One of the commonest forms of offering at pilgrimage shrines was a wax votive, either in the shape of candles or trindles measured according to the height or breadth of the supplicant, or else a model of the limb for which a cure was sought. These objects were both numerous and sometimes very large (and wax was a valuable commodity). In 1307 the objects at Bishop Cantilupe's tomb included 1,200 wax images of parts of the body and limbs. The process of canonization of Dauphine revealed that the bishop of Avignon had promised a candle of twelve pounds if one of his friends recovered from a wound, and the abbess of Ste-Croix at Apt offered a wax bullock if the holy woman's intercession led to the recovery of a lost herd of oxen. Conditional promises of this kind (and they were made by all classes

of society), accompanied by appropriate acts of piety, constituted eighty-six per cent of the 221 miracles attributed to Louis of Anjou in the *Liber Miraculorum*, drawn up soon after his death in 1297 (the majority of which, 199 cases, were concerned with human cures).

For most medieval believers sainthood was a vital link in the chain attaching them to God, and the establishment of new saints and new pilgrimage centres owed much to popular enthusiasm. An illuminating example of the interweaving of high level diplomacy and popular devotion that went into making a new saint is the process by which Thomas Cantilupe was canonized. This bishop of Hereford, who died in 1282 and was canonized by papal bull in 1320, was one of the last to achieve official sainthood in medieval England. The irony is that by the time he did so his cult was in decline. Although Cantilupe's remains had been honourably interred in the Lady Chapel at Hereford not many months after his death (which took place in Italy), it was five years before any miraculous cure was attributed to him. Coincidentally, but surely not accidentally, this happened on 3 April 1287, the very day on which Thomas's successor in the see, Bishop Swinfield, moved the bones into a new tomb in the north transept. Once launched, the new cult moved off on a wave of popular local devotion. There was a spontaneous burst of miracles among the visitors to the new shrine, most of whom were humble local people living in the vicinity of Hereford. Of the total of some 470 miracles attributed to Cantilupe in the extremely lengthy process of canonization, about two-fifths (194) took place in the first two years. In 1307, when the papal process of enquiry finally started, the tale of miracles was petering out and the flood of local pilgrims abating. By the time that Cantilupe's relics were translated into a still more splendid new shrine in 1348, the popular enthusiasm on which the whole process rested had faded away and Cantilupe, though doubtless cherished as a local father of the church of Hereford, was no longer the wonder-worker he had been.

The great preachers of the 15th century show us another form of popular piety on the move. The most famous of them were itinerant apostles, who not only took the word to many places, gathering vast congregations of auditors as they went, but also in some cases attracted trains of followers. St Vincent Ferrer (d. 1419) reached the ears of millions during his twenty years' preaching through Provence, Savoy, Dauphiné, Castile, Aragon, Catalonia, Normandy and Brittany. His call to repentance was responded to with scenes of communal flagellation. Apocalyptic messages, the news that the reign of Antichrist was about to begin, fell on willing ears in all parts of western Christendom. The Dominican Manfredi of Vercelli, preaching this word

*S. Bernardino of Sienna (d. 1444, canonized 1450), the most
eloquent preacher of his age – a woodcut of 1454. He holds his
emblem, the sacred monogram* IHS, *in his right hand.*

*The foolish preacher, inciting the people to violence: a satirical
woodcut from Sebastian Brant's 'Ship of Fools', 1494.*

in Lombardy in the same period, soon found that he
had a following of up to a thousand *simplices*, a large
proportion of them women who had left their husbands
in the holy cause. The potential sect was dispersed by
Pope Martin V, who summoned Manfredi to Rome in
1424.

The anxieties and enthusiasms of lay people were
readily galvanized into action by the electric powers of
pulpit orators. S. Bernardino, the greatest preacher of
his age, managed to reach the ears of countless auditors
in Italy without passing the bounds of orthodoxy,
though he, like Vincent Ferrer and Manfredi of
Vercelli, had to explain himself in the highest quarters.
Bernardino, magnetic in his down-to-earth vernacular
passion, brought believers in their thousands to mass
repentance and self-flagellation, but it was his popu-
larization of the cult of the Name of Jesus, making the
monogram of the Holy Name familiar in the piazzas of
northern Italy, that brought charges of heresy and
idolatry against him. His name was cleared, and the
church's eventual endorsement of the cult that S.
Bernardino did so much to extend is an outstanding
example of a popular devotion reaching liturgical use.
A cult that had its starting-point among the Spiritual
Franciscans (of whom more later) gained currency from
mass homiletics and arrived, before the end of the 15th
century, with its own office and mass. In the 16th
century the Franciscans gained official recognition for
the feast of the Name of Jesus.

The treatment of the dead shows the currents of
influence moving in the reverse direction. We can see
here how official dogma promoted a welter of
foundations that affected the whole of society from top
to bottom, clerical and lay alike, across the whole of
Europe. The pursuit of the security of souls was
perhaps the most common and binding passion of
western Christendom in the later Middle Ages, and it
owed a great deal to ecclesiastical formulation. The
doctrine of purgatory, though itself provocative of
anxiety, also offered a means of relief to the living, who
could both hope for the ultimate redemption of
endangered souls and themselves assist that end. The
church's teaching on this topic, evolving from the
patristic period, was not defined until the Council of
Lyons (1274). The concept of a treasury of merits which
could be unlocked and spent on behalf of the suffering
souls of the dead held the living thereafter in a terrible
grip, for it seemed obvious that the more one could
provide for one's own soul, or for the souls of others
one cared for, the less the agonies of posthumous
redemption in purgatory, where (according to St
Thomas) the smallest pain was greater than the greatest
on earth.

Purgatory both consoled and terrified. Michael

Magot, a lay brother, was able to comfort the Franciscans of Toulouse in 1334 when one of their members died before completing his confession. There was no need to worry, said Magot (to whom prophetic powers were attributed for his words at this emotional moment), God had taken into account the deceased's intention to confess. 'So he is really in the way of salvation?' asked the superior anxiously. 'Yes he is', Magot was able to reply reassuringly. The brother had escaped the danger of damnation, 'but he suffers great purgatorial pains'.

To provide for the souls of the dead was just as important as provision for the living, and (in a period that remembered obits more than birthdays) this was an assumption common to all classes. When Sir John Bosville killed Thomas del Hill and Robert de Derley, it seemed right in 1367 that 30 of the 160 marks he provided as compensation should be spent on masses for the souls of his victims – half the amount that went to dependants of the slain. Fears and worries over the souls of the dead (shriven and unshriven) produced, particularly from the 14th century, an enormous number of foundations, large and small, by which the living and dying provided intercessory prayers. Confraternities, which were established with regional variations all over Europe, existed, among a variety of other purposes, to maintain obsequies and prayers for their members. They were to be found in small villages as well as in towns, and people of all kinds belonged. By means of joining a confraternity even quite humble persons, including those who were too poor to pay the entry fees and dues, could provide themselves with a form of spiritual security. Whereas cathedrals were the monuments to the piety of an earlier age, the foundations typical of this period were the countless confraternity and chantry chapels constructed for the most part inside existing churches. Lay piety, in invading the church, turned inwards. The forms of spiritual self-help were multiplying.

Spiritual inflation

The sheer popularity and proliferation of some of these devotional forms is indicative of instability. The late medieval church was caught up in an inflationary spiral of a dangerous kind. Its pieties were subject to multiplication of the sort that inescapably leads to devaluation and to the disquieting effects with which we are all familiar. The fewer the higher, the more the lower was an observable law, even then, and was seen to apply to people, to practices and to things.

The enormous numbers of people who were admitted to lower clerical orders, many of whom never reached or aspired to the priesthood, meant that the percentage of clergy to people was seemingly ever on

Holy dying: the sinner, having confessed, and trusting in the sacrifice of Christ, commits his soul (the tiny naked figure emerging from the head) to the angels, while frustrated demons howl with disappointment: Paris, 1493.

the increase (in a manner somewhat analogous to government bureaucrats today). It also had the effect of bringing into the clerical estate many men who were indistinguishable from laymen. The fact that one could join the ranks of the church and receive its distinctive mark of the tonsure without abandoning secular life or marriage, indeed without any kind of meaningful commitment, reflected back on popular views of the priestly calling. It was not altogether surprising, given the large numbers of most unpriestly persons who had received the first tonsure for the most worldly reasons, if there was not always a clear understanding of the precise requirements of a spiritual vocation, or if ordination failed to command due respect. Schoolboy choristers might be tonsured at the age of seven years, and this purely technical ceremony could serve unworthy purposes in later life, if it became convenient to claim benefit of clergy. Ignatius Loyola, tonsured in his early years, used this device to escape the consequences of a youthful crime of violence. The fact that a provincial synod at Paris, in 1429, found it necessary to remind candidates for the order of subdeacon that this involved a vow of celibacy shows the perennial problem of the supposed line between major and minor orders – a line that Innocent III redrew, in 1207, when he made the subdeacon, hitherto a minor order (not involving continence), into a major one. Early 16th-century reformers who drew attention to this damaging state of affairs may have exaggerated in seeing the minor clerical orders as an 'asylum for scoundrels', but their consensus of criticism indicates the conspicuousness of the problem. The fact that so many lesser clergy were of the people in everything but name affected the nature of all popular religious movements, which were never purely lay, and ensured that the anticlericalism they so often expressed was always in part a reflection of the church's intramural divisions. Also, which was more important, disrespect for the clergy undermined their ministry, informing views like those of heretical villagers in the diocese of Pamiers in the 1320s, who parodied the elevation of the host, calling the sacrament a slice of turnip, and questioned the value of all this 'singing of clerks and chaplains', who 'shout "ho, ho, ho" for all they are worth'. The church's final sanction, excommunication, was presented as an invention for clerical domination: 'Excommunication doesn't hole your hide' – words to comfort a wretched man who had been under ecclesiastical ban for three years for failure to pay a minor debt.

Sainthood, like clerical orders, might be cheapened by proximity. This, too, was suggested by contemporaries, who thought that too many saints were being canonized. On one historian's count, 211 individuals who lived between 1300 and 1500 were canonized or beatified either then or later. This figure does not include the many more who were advanced for this honour and failed to reach it. Increasing numbers of ordinary people, laymen and laywomen, lived with the feeling that sainthood (or beatitude) might lie just round the corner of daily experience. Many believed they had seen it, and a sizeable proportion of those for whom claims of sanctity were made remained relatively unknown outside the areas that venerated them. Such for example were Thomas de la Hale, a monk of Dover murdered in 1295, Douceline de Digne, who was the centre of an early 14th-century cult at Hyères and Marseilles, and Dorothy of Montau, revered at several places in Prussia besides Marienwerder, where she died in 1395.

There were surely as many failed saints in this period as successful ones and the numbers of both must greatly have exceeded the total of the previous two hundred years. Successful canonization depended on papal authority, but the faithful believed in more saints and

miracles than ever came to be inscribed in official catalogues. In England alone one can set beside the nine successful processes of canonization between 1198 and 1500 another ten that failed. Technical failure, as everyone knew, did not prevent celebration, witness the image of 'St Richard' that stood to commemorate Richard Rolle in the chapel at Hampole, and the pilgrimages that were made to the remains of Henry VI in the abbey of Chertsey.

Ecclesiastical and popular canonization had never entirely coincided, and by 1500 they were dangerously at variance. Here, as elsewhere, there was an all too obvious discrepancy between official theory and popular reality. Endorsement by the church was certainly no bar to enthusiasm, but it could also be disillusioning. 'Good woman, do you believe this king's son has so quickly been made a saint?' a middle-aged woman caustically asked her cousin, who was offering a candle at the Franciscan church in Marseilles. The latter was giving thanks for a cure to St Louis of Anjou (son of Charles II), who, having died in 1297 aged twenty-three, after a meteoric career as Franciscan and bishop of Toulouse, was canonized in 1317. 'The Friars Minor', continued this critic, 'say it and preach it to get the profits of wax.' New saints by no means necessarily contributed to the lustre of the church. 'The other saints who are in paradise won't have much to do now, seeing that St Louis takes care of everything', jeered a stonemason of Marseilles, meeting a crowd of people processing one Sunday with candles and images to honour the saint.

These local scoffers (whose blasphemies were miraculously punished) expressed doubts that were related to the worries of elevated church reformers. There were dangers in making too many modern saints. The canonization in 1391 of a widowed mother of eight, who had died less than twenty years earlier, greatly troubled Henry of Langenstein and John Gerson. Gerson was not alone in thinking the widely circulated *Revelations* of St Bridget of Sweden unsuitable hagiographic material. The case was reopened at the Councils of Constance and Basel and St Bridget's *Revelations* were supported by papal theologians, but questioning of this kind did the church no good.

The same divergence between theology and popular practice is observable in the use of religious images. The church's sanction of the plastic arts moved far between Gregory the Great's endorsement of 'laymen's books' (imagery as instruction for the illiterate) and the treatment of this question by Thomas Aquinas in the 13th century. It was not only that the images in churches (paintings, stained glass, statuary, crucifixes) changed in kind and became more common. There was also a continuous tendency for people to use imagery in ways other than the church intended. Images expressed, as well as informed, popular theology and in doing so were capable of anticipating (or by-passing) official doctrine. There were saints who owed their existence to popular misreadings of art, as well as artistic conventions that derived from misreadings of texts. St Wilgeforte or Uncumber (supplicated by women who hoped to be relieved of their husbands) apparently originated in early crucifixes that portrayed a long-haired, bearded Christ, robed to the ankles. Artists followed (and catered for) the conventions of the people, as well as the dictates of patrons. It was objected that Catherine of Siena (d. 1380) had been widely depicted 'in the manner of those blessed by the church' before her canonization, which took place in 1461. These images – to be found as far afield as Poland, Dalmatia and Slavonia – were of all kinds, tablets and cards and on cloth as well as in books and on walls. It is clear that the lost evidence of the religious life of the people includes a large amount of portable domestic imagery, which antedated cheap woodcut (and later printed) reproductions. There were also enormous numbers of religious representations in many other secular settings: in streets, on bridges, or at country cross-roads – where one might find, for instance, a huge depiction of St Christopher to satisfy the belief that the day one caught sight of it one would be protected from sudden death.

Imagery proliferated like a natural growth, thanks as much to believers' enthusiasm as to clerical sponsoring. Bernard of Angers, who, in the early 11th century, was amazed at the almost pagan veneration of images of saints he discovered in Auvergne, tells of this accelerating process. 'Hitherto', he wrote, 'I have always believed that the veneration of images and paintings of the saints was improper, and to raise statues to them would have struck me as absurd. But this is not the belief of the inhabitants of these parts, where every church contains a statue of its patron made of gold, silver, or base metal, depending on the wealth of the church.'

The church, like Bernard, was converted by its members. The testimony of its acceptance was the intricate theory of image-worship expounded by high medieval theologians: the idea that the honour given to the image passed to its prototype, and the concept of different kinds of worship. The terms *latria*, *dulia* and *hyperdulia*, learnedly explained by Aquinas and others, remained as remote to most worshippers who lit candles before images as the theory of electricity is to most of us when we switch on the light. For the unsophisticated believer who knelt before a statue there existed a practical identity between the image and the saint. The sculpture of Our Lady at Rocamadour or at

St Anthony, supposed father of monasticism, vested as a monk. Many cures were attributed to the saint after his miraculous healing in the 11th century of the disease known as St Anthony's fire. Behind him in this 15th-century woodcut hang miniature limbs and organs – thank offerings for cures that he effected.

Walsingham *was* the Virgin in that it spoke directly to the pilgrim's needs and answered his or her prayers. The Virgin of Impruneta was the Florentines' *Nostra Donna* who came to the city's aid to bring or stop the rain. An image was an instrument of holiness through which believers reached towards God, and pilgrims expected to 'see' their saints.

Not surprisingly, holy icons grew in number, far beyond the powers of ecclesiastical control. Certainly there were efforts to put a stop to burgeoning local cults, such as the steps taken by the archbishop of York, in 1313, to prevent the 'great concourse of simple people' who were visiting an image of the Virgin 'newly placed' in the church of Foston; or the bishop of Lincoln's enquiry, in 1386, into the complaint that in the parish of Rippingale 'many of our subjects have made for themselves a pretended statue', to which people were thronging and reporting miracles. In this

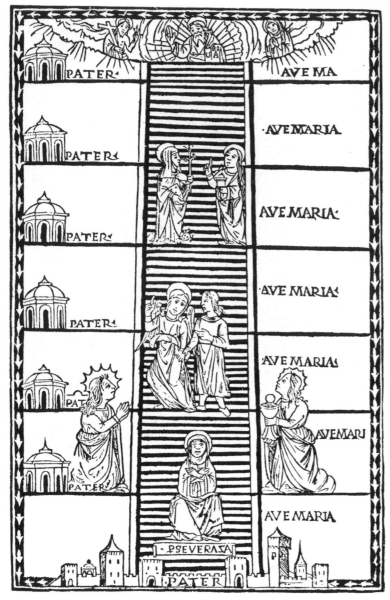

The mechanical repetition of prayers was one aspect of spiritual 'inflation'. This Italian diagram of 1512 suggests how the ladder of salvation could be climbed by Pater Nosters and Ave Marias: the more prayers, the closer to heaven.

so widely that an image should be set at every church, every chapel, every street's end, or every hedge's end in the country', for then undoubtedly they would be 'of little repute, and would be unesteemed because of the great number of them'. 'Plenty is no dainty' – which was another way of saying that you can have too much of a good thing.

Lastly, one may notice how this arithmetical piety affected the salvation of souls. Thanks to the reckless rivalry of popes, religious orders and pilgrimage towns competing for the alms of the faithful, grants of indulgence multiplied. The numerous crusades preached by the popes and antipopes of Rome and Avignon made indulgences notorious. Plenary indulgences, once restricted to a Crusade, were now given for pilgrimaging to Roman basilicas during years of jubilee (which also increased in frequency); famous relic collections could offer indulgence to those who came to their displays. Flurries of investment produced absurd numbers of indulgences and masses. The great were able to buy masses in thousands to secure a near-infinity of release. Cardinal Albrecht of Brandenburg managed to amass more than 39 million years of indulgence in Halle, and Henry VIII, England's first iconoclastic monarch, who had much to atone for, ordered daily masses to be said for as long as the world should endure. The church positively encouraged anxious belief in the quantitative value of such prayers. Do not imagine, said Archbishop Pecham in 1281, that one mass said devoutly for a thousand people procures them the same benefit as a thousand individual masses said with equal devotion. Ordinary mortals could not aspire to these astronomical sums, and in this period of numerical devotion they might well have agonized. They did their best. Hence the growing number of confraternities, so many that some towns may have reached saturation point in the 15th century. There were too many such foundations, thought Nicholas of Cusa, and John Gerson indicated the superstition of totting up indulgences till they reached 20,000 years.

Holy poverty

Among the most dramatic manifestations of popular piety on the move were the spontaneous demonstrations that took place in the face of the terrible mortality of the Black Death. Flagellants, groups of men and even women who inflicted penance on themselves in public, scourging their bodies till they drew blood, appeared in various parts of Europe in 1349. Flagellation (a gestural imitation of Christ) was itself neither new nor scandalous. It was a recognized monastic practice, and Franciscan piety expressed itself in this kind of sacred exhibition. Enacting as well as meditating on Christ's scourging was an acceptable

instance local initiative (abetted by the rector) was such that it thwarted episcopal condemnation by gaining papal licence to found a new chapel for this – purportedly hundred-year-old – holy cross. Despite some attempted restraints, the increase of imagery continued and sometimes seems more geometrical than arithmetic.

Some contemporaries were worried, as they were over new saints, about the cheapening of respect. It was a point made by Bishop Pecock, who went out of his way to defend church imagery against the attacks of the Lollards. Images, he wrote, should 'not be multiplied

Christian devotion. Why then should anyone have been alarmed at the spectacle of bands of devout lay people practising such public penance to appease the wrath of God evinced in the plague, calling all sinners to repentance? An eye-witness description of Flagellants in Verona in 1396 shows that they were not disorderly: 'six hundred people, going two by two, beating flails made of iron chains through the city, making a procession with crosses and habited priests, doing their penance and bearing the body of Our Lord', all being vested alike, their faces covered save for the eyes, and 'singing, as they beat themselves, one song together'.

The church, alarmed, saw a double threat in the Flagellants, who were formally proscribed by Clement VI in 1349. Firstly, there was the fact that these penitents seemed in some cases like a sect with its own organized rules, discipline and habit. Secondly, there was an appearance of doctrinal error in that flagellation, instead of being simply an ascetic practice, looked like dispensing with sacramental penance, rivalling, if not despising, part of the church's ministry; the fervent participants seemed to be both aping the church and detracting from it. The Flagellants, in the Low Countries and Germany, in 1349–50, and elsewhere thereafter, presented a challenge that was always fearful to church authorities and urban rulers alike; they were the lower orders – 'the multitude of simple men' – on the move. The dynamic potential of the people lay in their ability to take themselves and their ideas into towns and areas where they were not known, disappearing into the dangerous anonymity of the urban world in which individuals could easily attract followings. In a country where he is unknown, ran a satirical Czech verse of about 1360, the heretic remains hidden for two or three years and finds supporters.

As mistrust increased towards the claims of wealth and office, the entitlements of rank and parchment formulas, so the poor correspondingly gained new respect. Poverty had its own dignity. It had been sanctified by Christ, who in himself and in his words made it a spiritual pattern. This perennial Christian message gained fresh momentum in this period. The revulsion that it was natural to feel from above towards the tawdry masses of the rude people was turned to new account. The sense of Christian mission was pointed towards 'the poor in their hovels, overburdened with children', those 'halt old men and maimed, who all day and night cower continually before the altars, and in the crypts; and such folk as wear old mantles and old tattered frocks, and naked folk and shoeless, and covered with sores, perishing of hunger and thirst, and of cold, and of little ease'. It came to seem in certain quarters that the only authentic religious experience was to be found among such people. The conviction

that 'none are sooner saved or firmer in their faith, than ploughmen and shepherds and poor common labourers' was not confined to *Piers the Ploughman's* visionary gloss on St Augustine. God still spoke to the present age, but his words were only heard by the humble – the 'poor men', the 'simple priests' and self-disciplined mendicant 'perfects'. These were all contemporary self-descriptions used by those whose choice of life (the imitation of Christ) ended in some kind of separation from the church. Of course, when voiced by those who were themselves inexorably poor, there was an inevitable note of social criticism in popular insistence that the clergy should live in voluntary poverty. But the larger view of the evangelical vocation went beyond the carping of the jealous. It was believed that divine truths were vouchsafed to the simplest hearers – and they were gospel, not theological. Their immediacy was that of experience, not learning.

The example of one man had an enormous influence on this idea of poverty. The unaffected simplicity of Francesco Bernardone, after his dramatic wedding of himself to 'Lady Poverty', caught the imagination of contemporaries and met with a wide response. But the practical difficulties encountered by St Francis and the Franciscans in attempting to imitate Christ, reflect the paradox of the later medieval church: the more popular and successful the pursuit of evangelical life, the greater the likelihood of a condemnation for heresy.

The issue seems simple enough. Christ forsook possessions and expected his disciples to forsake all: renunciation of goods was part of the imitation of Christ. Such was the assumption of St Francis, and his way of life was premised on it. But the more Franciscans there were the more impossible it became to live with undefined beliefs, and between the death of Francis in 1226 and the death of Pope John XXII in 1334 numbers of people, including the pope himself, came to be charged with heresy for their view of what Christian contempt for temporal goods should amount to.

The main friction was that between the two wings of the Franciscan friars: the Conventuals and the Spirituals. There was much basic agreement between them, for they both started from the belief that Franciscan poverty uniquely exemplified the poverty of Christ, and both regarded the complete renunciation of all dominion, whether corporate or individual, as essential to evangelical life. Beyond that agreement, however, started critical differences about the nature of usufruct and the rights involved in the use of consumables – points that may now seem like legal quibbles but which concerned basic day-to-day practicalities and which ran into important points of doctrine. Was it possible to deny dominion (some right of property) over things consumed by use? Could the Franciscans' claim that they enjoyed only a bare use (*nudus usus*) in their goods, by virtue of the ownership of them being vested in the Holy See, be other than a legal fiction?

The question became clouded by the conspicuous acquisition of buildings and funds by the Franciscan order in the late 13th and early 14th century, which made the denial of property rights seem the most blatant artifice. The fact remained that, despite the self-evident difficulties of establishing an order which could maintain the hand-to-mouth existence implied in absolute poverty (living on alms, having no settled abode), this was an ideal that continued to have a tremendous appeal. Perhaps it was the very non-institutional (if not anti-institutional) aspect of the call that made it so powerful. This sort of abnegation implied the renunciation of office and governance, as well as of taking thought for the morrow. The fact that it could not be institutionalized enhanced its vitality, as well as its danger. The very call to regenerate Christian life in this way was a challenge to the church, which could only control it by transforming it. Absolute poverty, in short, revealed the inherent contradiction between church and Gospel, scripture and tradition. To be too faithful to Christ was to question the organized church.

It is no accident, therefore, that in varying ways and degrees the *imitatio Christi* ended in charges of heresy. It had done so already in the 12th century, after a rich merchant of Lyons, called Valdes, inspired by hearing the story of St Alexius, abandoned his wealth and property to take up a life of evangelical poverty. He wanted both to know Christ and to follow Christ and commissioned translations of Scripture so that he could himself learn and preach the Word of God. Others were eager to do the same and soon the voluntary mendicant attracted followers and had the beginnings of a movement. But was it right to teach the Word of God publicly to the people without the authority of the church? Members of the clergy certainly thought not. Valdes's followers took their case to the Third Lateran Council in 1179, where Alexander III endorsed their ideal of evangelical poverty but placed the activity of preaching firmly under clerical supervision. It was not long before fidelity to the call to preach took Valdes's disciples into excommunication and schism.

If there was always a grey zone between orthodoxy and dissent, the situation was changing fast between the renunciations of Valdes and Francis. The determination of the border that separated the heretic from the body of the faithful, subject at the best of times to the accidents of ecclesiastical politics, was affected by the church's preparedness and expectations. In 1200

Innocent III was still prepared to allow the third order of the *Humiliati*, with their artisans and humble lay members, the right to pious exhortation under episcopal supervision. Such a breaching of the fundamental principle that preaching belonged exclusively to those in orders became increasingly unthinkable after 1215, with the issue of the ban on the founding of new religious orders. In the 12th century a popular heretical movement (as opposed to individual heretics) had been a new phenomenon. The early years of the 13th century produced a proliferation of new religious groups and, above all, saw the spread of Catharism in Lombardy and Languedoc. By the 1230s the church had developed institutional forms specifically designed to deal with a heretical movement. The Inquisition never operated as effectively in northern Europe as it did in the south, but the fact of its existence had an enormous effect on the climate of heretical expectation. The grey zone had, as it were, been institutionalized.

Not all heresy was popular, but it became increasingly likely that a popular religious movement would be declared heretical, increasingly difficult for aspiring laymen and laywomen to lead a life dedicated to holiness while still living in, or only half withdrawn from, the world. To be too ascetic might be dangerous. 'Hear me, my lords! I am no heretic: for I have a wife and cohabit with her and have children; and I eat flesh and lie and swear and am a faithful Christian.' In this manner a 13th-century suspect hoped to convince the inquisitors of his orthodoxy. Once popular heresy was recognized, it became possible, like a new species, to find it anywhere. Thus the censuring of the writings of Petrus Johannis Olivi in 1283 was largely influenced by the fear that his humble followers in Provence (where the call of the Spiritual Franciscans had such success) would start another sect of poor men, as Valdes's preaching had done a hundred years earlier. Zealots of this kind, estimable though their intentions might be, constituted a threat to order. John XXII therefore condemned the doctrine of absolute poverty and moved firmly against the Spiritual Franciscans, four of whom were burned in Marseilles in 1318.

The bull *Cum inter nonnullos*, issued in November 1323, condemned as heretical the belief that Christ and the apostles had owned nothing, and also the assertion that they had held no rights over the goods they used. 'Since it is the case that among various men of learning it is often doubted whether the persistent assertion – that our redeemer and lord Jesus Christ and his apostles did not have anything, either privately or in common – should be deemed heretical ... we ... declare by this everlasting edict that a persistent assertion of this kind shall henceforth be deemed erroneous and heretical,

There were many editions of 'The Imitation of Christ'. This woodcut comes from an English edition dated c. 1518. Round the border are the symbols and instruments of the Passion – some of which were themselves objects of devotion – the scourge, the nails, the crown of thorns, the sponge, the dice, the ladder, etc.

quiet meditative life, combining communal work with devotion, untrammelled by formal rules and regulations, became possible for groups of lay people in the Low Countries. 'Christ is our rule; his life and doctrine are our breviary for life. . . . This is the Book of Hours common to clerks and laymen.' Thanks to Jan van Ruysbroeck, who wrote these words (d. 1381, at Groenendaël, where his small apostolic community had come together), and to Gerard Groote (d. 1384, at Deventer, where he had turned his house into a refuge for pious women), there began a movement that enabled people of both sexes to lead a shared devotional life without transgressing either the prohibition of 1215 against new orders, or the ruling of 1323. What became known as the *Devotio Moderna* consisted of groups of men and women who lived together in poverty and obedience, but without formal vows, and their ability to do so depended on the ruling that in thus following evangelical precept they were not forming a new order. Ordinary working people thereby found new opportunities for their religious aspirations. The number of houses grew under the direction of Florentius Radewyns and his successors, recruiting clerks as well as lay people, some of them humble peasants and brewers. Among such *pauperes* in the fraternity at Deventer was the son of a blacksmith, Thomas à Kempis, who wrote in *The Imitation of Christ*, 'keep company with the humble and simple'.

Popular heresy

In other movements evangelical fidelity caused a breach with the church. This divide between scripture and tradition lay behind the two major heretical movements that appeared in the late 14th and early 15th century. Both were popular movements, attracting much support among ordinary trades and work people as well as lower clergy. In both cases the initiative, and initial fears of heresy, started in academic circles and intellectual theology, but it was the currents of belief and agitation that ran through the people that attracted such attention. Although their personalities, lives and deaths were very different, John Wycliffe (d. 1384) and John Hus (d. 1415) shared a fierce concern for moral regeneration, an impassioned desire to redeem contemporary Christendom, and both took Scripture as their starting-point in redefining what was meant by the church. From these learned Latinate beginnings grew the popular followings of Lollards and Hussites, owing their success and survival to lively vernacular preaching and a corpus of vernacular writings that made popular theology, as well as much scriptural learning, available to humble (often self-educated) Christians. In England, though the sect went on through the 15th century, it

since it expressly contradicts Holy Scripture. . . .' It was a declaration that dealt decisively with the immediate troubles in the Franciscan order, but it could not shut the door on further controversies of this kind. William of Ockham was one of the men of learning who acted on his conviction that the pope's own edict was heretical. Just as important – perhaps more so – were the various other quite unlearned people who in subsequent years preferred the Word of Scripture to papal arbitration on the life of Christ and the disciples.

There was one remarkable movement in this period that managed to promote the shared evangelical existence without falling foul of the law. This community, less easily defined than some others (though it had a contemporary title), reflected the widespread desire, evident in all classes, to escape the frustrating world of externals for internal religion. A relapsed – as did the Waldensian following in Germany – into a sort of sectarian underground, of sporadic strength. In Bohemia, where there was an ongoing tradition of moral reform, as well as a more conspicuous background of political upheaval and uncertainty, heresy advanced to the point of schism and counter-church.

The Bohemians' biblical enthusiasm and millennial eschatology combined to produce the remarkable phenomenon of Tabor and other hilltop religious communities consciously modelled on apostolic Christian example. Owing to the skills of their military leaders (specially Žižka and Procop), as well as to the peculiar unsettlement of Bohemia and the contemporary papacy, the Hussites managed to do something that had never been done before in the history of the church. They reached the point of negotiating with the leaders of the church for their own religious platform. After a series of crusades had been launched unsuccessfully against the heretics, a combination of conservative forces finally defeated the Hussite radicals at the battle of Lipany in 1434. This defeat helped to bring about the agreement between the Bohemians and the Council of Basel on the basis of the so called Compactata. It was the first time a popular heretical movement had reached such a level of power: the first time that a split in observance received formal recognition.

The Compactata, a form of the earlier programme of the Four Articles of Prague, represented the minimum demands of the Hussites. These four articles, which tell us a good deal about the movement, return us to our starting-point, for they reflect that dialectical bond between popular religion (or popular heresy) and the church structure. The first point, utraquism, was the right of all believers to communicate in both kinds (bread and wine), *sub utraque specie*. This was fundamental to the Bohemian reform which from its beginnings had produced demands for more frequent communion, and which led among the Taborite radicals to congregational celebrations on open hilltops. The other three points were free preaching of the Word of God; the call for all priests from the pope downwards to give up their 'pomp, avarice and improper lordship'; and the correction of public mortal sins. At best it was a partial programme that summarized aspects of the tremendous surge of activity that transformed the Bohemian church in this period, doing away with monasteries and religious foundations (including the archbishopric of Prague, which was forcedly vacant between 1431 and 1516), destroying many images and relics of saints, killing religious, and everywhere making the cult of the Word prominent, whether in great preaching like that of Hus in the Bethlehem Chapel, or in vernacular writings like those of the laymen Thomas of Štitny and Peter Chelčicky.

Lollardy, imperative though it sometimes sounded and programmatic though it sometimes was, never commanded this extraordinary influence on ecclesiastical affairs. But if we compare this movement's aims with those of the Hussites, we can see something of the various strands of which popular heresy was compounded. The question of the Eucharist was as important in England as in Bohemia. Though a consensus on this matter is hard to arrive at, Lollards – often in earthy rural terms – followed Wycliffe in finding difficulties in the doctrine of transubstantiation, and the denial of this doctrine was one of the ways in which adherence to the sect could be determined. 'God made man, and not man God, as the carpenter doth make the house and not the house the carpenter', was a crude way of saying something like what Wycliffe was thought to have said; that the consecrated host was not Christ and could not be an accident without a substance; that the words of administration could not miraculously annihilate the substance of the bread. The Hussites who gave the cup to the laity and the Lollards who denied transubstantiation were both, in effect, rejecting the distancing of sacrament from people, brought about by previous centuries. Scholastic logic applied to the doctrine of the Eucharist enhanced the miracle of this sacrament and helped to make it an ever more remote and clerical rite; the congregation was expected to participate by seeing, not by understanding, and the layman's role in the Eucharist was of a completely different order from that of the ministering priest. The heretical call in both cases amounted to a demand for greater participation, a refusal of the people to remain passive spectators at sacramental celebrations. While both English and Bohemian heretics refused to accept this clerical arrogation of the rite, they did so in quite different ways. Hussite utraquism was an expression of moral reforming ardour, and celebration in both kinds, though it involved no doctrinal unorthodoxy, constituted a demonstration of religious independence. Yet the Bohemians were here linked with many reformers of contemporary Europe, who shared this Eucharistic fervour, and, to the extent that it answered devotional needs, Hussite utraquism was swallowed up as time went on by other reforming developments. In England, meanwhile, where the moral drive was weaker, Eucharistic heresy remained more negative and lacked the initiative to build a new ceremonial.

The free preaching of the Word was a matter on which agreement was total. This was where Hus and Wycliffe had their greatest effect. Lollards and Hussites alike saw the church as the ministry of the Word and believed that the duty and freedom to preach was the essence of priesthood. Commitment to this call as a Gospel command that overrode all ecclesiastical powers helped to send Hus to the stake and promoted the idea that men and women of virtuous life were more truly priests than any ordained by the church. 'I held and affirmed that every true man and woman being in charity is a priest', confessed a 15th-century English heretic, and there were plenty of humble people of both sexes at this time who were busy studying and teaching the Word of God. It was preaching, and the writings, handbooks and translations that served the task of evangelization, that attracted congregation after congregation and turned ideas into movements. This was an age in which many people yearned to hear as well as to see. The preacher (whether a S. Bernardino or a Hus) could gratify an appetite that could not be satisfied by going to church to kneel before a Virgin or to watch a mass: the appetite to understand.

Dissatisfaction with the church stemmed from spiritual angers, as well as from spiritual hungers. Where the Hussites sacked monasteries and killed monks, the Lollards hoped and sometimes planned, but without results. Many words were spoken and much ink used in castigating the pomp and pride of churchmen, with their extensive properties and excessive trains of horses and servants. Anticlericalism was always a strain of heresy, and the signs of it were clear to read, in England as in Bohemia. 'I trusted to God to see no church standing nor priest living within three years', said a Lollard. Millennial eschatology could make the most unreal of dreams seem reachable, and though such beliefs were less in evidence in England than elsewhere, aims of massive destruction were in the air. The idea of making priests' heads, like sheep's heads, three a penny, floated among the jetsam of proletarian gossip, occasionally resulting in radical action. It attached itself easily to that other ancient argument, 'when Adam delved and Eve span, who was then a gentleman?', premised on the idea of a golden age of paradisal equality. Though their world was far from paradisal, the Hussite radicals at Tabor, with their pooling of resources in common chests and their belief that 'there is nothing mine and nothing yours', got nearest to making a new, more biblically just society.

Popular heresy was thus an expression of hostility towards the clerical church. At the same time it turned against the forms of popular piety. Lollards who talked jeeringly of the 'witch of Lincoln' or the 'lefdy [lady] of Walsingham', and Prague labourers who pawned their crucifixes were ready to jettison the whole apparatus of image-worship and pilgrimage. They rejected both the famous Marian shrines cultivated by late medieval pilgrims, and even the worship of the crucifix, the

central Christian image. Our Lady of Willesden, said Elizabeth Sampson in 1508, 'was a burnt arsed elf and a burnt arsed stock; and if she might have helped men and women which go to her on pilgrimage she would not have suffered her tail to have been burnt'. 'If you want to see the true cross of Christ', the wife of a Norfolk village wright told a Norwich housewife, 'I can show it to you here in your own house.' She did so, stretching out her arms. 'This is the true cross of Christ, and this cross you can and ought to see and worship every day here in your own house, and so you labour in vain when you go to churches to worship or pray to other images or dead crosses.' It was the same message that had been taught more than a century earlier by Cathar perfects in Pyrenean villages: 'Do you believe that these bits of wood can perform miracles?' Farmers were given a lesson that could well have come from Isaiah. 'You carved with your own axes the statues of saints in the "house of idols" and then you worship them!'

Where ecclesiastical reformers were worried and tentative (admitting abuse and suggesting the need for more instruction) popular heretical movements pointed to radical solutions. Iconoclasm, the erasure of imagery as offensive to Christianity, was a feature of all the main medieval heretical movements, which broke and burnt crucifixes and images of the Virgin and saints. The idea that art and Christian religion were inherently contradictory, that visual and other sensory aids to worship either (at best) detracted from the spiritual or (at worst) induced idolatry, was confined in the later Middle Ages to the sphere of popular heresy. Lollards here went beyond Wycliffe, Hussites beyond Hus. To be sure, there were also plenty of heretics whose criticisms of church art were more moderate, who suggested that the historical criterion of imitating Christ should apply to representation as much as to life. Kept within such limits, depicting Christ and the saints in the poverty in which they had lived, 'not wantonly or falsely adorned' in such a way as to seduce and mislead believers, imagery might be tolerable. There was also the social argument claiming then (as it still does) that Christian art is a denial of Christian charity. Feeding the hungry and clothing the naked should take precedence over gilding statues and decorating walls. The only true image of Christ was man himself and the only true form of pilgrimage was that 'to poor men'.

Church and people

In a variety of ways, through the pious expressions and foundations of the orthodox, and in the clamorous demands of the unorthodox, by retreating from the world, and by trying to take it over, the lay people in the later Middle Ages made themselves and their religious needs more known. It was very much an age of the laity. It was also an age in which the *menu peuple*, the humble anonymous Christians, made an unprecedented mark on the church through popular movements of which the hierarchy could not fail to take cognizance, even when it failed to lead and control them.

The renewal of the church, the call to evangelical regeneration that is the essence of the Christian faith, was expressed in this period from below. The voice of secular men and women, commanding attention, demanding instruction and spiritual assurance, becomes audible as never before in the 14th and 15th centuries. At the centre of all religion of the people lies the search for direct spiritual experience. It may be the miraculous or the practically pious; seen or heard, acted or received. In every case the reality of the experience is more important than ecclesiastical or clerical forms. A great deal of the piety of the people remained devoutly orthodox, whether enlarging ever more vertiginously the numerical devotions sponsored by the church, or making for the retreats of individual, internal religion. The advance of the people in education, aspiration and enthusiasm, coinciding unfortunately with the church's marked lack of institutional resilience, allowed them to play a disproportionate part in the development and counter-development of Christianity and its culture. Both the making of saints and the representing of saints reflected popular pressures. The multiplication of images, the enormous growth of the arts of the church, like the proliferation of persons blessed by popular esteem, show the appetites of believers outdistancing ecclesiastical provisions.

Ordinary believers also found for themselves a spiritual independence that was remote from the ecclesiastical hierarchy. Evangelical knowledge (derived directly from the page or otherwise) yielded remarkable initiatives and experiments, whether on the material level of redistributing church property, or the spiritual level of giving ordinary men and women an active share in the ministry of the Word. Women found in heresy a recognition of ability, and opportunities for religious enterprise that were hard to find within orthodox forms, and we may see in these beginnings a contribution to that long, still ongoing quest for sexual equality that has gathered strength from the Christian ethic.

Christianity, the religion of a book of singular diversity, began in this age the earnest exploration of its sources that was to prove so problematical. The Christian call to renewal centres on Scripture, but, whatever the concentration on the evangelical law, that could not be taken alone: it was necessary to reconcile the requirements of the old law with the new, to strike a balance between the two Testaments. Though it was not till later that Christendom divided over the interpretation of its sources, the popular movements of the later Middle Ages (followed, quite differently but just as importantly, by Humanist scholars) had embarked on that fresh pursuit of biblical patterns. And already there were hints of the potential conflict stemming from the Christian graft on Judaic roots.

The survival – and the vitality – of the Christian faith has always rested on more than the institutions of the church. In all periods (including our own) in which the faith has seemed at risk, the responsibility for recovery lies as much with the community as with the hierarchy. Salvation, the starting-point of the faith, comes back to the individual, and there were many individuals among the people in this period who aspired to the redemption of the church, as well as of themselves.

Christianity will exist as long as there are believers. As Dante put it: 'the form of the church is nothing other than the life of Christ, understood in both words and deeds. For his life was both the conception and the pattern of the militant church.' Though it was once highly dangerous to say so, the structured hierarchy is dispensable, and it sometimes seems as if the church is most alive when that hierarchy, subject to Gospel appraisal, is most in question. Whether or not one thinks that the Christian message is itself social, giving a sense of community, dignity and equality to the humble, it was the movements from below that did the most to widen the Christian horizons of this age. Granted – and the history of the times proved it – a purely popular religious movement could not change ecclesiastical forms, but there is a sense in which popular religion both made and unmade the church. We can see in the later Middle Ages the power of the Christian mission to revitalize society, as well as the power of society to revitalize the church. Much of the best that remains to us from that time derives from this fruitful dialectic.

CHRISTIANITY AT THE CROSSROADS

7
The age of the Reformation

8
The social impact of Puritanism

THERE HAD BEEN CRITICISMS of the church before Luther. That the church was too rich, that many of the clergy were corrupt, that individual popes were fallible – all this was commonplace throughout the later Middle Ages, as the previous chapter has shown. But most of the criticism came from inside the church, and the cry was for reform not rebellion. Protesters did not make Protestants. So when Luther nailed his Ninety-five Theses to the door of Wittenberg castle church it was an act of opposition but not of defiance. As a priest and an Augustinian, Luther wanted abuses to be corrected. Above all, he pleaded for deepened spirituality. He did not want to cut himself off from the church.

One of the reasons why the effect of Luther's criticisms was different from that of any in the past was the attitude of the secular powers, the princes and electors of Germany. For the first time, laymen were prepared to support a reform movement not just to the point of clashing with the church but to the point of rejecting it altogether. Nowhere in Europe did the reformers succeed without the backing of the princes. The reasons for Luther's original attacks are clear and relatively simple. The reasons why they led to western Christianity's most serious crisis for a thousand years are much more complex.

Historians have produced an array of possible and plausible explanations. It is admitted by all parties that the church was in need of reform; its upper ranks had become worldly and ambitious, the lower ignorant and idle; an entrenched papal hierarchy showed little sign of correcting its own abuses voluntarily; while tithes and ecclesiastical dues paid to Rome constituted a drain on national revenue with no tangible return. Marxist historians go further and argue that a new commercial class was emerging which had no political role in the old feudal system, and which could exercise power only by radically changing society. The church stood in the way of change and must therefore be swept away. Historians of ideas point also to the rise of Humanism, the rediscovery of classical culture, which even in devout Catholics (like Erasmus) produced a broadening of perspective and an intellectual climate unfriendly to dogmatic theology.

The Reformation changed the map of Europe. It also changed people's lives. Luther's commitment, over the heads of churches, councils and popes, to the Bible, God's will and the individual conscience was taken to lengths that he himself would never have dreamed of. One of its consequences was Calvinism, the stern doctrine of 'election' and absolute ethical commitment. Another was Puritanism, in a way a British analogue to Calvinism, much akin to it as regards its ethical commitment. Later, as an instance of Puritan morality in practice, we shall look closely at the private life of a single family, that of John Winthrop and his wife. Carried across the Atlantic with the early settlers to New England, their faith – in the Bible and their own inner light – was to mark the beginning of a new chapter in the story of Christianity.

The role of the princes
in sustaining the movement of reform is underlined in a number of pictures by Lucas Cranach the Elder, who is almost official painter to the Reformation. In this one (*opposite*) Luther's patron John Frederick the Magnanimous, elector of Saxony, is shown with Luther (on the extreme left), Zwingli (next to the elector on the other side) and Melanchthon (on the right). It was John Frederick's uncle, Frederick the Wise, who after Luther's condemnation by the Diet of Worms in 1521 spirited him away to his castle, the Wartburg, and thus to safety. Frederick's support of the reform movement was more than a purely theological quarrel, and the movement as it gathered strength depended more and more on the involvement of the secular powers. The painter Cranach was himself part of this involvement. He served as councillor and burgomaster of Wittenberg at various times between 1519 and 1544, was a personal friend of Luther and designed title pages and illustrations for many of his books and pamphlets. (1)

Protest and reform

Luther's initial anger was directed at what he saw as an abuse of the church's ministry, namely the sale of indulgences. But in questioning the theory behind indulgences he was in fact running the risk of undermining the whole basis of the church's claim to authority.

The new apostles: Cranach's highly unconventional altarpiece for the castle church of Dessau (*opposite*) portrays the reformers gathered at the table of the Last Supper. All the figures except Christ and Judas are portraits. Next to Christ on the left is Prince George of Anhalt; then Luther; then Johann Bugenhagen. On Christ's other side is Melanchthon. Joachim of Anhalt, who commissioned the picture, is in the left foreground. The steward opposite him is a self-portrait of Cranach the Younger. (4)

Luther's words made their first impact at Wittenberg, where he was a sub-prior and professor of biblical studies. Another painting by Cranach is a schematized presentation of his teaching: Luther on the right, his congregation on the left and in the centre Christ crucified – for Luther the necessary and sufficient pledge of man's salvation. (2)

Christ's poverty contrasted with the church's wealth: a recurring criticism during the later Middle Ages which grew into a wave of protest at the Reformation. This coloured woodcut, with its rhyming caption proving that the pope is 'far from the Lord', originated at Augsburg, one of the storm centres of revolt.(3)

Siehe an Christum dieß Bilde recht. — Hie reit der Herr und auch der Knecht.
Der Herr auf einem armen Thier — Der Knecht mit höchstem Pracht u. Zier,
Der Herr trägt auf ein' Dornen Kron — Der Knecht ein' dreifach gülden Kron,
Der Herr war arm auf dieser Welt — Der Knecht hat groß Gewalt u. Geld,
Der Herr hat nicht da er's Haupt hinlegt — Den Knecht man auf den Aehseln trägt,
Der Herr sein' Jüngern wusch die Füß — Dem Knecht sein' Fuß man küssen müß,
Der Herr seit hie viel' Schand und Spott — Der Knecht sich ehren läßt als Gott,
Der Herr giebt uns sein' Gnad umsonst — Der Knecht um Geld Ablaß u. Gunst;
Drum merk aus diesem Beispiel ebn — Ob sich vergleich ihr Lehr und Lebn
Und dabei kanust du nehmen ab — Was Unterscheid es bei ihr' hab,
Und daraus schließen gwaltig frey — Daß der Knecht wider den Herrn sei.

The Bible in German

Luther's translation of the Bible proved to be one of the most influential elements in the emergence of a single German language.

No longer the preserve of the priest and the scholar, the Scriptures were now accessible to the laity. And if the Bible contained the Word of God, why should not the lay community decide its own religious affairs? *Above:* title page of the first edition, 1534. *Left:* a full-page woodcut showing God creating the world. (5, 6)

While the Old Testament has over a hundred illustrations, the New contains only portraits of the evangelists at work. This shows St Luke with his emblem, the ox. (7)

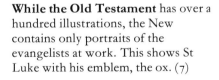

Private devotion now became the centre of religious life for many Christians, instead of the sacraments offered by the church. Its atmosphere of calm piety is beautifully caught by the painters of the Dutch school. The elderly lady (*right*) in a portrait by Gerard Dou is reading a lectionary in Dutch, a series of lessons and biblical excerpts arranged for each day. (8)

The Swiss reformer Zwingli had reached conclusions similar to Luther's even before 1519, but Luther's example encouraged him to proclaim them. He certainly studied Luther's works closely. A copy of the latter's book on the Gospels and Epistles (1522) is covered with marginal notes, in Latin, by Zwingli. (9)

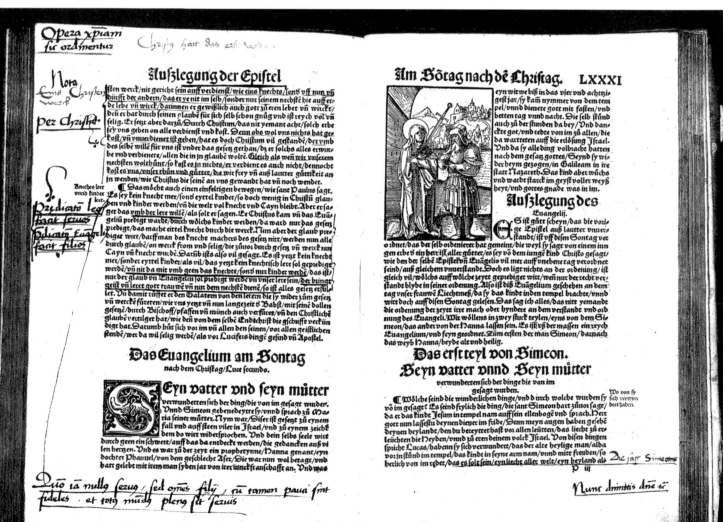

Calvinism: the majesty of God

Zwingli had gone further than Luther on such issues as the Eucharist and the simplicity of worship. Calvin went further still. He delineated the sweep of the reformers' theology with consistency and harmony, rooting his theology in the absolute subservience of man to God's sovereign will.

As a young man in 1535, Calvin (*left*) arrived at Geneva. Within a few years he had made it the setting for a radical experiment in realizing the City of God on earth. (10)

Calvinism spread to France, the Netherlands and Britain. A rare painting from Lyons of 1564 shows a Calvinist congregation (*right*) listening to a preacher. The pulpit, not the altar, is the centre of worship. (12)

The sermon would apply biblical precepts to the moral and social life of the community. *Below:* a Limoges enamel plaque of Pierre Viret of Lausanne preaching to an audience that includes Calvin and Theodore Beza. (11)

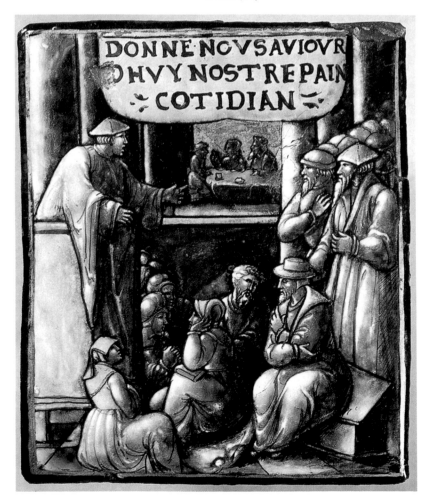

Confession of faith

The Augsburg Confession, read before Charles V in 1530, was a moderate document, drawn up to minimize the differences between the two sides. But still agreement could not be reached. When it was rejected, the reformers' growing radicalism soon rendered it out-of-date.

In 1534 Augsburg became Protestant. One of the results was to take charity out of the church's hands and place it in those of the civil authorities (*above*). The pine-cone is the emblem of Augsburg. (14)

The emperor sits enthroned listening to the Confession, with its assertion that 'man is saved by faith alone'. In front of him stand the princes and electors who supported Luther. In the background are depicted the services of the reformed church with biblical quotations justifying each – catechism, marriage, church music, baptism, preaching and communion. The last is shown being taken in both kinds (bread and wine), and there are long extracts from Luther's works explaining his doctrine on the subject. Under the altar are the names of theologians who differed from him and who are being consigned to perdition. (13)

The three essential parts of Protestant worship were baptism, preaching and communion, taken in both kinds. This altar frontal of 1561 (*below*) is among the earliest works of the Reformation in Denmark. (15)

A new iconography evolved to meet the needs of Protestant theology. In this design for a memorial, dating from the early 17th century, two central panels, with Christ in a niche between them, commemorate the deceased. The main picture shows the sacrifice of Isaac, supreme example of unquestioning faith. To left and right are the two trees of 'Belief' and 'Unbelief', the first tended by Abraham, the second by the devil. Roundels in the branches illustrate the effects of the two ways of life. These are based on the Acts of Mercy (see p. 125), Christ as a poor man being fed, clothed, comforted, etc. on one side and rejected and refused on the other. (16)

'O man, thou wretched creature.'

If the sacraments and the church could no longer guarantee forgiveness, how was man to be saved? By faith, by overcoming temptation and by appealing direct to Christ's mercy.

The assaults of sin continue to the moment of death. Protestantism was in many respects like a return to early Christianity (see p. 101). For Luther, too, man was more like someone on a precarious ladder from which he could fall at any moment, than someone huddling thankfully within the cloak of Mother Church (p. 13). The elaborate picture shown *left* was painted in England probably about 1600. Man, in the centre, is raised up by an angel whose shield bears the words 'Temperance, good reasons, chastity, alms deeds, compassion, meekness, charity and patience' (spelling modernized). Beside him a temptress shoots the arrows of Gluttony, Sloth and Lechery; a miser (with crossbow) shoots Covetousness; a devil three more arrows called Pride, Wrath and Envy; and death, the skeleton, raises his lance and brandishes his shield with the words: 'Behind they steal, a corporal life to deflower'. The long inscription at the bottom spells out the same lesson. (17)

Moral exhortation surrounded the Protestant on every side. Books and pamphlets developed the theme at endless length; long sermons hammered it home; images and aphorisms cried out from the walls of churches, from the façades of houses, even from the humblest objects of daily use. The German 17th-century tiles (*left*) are typical; they form one section of an extensive scheme covering a large household stove. In the centre the soul is forged in the fire of the world (*mundus*), surrounded by the Good Angel (sprinkling water), mortality (from whose bellows issue Temptation and Vanity), Satan and The Flesh, the whole being captioned 'the test of faith'. On each side stand allegorical figures of Justice and Faith. (18)

The great experiment

The colonization of North America was much more a religious than a political act: the idea of a nation founded in pursuit of a moral absolute.

John Winthrop was born in 1588, and for over forty years lived quietly in Suffolk attempting to practise his strict but humane Puritan creed. This part of his life is covered in detail on pp. 205–8. In 1630, after the death of his second wife, he sailed for America, becoming a leading citizen of the new colony and governor of Massachusetts. (19)

Before setting out for America the English Puritans had tried to establish a community in Holland. From here they sailed in 1620 (*below*), calling at Southampton on the way and renaming their ship the *Mayflower* before beginning the dangerous voyage across the Atlantic. (20)

The plain churches of colonial America still bear witness to the values that created them – a plain life and plain doctrine. *Right:* the Old Ship Church in Hingham, Massachusetts, 1681, the oldest church in America to be continually used. Following its tradition of distinctly liberal theology, it became Unitarian and today is called a free church. *Far right:* the Quaker meeting-house in Pembroke, Massachusetts, built in 1706. Here in the Plymouth colony the Friends were not persecuted, and for nearly two hundred years their society flourished. (21, 22)

The setting of worship was dramatically transformed by the Reformation. Paintings, statuary, stained glass; the Virgin, the saints, the relics and shrines of martyrs – all were swept away as the trappings of superstition. In their place came an austerity, a sense of inner peace that could in its way be equally moving. The painters of Holland, such as Pieter Saenredam, sought to convey this atmosphere in their quiet pictures of church interiors. We are looking west; the altar has been deserted and the congregation gathers round the pulpit. (23)

From the Bible alone a multitude of creeds could legitimately be derived. The Anabaptists and Mennonites were among those who attempted to live according to purely biblical precepts. One of Rembrandt's most powerful pictures shows a Mennonite preacher expounding the Scriptures. Conservative and uncompromising, the Mennonites were soon to leave Europe and find a new home in America, where they still flourish. (24)

7
The age of the Reformation

HANS HILLERBRAND

I N THE AUTUMN of 1517 nobody in Germany (nor Europe, for that matter) had heard of Martin Luther. Charles I (later the Emperor Charles V) had succeeded as king of Spain, Henry VIII was happily married. Culturally, the great names of the day were Erasmus, Raphael, Michelangelo, Dürer. And while some people were uneasy about the state of society and the church and talked reform, generally conditions were stable.

That year, however, a string of events began – precipitated by Martin Luther – that was to over-shadow everything else. The Reformation of the 16th century turned into one of the most significant epochs in the history of Christianity and of European society. The reasons are obvious. Europe was dramatically altered. The relationship of church and state underwent a change, even as new theological perceptions of society were formulated by the reformers. Wherever Christianity exists today – in Europe, North America and the developing countries – numerous Christians are the spiritual descendants of the reformers of the 16th century. The generic appellation, Protestant, to denote one of the three major branches of Christendom, was employed in the 16th century to describe the adherents of the Reformation, the reformers of (or 'protestants' against) the Catholic church. All Protestant churches, or denominations, from the Lutherans, Presbyterians and Anglicans in the 16th century, to the Baptists, Congregationalists and Methodists in the 17th and 18th centuries, can be traced, directly or indirectly, to the Reformation.

Historically, the Reformation meant the end of the dominant importance of the Catholic church in European society. Christendom was divided – beyond the separations recounted earlier in this volume – into several ecclesiastical factions. Even though in most European countries a single religion – held to be *the* Christian religion – continued to be the embodiment of Christianity and was declared normative for all citizens, these divisions were of profound consequence for the continuing role of the Christian faith. The concurrent presence of competing and conflicting interpretations assuredly lessened the Christian claim to universal truth. For European intellectuals the division of Christian truth – precipitated by the Reformation – became a reality of increasingly incisive importance.

The looming crisis

Narratives of the Reformation customarily begin by describing conditions in the late 15th and early 16th century, in order to suggest – perhaps even to demonstrate – that the outbreak of the controversy can be related to the position of church and society at that time. In traditional Protestant historiography this approach took the form of juxtaposing the picture of a worldly and perverted church – within which was voiced a thousandfold cry for reform – and the revitalizing initiatives of the Protestant reformers. More recently, Marxist historians have argued that society, too, was in a state of crisis in the 16th century. A new class of entrepreneurial townspeople, with increasing economic power, found it difficult to relate to the feudal system in which they played no political role. The Reformation became the vehicle by which this new class expressed its economic and social self-confidence. Since the ideological underpinning for the feudal order was provided by the Catholic church, that order could not be repudiated without an attack on the church.

Catholic historiography has acknowledged the presence of perversion and abuse in the pre-Reformation church, but attributes the controversy above all to a blatant theological aimlessness in the decades before the Reformation.

The evidence is heterogeneous and ambivalent, but there is no doubt that the emergence of the Reformation must be seen in a broader context than the theological. Several features stand out. As far as the church was concerned, there was an unhealthy preponderance of nobility in higher positions, along-side an uneducated lower clergy, whose qualifications were often restricted to a rudimentary knowledge of Latin, necessary for the ritual of the mass. The higher clergy tended to be preoccupied with matters of prestige and power rather than spiritual edification, while the illiteracy and ignorance of local priests were out of step with the heightened self-consciousness and expectations of the people.

What little we know about popular religion is not very inspiring. There was widespread ignorance of basic points of theological doctrine. Even such fundamentals as the Ten Commandments or the Lord's Prayer appear to have been stark mysteries for most

Among the telling contrasts used by the reformers was that between Christ driving the money changers out of the Temple and the pope using it as a place to amass wealth by selling indulgences. This pair of woodcuts by Cranach of 1521 is part of a series.

people. At the same time, people were increasingly preoccupied with certain external manifestations of the Christian religion, of which the waves of pilgrimages and the intensified veneration of relics were dramatic expressions. Relics were collected by the rich and passionately venerated by rich and poor. The castle church in Wittenberg boasted a collection of several thousand relics, including splinters from the cross, pieces from Jesus's winding sheet and earth from the spot where Jesus ascended into heaven.

The political authorities, both the territorial rulers and the city councils, were dissatisfied with the traditional fiscal and legal prerogatives of the church and engaged in a persistent effort to acquire as much authority as possible over matters traditionally governed by the church. While outright confrontations between the church and the political authorities were few, there was a large amount of tension and a good deal of anticlericalism.

In theology, much uncertainty and confusion prevailed. Diverse points of view were propounded side by side, while clear pronouncements on what constituted orthodoxy were lacking. The crucial question – whether pope or council possessed primacy of authority – remained unresolved.

The church faced a barrage of forces in society: the political authorities, intent on controlling the church to the greatest extent possible; the intellectuals, Humanists, townspeople, repelled by the heavy hand of the church and seeking to remove it; and, finally, the common people, many of them illiterate, often uninterested in religion or, for that matter, grossly vulgarizing it. There was an imbalance between the impressive splendour of the hierarchy and the poverty of the people, between the learning of the theologians and the ignorance of parish priests, between the yearning for spirituality and the insistent fact of worldliness.

In this setting the desire for reform was frequently voiced. Its common denominator was the denunciation of 'Rome', for its alleged greed, corruption and lack of spiritual values. While the intensity of this concern must not be overstated (thereby implying that all people were so deeply burdened by the perversion of the church that they only had a single yearning: reform), there can be little doubt that there were vocal critics, just as there were sundry efforts, individual and collective, at renewal. The church was slow in responding to these concerns, though some impetus came from the Fifth Lateran Council, which convened in 1512. Only in Spain, where Cardinal Cisneros could mobilize governmental support for his efforts, did meaningful reform take place. In France, not much happened, even though the Concordat of 1516 had entrusted the king with extensive power over ecclesiastical affairs, including the authority to fill high ecclesiastical positions. In Germany, the formulation of 'grievances against the apostolic see' was periodically undertaken with great enthusiasm but with few practical consequences.

Politically, society was characterized by tensions that, though they were neither more nor less pronounced than in earlier decades, proved significant for subsequent events. They had to do with the distribution of power, particularly between the ruler and the nobility. In Germany, the relationship between the emperor and the territorial rulers, and between the territorial rulers and the estates in their territories, posed unresolved problems. Each side groped for additional power. Related to these issues was the need to raise more revenues to support larger governmental bureaucracies, armies and royal life-styles. In the towns tensions grew between the ruling elites and those who were deprived of participation in the government.

Intellectually, the atmosphere was influenced by Humanism. Beginning narrowly, with philological – antiquarian concerns, Humanism increasingly affected a wide range of reform – sometimes vague, sometimes specific – which combined a self-conscious return to Christian origins with a commitment to secular values and responsibilities. There was not much cohesiveness to the movement, and neither the Humanists nor their contemporaries were fully aware of the startling changes that it implied. But the rise of Humanism meant that European society on the eve of the Reformation nourished ideas such as the assertion of individuality or the use of the distant past as a basis for criticizing the present, which enhanced the potential for change.

The point must be made, however, that prior to the Reformation European society was not beset by a universal crisis or even by a subjective sense of such a

The Lord's Vineyard: an elaborate allegory attacking abuses in the church. The text is from Matthew XV: 'Every plant that my Heavenly Father has not planted shall be uprooted.' Four such 'plants' are shown in the background. They are dead trees, watered and tended by pope and monks (one of whom is scooping water from a dry well), and the fruits they bear are rosaries, reliquaries, cardinals' hats, papal bulls – the paraphernalia of superstition. God the Father is himself uprooting one of them. In the foreground, angels throw the dead wood on a bonfire, to make way for the true vines, nourished by the water of life that flows from beneath the cross. Below: another allegory in a similar spirit. Christ leads simple believers to the light, while monks and schoolmen blindly follow Plato and Aristotle into the abyss.

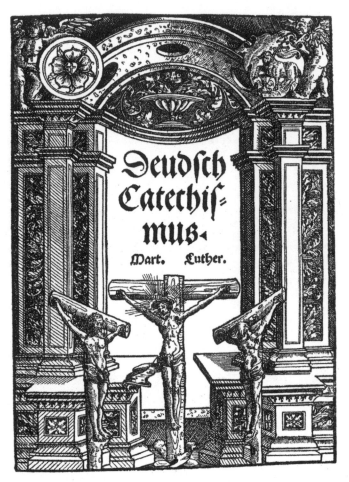

Luther's German Catechism ('Deudsch Catechismus'), published in 1529, laid the groundwork of Protestant religious education. Luther was immensely prolific: his collected works run to almost one hundred volumes.

crisis. Whatever the dissatisfactions and tensions, they were local and restricted. The absence of a universal vehicle of communication – in Germany a common language or a widely used printing-press – meant that no universal crisis of society could manifest itself. It was part of the significance of Luther and other reformers that they were able to do exactly that.

'Here I stand'

Into this setting burst the Reformation. Its initial phase was dominated by Martin Luther, a professor of theology at the University of Wittenberg. Luther had attained his doctorate in theology (and the teaching position that accompanied it) in 1512, and was, despite his youth – he was born in 1483 – in the process of acquiring the reputation of an insightful theologian.

Martin Luther not only dominated the controversy, he also precipitated it. In October 1517, he formulated Ninety-five Theses for an academic debate on the topic of indulgences. The teaching of the church on this matter was subtle and full of nuances, but the popular belief was that forgiveness of sins could be obtained simply through the payment of money to the church.

Luther's Theses were meant to clarify the church's teaching and to do away with vulgar and erroneous notions. Much to his surprise, they promptly became a matter of controversy. 'Had I known,' he wrote in later years, 'when I began to write, what I am now aware of, namely that people proved hostile to the Word of God and opposed it, I assuredly would have remained silent, for I never would have been so bold as to attack the Pope and all people.'

The impact of the Ninety-five Theses needs explanation. Although Protestant partisans soon insisted that 'the Theses spread throughout Germany as if angels themselves had been the messengers', the response, in fact, came slowly. Yet it did come, and ever more extensively. The reasons were several. Some saw Luther as a German nationalist, others as an opponent of the papacy, still others as a proponent of genuine spirituality. Above all, the controversy was fanned because Luther, with his pronouncement, had unwittingly stirred up a hornet's nest. The sale of indulgences, most notoriously through a Dominican friar named Tetzel, was part of an elaborate fiscal and political triangle involving the papacy, the southern German banking house of Fugger and Archbishop Albert of Magdeburg. The objective was to obtain for Albert the prestigious archbishopric of Mainz. Since Albert was below the prescribed canonical age for this appointment, a papal dispensation was necessary. It was given with the understanding that a special papal indulgence would be sold in northern Germany, and that the proceeds would be divided between the papacy and Albert. Luther's public protest raised the spectre of the failure of this arrangement; the haste with which heresy proceedings were commenced against him was understandable.

These proceedings immediately added an official ecclesiastical element to what might have been an academic controversy; and that controversy itself increasingly touched on more fundamental issues. Its high point came at Leipzig, in July 1519, with a disputation between Luther and a fellow theologian, John Eck. The disputation attained notoriety because Luther asserted at one point that popes and ecumenical councils can be in error – an assertion that clashed headlong with orthodox notions about the authority of the central church.

Luther's excommunication, which came in January 1521, after months of curial deliberations, was thus altogether to the point, even though the specific censures showed a cavalier, if sloppy, treatment of Luther's ideas, giving grounds for the notion that Luther had not been afforded a fair hearing.

Nevertheless, the excommunication should have settled the whole matter. The heavy legacy of 15th-century conciliarism, however, suggested that the definitive judgment could only come from an ecumenical council. At this point the local princes intervened, not just because they believed Luther deserved a hearing, but also because they wished to emphasize their own powers and to keep the authority of the emperor carefully circumscribed. Luther's own ruler, Frederick the Wise of Saxony, was well aware of Luther's popular support; and there were also long-standing grievances against Rome.

Luther was, therefore, summoned before the German diet at Worms to be heard. When asked to recant in front of the emperor and the dignitaries of the empire, Luther retorted with the famous words: 'Here I stand. Unless I am convinced by Scripture or by plain reasoning, I will not recant.' Protracted negotiations followed but proved unsuccessful. In May 1521, the diet affirmed, albeit under dubious legal circumstances, the ecclesiastical verdict against Luther and declared him a political outlaw.

Martin Luther was now both religious heretic and civil outlaw. He should have been apprehended and put to death. But Elector Frederick promptly spirited him into hiding, and safety. Residing, as 'Knight George', at the Wartburg castle, in the Thuringian woods, Luther witnessed how the movement of reform continued to spread. There was, in other words, a cause that went far beyond his personal involvement. In a variety of ways, Luther's words were echoed a thousandfold throughout Germany. As he himself put it upon his return to Wittenberg: 'I did nothing. And while I slept, or drank Wittenberg beer with my friends Philipp and Amsdorf, the Word so greatly weakened the papacy that no prince or emperor ever inflicted such losses upon it. I did nothing.'

Luther had served as a catalyst for a variety of concerns – German nationalism, anticlericalism, the yearning for a reform of society and the church and, last but not least, a yearning for meaningful religion. He did not solicit or want this varied support and he was – largely, at any rate – innocent of its steady increase. It was, nevertheless, a reality, and Luther's contemporaries rallied to the notion that society was in a crisis. Luther's intent had been to reform and renew religion. That is how the controversy erupted; that is how it initially flourished. But its scope quickly widened. Nobility, townspeople, clerics, Humanists, even peasants, responded with their frustrations, grievances, anxieties, and made Luther's language their own. Some became ardent and vocal partisans of the cause. They were ministers and intellectuals, and thus Luther received dozens of comrades-in-arms who interpreted and propagated the ideas of reform in local settings.

Luther and his fellow reformers took to com-

It was the sale of indulgences by the Dominican friar Johann Tetzel that sparked off the whole Reformation controversy. He is shown (above) preaching while his subordinates do a brisk trade in a church, and (below) riding the Apocalyptic Beast, wooing money from the simple peasantry. In both, the papal bull, hung with seals, is prominently in evidence.

O ihr deutschen mercket mich recht/
Des heiligen Vaters Papstes Knecht/
Bin ich/und br ing euch jtst allein/
Zehn tausent und neun hundert carein/
Gnad und Ablaß von einer Sünd/
Vor euch/ewer Eltern/Weib und Kind/
Sol ein jeder gewehret sein
So viel ihr legt ins Käftelein/
So bald der Gülden im Becken klingt/
Im huy die Seel im Himel springt/

municating their ideas in the vernacular, addressing themselves to the people as they discussed the issues of the Christian faith. What might have been an esoteric theological controversy among professional theologians expanded in ever-wider circles and captured the imagination of the people. By 1525, hundreds of thousands of copies of the writings of reformers were in circulation. The format employed was not the weighty tome but the slender pamphlet of eight or sixteen pages, as often as not illustrated with woodcuts.

The titles of Luther's tracts epitomized both his concerns and his appeal: *An Exposition of the Lord's Prayer, A Sermon on Grace, Concerning the Proper Way to Pray, Concerning Good Works*. While these tracts embodied theological perspectives, their overt concern was spiritual. Luther sought to enhance the spiritual life of the people rather than to expand theological doctrines. Luther himself was a genius and master in the use of simple, yet electrifying language. Take these words from a 1522 sermon: 'In short, I will preach it, teach it, write it, but I will constrain no man by force, for faith must come freely without compulsion. Take myself as an example. I opposed indulgences and all the papists, but never with force. I simply taught, preached and wrote God's Word.'

Underneath the diversity of themes put forward by the reformers lay a new standard of authority, the Word of God. Needless to say, it had been the basis for theology all along, but the Word had always been conveyed by church and tradition. Now the reformers raised the Word to absolute prominence. What counted was Scripture *alone*. Concomitantly, the reformers made the dramatic assertion that it would be understood by all, by peasant and artisan no less than by scholar and theologian. The exposition of the Christian faith thus became the province of all people, much to the exasperation of the Catholic leaders, who complained that 'even women and bakers' debated points of theology. The practical obstacle of the absence of a vernacular version of the Bible was soon overcome by a German translation, which is often acknowledged to have been Luther's most revolutionary achievement, profoundly affecting the evolution of the German language.

The reformers' emphasis on the universal accessibility of the Word was paralleled by their postulate of the 'priesthood of all believers', which repudiated the special status of the clergy and made all men and women equal in the sight of God. The reformers propounded a religion of the laity. Quite appropriately, many of their pamphlets addressed themselves to the 'Christian Man'. At least in the early years of the controversy Luther advocated the election of the minister by the congregation.

Social consequences

In addition to the religious and theological concerns put forward by the reformers, there were social and economic concerns. This broader appeal was exemplified by Luther's treatise, *To the Christian Nobility of the German Nation*, of 1520, which set out a lengthy list of urgent social and economic reforms, quoted extensively from the traditional grievances and even commented on the importation of spices and the reform of the university curriculum.

The uprising of the German peasants in 1524–25 must be seen in this context. First in south-western, then in southern and central Germany, peasants took to arms with a large variety of grievances, as they had done in previous decades. Initially, their uprising was graced by a measure of success, but in May 1525 they went down in disastrous defeat, no match for the well trained forces of rulers. Significant as an expression of the social and economic tensions in German society, the uprising was crucial for the course of the Reformation. Most of the peasant grievances (as preserved in the documents) remained within the context of traditional statement, but the most important pronouncement, *The Twelve Articles*, delineated a programme of reform that related social and economic goals to the proclamation of the Reformation. The Bible was to be the norm for society, and its principles were to govern all political and economic relationships. This seemed straight out of Luther's book; what had been at first sight another peasant uprising became publicly tied to the Reformation. Luther was appealed to by the peasants as arbiter. At first he commented cautiously, but then, in a tract entitled *Against the Murderous and Plundering Hordes of the Peasants*, divorced himself with scathing anger from the rebellious peasants: 'Stab, smite, slay, whoever can. If you die in doing it, well for you! A more blessed death can never be yours', he exhorted the rulers – who hardly needed his admonition.

Luther's siding so ostentatiously with the authorities cost the reform movement a good deal of popular enthusiasm and support. Where it continued in subsequent years, it was mainly in areas, such as northern Germany, that had remained untouched by the uprising. More importantly, the impact of the reform movement on social issues was dramatically narrowed. It returned to being a movement whose concerns were religious and theological.

For Catholics, the uprising was proof positive that the Reformation was a rebellion that entailed the disruption of law and order. Thus, the answer to the paramount question – how to avoid future recurrences – was thought to lie in the suppression of the Lutheran Movement which, so it was argued, had caused the conflagration. Soon after the defeat of the peasants several Catholic rulers sought to form an alliance towards that end. Lutheran rulers, on the other hand, faced the possibility that, under the pretence of maintaining law and order, they might be confronted with a military attack. The exploration of the possibilities of an alliance was their response. The course of the reform movement had become embedded in power politics. To be sure, the steadily increasing role of the rulers in ecclesiastical affairs had been, as we noted, an important characteristic in the time before the Reformation. Nothing changed. In order to succeed, the Reformation required the support of the political authorities, who showed themselves willing, even eager, to become involved. Such disposition fit harmoniously the rulers' quest for fuller control and power, not to mention the additional advantage of tangible benefits, such as the confiscation of monastic property. In the cities, the situation was more complicated in that the ruling groups did not uniformly support reform and change. Even there, however, the course of religious agitation was accompanied by politics – the desire on the part of some for fuller participation in governmental affairs.

The controversy had a fairly distinct pattern pertaining to the structure of ecclesiastical change. At the beginning there had been intense agitation for reform. While essentially religious and theological, this agitation also focused on larger social issues, which were clad in appropriate theological language. Under the impact of the Peasant's War, the concerns became more narrowly religious. At the same time, it became evident that there were practical ramifications to the message of religious renewal: if monasticism or the celibate clergy were unbiblical, should the monasteries be closed and the clergy be allowed to marry? What about the continued celebration of the mass, which was considered unbiblical? A large variety of changes was advocated by the reformers, but the actual authorization and implementation of the changes came from the political authorities. They thus played a crucial role in the course of events – positively or negatively – as partisans or as opponents of the reform movement.

Differences were appearing within the reform movement itself. One had to do with the timing of change. Those eager for immediate and comprehensive change faced those who felt it best to make haste slowly. Those with little regard for possible disruption and turmoil faced those who felt that orderliness best assured the desired change. Luther's colleague, Andreas Carlstadt, who sided with the impatient reformers, published a tract with the apt title *Whether it is Proper to Make Haste Slowly*. Other differences were theological. By 1523 it had become evident that the reformers' common opposition to Rome and the

The uprising of German peasants in 1524 was only one of a series of such revolts going back to the Middle Ages. For the first time, however, the peasants' demands included religious as well as economic grievances. Many of them expected Luther's support; they were cruelly disappointed.

papacy did not entail a common set of theological affirmations. Quite the contrary: differences of perspective and emphasis were becoming increasingly obvious, exhibiting the rather embarrassing spectacle of a division within the ranks of truth.

One of these stands out: Huldrych Zwingli, reformer of Zürich. Zwingli had come to Zürich in 1519 as 'people's priest', or preacher, at the Great Minster. Even though he subsequently denied that he had been influenced by Martin Luther, there is no doubt but that the Reformation controversy prompted him to express his opposition to the Catholic church. His persistent agitation brought Zürich City Council, in 1523, to convene two public disputations to determine the true Christian religion. If the outcome of both occasions was hardly surprising – Zwingli was the overtowering figure and the city council opted to support him – the premise was truly revolutionary. A community, convened by its political authorities, asserted its right to determine the faith, as if church, papacy and councils did not exist. No wonder that the Catholic partisans refused to be drawn into an affair the premises of which they had to reject.

The general pattern of ecclesiastical change in Zürich conformed to that elsewhere, except that Zwingli's presence led to its astoundingly speedy completion. By the spring of 1525, the changes (such as the abolition of the mass, the removal of the images, the institution of the new marriage law) had been completed; Zürich had accepted the Reformation. Indeed, the reforms had taken place with a consistency and comprehensiveness absent elsewhere. More important was Zwingli's emergence as Luther's foremost theological opponent from within the reform movement.

The specific issue was the Lord's Supper, and the disagreement arose over Zwingli's insistence that Christ was only spiritually present in the communion elements of bread and wine, whereas Luther argued, despite his repudiation of the Catholic notion of transubstantiation, that the body and the blood of Christ were truly present. The controversy became more vehement as time passed, but neither the intensity nor the quantity of the arguments put forward produced agreement. By 1529, Protestantism was a house bitterly divided.

At that juncture, Landgrave Philipp of Hesse, the youthful but important political leader of Protestantism, intervened to effect conciliation. His motivation was eminently political. Convinced of the political danger emanating from the Catholics, he believed that the future of the reform movement rested in a political alliance, which was impossible as long as theological

Town councils were now taking religious decisions into their own hands – an unprecedented step. In 1523–25 the Zürich City Council voted to accept the Reformation, suspend the mass and place itself under Zwingli's spiritual leadership. This woodcut shows such a meeting in a Swiss town.

discord prevailed. A colloquy held at Marburg, in October 1529, was intended to resolve the disagreement. It did not. Both sides represented not only divergent theological positions but also different political programmes. The Saxon point of view, shared by Luther, was that the gap with the Catholics could be bridged; either they would see the error of their ways or an ecumencial council would rule in the reformers' favour. The insistent assertion of the orthodoxy of the Lutheran Movement would pave the way to reconciliation. Zwingli, on the other hand, shared Philipp of Hesse's sentiment that conciliation was unlikely and that only a policy of political strength would assure the survival of the reform movement. Philipp and Zwingli were the losers of Marburg.

Another aspect of the Reformation was manifest at that time: its radicalization. The main thing the reformers had in common was repudiation of the Catholic church, a negative basis that invited division. Initially, disagreement was personified by Thomas Müntzer, minister in the Saxon town of Allstedt. He accused Luther of preaching a faith without suffering, and soon explosively and openly disagreed with the Wittenberg reformer. Not long thereafter, disagreement surfaced in Zürich among the followers of Zwingli. Some were determined to establish a true church (through believers' baptism), while others had intertwining religious and social objectives, with the tithe the crucial issue.

The Zürich authorities were unwilling to accept this radical notion of reform and were prepared to use force to retain the uniformity of religious sentiment. Persecution set in, and was to follow the Anabaptists – as they were called because of their stress on adult baptism as the sign of a voluntary acceptance of the Christian faith – wherever they made their appearance. It was meted out by Catholic and Protestant authorities alike, an indication that the retention of a single form of religion continued to be seen as the way to preserve order within society and to demonstrate the oneness of truth.

Originally, the adherents of the Anabaptist Movement included all classes of society, with a heavy representation of intellectuals and Humanists. Soon, however, the movement was recruiting its followers mostly from the ranks of the artisans and the peasants. It was never very substantial, even though it spread rapidly into southern and northern Germany, Austria, Moravia and the Low Countries. In contrast to the stately forms of church life, both Catholic and Protestant, a temporizing quality characterized the Anabaptist Movement. Organizational structures were slow in coming, and there was no trained clergy or church buildings.

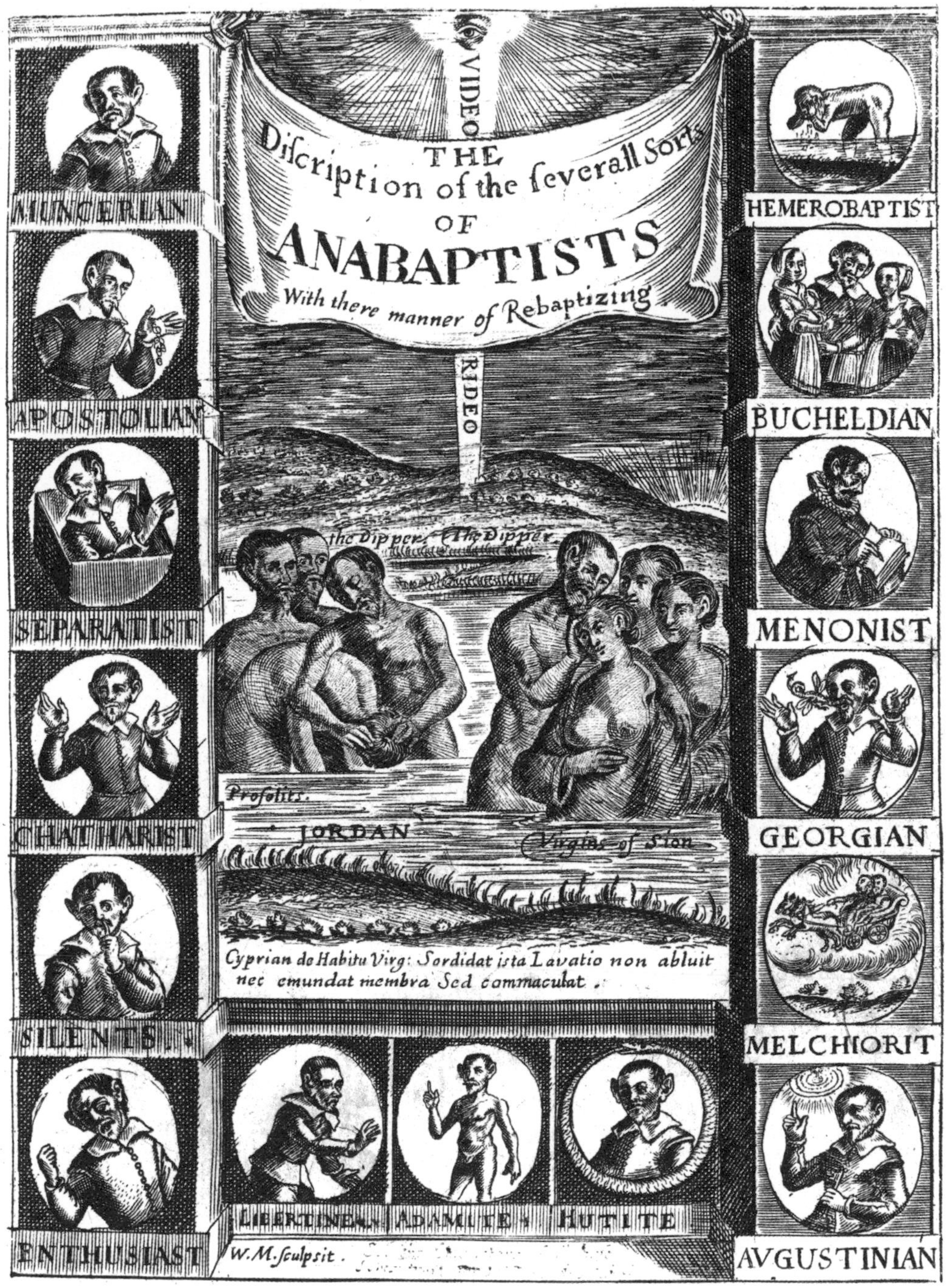

THE
Discription of the severall Sorts
OF
ANABAPTISTS
With there manner of Rebaptizing

VIDEO

MUNCERIAN
APOSTOLIAN
SEPARATIST
CHATHARIST
SILENTES
ENTHUSIAST

HEMEROBAPTIST
BUCHELDIAN
MENONIST
GEORGIAN
MELCHIORIT
AVGUSTINIAN

the Dipper. The Dipper
Proselits.
JORDAN
Virgins of Sion
Cyprian de Habitu Virg: Sordidat ista Lavatio non abluit
nec emundat membra Sed commaculat.

LIBERTINE. ADAMITE. HUTITE
W. M. sculpsit.

The Anabaptists represent the radical wing of the Reformation. Drawing their support largely from the labouring and artisan classes, they stressed the voluntary receipt of baptism by adults and a simplified Christianity based on the New Testament. Fervent enthusiasm made up for the lack of a sophisticated theology, but from the beginning they encountered the hostility of the more moderate reformers. An English tract of 1645 called 'The Dipper Dipped' ridicules their baptismal rites and gives satirical portraits of the sects that proliferated around them.

Anabaptism was truly a people's movement; it could boast a handful of trained theologians among them, but laymen assumed leadership roles. The dissemination of Anabaptist ideas took place clandestinely. A few secret printing-presses published Anabaptist tracts and pamphlets, which, together with the preaching of itinerant Anabaptist preachers, provided the theological mainstay of the movement.

The most dramatic event in the history of the Anabaptist Movement occurred in the north-western German town of Münster in the early 1530s. Under the leadership of one of the town ministers, Bernhard Rothmann, the Anabaptists succeeded in persuading the authorities to embrace their tenets. This victory led to a steady influx of persecuted Anabaptists from elsewhere. The city itself undertook more extensive changes, especially after the prince bishop laid siege: communism was introduced as was polygamy. Both measures received their impetus from the economic and social realities created by the siege, though Scriptural mandates were cited to justify them. In the spring of 1535 the siege proved successful and the Anabaptist kingdom came to an end. As a result, Anabaptists everywhere had to reconsider their attitude to the role of force. A former Dutch priest, Menno Simons, consolidated the shattered and confused Anabaptists along the lines of a quiet, peaceful Christianity. The movement undoubtedly played a major role in providing a religious outlet for those who sought a form of religious expression more intimate and more serious than that provided by the major branches of the Reformation.

From words to arms

We return to events in the Germany of the 1520s, when practical consequences of the Lutheran proclamation were increasingly drawn. Monasteries were dissolved, the celebration of the mass discontinued, episcopal jurisdiction rejected. These changes were not meant to mark a permanent divergence or separation from the Catholic church, since it was expected that Catholics would sooner or later follow suit. The rulers who implemented the ecclesiastical changes meant to demonstrate their pivotal role in the structuring of ecclesiastical affairs. A diet at Speyer, in 1526, accordingly concluded (the emperor was absent) that each ruler should deal with matters of ecclesiastical change as he could answer before God and the emperor. Three years later, the majority of the estates – it must be noted that ecclesiastical rulers held only slightly less than half the seats in the diet – had second thoughts and reaffirmed the Edict of Worms of 1521. Luther's followers protested against this decision, since 'in matters of conscience it is not proper to rule by majority vote', and were promptly labelled 'Protestants'. Legally, matters were at a stalemate.

In 1530, after an absence of almost a decade, Emperor Charles returned to Germany and convened another diet, at Augsburg. He at first proved conciliatory, but then quickly took a rigidly Catholic stance. An even more rigid stance was taken by the German ecclesiastical rulers; they had forced the emperor to abandon his conciliatory approach and eventually brought about the failure of the effort to resolve the controversy.

The Lutherans were persuaded that the best strategy was to emphasize their common ground with the Catholics. Perhaps with an eye to its effect on the rest of Europe (convinced that the Catholics would not agree with anything) they submitted an extraordinarily conciliatory statement of their belief – the *Augsburg Confession*. Surprisingly, negotiations brought a great deal of agreement. Only two issues remained unresolved: the married clergy and episcopal jurisdiction. But further progress proved impossible; the emperor asserted that the Protestants had been shown the error of their ways and ordered that they undo the ecclesiastical changes in their territories within six months.

In response, the Protestants quickly formed a military alliance, the League of Schmalkald, which meant that any effort on the part of the emperor and the Catholic estates to suppress the Reformation was bound to lead to armed conflict. A second element now intervened to render the emperor's actions less effective than usual: the Turks resumed their military offensive against central Europe. Charles, who was very conscious of his role as emperor of all of Christendom, desperately needed all the support he could get, including that of the Protestants. There was no way to put teeth into his ultimatum to them. The Turks thus proved a major factor in the course of events of the Reformation. In 1530, and several times later, the Turkish military threat hung over the religious controversy and confronted both sides with the duty of placing their common political solidarity above partisan religious interests.

In the decade that followed, when the emperor was preoccupied with non-German affairs, Protestantism scored further successes. Most of the imperial cities turned Protestant and, accordingly, the Reformation has been labelled an 'urban event'. The cities became Protestant amid extensive discussion, agitation and legal manoeuvring, all of which left an extensive documentary record that tells us a great deal about the momentum of change. We are able to gauge the impact of the proclamation of reform and renewal, and the evolution and crystallization of support among the ruling elites of a town; and also to follow the quest for ecclesiastical change, formulated in such phrases as 'proclaiming the Gospel' and repudiating 'man-made traditions'.

In the long run, however, the large historical significance of the Reformation derived from the territories and their rulers. In the three decades between the first diet at Speyer (1526) and the Peace of Augsburg (1555), during which a steadily spreading Protestant Movement sought to secure legal recognition, the dominating forces were the rulers.

By the early 1550s it was obvious that legal recognition could no longer be avoided. The Peace of Augsburg, concluded in the emperor's absence after lengthy negotiations, sealed the age of the Reformation in Germany by affording legal recognition to the Protestants. The freedom to choose ecclesiastical sides remained restricted to the rulers. Once they had decided, their subjects had to follow. This stipulation meant that political power in Germany would remain in the territories.

Calvin's theocracy

By that time, the pivotal figure in the Reformation (Luther had died in 1546) had come to be a Frenchman: John Calvin, minister in Geneva. His impact was so profound, so far reaching, that – from a European perspective – he came to epitomize the Reformation.

Calvin's contribution to the Reformation was twofold. First, he provided a theological synthesis of Protestant thought, which, because of its comprehensive and harmonious elaboration, proved its most eloquent and persuasive expression. His *Institutes of the*

Christian Religion, first published in 1536, was *the* text of the Reformation. Second, his thought fashioned a movement that, from its centre in Geneva, spread throughout Europe, so that Calvinism came to be seen as the Reformation in its purest form.

Born in 1509, Calvin appeared on the scene in the mid-1530s, almost two decades after Reformation controversy had first broken out. Having experienced what he himself called a 'sudden conversion', he fled his native France and, stopping accidentally at Geneva, he became minister of the newly reformed church there. In Geneva, as elsewhere, the Reformation had been introduced in a political context. There was a strong sentiment that Geneva should free itself from the secular rule of the bishop. The acceptance of Protestantism thus reflected a political no less than a religious judgment.

Determined to implement what was at that time a modest programme of reform, Calvin promptly ran into conflict with the authorities, who were sensitive to political ramifications of religious decisions, and wished to avoid moves that would cause undue complications. Calvin was expelled, then asked to return. Until his death, in 1564, Geneva was the site of his endeavours – an alien in a city whose citizenship he did not receive until many years later, in constant conflict with the factions of power, much maligned, but doggedly persistent and eventually victorious.

Calvin's secret lay not only in the stubbornness with which he pursued his goals but also in the assertiveness with which he interpreted the Gospel. He evoked, in a majestic sweep of God's dealings with men, the vision of the elect whom God had chosen for eternal salvation. And this vision assigned to the elect the task of subjecting the world to God's will. The believers were soldiers of Christ, engaged in a mortal struggle against evil. The Calvinist exercise of religion was vibrantly serious; it meant a life devoted to high principles of religious as well as moral provenance; it meant to subject one's own life and that of the entire comunity ever more fully to God's mandates. This communal aspect was important, since it constituted Calvin's novel contribution. Luther had confined himself to the vigorous enunciation of principles, but had refrained from issuing mandates for society. Calvin, on the other hand, had a blueprint of how God's will was to be concretely manifested. His was not only a blueprint, to be rigidly and determinedly followed, it was also an ethos. The clock makers in Geneva may not have improved their technical skills nor the French Calvinist entrepreneurs received new expertise in double-entry bookkeeping; however, they lived in an atmosphere where stewardship of time, certainty of purpose, and high moral standards were greatly valued. Such civic virtues were never an end in themselves; they were the consequences of prior religious commitment.

Many observers have taken note of this Calvinist ethos, relating it to the rise of capitalism or to the revolutionary liberalism of 17th-century England. There can be no doubt that Calvinism proved singularly able to relate to pressing social and political issues facing society, as the Lutheran Movement had done in Germany at the outset of the controversy. And through the doctrine of election, it gave its adherents that sense of self-confidence and certainty, determination and commitment of which we have spoken. Calvin's influence was also of crucial importance in France, where the question of success or failure of the movement of reform and renewal still hung very much in the balance. Here, too, the religious issue had political consequences. The French Calvinists found themselves, after 1559, taking sides in the constitutional controversy dividing the country: the exercise of the regency on behalf of the minor king. In so doing, they amassed new and increasing support.

In Geneva itself, Calvin was stubbornly determined to put his notions of a truly reformed church into practice. These included, quite prominently, the practice of church discipline, exercised by the 'consistory', a body of laymen and clergy, which met regularly to monitor the faith and morals of the citizens. The rules were many and the restrictions extensive (Geneva has been called a theocracy), but it is necessary to keep in mind that a strict supervision of social mores was rather standard in those days. What made Geneva different was the particular ethos that informed the policy: the convergence of secular and religious concerns.

Calvin's Geneva was the hub of the wheel, the spokes of which reached to the outer rim of Europe. Ministerial students came from all over Europe, absorbed the new gospel and then returned to their native lands as ardent and zealous missionaries for a great cause.

Widening circles: the English Reformation

By this time, the Reformation had become a movement of European dimensions. Everywhere, in Switzerland, France, England, the Netherlands and Sweden, reformers appeared on the scene, each one echoing in his own way Luther's message of reform. The question has been asked whether the Reformation in Europe really began with Luther, or can be traced back to more remote origins. The idea of justification by grace, for instance, can be found in certain pre-Reformation thinkers, such as the Frenchman, Jacques Le Fèvre of Étaples. Indeed, some early critics and reformers outside Germany had put forward propositions

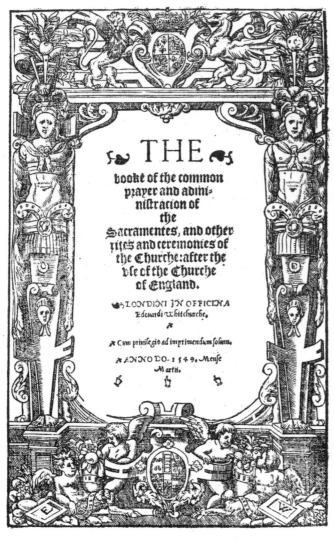

Title page of Cranmer's first 'Book of Common Prayer', 1549, a milestone in the English Reformation. Doctrinally it sought to incorporate some Lutheran and Calvinist interpretations, while retaining a foundation of Catholic liturgy.

uncannily similar to those of Luther. But it was Luther's preaching that turned fragmented apprehensions into a universal sense of crisis. What was transmitted from Germany to the four corners of Europe was not a specific set of notions of reform or renewal, nor even specific theological propositions (though this was undoubtedly the case to some extent), but the idea that Germany, that society generally, was in a state of crisis. Plus something else: an intense and emotional anticlericalism, with its ringing insistence that the pope was Antichrist.

England is a good case in point. The 1520s brought sundry manifestations of reform, nurtured by native sentiment, but precipitated by developments on the continent. How events would have unfolded of their own momentum must remain conjecture, because towards the end of the decade an altogether new element appeared, which was to overshadow English affairs for some time to come: Henry VIII's 'great matter', the annulment of his marriage to Catherine of Aragon in order to leave him free to marry Anne Boleyn. Henry needed the consent of the papacy for the annulment, but for political reasons Rome dragged its feet; Catherine was the emperor's aunt and the papacy could ill afford to alienate the emperor. After several years of unsuccessful manoeuvring, the king decided to take things into his own hands. He did so by insisting on his full jurisdiction to adjudicate English affairs, disavowing the authority of the pope, whose concurrence he had earlier sought. In what followed, the king used Parliament to force through not only administrative but also ecclesiastical changes.

Thomas Cranmer, the king's choice for archbishop of Canterbury, and Thomas Cromwell, the king's secretary, put these changes into effect. One provided the theological, the other the administrative, rationale. Henry skilfully used Parliament to vindicate his objectives by a series of statutes severing English ties with Rome. The most famous declared Henry to be the 'Supreme Head of the Church on Earth', a role that other rulers throughout Europe had begun to assume wherever the Reformation had found acceptance, though they did not claim that pretentious title. Theological changes were virtually non-existent and, where they did occur, they were nowhere as dramatic and comprehensive as on the continent. The English people merely had to disavow the jurisdiction of the 'bishop of Rome' and not question the king's title of 'Supreme Head of the Church'. That was all.

But there were changes. The dissolution of the monasteries in 1535 stands out, the social consequences of which were enormous.

Soon afterwards the king commissioned an English translation of the Bible, thereby not only bowing to the sentiment of the reformers but also concurring with the notion that people, acquainted with Holy Scripture, would readily support the case against Rome. The key figure of the new attitude was Erasmus, whose Christian Humanism epitomized a disposition essentially Catholic, yet open to reform and primarily concerned with the moral life. Such views could include the idea that ecclesiastical practices could be changed without sacrificing orthodoxy.

Henry VIII's Great Bible of 1539 made the Scriptures officially available in English for the first time. By an act of Parliament, Henry had been declared 'Supreme Head of the Church', and on this title page he is depicted handing down copies of the Bible to his archbishops, who distribute it to the priests and so to the people.

The king's own theological sentiment was conservative. It found expression in 1539 with the Six Articles Act, which, under its six headings, affirmed normative Catholic doctrine, including transubstantiation and clerical celibacy. The penalties for violating the act were severe, though they were hardly ever applied. Henry walked a tight-rope between two extremes, repudiating the papacy but not veering too far in the Protestant direction. He succeeded remarkably well, although his delicate balancing of ecclesiastical temperaments on the council of regency for his minor son, Edward, proved to be a failure. When Henry died, in 1547, and Edward VI succeeded him, power was quickly seized by men of reforming zeal and what had not been accomplished during Henry's reign was now undertaken. A new order of worship with a distinctly Protestant ring – *The Book of Common Prayer* – was promulgated in 1549, a truly creative document, which fused the best of diverse liturgical traditions into a statement of aesthetic beauty and theological cohesion.

After a great deal of meandering and a minimum of theological discussion, England had become moderately Protestant. As was the case in most countries that accepted the Reformation, however, agitation for further change continued. Its advocates were committed to the proposition that true religion had not as yet been fully and purely established. They soon became known as Puritans, who were to restore pure religion (see Chapter 8). Most of the issues were clerical, such as the propriety of clerical vestments. Despite such Puritan agitation, the Elizabethan settlement remained intact, and, after the turn of the century, it did what it had done everywhere else – it related to political considerations. Puritanism became a political phenomenon, and as such a major force in 17th-century England.

The new face of Europe

The transformation of the religious phenomenon into a political one was very characteristic of the Reformation as a whole. The course of the Reformation in France, Sweden, the Netherlands and Poland (to name the major areas of Reformation activity) had one common denominator: the convergence of religious and political factors and forces. The Reformation neither created nor did away with existing social and political tensions in society. It cultivated them. Where controversy in society existed, the reformers embraced one side; or, concomitantly, one side would connect with the reformers. In either case, the outcome was that the acceptance of the Reformation became at once a political choice and the solution to a specific problem. France is a good case in point: here three decades of

reform agitation had, by the middle of the century, led to a stalemate, since the king was unwilling to accept the 'new faith'. In the serious constitutional issue raised by the succession of the minor, Francis II, in 1559, into which the Protestants were inescapably drawn, they chose the side of those who opposed the regency of Cardinal Guise, since he represented the Catholics. The political controversy thus had a religious component; the success of the one was at once the success of the other.

In all this, the overtowering role was played by the political authorities. In Europe as a whole no less than in Germany, the ruler's verdict determined the formal outcome of the quest for reform and renewal. Reformed religion was never successfully established anywhere against a ruler's will.

The political leaders who spearheaded the Protestant cause – Philipp of Hesse, Henry VIII, Gustavus Vasa of Sweden – were not notably religious men. This is not to deny their sincerity, but only to suggest that their religious beliefs and commitments had to be integrated with other aspects of their rule.

We have described the course of events that changed the ecclesiastical configuration of Europe. At the beginning stood a religious movement for reform and renewal, which soon became involved with broader social concerns.

The Reformation was successful because it brought with it a spirit of freshness that contrasted with the staleness and routine of existing life. Freshness bred vigour, and vigour bred enthusiasm. Underlying all was a sense of certainty on the part of the adherents of the movement of reform. Catholics spoke disparagingly of 'the vain confidence of the heretics', but it was precisely that confidence that inspired their enthusiasm. Protestantism was a religion of liberation and emancipation.

It is a romantic notion, engagingly held by Protestants, that the Reformation was a popular movement in the sense that it evoked a universal appeal – as if every man and woman was not only concerned about religion, but also enthralled with Protestantism in one of its forms. The notion overstates reality. The evidence suggests that most people remained singularly uninterested in the Reformation controversy, and were often blatantly misinformed about religious affairs. Given the low level of literacy in the 16th century, this fact should not come as a surprise.

It is nevertheless true that there was much popular enthusiasm and support for the new gospel. The theological controversy was not fought by professionals and churchmen but by men (and women) from all sections of society. In that sense, the Reformation was a popular movement.

The social consequences of the ecclesiastical changes must be noted. The most dramatic one was the division of western Christendom into several competing factions, though it is evident that the 'unity' of western Christendom prior to the Reformation was so beset by internal tensions that one may hardly speak of it with great confidence. Another consequence was the laicization of religion. Everywhere that the Reformation gained a foothold, the laity played a crucial role. Initially, the entire spectrum of society was represented; one Catholic partisan observed with evident frustration that 'even women and simple folk' participate in the religious controversy. Eventually, such lay involvement declined at the popular level and came to be replaced by representative bodies or by government. In England, the king became the 'supreme head' (or 'governor') of the church. In Germany, the territorial ruler became the 'summus episcopus'. In Geneva, and wherever Calvinism took root, consistories and elders provided the avenues for laymen to help direct ecclesiastical affairs. To be sure, this was a far cry from the 'priesthood of all believers', which Luther had so exuberantly enunciated at the outset of the controversy. It provided, however, a much broader role for the laity, and thus a change from the situation prior to the Reformation, where the involvement of political authorities in ecclesiastical affairs occurred in settings of tension and conflict.

The Reformation also secularized religion. The area of religious commitment ceased to be the monastery, the pilgrimage and the priesthood. It came to be the market place, the family, the daily round of responsibilities that Luther, with a creative turn of phrase, called 'vocations'. The proper exercise of one's vocation – as parent, artisan, citizen – became the distinguishing mark of the Christian. Luther put it like this: 'Along comes the clever harlot, namely natural reason, looks at married life, turns up her nose and says: "Why, must I rock the baby, wash its diapers, change its bed, smell its odour, heal its rash, take care of this and take care of that, do this and do that? It is better to remain single and live a quiet and carefree life. I will become a priest or a nun and tell my children to do the same."

'But what does the Christian faith say? The father opens his eyes, looks at these lowly, distasteful and despised things and knows that they are adorned with divine approval as with the most precious gold and silver.'

The traditional world-view remained intact. That the Bible was the Book of Books, the guide for understanding *all* of life – history and geography no less than theology – continued to be the central assertion. The Reformation reinforced the conservative propensity of society, enhancing the values of the past, of the old, of tradition. The reformers' stress on apostolic Christianity and their opposition to what they called recent innovations epitomized this. On the other hand, the essence of the Reformation was that it questioned, challenged, repudiated the status quo. As long as religion remained the central preoccupation of European society, the conflict of values inherent in this situation would remain. The age of the Reformation only ended when, in the course of the 17th century, new developments – notably geographic and scientific discoveries – posed new issues.

Study of the Bible by laymen is one of the keys to the Reformation. Tyndale's English translation of the New Testament was first published in 1526 and although at first illegal became one of two sources for Henry's Great Bible and eventually for the Authorized Version. This title page of the second edition is faced by a later portrait of Tyndale.

THE
Pilgrim's Progress
FROM
THIS WORLD
TO
That which is to Come:
Delivered under the Similitude of a
DREAM,
Wherein is Discovered
The Manner of his setting out,
His Dangerous JOURNEY,
AND
Safe Arrival at the Desired Country.

By *JOHN BUNYAN.*

The Thirteenth Edition with Additions, and the Cuts.

I have used Similitudes, Hosea 12. 10.

Licensed and Entred according to Order.

LONDON,
Printed for *Robert Ponder,* and are to be Sold by *Nich. Boddington,* at the *Golden Ball,* in *Duck-lane.* 1693.

Bunyan's 'Pilgrim's Progress' is the enduring legacy of the Puritan revolution, and in it the theme of life as a journey that can end in either heaven or hell – a theme that we shall see reappearing at every period of Christian history – assumes its most deeply felt and powerful form. Christian's resolution to save his soul, his meeting with and defeat of various temptations and his triumphant arrival at the Heavenly City were studied in every Puritan household. Bunyan's own spiritual history, which he relates in 'Grace Abounding to the Chief of Sinners', included all the typical experiences of conversion – the overpowering sense of guilt, the suicidal depression, the realization of God's mercy and in the end unshakeable faith in salvation.

8

The social impact of Puritanism

J. WILLIAM T. YOUNGS

THE PURITANS of Old and New England loved to find colourful images to describe the ideal union of God and man. Both the heavenly Lord and the human spirit were intangible and elusive, but through compelling phrases these unseen entities could be made visible and accessible. One of the finest of these word pictures was written by Thomas Shepard, a 17th-century minister at Cambridge, Massachusetts. 'As iron put into the fire seems to be nothing but fire,' he said, 'so Adam, beloved of God, was turned into a lump of love, to love God again.'

Although Shepard spoke of the biblical Adam, he was describing the proper condition of the Puritan saint. He had chosen his words carefully. He must often have watched blacksmiths at work, holding metal to flame until it glowed warmly, becoming fire itself. So God, like the flames, should enter into a Christian and transform him into a spark of divinity. This condition was the central goal of Puritanism.

The Puritan vision: God and the soul

Puritan history is the story of the attempt to unite God and man in Reformation England. Puritans believed that human beings were separated from the Lord by sin and that human happiness could be achieved only through overcoming that separation. Man and God had once been united in the Garden of Eden, and they would communicate again with the coming of the millennium. In the meantime, men must seek to reduce the distance between the ideal and the real. As individuals they should aspire towards personal salvation. And as members of communities they should attempt to create a more godly nation through personal virtue, family government, Christian labour, political morality and ecclesiastical reform.

The Puritan Movement may be said to have originated long before there were English Puritans. The aspiration towards perfect union with God finds antecedents in the lives of Paul, Augustine, Francis and Wycliffe, along with many other Early Christians. As a specific episode in Christian history, however, Puritanism began in 16th-century England. When Henry VIII divorced Catherine of Aragon, broke with Rome and established himself as head of the Church of England, he began an uneasy association between his realm and the Protestant Reformation. Henry was willing enough to destroy the monasteries, authorize an English translation of the Bible and remove Catholic images from places of worship. But by and large he adhered to traditional forms of worship and church government. His daughter Elizabeth realized that the only way to avoid religious turmoil was to steer a moderate course between Catholicism and extreme Protestantism. Under the Elizabethan Settlement of 1559 the church again broke from Rome and adopted a reformed prayerbook, but it retained many traditional elements.

Those Englishmen who in the late 16th century protested against the remaining Catholic element in the church became known as Puritans, a derisory name based on their seemingly excessive demands for a pure church. They opposed clerical vestments, signing with the cross in baptism, confirmation, kneeling at communion, retention of the term 'priest' to signify a minister, the saints' days, bowing at the name of Jesus, organs and singing in parts. All of these observances smelled of popery. The vestments put too much emphasis on the minister, distracting attention from God. The saints' days focused worship on men rather than upon God.

In addition, the Puritans insisted on an educated preaching clergy. They held that the essential element in Christian worship was the delivery by the minister of the Word of God. Men must be made in the sermon to comprehend fully their relationship to the Lord.

For several decades the Puritans tried unsuccessfully to win support for their reforms. In the 1560s and 1570s they sought to persuade Parliament to abolish clerical vestments and to adopt a Presbyterian form of government, placing control of the church in local congregations and ministerial associations rather than in an episcopal hierarchy. But Parliament upheld the status quo. At Cambridge, Thomas Cartwright, the Lady Margaret Professor of Divinity, delivered lectures in 1570 favouring Presbyterianism. He was removed from his post and went into exile in Geneva. During the years 1586–88, John Field led a movement to win nationwide support for Presbyterianism. His premature death in 1588 ended the attempt.

Despairing of victory, a few Englishmen decided to

The Orthodox true Minister,   the Seducer and false Prophet.

During the years before the Civil War tension grew between those for whom the Anglican church was an acceptable Protestant compromise and those for whom it did not go far enough. This anti-Puritan woodcut contrasts the 'orthodox minister' (Anglican) with the 'false prophet' (dissenter).

start secret reformed congregations of their own rather than wait upon a universal reformation. The most famous of these Independents, or Separating Puritans, is William Bradford, who, with other reformers, went into exile in Holland in 1607 and sailed for America thirteen years later on the *Mayflower*.

Most English reformers, however, could not accept such piecemeal attempts at reform. They believed they must reform society as a whole, not simply preserve themselves as a small remnant. In 1603, when James I ascended the throne, many Puritans felt that their time had at last arrived. James had been raised in Presbyterian Scotland, and would, it was hoped, carry on the Reformation in England. James met with Puritan representatives at Hampton Court in 1604 and promised to make some changes in the liturgy and the ministry, but he warned the Puritans that they must conform to the Church of England. And his new archbishop of Canterbury, Richard Bancroft, was even more hostile to the Puritans than his predecessor. Under Bancroft's regime, William Ames, the foremost Puritan theologian of his time, was forced into exile for refusing to wear clerical vestments and to use the sign of the cross in baptism, and other reforming ministers were driven from their pulpits.

The early history of Puritanism was, thus, a history of successive defeats in the arena of national policy. And yet in another sphere, that of personal conscience and conduct, Puritanism fared well late in the 16th and early in the 17th century. At Oxford and Cambridge Puritans held sway in several colleges. Emmanuel

College at Cambridge was founded by Sir Walter Mildmay in 1584 as a nursery of Puritanism. There and elsewhere Puritan theologians such as Laurence Chaderton, William Perkins and John Preston taught their students a distinctively Puritan view of the relationship between man and God.

Although they could not overtly attack Anglican vestments and ceremonies, the Puritan graduates of Oxford and Cambridge could preach Puritan doctrine in the great churches of London and the remote corners of the realm, and in so doing they could alter the complexion of English society. Their central theme was a Protestant description of God, sin and salvation.

Puritans described God as the creator and supreme ruler of the universe, so far above his creations that he was unseen and incomprehensible. He was like the weather in that no man could predict or guide his course. Men could not look upon the Lord any more than they could stare at the sun. And yet his very remoteness gave cause for admiration. As one minister wrote: 'We admire the luster of the sun the more in that it is so great we cannot behold it.'

Despite God's mysterious character, he was not cut off from the earth. He filled the world with his being, guiding human history by divine providence. The Lord was both infinitely remote and infinitely present. He could appear in nature, as he did when Anne Bradstreet in frontier Andover, Massachusetts, saw a beautiful sunset and wrote: 'More heaven than earth was here.' And if viewed properly, the whole earth testified to God's existence. Shepard declared: 'Can we when we behold the stately theater of heaven and earth, conclude other but that the finger, arms and wisdom of God hath been here . . . ? Who taught the birds to build their nests, and the bees to set up and order their commonwealth? Who sends the sun post from one end of heaven to the other, carrying so many thousand blessings to so many thousands of people and kingdoms? What power of man or angels can make the least pile of grass, or put life into the least fly if once dead?'

God was the source of life, strength, wisdom, happiness. He gave human existence its purpose and exhilaration. And yet many men and women failed even to recognize God's existence. Most were 'notorious worldings, that look no higher than their barns, no farther than their shops'. The Puritans regarded this absorption in the world as the essence of sin.

Sin was wrong because it distracted man from God. The sinner was 'a dead corps, lying rotting and stinking in the grave'. He might appear alive: frolicking in the tavern, fornicating with whores, cheating his fellows in business, grasping every sordid pleasure that came his way. But he was dead to the thing that mattered most, his relationship to God. Thomas Hooker, a 17th-century minister, described the sinner's plight in these words: 'Shame takes away my Honor, Poverty my Wealth, Persecution my Peace, Prison my Liberty, Death my Life, yet a man may still be a happy man, lose his Life, and live eternally: But sin takes away my God, and with him all good goes.'

The Puritans believed that most men and women ruined their lives chasing after the wrong objects. From morning until night they sought worldly pleasures. Good meals, fine clothes, elegant houses; these were their gods. But such things could not even satisfy men's material needs. 'Thy clothes may warm thee,' declared Thomas Shepard, 'but they can not feed thee; thy meat may feed thee, but can not heal thee; thy physic may heal thee, but can not maintain thee; thy money may maintain thee, but can not comfort thee when distresses of conscience and anguish come upon thee.'

God was the source of all that was good, but sin separated man from God. The human story might have ended there, but for a third element, salvation through Christ. Man was by nature 'dead in sin'. Cut off from God, he deserved only misery in this world and eternal damnation hereafter. But, for man's sake, Christ, the Son of God, had died upon the cross, taking upon himself the sins of man. God was willing to forgive and redeem those men and women who believed in Christ.

Puritans filled many sermons explaining the mystery of redemption. One could not win salvation simply by doing good deeds. Certainly God approved of righteous conduct. Redemption, however, came only when grace entered a believer's soul and allowed him to see the Lord. Men and women could prepare for grace by lamenting their sins and praying for pure hearts. But salvation came only through the free gift of God.

The Puritan saint so disciplined his mind that he waited continually upon the gift of grace. In his expectation he could be stern and introverted, fearful of giving himself over to frivolity and worldliness. He was taught to consider that there was 'a snare for him in every lawful liberty'. He must ask himself: 'May I not sin in my mirth, in my speaking, in my sleeping?'

This austere self-control led to the Puritan reputation for excessive sternness. It was said disparagingly that the Puritans disapproved of the cruel sport of bear-baiting not out of consideration for animals, but because the game gave pleasure to the audience. We should not, however, exaggerate the Puritan opposition to pleasure. Ideally, Christians would pursue a moderate path in all things. They would 'be merry in the Lord, and yet without lightness'.

The Puritan was not a 'killjoy', a person constitutionally unable to taste worldly pleasure. His attitude to the flesh is aptly summarized in the Puritan saying: 'Wine is from God, but drunkenness is from the Devil.' The

The Puritans were used to persecution. In the days of Queen Mary Tudor, the Duke and Duchess of Suffolk, with their child and child's nurse, fled the country and escaped to Germany.

things of the world were there to be enjoyed, but not to excess. Puritans disapproved of sexual relationships outside marriage; between husband and wife, however, connubial bliss was not only allowable, but positively expected. There were cases in Massachusetts Bay where judges scolded lethargic husbands and wives in court for not having sexual intercourse often enough with their spouses!

Men and women were free to enjoy food and drink and love-making as long as they recognized that these earthly comforts must be subordinate to a greater pleasure in God. All other joys were transitory, but this was eternal. 'This God is a joy in sadness, light in darkness, life in death, heaven in hell', said Shepard. 'Here is all thine eye ever saw, thine heart ever desired, thy tongue ever asked, thy mind ever conceived. Here is all light in this sun, and all water in this sea, out of whom, as out of a crystal fountain, thou shalt drink down all the refined sweetness of all creatures in heaven and earth forever and ever. All the world is now seeking and tiring out themselves for rest; here only it can be found.' Perry Miller, the foremost modern Puritan scholar, summarized this piety in a suggestive phrase: 'Men were made believers by an inward gladness.'

The main object of the Puritan religious life was to achieve 'inward gladness' by making the spiritual journey from the natural condition of sin to the supernatural state of grace. A central element in Puritan sermons was the tale of the saint's difficult progress to redemption. The soul was portrayed sometimes as a warrior fighting for a cause and sometimes as a poor pilgrim lost in a desert or confined in a jail. In a famous analogy, John Cotton likened the convert's journey to grace to a man's slow entrance into a body of water. First he 'wades in the rivers of God his grace up to the ankles'. Then he goes in up to his knees. Grace refreshes his legs but the rest of his body is still

Remember that thou keepe holy yͤ Sabboth Day
The profane Ifralite, that durft affay,
In gathering fticks, to breake the Sabboth day,
Is ftonde to death, for like Contumacy
The Lord hath fworne, that every Soule fhall dye.

A Woman and her two Daughters pill and dry
flax on the Lords day, are all burnt

*Puritan morality, from 'Divine Examples of God's Severe
Judgments', 1671. The Sabbath-breaker is stoned to death
(following the prescription of the Old Testament); women drying
and spinning flax are consumed by flames.*

untouched and so corrupt. Finally the man goes on until he is afloat in God's grace. 'There is such a measure of grace', says Cotton, 'in which a man may swimme as fish in the water, with all readinesse and dexterity.'

Puritan sermons abound in stories like these. One scholar has likened them to folktales because of their dramatic quality and their appeal to the common people of England and New England. Usually such narratives were blended with exposition of the Scriptures, exhortation to good behaviour, and other modes of religious edification. But in the most famous Puritan tale of all, John Bunyan's *Pilgrim's Progress*, the folktale of the Christian's journey to heaven stands on its own as a literary classic.

The Puritan saint was expected to walk through life as if on a journey to heaven. 'In whatsoever place thou art,' Puritans were told, 'whether alone or abroad, by day or by night, set thyself in the presence of God.' Long before some 'Pilgrims' made the physical journey to New England, Puritans thought of themselves as pilgrims. They lived in the world, but they attempted to set their hearts on heaven. This piety led to distinctive modes of behaviour.

In seeking frequent communion with God, Puritans ideally began each day by praying silently in their own beds. Then the father, as head of the household, would pray and read from Scripture before the whole family. These services would be repeated in the evening, and during the day the devout Puritan would try to find time for prayer and meditation.

Puritans regarded the whole Sabbath day as the Lord's own time. They frequently attended long church services in the morning and the afternoon, and they set aside the rest of the day for reading Scripture, discussing the sermon, meditating and other forms of serious devotion. One of their primary grievances against King James was that he encouraged his people to devote their Sundays after church to sports such as soccer. He believed that such exercises would strengthen his people and prepare them for foreign combat. The Puritans, however, devoted to Christian warfare against sin, regarded the king's suggestion as an abomination. One may imagine them listening in dismay to the howls of their neighbours engaged in village soccer.

Through family worship and honouring the Sabbath the Puritan demonstrated his love of God. His piety also required virtuous conduct in secular affairs. Above all he must regard his vocation as a holy duty. Housewifery, farming, trading and other enterprises were ordained by the Lord. A person must work hard and serve man and God in his calling. A merchant, for example, should not cheat his customers or charge them more than a 'fair price'. His purpose was not to enrich himself, but to serve his community.

Because Puritanism encouraged hard work and orderly conduct, it has sometimes been associated with capitalism. Certainly many Puritans did become wealthy because of their diligence and efficiency. They even regarded their riches as signs of God's approval. But we must not conclude that Puritanism led easily to materialism. The Puritans did not endorse wealth as an end in itself and sternly opposed the gaudy display of riches. As in other matters, they sought to pursue a moderate course, regarding wealth with detachment. Attractive though it might be, prosperity must not interfere with their relationship to God.

In such precepts we can see the broad contours of Puritan piety: the emergence of a historical movement, its essential doctrines and its code of behaviour. Let us consider now how these elements entered into the lives of two typical Puritans, John and Thomasine Winthrop. In the story of their brief life together we can gain a fuller appreciation of the character of Puritan society.

The Puritan microcosm: life and death in a godly household

John and Thomasine were both children of East Anglian gentry families. In the mid-16th century John's grandfather, Adam, had purchased a church property known as Groton Manor, when Henry VIII sought to further the Reformation and enrich himself by dissolving the monasteries. A second Adam Winthrop, John's father, inherited the manor. John Winthrop was born in 1588, the year that the English defeated the Spanish Armada.

The land where the Winthrops lived was in the southern part of Suffolk, not far from the border with Essex. The gently rolling country was covered with rich farmland, green marshes, ponds and forests of oaks, beeches and willows. The county was the first in England to enclose its fields; so the land was intersected with innumerable hedgerows that served as fences. It was noted for its mutton, beef, butter and cheese. It was a pastoral land, though the white gulls that fed on the Groton Ponds reminded the people the sea was only a few miles away.

John was raised on the manor until the age of fourteen, when he went to Cambridge to attend Trinity College. He stayed at Cambridge for only two years, returning when nearly seventeen to help his father run Groton. He so impressed his parents with his maturity that they consented to his marriage to Mary Forth, the twenty-year-old daughter of a neighbouring gentleman. John and Mary lived together for ten years until her death in 1615, when she left him with four children.

A Tudor father recites prayers before his wife and children: a woodcut illustrating a book of Psalms, published in 1563.

Although John lamented Mary's passing, in those days a bereaved spouse seldom remained single for long. Marriage was a practical as well as a personal and romantic relationship, for a wife's help was essential in raising children and overseeing a household. Thus, shortly after Mary's death, John began the courtship of Thomasine Clopton, whom he undoubtedly knew already. She was the daughter of William Clopton, the squire of a nearby estate. The couple married in the autumn, 1616. Thomasine was a good wife, 'industrious', 'plain hearted' and 'patient of injuries'. She showed her love of God in public and private worship, and cared for John's children as if they were her own. John was so attracted to her that he would recall, after her death, that their affection 'had this only inconvenience, that it made me delight too much in her to enjoy her long'.

During their year together John and Thomasine spent most of their time in the prosaic work of managing their country estate. The Winthrop papers and descriptions of other households allow us to draw a picture of their daily life. On a typical spring day they would awake with the crowing of the cock. They would dress quickly in their chilly room and hurry downstairs to a warm fire prepared by the servants. John's four children would soon arrive and huddle near the flames warming themselves, while the servants came in from the kitchen. Each morning Winthrop read to the family from the Bible and offered a prayer asking for God's favour in the day ahead.

Over breakfast John and Thomasine might discuss the day's activities with the children and servants. After they finished the meal, John would likely tour the manor to see that all was in order, inspecting cattle and pigs and supervising his servants in the fields or wood lot. On many spring mornings the air was damp and cold, but there were pleasant days when the sun broke through the clouds to the east and the wind bore the scent of salt water off the North Sea. Since most physical labour at Groton was carried out by servants, Winthrop could devote time to studying the Bible and other religious works. We may imagine him retiring to his study after touring the manor.

Thomasine would probably supervise the domestic chores, seeing that rooms were dusted, floors swept, butter churned and meals prepared. She might attend personally to a garden of flowers, vegetables and herbs. While men supervised grain cultivation, English women usually planted radishes, beets, carrots, cabbage, cucumbers, onions, melons, parsley, cloves and other garden crops.

At supper the family might discuss the day's events. John would again read from the Bible, and they would sing a Psalm. That spring, Thomasine learned that she was pregnant, and after they went to bed, she and her husband might discuss the new baby, John wondering whether she felt well, and Thomasine worried about the older children's reaction to a new brother or sister. John might tell her, as he later wrote in his diary, that his children already loved her like a mother.

On the surface, life at Groton Manor seems a kind of agrarian paradise. The family is close; everyone is well fed, clothed and housed; and the men and women spend their days in honest toil. John and Thomasine believed, however, that they must not become too absorbed in the pleasures of day-to-day life. Instead they should think constantly about their relationship to God.

John Winthrop's interest in religion began at an early age. When he was ten, he came to have 'some notions of God', but he characterized himself as being 'lewdly disposed', 'wild and dissolute' and dominated by a 'voluptuous heart'. This does not mean that he spent his time drinking, whoring and stealing. In fact, the only youthly sin he specifically mentions in his later writings is the theft of two books as a small boy. When Winthrop refers to himself as possessing a 'voluptuous heart', he is probably describing the course of his imagination rather than his actual behaviour. Although such activity may not seem to qualify as 'dissolute behaviour' today, this failure to master his desires grieved Winthrop. He believed that a good Christian would discipline his heart and think about God in all his free moments. There was sin, he believed, in 'all such works as are done to fulfil the will of the flesh rather than of the spirit'.

By the age of eighteen John Winthrop was deeply concerned with his spiritual condition. Now for the first time the Word came into his 'heart with power'. He would walk for miles to hear a good sermon and developed a reputation for giving spiritual advice to others. But he also became overly proud, and, since he realized that without Christ's grace all of his good works would not save him, he began to despair that perhaps he was only a hypocrite.

Throughout his twenties Winthrop's religious life consisted of alternating periods of assurance and doubt. He abandoned hunting and cards because he felt that they interfered with his religious life. He attempted to devote more time to prayer, meditation and religious reading, but frequently failed to meet his own high standards of behaviour. He accused himself of having become too frivolous in his relationships with friends and having eaten and drunk more than was appropriate. Once he condemned himself because during a church service his mind wandered to a journey he was about to take into Essex, and soon he was 'possessed with the world'. He sought to 'tame his heart' by regulating his diet, singing Psalms while travelling and reading tracts. But he found that complete abstinence from the pleasures of the world left him 'melancholy' and 'dumpish'. He found that complete asceticism was as destructive to his spiritual equilibrium as excessive worldliness. The problem was to find a moderate course between these two experiences.

The goal of Winthrop's constant self-regulation was a felt relationship with Christ. Puritans believed that grace came when one preferred heavenly to earthly treasures. Moments of spiritual illumination were rare but compelling. In 1612, for example, after comforting an old man with spiritual advice, Winthrop went to bed and dreamed that he was with Christ. 'I was so ravished with his love towards me', he writes, '. . . that being awakened it had made so deep an impression in my heart, as I was forced to unmeasurable weepings for a great while.'

Despite the experience of such periods of ecstatic acceptance, John Winthrop often felt that he was too concerned with the world. His religious life was a constant struggle to 'tame' his heart to a complete service to God. On the manor he was responsible for overseeing a complex economy, planting crops, buying and selling livestock, gathering rents and a dozen other duties. Important as these activities were, however, when he wrote about his own life or went to bed at the end of the day, his greatest concern was frequently whether his rebellious heart had indulged itself too much in the world.

We know less about Thomasine's religious life than we do about John's. But it is apparent that she, too, was a serious Christian and believed that salvation came through God's grace. John later praised her for her reverent attention to religious services at home and in church, and noted that she avoided 'all evil' herself and reproved sin in others. Undoubtedly, on many evenings after they had discussed crops, children or servants, they ended the day by praying or reading Scripture together. Together they would pursue the path of moderation.

John and Thomasine thus spent their days attending to matters temporal and spiritual. The year 1616 progressed from season to season. In the summer there were bright days interrupted occasionally by sharp storms of thunder and lightning. Then came the time to harvest and thresh the wheat. In October, grey clouds lay over the countryside, and crisp night air and geese flying overhead announced the approach of winter. The hearth with its crackling fire drew the family to it in the morning. John and Adam dragged their main pond, catching carp for dinner. In preparation for winter the family salted fish and pressed apples into cider to store in the cold cellar.

Thomasine was less active now. She spent time preparing for the new baby, making blankets and a bunting. With fewer chores she spent more time playing games with the children and helping them read. In November she had difficulty moving and sleeping comfortably. Then on Saturday, 30 November, she felt that her time had arrived. John summoned a midwife, who came to the house with several neighbour women, and encouraged Thomasine. They heated kettles of water while Thomasine bore her pains patiently, asking constantly about the child. People would later remark 'how careful she was' for the life of the baby in her travail. At last the infant was born, a tiny girl. She was washed by the women and then placed alongside her mother. John now entered the chamber and sat beside Thomasine and their new daughter. He offered prayers of thanks for the safe delivery.

That night John slept in a separate room leaving Thomasine under the watchful eye of a 'keeper', a woman who made sure that mother and child were well. On the following morning, a Sunday, John arose early and came to the room. When Thomasine awoke, he sat with her, and prayed for the continuing health of wife and daughter. After breakfast John, his parents and the other children went to church.

Later on Sunday, the child began to weaken, and on Monday morning the Winthrops' new daughter was dead. John later reported that Thomasine took the child's death with 'patience', by which he meant that she accepted the loss as God's will. In view of Thomasine's earlier concern for the child, people now 'marvelled' at her ability to accept its death.

But John had little time to think about the loss of his infant daughter, for his wife now grew ill with a violent fever and cough. The next morning these symptoms were allayed, but she was hoarse, her mouth was sore

and her throat bled. John began to fear for her life and on Wednesday sent for his cousin, a doctor.

When she heard that a physician was coming, Thomasine told John she expected to die. People were frequently not told the truth about their ailments, for fear of upsetting them, but Thomasine did not wish to be deceived.

'John,' she said, 'when cousin Duke comes, I hope that he will deal plainly with me and not fill me with vain hopes.'

Forced by his wife to acknowledge the seriousness of her condition, John began to cry.

Thomasine was moved by his concern and begged him 'to be contented', to accept her condition with patience, 'for you break my heart', she said, 'with your grievings'.

John replied: 'I can do no less when I fear to be stripped of such a blessing.'

Bedridden, seriously ill, Thomasine now sought to comfort her husband. John later recalled that 'always when she perceived me to mourn for her, she would entreat and persuade me to be contented, telling me that she did love me well, and if God would let her live with me, she would endeavour to show it more'. She urged him to pray for her and stay as near as possible.

At noon, Thursday, the doctor arrived, and after examining Thomasine he declared her condition was dangerous. When John told her this, she was 'no whit moved at it, but was as comfortably resolved whether to live or to die'. In this condition of resignation, of willingness to accept life or death from God, she fell asleep. She awakened at midnight feeling that death was near, and called to John to help her prepare. She wanted also to see two ministers and other friends and so desired 'that the bell might ring for her'. In the early morning hours the neighbours came one by one to talk by candlelight 'quietly and comfortably' with Thomasine. Then the bell began to ring. John tells us that 'some said it was the four o'clock bell, but she conceiving that they sought to conceal it from her, that it did ring for her, she said it needed not, for it did not trouble her'.

The ringing of the bell was a traditional way of telling a community that someone was critically ill. It allowed men and women in and around Groton, who already knew of Thomasine's difficulty, to visit her, or say prayers, or simply be concerned.

Certain now that she would die, Thomasine called all her family one by one to give them her final advice. Her parting words to her sisters included admonitions to serve God, marry for religious rather than worldly considerations, avoid lying and raise her children well. Then she spoke to her mother, noting that she, Thomasine, was the first child her mother would bury, and praying that she would not be 'discomforted'. Her mother, a pious woman, replied: 'I have no cause to be discomforted. You will go to a better place, and you will be with your father again.' The thought must have comforted the mother, but Thomasine, perhaps overly self-righteous now, noted that she would go to God and hence she would be with 'a better father than her earthly father'.

She then spoke to members of John's family, thanking his parents for their kindness and blessing the children. She spoke to the servants, praising some and scolding others and encouraging them to behave well and observe the Sabbath. Finally, she told the woman who had served as her keeper not to blame herself if she died.

Thomasine was still in great pain. Her breasts were so swollen that her friends cut her waistcoat to give her some relief. She uttered many prayers and exhorted those around her to prepare to die telling them they did not know 'how sharp and bitter the pangs of death were'. Reflecting on the church she asked God to 'bless good ministers, and convert such ill ones as did belong to him, and weed out the rest'.

Now it was apparent that 'God had given her victory' in her spiritual struggle. In the afternoon her pains lessened, and she told John she expected to live for another twenty-four hours. Through the afternoon and into the evening he read the Scriptures to her. Thomasine was attentive, asking John 'earnestly' to read on whenever he paused and remarking on his texts. 'This is comfortable', or 'this is a sweet Psalm', she would say.

In the evening the Rev. Sands came and prayed. Thomasine took him by the hand and bid him farewell. Then John retired leaving his wife in the care of a woman who continued to read to her into the night. Thomasine frequently asked about John; at two o'clock in the morning, he got up and came to her again.

It was now Sunday, and at times Thomasine had doubts again about her conversion, saying that the devil wanted her to cast off her 'subjection' to her husband. At noon when others were at dinner, John and Thomasine continued to talk. John assured her of Christ's love for her and told her 'how she should sup with Christ in paradise that night'. From the Groton Manor in Suffolk, England, she would actually go into the presence of Abraham, Isaac, Jacob and the other prophets, apostles and saints. This thought so encouraged Thomasine that she said 'if life were set before her she would not take it'.

Thomasine and John conversed through the afternoon. He told her that the previous day had been the first anniversary of their marriage and that now she was going to Christ who would 'embrace her with another manner of love'. She misunderstood him and replied: 'O husband, I must not love thee as Christ.'

After a while she could no longer speak, but lay back with her eyes 'steadfastly' upon John, as he spoke to her about the promises of the Gospel and the 'happy estate' she was 'entering into'. If he paused, she would signal him feebly with her hands, urging him to continue. At five o'clock on Sunday afternoon, a minister came to pray with her. At the end of the prayer she sighed and fell 'asleep in the Lord'. Three days later, she was buried beside John's first wife in Groton chancel. Her child was taken from its tiny grave and laid by her.

In the days that followed, Winthrop thought often about the course of his life. A small sin committed many years before troubled him. As a boy visiting a house, he had spied two small books. Reasoning that the owner had thrown them away, he took them with him. The memory of that act grieved him, especially in times of affliction. Now, troubled once more, he made 'satisfaction' for the books, probably by paying something to the former owner.

In January 1617, Winthrop attended a court session, usually an occasion for entertainment and frivolity as well as judicial business. This time he felt detached and was bemused by the respect paid by other men to wealth and pleasure. Later on a trip to London he noted that he used to 'lose all my time in my journeys, my eyes running upon every object, and my thoughts varying with every occasion'. But now he passed the time in prayer, Psalm singing and meditation.

In later years Winthrop would identify this period as his time of greatest piety and he felt powerfully that Christ accepted and loved him. This was not merely an intellectual conclusion, but rather a pressing conviction of Christ's presence. 'I was now grown familiar with the Lord Jesus Christ,' he wrote, 'he would oft tell me he loved me. I did not doubt to believe him. If I went abroad he went with me, when I returned he came home with me. I talked with him upon the way, he lay down with me and usually I did awake with him. Now I could go into any company and not loose him.'

Holy commonwealths:
Puritan progress in England and America

In the story of John and Thomasine Winthrop we see how Puritanism could transform daily life. The Winthrop history is on one level an account of prosaic secular events: tending an estate, governing a household, bearing a child and enduring death. It is also, however, the story of a Christian pilgrimage. Through prayer, Bible reading and meditation John and Thomasine tried to bring God into their daily lives. Perhaps they were never able to glow continually with God's love like the iron in the blacksmith's fire, described by Thomas Shepard. But they were able to view the end of life as a transformation rather than a termination. Here was the moment when the longed for union with God could become a reality.

In their daily lives and in their confrontation with death, John and Thomasine Winthrop exhibited a precept articulated by William Perkins, one of the foremost Puritan theologians of the 17th century: 'In whatsoever place thou art, whether alone or abroad, by day or by night, and whatsoever thou art doing, set thyself in the presence of God, let this persuasion always take place in thy heart, that thou art before the living god.' In the years when James I ruled England, the Puritan endeavour to live in 'the presence of God' shaped the course of life in many English households. Thousands of families like the Winthrops were willing to nourish their Puritan piety at home without concerning themselves greatly about reforming the nation as a whole. Certainly they disliked the episcopacy, the King's Book of Sports and the 'popish' elements of the church service. But Puritan ministers were generally free to preach as they wished, and in obscure parishes or areas ruled by sympathetic bishops they could even modify the service and preach without clerical vestments. Puritan families like the Winthrops could practise their piety freely, worrying far less about bishops and kings than about sinful souls.

In 1620, most Puritans probably believed that history was on their side. If they tended their own souls and gave a proper example to others, England would eventually become a Puritan nation. Their influence was already felt throughout the realm, especially in London, East Anglia, Lincolnshire, the West Riding, the Midlands and the south-west. Although Puritanism did not appeal exclusively to any class, it was particularly attractive to artisans, small merchants, lawyers and the yeomen and lower gentry of the countryside. Its emphasis on self-discipline and hard work and its suspicion of worldly pomp and power were especially congenial to middle-class Englishmen. But there were also upper-class Puritans, men like the Earl of Essex and the bishop of Lincoln who, for reasons of their own, favoured the reform movement.

These men and women had begun to make England a Puritan nation. In the later part of the 1620s, however, official resistance to their ideas became more rigid. Charles I came to the throne and with the help of William Laud, who became archbishop of Canterbury, he attempted to suppress the unruly Puritans. Laud was determined that the discipline, organization and ceremonies of the Anglican church should reflect what he called 'the beauty of holiness'.

Laud's idea of religious beauty seemed to many Englishmen to presage a return to Rome. Although

The emigration of Puritans was the result of persecution at home, of which the sentences on Prynne, Bastwick and Burton are an example. In a popular print, Archbishop Laud is shown dining on the victim's ears, cut off in the pillory.

actual Catholics in England were persecuted with an increased vigour, the government seemed determined to bring the church closer to Rome. King Charles married a French Catholic princess; England refused to assist the Protestant side in the Thirty Years' War, which began in 1618; and Laud seems to have contemplated some future union with Rome.

In doctrine, the church began leaning towards Arminianism, a belief anathema to the Puritans, which stressed the role of human ability in the process of conversion. The Puritan doctrine of predestination, the view that God alone had the power to determine who was saved, was outlawed at Oxford and Cambridge in the late 1620s. Throughout the land church altars were raised and set off from the congregations, a gesture suggesting a Catholic conception of the power of the priesthood. Laud visited many churches seeking out recalcitrant Puritans, imprisoning the Puritan bishop of Lincoln and punishing men such as William Prynne, who criticized his policies. Using the Star Chamber, the Court of High Commission and regional ecclesiastical courts, he applied the full authority of church and state to discourage dissent.

What could the Puritans do? They sought redress in Parliament, but in 1629 Charles dismissed Parliament and began to rule without it. Few Puritans were so bold as to contemplate revolution at this early date, but many now found life in England intolerable. How could one 'live in the presence of God' when Antichrist seemed to have taken control of church and state? In this seemingly hopeless situation many Puritans looked westward to where the vast lands across the Atlantic appeared to have been set aside by God as a refuge for oppressed Christians.

William Bradford and the Pilgrims were the first to go to America. Having left England in 1607 to begin a new life in Holland, they had become disenchanted a decade later with life on the continent. They could worship freely, but their children seemed likely to become more Dutch than English. The Pilgrims wanted to be both English and Puritan. Apparently the only place where they could be both was in the New World.

The decision to migrate did not come easily. The Pilgrims initially imagined America as a hostile wilderness where there were 'only savage and brutish men which range up and down'. After a difficult voyage of sixty-six days during the autumn of 1620, they arrived at Cape Cod in New England, where they 'fell upon their knees and blessed the God of Heaven'. But the voyage was only the beginning of their difficulties. Englishmen had colonized Virginia thirteen years before, but those settlements were five hundred miles away. Along the sandy shores of Massachusetts Bay they could expect, in Bradford's words, 'no friends to welcome them, nor inns to entertain or refresh their weather beaten bodies; no houses or much less towns to repair to, to seek for succour'.

During the harsh first winter in New England half the *Mayflower* colonists died. But the sixty survivors planted crops, built houses and began Puritan life in the New World. They called their infant colony Plymouth Plantation. In the winter of 1621, when the crops were in, they held a feast of thanksgiving, establishing a precedent for the annual Thanksgiving celebration that would become in the 19th century a distinctive American holiday. The Puritans themselves, however, never held regular annual feasts; they had days of thanksgiving and days of fasting too, depending on their worldly circumstances. If they had experienced good fortune they gave thanks to God. But if they encountered hardships they held fasts to acknowledge their sins. A set thanksgiving holiday would have seemed to them an empty ritual. God and not the calendar would give them their occasions for feasting.

William Bradford became governor of Plymouth Plantation, and with several hundred other colonists, who came to New England during the 1620s, he established the first permanent Puritan settlement in America. In the meantime, the political situation in England had worsened and many more Puritans began to consider migration. Among them was John Winthrop and a group of his friends, who obtained a charter in 1629 to establish the Massachusetts Bay Colony.

On 29 March 1630, Winthrop set sail in the *Arabella*, leading a fleet of seven ships and a thousand Puritan immigrants to America. The trickle of migration that had peopled Plymouth Colony had become a torrent. In the next decade more than thirty thousand Englishmen would migrate to New England. They came for many reasons, not the least being the promise of ample land.

But the leaders and most of the followers in the migration were motivated primarily by the desire to create a Puritan commonwealth in the New World. Many, like Winthrop, had to convince themselves that they were not deserting England by coming to America. They claimed that they were still Englishmen and even members of the Church of England. But they believed that in America they could establish a society so faithful to the rules of God that other men would see and imitate them. They would reform the Old World by going to the New.

In a sermon delivered at sea aboard the *Arabella* John Winthrop urged his fellow passengers to be 'knitt together in the Bond of brotherly affection'. Even as the ship bore these Puritans away from England, Winthrop assured his audience that they would not be hidden from their fellow countrymen. 'Wee must Consider', he said, 'that we shall be as a Citty upon a Hill, the eies of all people are uppon us.'

Thousands of other American Puritans shared Winthrop's vision of the holy commonwealth. During the 1630s they peopled not only Massachusetts Bay, but established other colonies in Connecticut, Long Island (later a part of New York) and even the Caribbean. Through their organization of the church, the state, the town and the family, they gave their communities an indelible Puritan stamp.

For the first time in their lives, men like John Winthrop and Thomas Shepard were able actually to create religious institutions consistent with their own views of God's will. Far away from the interference of bishops, the Puritans founded Congregational churches, which were established by law, virtually autonomous bodies governed by the members of each parish rather than by an episcopal hierarchy. No ornate images drew the people's attention from the Word of God. Instead, the church structures were plain wood buildings, known sometimes as 'the Lord's Barns'. All the citizens were expected to attend church on the Sabbath, but only a small group of what the Puritans called saints were allowed to take communion and vote in church affairs. The saints were men and women who could demonstrate not only that they had learned the principal Christian doctrines, but also that they had experienced a work of God's grace in their own souls. Although these high admission standards left the majority of Puritans outside the circle of full membership, most New Englanders appeared to approve of the requirement, hoping eventually to meet the test.

The Puritan colonies were governed by the saints. In Massachusetts Bay Colony only full church members could vote in elections for representatives and the governor. Although the colonies were not theocracies in the strict sense of being ruled by men who were both governors and ministers, church and state did work closely together. The Puritan governments passed laws supporting the church, sanctifying the Sabbath, preventing vice and enforcing Christian charity in business. The ministers, in turn, preached sermons reminding the people of their duty to uphold their rulers. In order that educated ministers might never be lacking, Harvard College was founded in 1636.

If the Puritan church and state sought to stand in the presence of God, so too did those smaller units of Puritan society, the town and the family. In the 17th century, the typical New England village had no more than a few hundred residents, who governed themselves in town meetings attended by most of the adult males. In many villages the typical family reflected the strength and the cohesiveness of Puritan society.

In Andover, Massachusetts, for example, public records indicate that fathers exercised firm control over their children for many years after adolescence. Young men did not tend to marry until they were in their mid-twenties and young girls in their early twenties. Even after marriage young men settled on their fathers' farms, not owning land of their own until middle age. We may tend to think of frontier life as contributing to early marriage and freedom from parental control, but Puritanism, with its emphasis on the acceptance of godly discipline, apparently offset this tendency and contributed to the patriarchical quality of life in Andover and other New England villages. The Puritans had crossed an ocean to escape the discipline of Old England, but in America they quickly established an orderly orthodoxy of their own.

In the 1630s, many of the leading figures in the Puritan movement, especially among the ministers, left England. But with the 1640s and the beginning of the English Civil War the prospect of a new holy commonwealth in England itself loomed before the Puritans. In 1640 Charles I, needing funds to quell a revolt in Scotland, convened Parliament, ending eleven years of personal rule. It was soon apparent that the members of that long-slighted body were more interested in reforming England than in fighting Scotland.

Charles dissolved Parliament only to face further criticism from a newly elected Parliament. In 1641 the members of the 'Long Parliament' voted in favour of the Grand Remonstrance, a bill containing some two hundred reforms including the abolition of the courts of Star Chamber and High Commission, the extinction of the episcopal hierarchy and the recasting of the order of worship. Within a year the breach between Charles and the Puritan-dominated Parliament had resulted in Civil War. And in 1643, Parliament negotiated a military alliance with Scotland, the Solemn League and

Four scenes from the religious conflicts in England during the 1630s – from the attempt to impose uniformity of worship throughout the country, through the imprisonment and release of the three dissenters, to the departure of Queen Henrietta Maria, prelude to the Civil War.

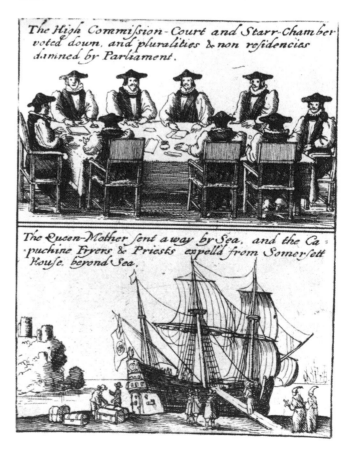

OLIVARIVS CROMWELL EXERCITVVM ANGLLÆ TENENS ET GVBERNATOR HIBERNIÆ OXO REIPVBLICÆ DVX GENERALIS. LOCVM-NIENSIS ACADEMIÆ CANCELLARIVS.

Oliver Cromwell, the Puritan man of action, came to the fore during the war and was soon the most powerful man in England. Cromwell's piety was stern and realistic, the New Testament combined with law and order. The more extreme forms of Utopianism received no sympathy from him, and what might have been a time of revolutionary social and religious experiment was subdued into merely another kind of conformity.

Covenant, promising to refashion the church in England following the example of 'the best reformed churches' and the Word of God.

In the turbulent years that followed, Puritans would come to govern all of England. But first they must create and govern an army. Under the influence of its foremost leader, Oliver Cromwell, the Puritan forces became not merely the agent of change, but also its embodiment. Within the army itself the Puritan ideal of standing, in William Perkins's phrase, 'before the living God' became a principle of martial discipline.

Cromwell was eminently suited to emerge as foremost spokesman of the Puritan revolution. Like John Winthrop he may be described as a 'typical Puritan'. He was the son of a country gentleman who had acquired his estate through the dissolution of the monasteries. As a young man, Cromwell endured a

long period of self-doubt – almost a prerequisite for Puritan sainthood – and considered himself 'the chief of sinners'. When he was about thirty, however, he felt that God had forgiven his sins and accepted him as one of his own chosen people.

Cromwell was soon active in the Puritan movement. In 1628 he argued in Parliament against the episcopacy and the prayerbook. He favoured a preaching clergy and gave money to support Puritan lecturers who operated on the fringes of the established church. As a member of the Long Parliament he favoured the Grand Remonstrance and later implied that he might have joined the migration to America had it not passed.

He began his service in the Puritan, or 'Roundhead', army as a minor cavalry officer. But he soon created a notable force that tipped the balance for Parliament in several battles. His cavalry was a remarkable combination of religious zeal and military efficiency. Cromwell believed the army should put into practice in its own ranks the Puritan discipline for which it fought. Accordingly he fined soldiers who swore and imprisoned those who drank excessively. He urged Parliament to dismiss officers whom he considered profane and favoured the promotion of honest devoted Puritans, preferring 'a plain russet-coated captain that knows what he fights for and loves what he knows' to a gentleman who lacked enthusiasm for the cause.

When in 1649 Parliament had prevailed over the Royalists and executed Charles I, Oliver Cromwell was the most powerful man in England. But the next nine years proved that it was more difficult to rule England than to defeat her former rulers. Unable to choose between supporters who favoured a republican government and those who wanted to establish a new monarchy with himself as head, Cromwell accepted the anomalous position of Lord Protector. Failing to stabilize relations with Parliament, he ruled through his major-generals.

The ideal of a holy commonwealth in England proved elusive in spite of the Puritan victory. The revolution had given heart not only to moderate Puritans, but also to thousands of men with diverse visions of the ideal society. In 1647 many of these 'masterless men', as Christopher Hill calls them, joined ranks in the Leveller Movement and attempted to win the army over to a programme of radical reform, including universal suffrage and a written constitution. They were thwarted when the officers, including Cromwell, reasserted their control of the army. But they continued to agitate for their reforms, and their spiritual heirs, the Diggers, began to establish a collection of democratic commonwealths by taking over unused lands and establishing tiny republics of their own.

These political reformers regarded the Protestant emphasis on the equality of men before God as implying equality on earth. Other reformers found additional meanings in the Protestant notion of man's proximity to God. Under the leadership of George Fox, the Quakers emerged as a new religious body, emphasizing direct and often ecstatic communion between man and God. Quakers found no need for ministers, believing that, in a congregation of the faithful, God could speak through any member. Other sects even abolished the Bible itself, regarding it as an unnecessary intrusion into the felt relationship between man and God.

Such fervent feelings of God's closeness led also to diverse forms of millenarianism, to the notion that the Lord would soon appear in history to redeem a fallen world. Fifth Monarchy Men claimed that Christ himself

The Quakers (properly the Society of Friends) and the Levellers represent equally radical attempts to create new communities. But whereas the Quakers confined their changes to the act of worship, dispensing with all forms of priesthood whatever, Levellers (below) were concerned to change society and quickly ran into opposition.

would soon rule in England. American Puritans inadvertently fed these expectations in the 1640s by beginning to convert Indians to Christianity. Many Europeans believed that the Indians were actually descendants of the Ten Lost Tribes of ancient Israel; the Bible had foretold that the conversion of the Jews would come before the millennium. Minds feverish with the expectation of God's imminent arrival could easily construe Puritan preaching in distant wigwams as an antecedent to the Lord's arrival on earth.

Cromwell sought to steer a moderate course among the various factions of religious belief. The sects all shared the Puritan longing for direct, personal communion with God. Cromwell favoured allowing many 'the liberty they fought for'. During the Protectorate, Congregationalists, Presbyterians, Quakers and even Anglicans and Catholics worshipped in some degree of liberty. Nevertheless, through the major-generals Cromwell imposed a Puritan seal on English society. By closing ale houses, suppressing cock fights and imposing other social reforms, they sought to recast English society in the sober hues of Puritan moral discipline.

Ironically, Puritanism as a political movement may be said to have brought about its own decline in both Old and New England. Many Englishmen grew weary of the extremes of authority and chaos – the rule by major-generals and the turmoil of sectaries – released by the Civil Wars. After Cromwell's death in 1658 the nation slipped almost inevitably into the frame of mind that made possible the Restoration of the Stuart monarchy in 1660 in the person of Charles II. In the New World, Puritans continued to rule in Massachusetts until 1684, when the original charter was revoked and the crown began to appoint governors for this, the

chief, Puritan colony. But even before that defeat, Puritan New England had lost much of the fervent zeal of the first generation. After Parliament had adopted toleration, it was clear that England was not going to follow Winthrop's 'Citty upon a Hill' in seeking to establish one true religion. On the personal level, fewer New Englanders were able to come before the church and describe an experience of the living God, and the churches began to adopt the 'Half Way Covenant', whereby descendants of the saints were given some church privileges even if they had not undergone conversion.

Such changes suggest that the Puritan impact on society may have been short lived. Indeed, William Goffe, a Puritan regicide, claimed as much in 1688. Writing in frontier Massachusetts, to which he had fled after the Restoration of Charles II, he lamented: 'These are dying times wherein the Lord hath been and is breaking down what he hath built and plucking up what he has planted.'

Accounts of religious demise were common but premature, for the social impact of Puritanism long outlived the short period of Puritan rule in England and America. The Puritan aspiration to conform the totality of life to the rule of God nourished enduring features of English and American life. Puritanism contributed to a propensity for sobriety and self-scrutiny that forms one strand of English and American character even today. At the same time, the expectation of the union with God encouraged the personal ecstasy of the great revivals that swept through England and America in the 18th and 19th centuries. In such ways the Puritan yearning for a more perfect union with God would continue to nourish both a temperate sense of life's frailty and a blissful appreciation of its wonder.

COUNTER~ REFORMATION EUROPE

9
Religion in the age of the Baroque

THE REFORMATION was a traumatic experience for the Catholic church. Faced with the loss of large parts of northern Europe to Protestantism, it reorganized its forces and redefined its terms, emphasizing rather than blurring the line between the two sides. Where the north valued independent judgment, the south insisted upon obedience; where the north stressed the *symbolism* of the liturgy, the south reaffirmed its sacramental *reality*; where the north pinned its hopes either on good works or on apparently arbitrary 'election' by God, the south pointed to his overflowing love available to all mankind. This whole movement, which we know as the Counter-Reformation, was one of intense practical and intellectual activity. The Council of Trent formulated doctrine and issued regulations for conduct, while new religious orders – Jesuits, Discalced Carmelites, Oratorians, Theatines – combated heresy in Europe and paganism abroad.

It was also a time of artistic activity. The Baroque style, which came into full flower towards the beginning of the 17th century, can be seen as the response to a particular set of needs. Unrestrained, passionate, vibrating with colour and movement, it is the antithesis of the quiet introspective style of the north. It was, above all, a medium for religious experience – the rapture of personal revelation, the ecstasy of communion with God, the bliss of eternal happiness. Although this entailed a degree of unreality (both St Teresa and St Ignatius, for instance, were actually tough, hard-headed administrators, but in art they are normally represented in the throes of mystical delirium), it did serve as powerful Catholic propaganda – in the original sense of *propaganda fide*, propagating the faith. Art transfigured reality, as the supernatural transfigured the natural.

Painting was not alone in being pressed into service in this way. Sculpture, architecture and even town-planning proclaimed the same message of cosmic order and Catholic supremacy. The Jesuits especially were adept at promoting religious drama, poetry and music. An element of mystical devotion was also brought to wholly utilitarian enterprises such as education, social services and scholarship. The spiritual heights that were reached during the age of the Baroque left Christianity permanently enriched.

The Virgin interceding
for the city of Naples (*opposite*), by Domenichino, is completely typical of Counter-Reformation imagery in its combination of hard allegorical message with direct assault on the emotions. Bottom left, an elderly canon holds a reliquary. Behind him, Prayer, face upraised, appeals to heaven on behalf of Naples. At the top, her intercession is reinforced by the Virgin, who pleads before Christ. On the right, the prostrate bodies of Luther and Calvin are being trampled on by an angel bearing the banner of the Immaculate Conception. (1)

LVTER   CAL

Christian charity

To both Catholic and Protestant, the exercise of charity was not merely a social duty – it was a way of approaching more nearly to Christ. The Baroque age is marked by an increase in the number of charitable foundations and by a more dedicated, more specifically religious approach to the problem of poverty.

The sisters of Charity, founded by St Vincent de Paul about 1620, typify the sense of mission that the 17th century brought to poor relief. In this scene (*left*), painted after he was canonized in 1737, 'Monsieur Vincent' is seen receiving the rings and necklaces of Parisian ladies, while in the foreground the sisters take in foundlings abandoned in the streets of the city. (2)

St Elizabeth distributing her jewels to the poor (*opposite*). St Elizabeth was a Hungarian princess of the 13th century, who after the death of her husband devoted her whole life to helping the sick and needy. Popular throughout the Middle Ages, her cult gained momentum in the 17th century, when she was regarded as the patron saint of charitable foundations. In a rather schematized painting by Master Pepin of Antwerp she is seen handing out gifts from a well stocked treasury. Realism comes in, however, in the depiction of the crowd, where anger, greed and jealousy seem to outweigh gratitude. (4)

In the north charity was less involved with the church, but was equally based on piety. Nikolaus Elias's painting (*left*) of four governors and the secretary of a workhouse in 1628 catches the sense of civic satisfaction that went with good works in the Protestant Netherlands. (3)

'So long as you did it for one of these, the least of my brethren, you did it for me.' The passage in St Matthew, from which the seven Acts of Mercy are taken, emphasizes the parallel between charity and the example of Christ. *Right :* two typical panels by a Dutch 17th-century painter, Michiel Sweerts: *Visiting the Sick* and *Clothing the Naked*. (5, 6)

The Eucharist, or Holy Communion, is the central rite of the Catholic church and of many Protestant ones. But whereas most Protestants regard it merely as a symbolic act of remembrance, Catholics believe that the bread and the wine literally *become* the body and blood of Christ.

◁ **The consecrated bread,** the host (*hostia*, victim), is surrounded by liturgical ceremonies that underline and express its miraculous nature. Placed in a transparent monstrance (from *monstrare*, to show), it was exhibited to the faithful and, on exceptional occasions, administered to a communicant. In this detail (*left*) from a painting by the Spaniard Coello it is about to be given to Charles II of Spain. (7)

Souls in Purgatory (*above*) can hope for release only through Christ's blood, represented as flowing from the chalice of wine and the consecrated wafer. Or in more theological language: the sins of men always outweigh their merits; the merits of Christ, however, are infinite, and it is by his sacrifice that men are saved. (8)

The body of Christ

A silver monstrance from Holland (*left*) surrounds the wafer with angels and other symbols of holiness. The Roman imperial crown at the top is an instance of that close association between empire and papacy which was part of Counter-Reformation policy. (9)

The spiritual nourishment afforded by the Eucharist finds a symbol in the fruits of the earth. In this striking image by Jan de Heem, 1648, the chalice is flanked by overflowing cornucopia – food for the body standing for food for the soul. (10)

The missionary church

China and India were among the countries where Jesuit missionaries followed hard upon the explorers' heels. Alone among a vast, unsympathetic population, their success depended upon persuasion, argument and tact. Matteo Ricci and Paolo Magno (*above*) adopted a completely Chinese way of life, bridging the gap between cultures rather than crudely attempting to impose their own. In Goa (*below*) the altar of St Ignatius shows that the seeds planted in the 17th century continue to bear fruit. (12, 13)

Ignatius of Loyola founded his Society of Jesus, the Jesuits, in 1540, at first simply as a body of totally dedicated men for the pope to employ as he thought fit. Exactly answering to the needs of the time, it quickly became one of the most powerful forces in Christendom. Through intellectual energy and practical shrewdness it came to dominate the universities, schools and courts of Catholic Europe; through unstinting labour it won the loyalty of the poor; through courage and sacrifice it spread the faith to parts of the world whose very existence had until then been barely realized. (11)

In Mexico conquest by Spain had been followed by the mass conversion of the people by Dominicans and Franciscans. By a curious paradox, their ruthless rejection of all compromise with local tradition gave them a ferocity that can itself seem faintly Aztec. *Left:* bone carving of St Dominic holding a skull. (14)

A Chinese bishop carved in ivory about 1700 in Canton (*right*) has an elegance that brings it closer to Manchu art than to European Rococo. (16)

Among the Incas of Peru, Christianity was again an imposed religion. *Below:* a Corpus Christi procession in Cuzco about 1660. Corpus Christi – the Body of Christ was one of those feasts that acquired new, more emotional overtones in the age of Baroque. (15)

9
Religion in the age of the Baroque

JUDITH HOOK

THE ONE UNIVERSALLY FAMILIAR ASPECT of the religious history of the 16th century is that this was the age of the Reformation: a period of crisis in which every established Christian tradition and convention was called into question, when the western church was rent in half by the schism between Protestant and Catholic, and all authority in both church and state was challenged. However, while in Protestant Europe this crisis continued unabated until at least the end of the 17th century, by 1600 the Catholic church appeared to have emerged from its crisis, stronger than ever before. As a result of the Council of Trent it was possessed of a series of theological definitions which, on a number of crucial issues, were more precise than any had been in the past; the authority of the episcopate had been reasserted; the rule of the papacy immeasurably strengthened, and new creative forces released in the church.

Notable practical successes had accompanied these changes. A church which, in the 1520s and 1530s, had everywhere appeared on the defensive now effectively moved to the offensive. Italy had been totally recovered for Catholicism, as had large areas of Switzerland, southern Germany, France and Poland. The Treaty of Westphalia of 1648 had marked the end of Protestant progress in Europe and a general acceptance of the Catholic reconquests. Meanwhile, mainly through the activities of Jesuit missionaries, Christianity had been spread to new areas of the globe: the New World, India, Japan and even China.

Yet this picture of the Counter-Reformation triumphant, of a church assured in its position and daily making progress and new converts, masks a reality

which was as true of Catholic as it was of Protestant Europe in the 17th century. The Reformation, whether in its Catholic or its Protestant guise, had apparently failed to bring permanent enrichment to the spiritual life of Europe. For this reason, the key-note of the spiritual and so of the cultural life of Europe at the end of the 16th and the beginning of the 17th century was one not of assurance but of perplexity of spirit.

Religion, whether Catholic or Protestant, taught men that truth was a divine unity. Yet actual experience suggested that life was not ordered and united but disordered and fractured. In addition, as a result of intellectual advances, which the churches might try to curb, but which ultimately they could not control, the intellectual certainty of religion had disappeared for ever. Throughout Europe, scholars of all persuasions were increasingly led to the conclusion that, whatever the churches might continue to preach, reason and observation would never be able to offer final substantiation of divine truths. These, by their very nature, lay beyond reason and could only be discovered through faith and by revelation. John Locke, for instance, was to advance this argument from the Protestant viewpoint, claiming that reason could prove no more than the existence of God, and that all the rest of Christian belief came by revelation. From the Catholic viewpoint, Pascal was to argue that Christian truth was a denial of reason and that Christians should rejoice in its very irrationality.

An intellectual revolution

Such a view represented a major revolution in European thought, for all previous ages had assumed a unity of knowledge. Theology was regarded as the 'Queen of Sciences' because it was assumed that knowledge of the natural and supernatural worlds was co-extensive, that metaphysics was really but a superior and more advanced branch of physics. Now, for the first time, religion and science parted company, their divorce being aptly symbolized when the founding members of England's Royal Society specifically ruled that religion might not be discussed at their meetings.

The consequences of this intellectual revolution for the cultural history of Europe were manifold. One result, undoubtedly, was an increased emphasis on the

---

The Jesuit churches that sprang up all over Europe in the late 17th and early 18th century bear witness both to the speed with which the Society expanded and to the wealth that it could command. They were especially prominent in lands where Catholic and Protestant territory met, like the bridgeheads of an invading army. That at Antwerp lay almost on the border of the United Provinces. This interior view by Sebastian Vrancx shows it attended mostly by fashionable people and with a mass in progress. Above the altar is Rubens's famous painting of the *Miracle of St Ignatius* (now in Vienna) with the saint casting out devils. (17)

Bernini's masterpiece, a vast quadruple file of columns lining the piazza of St Peter's, was constructed (shown above) during the reign of Alexander VII (1655–67). Man's view of the divine is reflected in its order and symmetry.

assertion of truth. Such assertions are to be found on both sides of the religious divide but are particularly obvious in Catholic Europe. Here, the Protestant challenge was constantly met by the assertion of dogma as divinely revealed truth, as for instance, in the superb painting by Il Domenichino which shows Calvin and Luther being trampled underfoot by Catholic truth. At the same time, Catholic believers were also bombarded with heroic models who bore witness to the truths of Catholicism: exemplars of the glory of martyrdom, like St Lawrence; of repentance, like St Mary Magdalene – Crashaw's 'pretious prodigall'; of mystical union with God, like St Theresa of Avila.

Since divine order, truth and unity could not be proved, but could be asserted and reasserted in men's surroundings, and in the patterns of daily life, the external appearance of things became of paramount importance. In the words of the Spanish Jesuit, Gracian, writing in 1647: 'Things do not pass for what they are but for what they seem.'

Thus a beautiful and richly decorated church was not, as it might appear to Protestant eyes, a denial of charity and true religion, but a celebration of divine truth, because, as the Jesuit General John Paul Oliva explained:

In our churches, both Ignatius our father, and all of us, who are his sons, try to reach up to the sublimity of God's eternal omnipotence with such appurtenances of glory as we can [to the best of our powers] achieve.

A fine façade, in other words, was not merely a fine façade, but actual evidence of divine order and perfection. In such a world-view, symbolism obviously acquired a new importance. A cupola on a church was not merely an aesthetic delight but a statement about the nature of the universe, for its perfect geometrical form symbolized the idea of God. So, throughout this period, beginning with the completion in 1590 of Michelangelo's dome of St Peter's, cupolas were built on new churches or added to old ones, and from Rome the fashion spread rapidly not only in Catholic but also in Protestant Europe. Even in France, where classical impulses always remained strong, we find the same delight in the cupola, beginning with Lemercier's

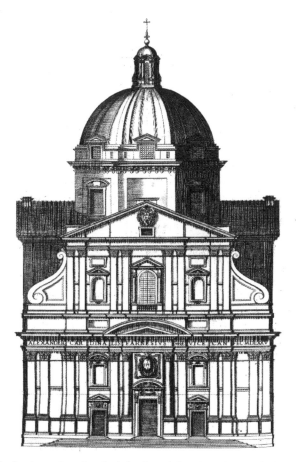

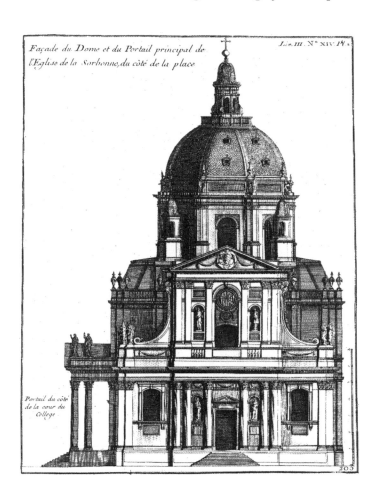

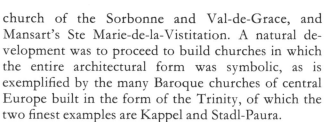

The Jesuit mother-church of the Gesù (above), with its splendid façade and great dome, was the prototype of the large congregational churches built in Rome during the Counter-Reformation. It set the style for Jesuit churches world-wide, and is echoed in the church of the Sorbonne (right) in Paris.

church of the Sorbonne and Val-de-Grace, and Mansart's Ste Marie-de-la-Visitation. A natural development was to proceed to build churches in which the entire architectural form was symbolic, as is exemplified by the many Baroque churches of central Europe built in the form of the Trinity, of which the two finest examples are Kappel and Stadl-Paura.

The second consequence of these intellectual changes was the restoration of emotion to religion, for, if the mind was inadequate to discover divine truth, this was not true of the heart which, it was believed, was capable of discovering and understanding all things in faith. Thus, Pascal argues: 'We come to know truth not only by reason, but still more through our hearts.' In line with such a view, spirituality had to be centred on the heart and sustained by a constantly renewed love. 'All is love,' said St Francis de Sales, 'in love and of love in Holy Church.' Single-mindedness of purpose and total self-commitment, born out of passionate love, became the distinguishing features of Baroque Christianity, whether manifested in the English Quaker Movement or in the Spanish Corpus Christi plays – the

autos sacramentales – of which Calderon de la Barca (1660–81) was the greatest exponent. His *El gran teatro del mundo*, published in 1655, is one of the most important of all texts for an understanding of Baroque sensibility, because it argues that religion, essentially, is not a matter for the intellect to understand but rather a mystery to be celebrated. In other words, in a world of unresolved mental paradoxes which teased the intellect, religion could be seen as resolving those paradoxes by asserting as a fact that paradox is truth.

The acceptance of this reality – that religion is, ultimately, something beyond reason – seems to have led, in turn, to a revival of mysticism and to the positive celebration of spiritual ecstasy that is so marked a feature of the religion of the later 16th and the 17th century. The value of the mystical experience was asserted most creatively in the Spain of St Theresa of Avila and St John of the Cross in the 16th century and in the France of the great Jesuit, Louis Lallemand (1588–1635) and the Carmelite, Jean de Saint-Samson (1571–1636). Mysticism was devalued when it degenerated into Quietism, that most distinctively 17th-

227

century movement, fathered by the Spanish priest Miguel de Molinos, who arrived in Rome in 1664. His *Guida Spirituale*, published in 1675, was an immediate best-seller but was, nonetheless, essentially a decadent book. With its emphasis on passive contemplation rather than active meditation, it lacked all the fervour and directness, and the common sense, of the works of the great mystics, and offered little more than an escapist form of devotion that could be practised at will. Nevertheless, the influence of the *Guida Spirituale* was very widespread indeed, and Quietism was therefore one of the most significant developments of Christian piety in the later 17th century, affecting both the Catholic and the Protestant worlds.

The new Rome

All these changes in religion and the religious life contributed to the most important cultural development of the 17th century: the reshaping of Rome as a Baroque city. For Rome was the cradle of Baroque art and there can be little doubt that the new Baroque style that developed there reflected a new kind of Catholicism. It is indeed for this reason that Baroque art is frequently, if erroneously, seen as Counter-Reformation art. The new values that were reflected in the new style should not, in fact, be confused with Counter-Reformation values, although some of the impulses that produced Baroque art can be traced back to the early 16th century. But the true Counter-Reformation popes and churchmen, with their intensely austere attitudes, would have been scandalized by the outpourings of sensuality, which are part of the essence of the work of such artists as Bernini and Borromini. The Christianity reflected in Baroque art was much more than a simple product of the Counter-Reformation; it was something new and different. It was human-orientated, taking as its starting-point the statement of St Francis de Sales: 'I am so much a man that I can be nothing else.' Although its basis was the individual, its emphasis was on universalism and uniformity, on the welding together of all Christian peoples to live in charity under the discipline and teaching of one standardized doctrine. Every aspiration was towards some all-embracing unity which is why Leibniz (1646–1716), who envisaged humanity as a whole with identical needs and desires, is the essential philosopher of the Baroque age.

Universalism and unity were desired. Disruption, disorder, disunity too often appeared the reality. Christendom was no more united in the 17th than it had been in the 16th century. Europe continued to be rent by warfare, and by warfare that in the first half of the century continued to have a religious dimension. Men still disagreed violently about fundamentals and persecuted each other because they disagreed. Faith and reason seemed often in disharmony. Yet, unity might still be asserted and the assertion might take the form of a new Rome, which, in the words of Pius V, would become 'a common country of all Christian peoples'.

The successful shaping of that new Rome was totally dependent on the fact that, in its creation, patron and artist shared a common vision. The leading patrons were all popes, cardinals or other high-ranking ecclesiastics, deeply imbued with both the political and the spiritual values of the new Catholicism and anxious that those values should be publicly exhibited. Many of the leading patrons were, in addition, bound even closer together by the common bond of exposure to Jesuit influence. It was, for instance, because he had been at a Jesuit school that Cardinal Ludovisi decided to build the order a new church in Rome in 1626, to be dedicated to St Ignatius and to be 'second to none for size and beauty'. Urban VIII, one of the chief creators of Baroque Rome, had also been educated by the Jesuits.

The architects and artists employed in the creation of the new Rome were supremely successful in interpreting the desires of such patrons simply because, for the most part, they shared their visions and their assumptions. They were men who not only thought deeply about religion but were actively involved in the spiritual life of Rome. Guercino, for instance, assisted at mass every day, and spent an hour in prayer before beginning work. Bernini was a man of deep religious commitment, who read a chapter from *The Imitation of Christ* daily. He was also a great admirer of the Jesuits and counted their General among his closest friends. While in France, he made a point of visiting Jesuit churches and spoke frequently of his sympathy with that order's ideals. It is totally consistent with his spiritual attitudes, therefore, that he should have refused any payment for the work he undertook for the Jesuits at S. Andrea al Quirinale, preferring to see that work not as an ordinary commission but as an opportunity to demonstrate the glory of God to the world. In all that he undertook, this remained Bernini's constant aim. For him, the truth of the unified vision of the world, which, as we have seen, lay at the heart of Baroque Christianity, was never in doubt, and each of his artistic undertakings was, in one way or another, an expression of his unified view of life. Beauty, for Bernini, lay only in unity and it was for this reason that he specifically rejected the legend that Zeuxis had made a Venus by combining the best parts of beautiful women, on the grounds that this was a denial of unity: the beautiful eyes of one woman could not, with sense or honesty, be joined to the beautiful face of another.

Caravaggio similarly shared the spiritual and cultural

Emphasizing the mystical aspect of St Theresa of Avila, Bernini's drawing, a study for the figure in S. Maria della Vittoria, captures the saint in the moment of visionary ecstasy that was mentioned prominently in her canonization. St Theresa joined the Carmelites at the age of eighteen, but in 1554 the experience of her first trance and direct communion with Jesus led her to found a new order. She devoted the rest of her life to opening new convents and organizing the order.

assumptions of his major ecclesiastical patrons. His belief that revelation was a natural experience that could be enjoyed at any human level was totally in accord with the spiritual values of his age. And his belief in a religion of and for the people, expressed throughout his paintings, although it shocked many of his contemporaries and not least those on whose behalf he claimed to speak, was in accord with all that was best in 17th-century Christian thinking.

The works of Baroque artists in Rome also manifested another important concept, which had been specifically reaffirmed by the Council of Trent. This was the view that the universe, and so, of course, the world, was essentially hierarchical. The increasing emphasis on such a world-view, boldly asserted on the painted domes of so many Baroque churches with their tantalizing glimpses into a divinely ordered heaven, was not only the main attraction of Catholicism to secular governments, but also the explanation of the success of a church that actively preached the value of authority and obedience, rather than sharing the Protestant bias towards freedom and individualism. This is not, of course, to suggest that the values of hierarchy and order were not understood in a Protestant world where, indeed, the vast majority held quite literally to the doctrine of Romans XIII:2: 'Whosoever resisteth the power, resisteth the ordinance of God: and they that resist shall receive to themselves damnation.'

But the whole tendency of Protestant thought, with its doctrine of the priesthood of all believers, was towards the value of independent judgment in political as well as in spiritual matters, and it was Catholic preachers, artists and writers who therefore proved the more satisfactory in depicting kingship as the embodiment on earth of divine order, and kings as answerable only to God for their deeds, since it was from God not man that they drew their authority. The archbishop of Vienne was able to tell Henri IV that his crown was 'the living image on earth of the eternal government which is in heaven', and Bossuet would argue:

A king's throne is not the throne of a man, but the throne of God Himself. . . . Royal power is sacred: God raises up kings as his ministers and reigns through them over nations. . . . Obedience to princes is therefore an obligation of religion and conscience. . . . An inherent holiness exists in the character of a king and no crime can efface it.'

The celebration of obedience

Thus it was the Catholic preachers who reiterated the value of obedience, which they portrayed as one of the chief Christian virtues. The celebration of obedience lay, indeed, at the heart of the new Catholicism, one of whose founding members, St Theresa of Avila, had, like her fellow Spaniard, St John of the Cross, come to believe that the soul's highest realization came not through ecstasy and the mystic experience but through total obedience, or the habitual conformity of the individual will to the divine will. And a doctrine of obedience also permeated the ethos of the Society of Jesus, whose members were the most important propagandists of the new-style Catholicism of the late 16th and the 17th century. Such an emphasis on hierarchy and obedience helps to explain why, to a struggling Catholic power, anxious to reassert its authority in the secular sphere, it might appear more useful to spend money on the restoration of a church or the building of a monastery than on increased military preparedness. This, at any rate, was the view of Alessandro Farnese, Governor-General of the Netherlands, who, in 1580, wrote to advise Philip II: 'Your Majesty desired me to build a citadel at Maastricht. I thought that a college of the Jesuits would be more likely to protect the inhabitants. . . . I have built it.'

Whether or not it was solely a question of the primacy given to the doctrine of obedience, there can be no doubt that the restoration of Catholicism tended to go hand in hand with the development of absolutism. Thus, for instance, the Treaty of Westphalia of 1648 led, in central Europe, to the effective restoration both of the secular ruler and of the church as an institution. Church and state worked together to bolster and reinforce each other's authority. While the church actively taught that the emperor was God's representative on earth, and that total obedience to his commands was divinely ordained, the state, for its part, reinstated the prince-bishops, restored church lands, re-established the old religious orders and encouraged new ones.

In France, also, the development of absolutism went hand in hand with the aggrandizement of the Catholic church, culminating in the Revocation of the Edict of Nantes in 1685. Here, the alliance between the secular authorities and the church was even personalized in the two cardinal-ministers, Richelieu and Mazarin. It is significant that both of these ministers paid considerable attention to the spread of Catholicism in France and to the regaining of Huguenot areas. Richelieu, for instance, did not merely destroy Huguenot political power at La Rochelle, but gave positive assistance to those who tried to further Catholicism within France.

He was always a great supporter of schemes to bring religion to the French people, and in 1638 even drew up an elaborate plan for the complete re-evangelization of the country; every year a number of missions would be preached in various districts, according to a predetermined scheme. Although nothing came of this project, Richelieu always remained a great supporter of the Congregation of the Priests of the Missions, to which he left a large legacy, and also always favoured any scheme aimed at improving the quality of the priesthood. A similar enthusiasm for such schemes is to be found, significantly enough, in Louis XIII, Anne of Austria and, of course, in Cardinal Mazarin.

Such alliances between the secular authorities and the church, in turn, facilitated the reconversion and, in certain areas, the first evangelization of many thousands of people. The main agent of this remarkable process was the greatest of the new orders founded in the course of the 16th and 17th centuries – the Society of Jesus. While it is indubitably true that the Jesuits aimed at gaining control of the minds and policies of the Catholic ruling class of Europe, their purpose in doing so was to further more universal ends. It is a popular misconception that the Jesuits were only interested in an intellectual and social elite. On the contrary, their mission was always to all men and they were among the first in European society to recognize what the real spiritual needs of Europe were in the late 16th and the 17th century. Most typical of their order were not the famous Jesuit confessors of princes, but fathers like St François Regis (1597–1640), who when still very young had determined to dedicate his life to the poor because they were 'the most neglected part of the flock of Christ'; St Francesco di Geronimo (1642–1715), who worked in the slums of Naples rescuing fallen women and preaching to prisoners and galley slaves; or St Peter Claver (1580–1654), who laboured for forty years in the slave-ships which transported Africans to South America. The many Jesuits who were martyred in the mission field are remembered and honoured. Less well known, though deserving of equal honour, are the many more who gave their lives labouring with the plague-ridden poor of Europe in the 17th and 18th centuries; 80 in the province of Lyons between 1628 and 1630, for instance; 77 in Andalusia in 1649; 59 at Naples in 1656; and 150 in Lithuania and Poland between 1708 and 1710.

Missions to the poor

Initially, neither Protestantism nor Tridentine Catholicism, which were urban-based, was a movement of the people; both were spiritually elitist. It was only in the 17th century that religion was restored to the people. Thus, the great Christian success story of the 17th

S. FRANCO SOLANO

Popular art often portrayed the activities of missionaries abroad. Here, St Francis Solano is shown in an 18th-century woodcut from Spain, baptizing the natives in the Americas.

The growth of the church in Japan produced a terrible counter-reaction, and proscription of Christianity in 1614 resulted in the torture and crucifixion of many missionaries, both Jesuit and, shown here, Franciscan, as well as many Japanese Christians. Crucifixion had not been known in Japan until this time and it is ironic that it should have been suggested by the Passion of Christ.

century must be the evangelization of the working classes of Europe together with the conversion of thousands of non-Europeans. The evangelization of the people became the first concern of Catholic and Protestant alike. The process itself was in a sense facilitated by the contemporary splitting apart of reason and faith. Thus, John Locke saw in his conclusion that the only dogma necessary to salvation was that Jesus was the son of God, a manifestation of God's mercy, since by it:

God seems to have consulted the poor of this world and the bulk of mankind. These are articles which the labouring and illiterate man may comprehend. This is a religion suited to vulgar capacities and the state of mankind destined in this world to travail and labour.

Though both the Catholic and the Protestant churches alike directed their attention to the problem of the religious education of the people, in the long run the Catholics seem to have been more successful in establishing a genuinely popular base. From the very beginning of the Counter-Reformation, the desire to bring Christianity to all men had become a central tenet of the Catholic faith. St Philip Neri's Oratory in Rome, one of the characteristic expressions of the early period of the Catholic revival, had, indeed, taken its origin from this impulse. The Oratory simply institutionalized what had previously been informal meetings between pious laymen who met together to preach and teach and pray and whose spirit was, essentially, democratic. Elsewhere, throughout the urban centres of Europe, countless other newly founded or revitalized religious confraternities served the same purpose of bringing living Christianity to the common man.

Meanwhile, the rural areas were being won by a series of missions. In France, for instance, St Vincent de Paul spent much of his life evangelizing the French peasantry; he established the Congregation of the Priests of the Missions – priests without parochial or other ties – who were sent out into the French countryside to preach to those 'who are almost abandoned, while the towns have a large number of doctors and religious to attend to their spiritual needs'. The lack of concern shown by the spiritual authorities for the condition of the French peasantry also inspired St John Eudes, the apostle of Normandy, who asked: 'What are so many doctors and learned men doing in Paris while souls are perishing in their thousands?' Eudes founded the Society of Jesus and Mary, which was dedicated to missionary work and the education of priests. Although some of the most spectacular missionary work of the century was thus undertaken in France, the problem of the peasantry was a universal one, as was recognized by Urban VIII in 1633 in his bull *Salvatori Nostri*, and the idea of the mission spread rapidly from France to the other Catholic countries.

The Society of Jesus

In these missions, the Jesuits naturally played a prominent part, for throughout the 17th century it was the Society of Jesus that proved pre-eminently suited to the task of reaching out to all men and women and making Christianity a living reality for them. Whereas the aim of many Protestant reformers often seemed to be to change the very nature of man, and to create a community of saints in this world, the Jesuits, by contrast, accepted man as he was – a fallen creature – and worked within this framework. Their intense humanism, which we have seen to be so characteristic of Catholicism at this stage in its history, engendered in the Jesuit fathers attitudes of versatility, adaptability, forbearance and compromise. On occasion, as Pascal suggested, when he accused the Jesuits of 'putting cushions under the elbows of sinners' and of making Christianity 'indulgent and accommodating', this standpoint even led them into positions that, to say the least, were morally dubious when seen in the light of Christian tradition. Their casuistry and abuse of the confessional did tend to make it appear as if for them

any conduct was permissible provided that a Christian attended mass regularly, and subscribed to orthodox doctrine; and many immoral actions were excused on the grounds suggested by the Jesuit theologian, Escobar, that 'Purity of intention may be justification for acts contrary to the moral code and the human law.'

In many ways there can be no doubt that the aim of the Jesuits was always to make things easier. But it was to fallen man, after all, that they addressed themselves. Thus, they did not seek to deny sensuality but made use of it to the greater glory of God. Such an attitude was, indeed, inherent in the origins of their order, for the major work of their founder, St Ignatius Loyola – *The Spiritual Exercises* – is a work that deliberately makes every possible use of a man's senses in order to create for him a vivid, personal and intimate spiritual experience. It was thus a work entirely in sympathy with that Baroque sensibility with which the Jesuit order in the 17th century is inevitably associated. It was in the same spirit that Father Louis Richeome (1544–1625) used to teach the Jesuit novices at S. Andrea al Quirinale in Rome to lift their minds to God by means of everything they saw, in their church, in the refectory, the corridors or the infirmary, using pictures, decorations, plants and even garden tools to direct their minds to God.

If, therefore, men and women enjoyed pomp, pageantry and splendour, the Jesuits would employ pomp, pageantry and splendour to direct the attention heavenwards. No better example of this exists than the Jesuit mother-church of the Gesù, and, in particular, Gaulli's spectacular *Celebration of the Name of Jesus*, in which every possible device of artistic persuasion is employed to convince the spectator that he is directly experiencing a vision of heaven. If men and women enjoyed the drama, then, unlike the Protestant saints, the Jesuits would not seek to close the theatres, but would, instead, write and produce dramas of their own that celebrated sacred themes. Indeed, the whole history of Jesuit interest in the drama provides an instructive illustration of their order's flexible attitudes. It was, in fact, an interest that developed very early for it arose naturally as the fathers discovered the need to provide for the students in their colleges some superior form of entertainment as an attractive alternative to the

Typically Baroque in spirit and in symbol, the 'Imago Primi Saeculi' was a volume published in Antwerp in 1640 to celebrate the centenary of the founding of the Society of Jesus. Holding a flaming cross and crushing Time underfoot, this image of the society on the title page would doubtless have shocked St Ignatius. The allegorical shields down the sides glorify the Society's achievements throughout the world.

IMAGO
PRIMI SÆCVLI
SOCIETATIS
IESV
A
PROVINCIA
FLANDRO-BELGICA
EIVSDEM SOCIETATIS
REPRÆSENTATA.

ANTVERPIÆ
EX OFFICINA
PLANTINIANA
BALTHASARIS MORETI,
ANNO SOCIETATIS SÆCVLARI
M. DC. XL.

seductive, and worldly, delights of carnival. For this reason the students at the Collegio Germanico in Rome were first permitted to perform sacred dramas in the 1560s and they were soon followed by the students at the Collegio Romano. What was born of necessity was then improved and developed to become a sophisticated tool of instruction and indoctrination, and the sacred dramas were soon introduced into Jesuit colleges throughout Austria, Germany, France and Spain, everywhere adapting certain basic themes to the demands of prevailing local dramatic traditions.

The same qualities of adaptability were what made the Jesuits so eminently successful in the overseas missions. This aspect of the work of the Society of Jesus is perhaps the best known of their activities in the 17th and 18th centuries. Certainly, the missionary impulse was always very strong within the order. Letters flooded into Rome from Jesuits in the provinces imploring the General to send them to work among the heathen and it was overseas that many of the greatest successes of the Jesuits were achieved. These successes again depended, essentially, on the tact which the Jesuits always showed in preserving native art and culture. It is interesting, for instance, to compare the relative success of the Dominicans and Franciscans with that of the Jesuits in their respective missions in China. There the older orders largely failed because, bent on a total evangelization of the native population, they would admit of no compromise with local traditions. By contrast, one of the first of the Jesuit missionaries, Matteo Ricci, always dressed in Chinese fashion, made himself totally familiar with Chinese patterns of thought and devoted his life to trying to bridge the gap between Confucianism and Christianity. Similarly, Roberto de'Nobili, who followed St Francis Xavier to India, adopted the dress of a typical Indian ascetic; he became an expert in Indian culture and made himself agreeable to the many Brahmins he converted by persuading them that Christianity was but a more perfect form of the Hinduism they already practised.

By such means the Jesuits made themselves the most successful spiritual force of the Baroque age and won the great wealth and power for which future centuries would condemn them. Cardinal Ludovico Ludovisi once confessed that the great admiration he had for the Jesuits stemmed from the 'power and authority that they have over nearly all princes', and it is certainly true that as confessors they enjoyed the ear of virtually every Catholic ruler. It is equally true that the education of the ruling elite of Catholic Europe became a virtual Jesuit monopoly. Jesuit colleges, seminaries and universities provided an ideal Catholic education throughout the world, and nowhere more significantly

than in central Europe. Here the Jesuit schools played a particularly vital role in the reawakening of the Catholic faith and their value was recognized by the secular rulers who financed them.

So successful were the Jesuits that their cultural influence became all-pervasive. Not only in Europe but in Mexico, Goa, Peru and the Philippines there rose, in imitation of the Gesù, churches which are immediately recognizable as Jesuit churches, with their imposing façades and spacious interiors, designed to aid audibility, and to direct the attention of the viewer to the high altar. The Jesuit cult of martyrdom for the sake of the faith, illustrated at its most gruesome in a series of narrative frescoes for the English college at Rome, was inspiring enough for that cult to become a dominant theme in European literature, producing at least one masterpiece in Corneille's *Polyeucte*. The great Jesuit theologians and thinkers, Molinas, Bellarmine, Suarez and Gracian, determined the intellectual patterns of Catholic Europe for more than a century while *The Spiritual Exercises* established the new patterns of personal devotion which developed in the 17th century.

Spiritual exercises

Such new forms of religious devotion were a marked aspect of the new Catholic sensibility. Their central feature was, without doubt, the new emphasis on the Eucharist, which the Council of Trent had restored to its position as the primary act of worship. Particularly striking is the new value given to frequent communion. This aspect of religious practice is the one that most clearly marks the divide between the medieval and the modern world; in the Middle Ages it was entirely normal to communicate only once a year at Easter; but from the 16th century onwards it became equally normal to communicate weekly or even, in many cases, daily. The new devotion to the Eucharist was reflected in the countless confraternities, founded in the course of the century, which were dedicated to the Blessed Sacrament; in the Benedictine nuns of the Holy Sacrament, approved by the pope in 1661, who passed their entire lives in adoration before the reserved host; and in the vast number of paintings, such as Domenichino's *Last Communion of St Jerome*, which focus attention on the Eucharist.

The Jesuits adapted the use of drama to their own ends, with religious entertainment lavish enough to rival anything secular. A Theatrum Sacrum was devised for every festival, in which cut-out figures and backdrops were arranged in the churches, and lit by candles to enhance the effect of reality. This engraving of such a scene by Bibiena shows Christ being crowned with thorns, as it would have appeared on a Baroque stage.

Et Milites
plectentes Coronam
imposuerunt
Capiti eius
Jo Cap 19.

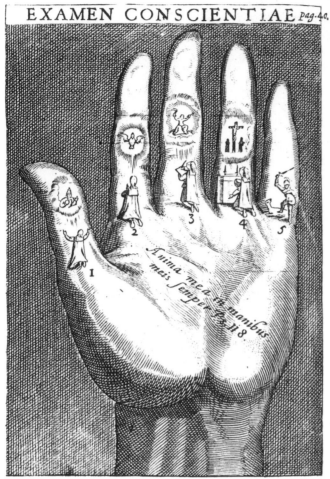

EXAMEN CONSCIENTIAE *pag.40.*

1.Gratias age. 2.Pete lumen. 3.Examina 4 Dole. 5.Propone.

'Though constantly I take my life in my hands, yet I forget not your law' (Psalm CXVIII). Encouraging the creation of vivid and concrete images, a 1689 edition of Loyola's 'Spiritual Exercises' contains such illustrations to aid meditation as this step by step diagram for examination of the conscience: give thanks, seek the light, self-examine, sorrow and sacrifice.

Perhaps the most Baroque of the new devotions of the 17th century, and the one that may ultimately prove to have had the most enduring influence, was the development of devotion to the Sacred Heart of Jesus. The new cult grew rapidly after a series of visions had been experienced by a French nun, St Margaret Mary Alacoque, between 1673 and 1675, in which Christ required her to 'Behold this heart which has so loved man.' By 1743, some seven hundred confraternities in Europe, India, China, Mexico, Turkey and Persia had been dedicated to the Sacred Heart and, ever since, the wounded, physical heart of Christ has proved an enduring symbol of the reciprocal love of God and man.

In order to persuade people to participate fully in these new cults and devotions, every artifice was employed, and this often explains the development of those characteristic forms of art and architecture that we call Baroque. This was an art that made a deliberate and overt appeal to the senses and to the emotions, restoring sensuality and colour to the churches of Catholic Europe. Here, services were deliberately made more attractive by fine music; churches themselves were designed and decorated in such a way that their theatrical elements served to make a direct appeal to the emotions; lavish use was made of the most costly materials, while everywhere a universal religion was given a local appeal through the emphasis placed on the cults of local saints. Popular participation in religion was everywhere encouraged. In Brittany, for instance, Michel le Nobletz (1577–1652) taught the peasants to sing hymns in their own language, not just in church but in the open air and along the roads, while one of his disciples, the Jesuit Father Manoir (1615–83), invented the Procession of the Passion, in which the priest took the part of Christ. A simultaneous development of a similar nature was the famous Passion play of Oberammergau, which began in 1634 when a group of peasants who had been delivered from a plague epidemic took a vow to perform a Passion play once every ten years.

Religion was thus made joyful, exuberant and moving, and consequently in many parts of Europe exercised a profound appeal by providing the only real consolation for lives otherwise composed of grinding toil and unremitting poverty. It was for this reason, no doubt, that the most spectacular successes of Catholicism occurred in those areas of Europe that suffered the worst devastation during the Thirty Years' War (1618–48): southern Germany, Poland and Bohemia.

Preachers and teachers of the new Catholicism working there were fortunate, ironically, in that it was an area in which Baroque art, with all its inbuilt techniques of persuasion, could be most effectively employed, simply because the physical devastation had been so extensive. Virtually the whole of Catholic central Europe had to be either restored or rebuilt. In consequence, a style which originated in Italy, and in Rome in particular, would come to dominate this area, which is now a world of magnificent Baroque churches, abbeys and chapels.

The reason that the new style could be so successful was its infinite adaptability to local traditions, techniques and styles. It could be modified to reinterpret any vernacular experience. Thus, for instance, we find in Bohemian Baroque painting a repeated emphasis on early medieval Czech saints, St Nepomucene, St

Wenceslas and St Ludmilla. Typical of such work was that of the great Czech painter, Karel Skreta (1610–74), who painted a series of episodes from the life of St Wenceslas for the cloisters of the Zderaz monastery; or that of the first Czech stone sculptor, Johan-George Bendl (1625?–80), for whom St Wenceslas was also a favoured theme. Similarly, in Poland, the new Baroque art was used to revive such traditional Polish cults as that of devotion to St Edwige.

Baroque architecture proved as adaptable to vernacular traditions as did Baroque painting. Thus, Baroque style as interpreted in the German tradition retained a flavour of the Gothic, while remaining essentially modern. Although the famous Jesuit church of St Michael in Munich was designed with a classical tunnel-vault, that vault was carried by tall piers which derived from traditional German Gothic structures. The same was true of the Jesuit church at Dillingen, built between

1610 and 1617, and which was to serve as a model for a number of other Jesuit churches throughout Swabia, Bavaria and Austria.

On the other side of the Atlantic, in Spanish America, Baroque was proving itself to be equally adaptable to native traditions. In the early years of the conquest and evangelization of Spanish America, such churches as were built tended to be strictly utilitarian, makeshift constructions. It so happened that the first permanent churches and monasteries erected there were all built at a time when Baroque was the fashionable style in Europe. Thus these are Baroque buildings, but modified by native traditions as, increasingly, Indian artists and craftsmen came to be used in building and decoration, imposing the luxuriant ornamentation that is so much a feature of colonial Baroque art.

The persuasive quality of Baroque art may justifiably

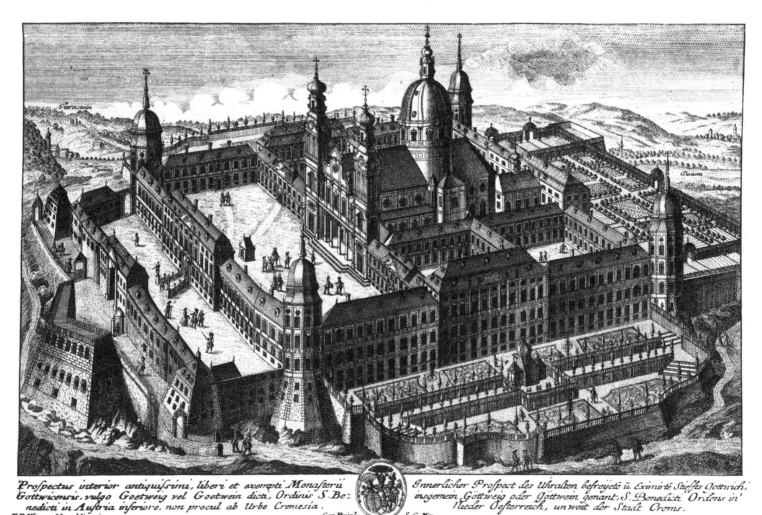

Prospectus interior antiquissimi, liberi et exempti Monasterii Göttwicensis, vulgo Goetweig vel Goetwein dicti, Ordinis S. Benedicti in Austria inferiore, non procul ab Urbe Cremesia.

F.B. Werner. Silos delineavit *Cum Privil.* *S.C. M.y*

Innerlicher Prospect des Uhralten befreyeto u. Exinnité Stieffts Gottwich, insgemein Göttweig oder Göttwein genant, S. Benedicti Ordens in Nieder Oesterreich, unweit der Stadt Crems.

Ioh. Georg Merz, excud. Aug.V.

During the later 17th and early 18th century, the lands of central Europe that had been devasted by the Thirty Years' War carried out a vast programme of rebuilding, involving churches and monasteries of unprecedented splendour. Göttweig in Austria was designed by Lucas von Hilderbrandt but was never completed on the enormous scale shown in this engraving.

be seen as one of the major reasons for the successful re-Christianization of Europe, and the conversion of so many new Christians outside Europe in the 17th century. Another major reason for the success of Catholicism, in particular, lay in the rediscovery of the church's social role. The 17th century might well have taken as its motto the watchword that St Vincent de Paul gave to his Sisters of Charity – *Caritas Christi urget nos* – 'the Charity of Christ weighs upon us', for this was one of the greatest ages of positive, outgoing, Christian charity.

The central impulse towards such outgoing charity lay in the Christocentric character of so much of 17th-century piety and mysticism. Man's attention was fixed on the Christ of the Incarnation because it seemed that only Christ could bridge the vast divide between sinful humanity and divine infinity. But the concentration on Christ, the love of the Christ of the Incarnation, brought with it the logical obligation that man should show his love of Christ by actively imitating his human life. So it was that active, outgoing charity in the world became the most positive aspect of the Christian life. This age, therefore, in which one of the most popular of all handbooks to piety was St Francis de Sales's *Introduction to the Devout Life*, with its constant and positive advocation of the imitation of Christ, fully understood the significance of the instruction given by St Vincent de Paul to his Sisters of Charity: 'Visit the poor instead of praying. In this way you leave God for God.' And St Vincent was himself a model of charity with his self-appointed mission as the apostle of the poor; a man who, by choice, laboured in poor hospital wards, in the slums of towns and among the convicts of the galleys. Typical also of the Baroque age was the development of Pietism in central Europe, where a fervent introspection often issued in a practising,

charitable Christianity in which the laity were to play a most prominent part.

Finally, however, it would be wrong to forget the more negative aspects of Christianity in the 17th century. An age of great piety and charity was equally an age of great intolerance and persecution, of Catholic by Protestant, Protestant by Catholic. After the defeat of the Protestant forces in Bohemia in 1620, for instance, more than 30,000 Protestants were obliged to flee a country where Catholicism was made obligatory in 1627, and where after 1650 any non-Catholic was liable to be punished by life-imprisonment or execution. Two successive archbishops of Prague pleaded with the emperor against such a policy on the grounds that no heretic could be won for the faith except by gentleness, but such appeals fell on deaf ears. The same Catholic policy was applied to Hungary, provoking a bitter rebellion of the Hungarian nobles, which was cruelly suppressed. Meanwhile, for the Protestant part, the Geneva Consistory introduced the death penalty for Catholics in 1621. And such incidents would be multiplied in the course of the century. In many ways, therefore, the age of the Baroque, for all its artistic triumphs, for all the positive qualities that Christianity brought to the enhancement of life for the ordinary person, is an age that must also be remembered in the history of Christianity for its dismal record of wars of religion, persecution, torture and judicial murder. We need to remind ourselves that these less than admirable practices were engaged in by two sides, both claiming to live by the Christian creed, and both simultaneously dedicated to emphasizing all that divided rather than anything which united them. The great religious divisions of the 16th and 17th centuries proved to have an immensely creative impact on the culture and society of the time. But for that creativity a high price was paid.

Jesuit letters from Japan, published in 1580 in an Italian translation from the Portuguese, bear the stamp IHS on the title page, with the Sacred Heart of Jesus.

THE CRISIS
OF THE
NINETEENTH
CENTURY

10

*Christianity and industrial
society*

THE SOCIAL CHALLENGE of the Industrial Revolution hit the churches at a particularly difficult time. The progress of science was undermining some of their traditional teachings, and Christians had to decide whether to give up those teachings, to reinterpret them in the light of modern knowledge or to retreat into dogma. At the same time the critical examination of early church history and Christian origins was striking at scriptural authority. Even sincere believers had to wrestle with 'doubts' and not all of them came off victorious. Atheism was still a loaded word, but for the first time it became possible to ask whether men needed religion at all.

Christianity in the 19th century is therefore marked by two struggles – one to win back the masses to the churches, the other, within the churches themselves, to find a response to their common problems. In the event, each church went its own way. The Vatican, just as it had done during the Counter-Reformation, adopted a hard line; new dogmas such as papal infallibility deliberately closed the door on compromise. Mainstream Protestants tended to remain open-minded, but at the price of forfeiting doctrinal coherence (the official theology of the Church of England, for instance, is often hard to define authoritatively). Some nonconformist churches held on desperately to the literal truth of the Bible. In America new sects multiplied, some of them, like the Mormons, quite unlike previous forms of Christianity. Everywhere an urgent debate was taking place. Assuming that God's church was destined to endure, how far was it justifiable to introduce changes? To what extent were Christians involved in social problems such as poverty? Should the church be political? Should it try to discard its middle-class image? Could one be a Christian revolutionary? To each of these questions diametrically opposite answers were possible.

'Sunday',
a French allegorical landscape, forms part of a series to illustrate the Catechism. It is interesting to compare this with the 'Ladder of Heaven' reproduced on p. 101. In the 19th century the way to salvation looks smoother and the temptations less terrifying, but the end is equally in doubt. In the foreground the factory draws people away from Sunday worship by the never-ending lure of gain, while along the street the cafés make it all too easy to forget one's religious duties. Those who follow the path to the church on the hill (which is typically unappealing architecturally) seem to be either respectable bourgeois families and schools or country people coming in from their villages. (1)

A church for the people

In a world that was changing so rapidly and so radically, the great question for churchmen was how to adapt to modern needs without sacrificing essentials.

Social revolution was not just compatible with Christianity; to many it was a necessary consequence. When the citizens of the Halles district of Paris planted their 'Tree of Liberty' in 1848 (*left*), the curé of St Eustache was on hand to deliver a sermon and his blessing. Hopes were high for a Christian brotherhood. In a lithograph by Sottian of the same date (*below*), Christ personifies the revolutionary virtue of Fraternity, under whose beneficent rule the nations of the world come to hail the 'Rights of Man', represented by the statue on the left. In the foreground lie the abandoned regalia of monarchy. (2, 3)

Rich and colourful new churches were built in working-class neighbourhoods. G.E. Street's St Mary Magdalene (*left*) stood in what was then a poor parish of London near Paddington. Neo-Gothic architecture was part of a self-conscious revival of medieval forms of worship, curiously at odds with progressive thought in other areas. The stonemason of 1868 (*below*) is constructing his church by traditional methods. (4, 6)

Evangelical movements set out to convert the workers of town and country. In a state such as France (*above* and *left*) this involved challenging the resident Catholic establishment. Both illustrations belong to the 1890s. (5, 7)

Nostalgia for a simple, unquestioning faith that seemed to be passing away comes through in art and literature – mostly created by townsmen. *Above:* in Legros's *Ex Voto* a young girl accompanied by peasant women performs a vow before a wayside shrine. *Right:* Rudolf von Alt's watercolour of a cottage interior in 1853 reflects the life of those who live in it – a peaceful life where domestic order, nature and religion harmonize. (8, 9)

Faith and innovation

In the countryside social problems were less obtrusive, and traditional values were more likely to remain intact. It was the towns that presented the challenge.

The new proletariat had lost contact with Christianity: how to win them back? Priests went out to the factories and mines taking Christianity to the workers. *Right:* part of the pit-head of a Bavarian coal-mine furnished as a chapel for the miners. The Salvation Army (*below*, painting by Raffaelli) was founded by William Booth in London in 1880, to take Christianity to the streets. Organized on a quasi-military basis, it combined social work with a strong spiritual message. (10,11)

The class structure of worship

Jesus was a poor man, who came to the poor. The churches – even the more radical among them – were middle-class institutions. Painfully aware of this, they strove to bridge the gulf and speak to working people in their own language.

Priests and nuns in Catholic countries stood partly outside the class structure and there were strong bonds between church and laity. *Above:* a church primary school in Italy. (12)

'Reading from the Bible' (*right*) – a cameo from the Protestant north, where religion and respectability went hand in hand; the painter is the Dutchman, A.H. Bekker Korff. (13)

The cool eye of the age of realism could portray congregations as they were rather than as an ideal. *Below:* worshippers at an Italian mass range from devotion to indifference. *Below right:* communion in a Hungarian Protestant church. (14, 15)

In England the split between rich and poor, godly and godless, was perhaps more marked than elsewhere because it was the first country to be industrialized. In the latter part of the 19th century we find an artist such as William Frith looking back with longing to an imagined golden age in *The Village Pastor* (*right*): 'around the pious man, with steady zeal each honest rustic ran'. It is an illustration to Goldsmith's *The Deserted Village*, a poem nostalgic even when it was written in 1770. (16)

The gentry (*above*) might hold informal evening prayers in the drawing room when there was no chapel available. (17)

The outcasts (*above right*): in a night refuge in London, drawn by Gustave Doré in 1872, a minister reads the Bible to those at the bottom of the social heap. (18)

The middle class (*right*): a congregation listens to the sermon in a fashionable London church – serious, sincere, but not indifferent to social distinctions. (19)

At home the Vatican Council of 1870 (*above*) marked a stricter statement of the Catholic position. The dogma of papal infallibility was propounded as no more than a formal statement of something that had always been implicit in Catholic theory – that the pope, when speaking *ex cathedra* as the voice of the church, on a matter essential to Christian belief, could not err. But it was a contentious issue. Many cardinals maintained that the time was not ripe for such an assertion, and in fact a sizable body of Catholics seceded rather than accept it. Those that remained, however, closed ranks; criticism was silenced and unity promoted. (20)

Abroad the work of conversion went on, largely untouched by theological controversy. This painting, so characteristic of the self-confidence of its age, shows the baptism of a Maori chief in New Zealand in 1853. (21)

10
Christianity and industrial society

OWEN CHADWICK

THE COMING OF INDUSTRY caused a vast movement of population from country to town. All religious denominations were faced with extraordinary tasks of reconstruction and redevelopment. They must build new churches in new towns, decide whether to keep up old village churches in places where the people were far fewer, and invent new kinds of charitable relief to cope with the new kind of need. Throughout the 19th century churchmen were always behind the clock, always struggling to keep up with problems that constantly outstripped them, but making endeavours that were at times heroic.

The movement of population was also an uprooting. The villager who perhaps went to church in his village usually became a townsman who did not attend church in his town. The larger the town the smaller the percentage of churchgoers. Therefore the new towns confronted churches with a missionary challenge equal to that which carried Christianity into Africa. They had to win, or win back, a soul uprooted from his past home and past customs, living in a new world with new moral as well as physical difficulties, and with no social pressure to conform to the ways of the middle class.

In the early years of industry, many Christian observers attributed the falling off to desperate conditions of labour. But when conditions were better, and work prosperous and labour happy, the labourer came no more to church on Sundays than when he took home a wage below subsistence level.

In an urban society, the state had to take over a large part of what formerly was done by the family or clan – care of the old, care of orphans, education of children and adolescents, employment of released prisoners and rescue of social outcasts such as professional prostitutes, who increased greatly in numbers. The fundamental cause of all these changes was the fact that the home was no longer the place of work.

Poverty and the new cities

All Christians accepted Jesus's saying that the poor are always with us and that those who have must relieve those who have not. But some time in the 19th century members of churches began to see that the invention of machines and the development of industry had changed the way they had to look at this duty of charity. In the past the poor had been of two kinds: those who were poor because they could not help it (i.e. the sick, the widows, the orphans and the old) and those who were poor because they were idle or extravagant or drunk (i.e. all the rest). But now churchmen began to see that a lot of able-bodied men and women, diligent workers who were neither idle nor drunk, could still not help being poor. And they diagnosed that this state of affairs was caused by the new state of society and of work brought about by the invention of machines. Poverty was bearable when it was distributed over the countryside in cottages. It was harder to bear when concentrated in towns and the ghettoes of those towns.

Because poverty was caused by the 'system' and not by sin the system came under fire, first from the vociferous among those who were actually suffering under it, second from intelligent observers who cared for them and third from intelligent observers who feared for the state. The urban worker was at the mercy of the industrialist, who had a strong interest in keeping wages as low as possible; indeed, if he failed to keep wages low, he might have to close his factory and throw all his workmen out of work. So the first moral doubt that afflicted the churches in this new age was whether the wealth of the world was being distributed justly; and if not, whether Christians had any moral duty to try to change the system to make it more just.

Apart from naïve idealists, like Fourier or Proudhon, the theorists had two kinds of cure to offer society. One party, much the more uncommon, looked to the worker himself, his power to associate, to organize, if necessary to strike. The other looked to the state to interfere with the free operation of markets, wages and prices, though such a programme aroused the scorn of doctrinaire liberals because it imposed a solution from above, like a lord of the manor in the Middle Ages.

Both these parties, however, were minorities. The vast majority of churchmen during most of the 19th century thought that the question had nothing to do with them, and they had nothing to do with the question. They were not politicians or sociologists. Their task was not to solve the problem of poverty but to fight ignorance, or atheism, or Protestantism, or Catholicism, or deism, or undenominational education. As individuals, they might help poor people because

Where Christianity had once confined itself to the churches and cathedrals, it now emerged in unexpected surroundings, showing itself on the street corners at open-air sermons, such as this one depicted in a French engraving by A. Lançon.

they recognized the law of charity. But they did not think it possible to change the conditions of society so that the poor might be poor no longer. And the mood of Europe, Catholic or Protestant, after the French Revolution was not sympathetic to Christian leaders who tried to change politics or society because it was not sympathetic to anyone who tried to change politics or society. People wanted pious priests and godly pastors, and were offended by radical priests and political pastors.

The first hint of new attitudes came when some Christian thinkers baptized the idea of progress. Formerly they had seen it as a deistic idea. But in Germany most Protestant leaders were affected by an ideology that conceived of the human race as pursuing a perpetual course of development. In Germany the word *development* became a key motif of the new Protestant age. From Hegel downwards, Christian philosophers and theologians saw the guidance of God in or over the world, leading mankind nearer to the perfection that was the kingdom of God. Not without reason, they claimed Christianity to be the source of the moral principles on which European society rested. And then, looking ahead, they claimed that Christianity worked as an inward force, leading men onward and upward in the scale of moral duty and civilization.

This was an intellectual and not at all a revolutionary idea. Before long, however, the problem of the proletariat was such that the intellectuals were forced to focus on the existence of poverty on a vast scale; the poor, heaped in ghettoes, were omnipresent and menacing in the political landscape. The prospect of revolution is a little like the prospect of being hanged – it concentrates a man's mind wonderfully. On the very day when Paris started its revolution in February 1848, a wise and not at all extreme leader among the French clergy, the abbé Maret, laid down a theoretical principle, which is a sign of the emergence of new ideas about society: 'We regard the progressive improvement of the moral and material lot of the working class as the very end of society.' Two and a half months later the same author wrote: 'In the social character of our revolution we recognize its lasting glory and in that we see the truly firm ground for its alliance with Catholic Christianity.' This idea was neither Catholic only, nor French only. Very shortly after Maret, and stirred not by an actual revolution but by the threat of a Chartist one, the Anglicans Maurice, Kingsley and Ludlow took for themselves the name Christian Socialists.

Christian Socialism

Naturally, such principles were found most often among churchmen willing to baptize the coming democracies. Such men talked of the equality of men before God, and the need to embody this equality of creation within the structure of society. Their beliefs made them suspect to all who distrusted democracy. They were accused of thinking, not about the poor but about pauperism, of turning the old act of charity, which was the generosity of God, into a new social theory, which was a cranky and dubious ideology.

Sometimes the Christian thinker deserted his

Christianity when he found that the church rejected his standpoint and repudiated his arguments. Lamennais was the creator of French liberal Catholicism during the years 1827–32. Coming up against papal prohibition, he moved away to the political left, developed into a socialist and abandoned his priest's orders and his church. Had he been allowed to, he could have created a Catholic socialism. But Rome stamped upon the first signs of his movement in that direction and so the socialism of Lamennais was made to look incompatible with Catholicism. Similarly, in Lutheranism membership of the Social Democratic party was long regarded as impossible for pastors. Individuals were faced with a cruel choice. One man, Pastor Goehre, joined the party and was expelled from his church, and soon preferred his socialism to his Christianity. Another, Pastor Blumhardt, joined the party and was expelled from his consistory, but preferred to keep his Christianity and his socialism in alliance.

The Christian Socialists of France or Germany or Britain, later in Italy, became very critical of the hierarchy of their church. They moved among men for whom equality was of the essence; and the notion of hierarchy, especially within the more traditional churches, was anathema. They were apt to talk of simple priests leading the march towards a new social order. Though they were devout Catholics, and accepted the doctrines of the creed, they could be violent in their language against bishops or popes. Usually, and especially if they were middle class, like Frédéric Ozanam in France or Maurice in England, they knew almost nothing of economics and were content to concern themselves with large principles or aspirations. If they were pastors among the proletariat, however, they might share all the revolutionary drive of the extremist leaders, and preach on the basic right of man to live and, therefore, to take what was necessary to live. But if they were enthusiasts their enthusiasm did not always survive harsh realities.

The abbé Deguerry became a fiery republican at the 1848 revolution and hailed the new democratic age as the coming of the brotherhood of man. Then, when democracy vanished into dictatorship and empire, he lost his republican idealism and in the end was shot as a hostage by the Paris Communards in 1871. Usually such men were in revolt against their bishops, or synods, or consistories. On 29 April 1849, Paris witnessed a banquet of 'socialist priests', of whom three appeared in cassocks and thirty in lay attire; six hundred working men joined in the festivity, and drank toasts to 'Jesus of Nazareth, father of socialism' or 'the union of democracy and Christianity'. In his speech Father Montlouis told the banqueters: 'We want your freedom, we want no more to let men exploit men. It is

Hugues Félicité Robert de Lamennais broke with Rome when his policies were condemned by Pope Gregory XVI, and all his life remained faithful to his dogma of the sovereignty of the people.

time that the labourer enjoys the fruit of his labour, and that no capitalist shall grow fat upon your sweat.' When democracy ended in Louis Napoleon's coup d'état, the speaker disappeared into exile in Brussels. Such priests or pastors were accused of encouraging working men to sedition, or upsetting the order of society, or fostering class warfare, or corrupting their sacred office by mixing religion with political ambition. Bishops were known to demand more moderation in the language of curates when they talked of the mutual duties of masters and men, and, occasionally, bishops could bear the complaints and parish turmoil no longer and banned these priests from wearing cassocks or celebrating sacraments.

Yet such liberal clergy could appeal to a wider circle of sympathizers than those who were actually willing to risk disrepute or censure by undertaking propaganda for the political left. The abbé Migne is famous for his vast scholarly undertakings, which changed the study of Christian history. He needed educated workers and protected many a socialist priest who was under a cloud, hiring them to edit texts or check references. He paid them badly and was harsh in discipline, but he had a real though muted sympathy for their social aspirations.

Religion and class

Most strong churchmen throughout the 19th century probably voted for conservative parties. Conservatism stood for the home, the family, the force of history, the retention of all that was good in the past. This was probably truer of Catholic than Protestant countries, because the pope stood under radical onslaught from Italians and from 1849 to 1878 was the most conservative person in all Europe, condemning in the Syllabus of Errors (1864) not only communism and socialism but even toleration and 'clerical-liberal societies'. This general law, expressed ironically by the Germans of the Weimar Republic in the epigram, 'The Church is neutral in politics but votes for the Conservative Party', was nonetheless liable to infinite exception. Roman Catholics under governments not Roman Catholic – in Ireland, Poland, at times Belgium – easily found themselves linked to radical if not revolutionary parties. Popes disapproved or formally condemned such links but the needs of Ireland or Poland mattered more to the Irish or the Poles than the needs of Rome. In Protestant countries, all churches had a vocally radical fringe, usually but not always among the more extreme groups. In England, the most celebrated were Anglo-Catholics at one end and Primitive Methodists at the other.

Most churches, however, were under educated leadership and therefore likely to be middle class in feeling; they desired order and stood for peace instead of violence. They preferred a steady or organic development of society to sudden changes, which were liable to be accompanied by the spilling of blood. They fostered those personal roots, family ties, home links, which were so weakened by the ceaseless movement of people from countryside to town. They were inclined to suspect radical socialism, partly because they were middle class and partly because they stood for the unique value of the individual, and they disliked doctrines that, as they saw it, made the individual a nothing before the state.

This was the tension at the heart of the social work of the churches during the 19th century. They saw that the old methods broke down in the new cities; for example, the old methods of coping with prostitutes were not suitable when big cities created herds of them. Therefore, the churches felt they must demand state interference, state action, which originally they saw in paternalistic terms, that is, in the manner of the squire caring for the spiritual and physical welfare of his tenants. Little by little this paternalism became outdated; once they had accepted democracy, it was the interference of a democratic state that they had to demand. But their experience, their conviction of

individual worth, their concern for individual rights and their love of the freedoms of an older world made them fear the tyranny of a majority. The division in the minds of churchmen, and even in their souls, rested here. That the worker in a factory must not be turned into a piece of machinery, a commodity in the line of production, they were certain, and said loudly that this was wholly incompatible with the Christian ethic. But the only way to prevent the worker from being a piece of machinery belonging to an employer seemed to be to turn him into a piece of machinery belonging to the state, which, they were sure, was a solution equally abhorrent. On the one hand churchmen had to demand more power for the state; on the other they feared the extension of state power that would answer their cries for liberty and for the rights of every man before God. Throughout the 19th century this tension among church leaders was never resolved.

They engaged in various schemes of welfare, for instance, co-operative societies, which in England the Christian Socialists of 1848–53 made their chief practical programme, as did several French organizers who called themselves Catholics and socialists. These church leaders asked for grants from the state to accomplish their plans, but seldom received them. They worked for liberty of association, and some of them demanded a minimum legal wage. Neither their power nor their agreement should be exaggerated; they varied from country to country and from district to district. They accepted liberty, equality and fraternity, not only as Christian ideals but as goals that could not be achieved even partially without a foundation in the truths of Christian doctrine. How they should be put into practice varied according to different national traditions, different political circumstances, different social conditions and individual minds or experiences.

To define the relation of the church to the working-class world, that is, to a world in which the industrial worker had gradually accumulated much of the physical power in the state and nearly as much of the political power, is an immense and still insoluble problem for the historian. The European worker, or the American worker, normally had almost no relation to the churches; if he felt anything at all, it was likely to be hostility. If an individual worker or group of workers formed an exception to this rule, they were regarded as abnormal by everybody. They had trouble with their churches, aroused suspicion from the authorities in the state and created friction with their fellow-workers. It is easy to call the whole problem a uselessly academic exercise, like asking how dinosaurs would get on among modern whales. The churches, it might be said, lost or never had the industrial worker – the industrial worker cared nothing for the churches – hence the secularity of modern society, the weakness of modern churches and the melting-pot of modern moral attitudes.

No one, however, has yet proved that industrial cities and churches are by their nature incompatible. Jesus was a poor man, who came to the poor. The proletariat had a yearning for a better world, a kind of worldly eschatology partly derived from the Christian hope. It had no use for churches, but could identify with Jesus. In fact, one of their charges against the churches was that they had betrayed Jesus. Orators who blasphemed against his name gained no sympathy. Christians might offend workers by saying that poverty was not (or need not be) an ill, and that many good men had made themselves poor for Christ's sake. But they did not offend them when they said that riches meant danger, that it was easier for a camel to pass through the eye of a needle than for a rich man to enter the kingdom of heaven and that the rich must use their wealth as stewards of God for the benefit of the community. The *Magnificat*, Christian Socialists kept saying, was a hymn of revolution. Some held the view that to be a proletarian was necessarily to be irreligious; that irreligion was an integral part of the proletarian social structure. Others saw this irreligion as a matter of pure chance, that the proletariat was only a group of people, like newly discovered Mohicans or Maoris, whom the churches were obliged to bring to God; and one day, doubtless in the distant future, the churches would succeed with them as formerly they succeeded with Mohicans or Maoris.

In support of this latter theory, Christians pointed to the areas of irreligion that existed before the coming of industry, and claimed that what was now called 'de-Christianization' really meant the discovery of peoples or districts which had never been truly Christian. There is, in fact, a good deal of evidence in favour of such a theory, especially in France. The chaplain to the French army that occupied Moscow in 1812 painted a vivid and convincing picture of 400,000 men, both privates and officers, without the least interest in religion, though he saw many of them as they died.

An extension of this theory that pockets of irreligion, or semi-religion, existed also has a measure of probability. What had been called 'religion' was often in fact mostly superstition. God prevented the house catching fire, or warded off the evil eye, or healed a sick cow, or gave an infertile wife a baby, or made one pick the right number in the lottery. When education – not only education by the sons of Voltaire, but education by Christian clergymen – dissolved or cast shadows on these beliefs, then this kind of 'religion' dropped away and left nothing behind. The situation in the 19th century was the reverse of what it had been in the 18th.

The Roman revolution turned Pope Pius IX away from liberal policies and identified the papacy with the political reaction. A Dutch anti-papal cartoon of 1852 represents a scheming figure behind the mask of Christ, and so the hostility of much of Protestant Europe in these years.

In the 18th century the leaders of irreligion were bourgeois, the props of the churches were the people. As society industrialized, the classes changed places: the middle class became the mainstay of religion while the worker had no use for it.

Is there a link with political history? Recent research suggests that there is. The failure in the later part of the century of previously successful missions to the miners in the département of the Nord in France looks as though it must have been connected with the victories of the republicans at the elections of 1876 and 1881. Industry gave potential power to the have-nots. They were bound to fight the haves, whose power rested on inherited wealth – which meant to fight the middle class, rigged franchise and hierarchies of every description, including churches. This last aspect of the fight was at its most obvious in Italy and France, least obvious in the United States. Anticlericalism hardly existed in Britain and America and parts of Germany, but was a tormenting fact of politics in Italy, France and Spain. The main cause for this difference seems to have been less a different social structure than a different political history. Old-fashioned Protestant historians used to say that Italy, France and Spain were Roman Catholic countries, whereas Britain, the United States and Germany were simply countries that contained many Protestants. Undoubtedly the political style of any state was conditioned, among other things, by the nature of the churches in that state. But this facile Protestant axiom that anticlericalism thrives only in Roman Catholic countries has begun to look like a distinction without a difference. Whether he liked the parson or hated the priest, the male worker did not appear in church on Sundays.

In France the link with politics is clearest. Right into the pontificate of Pius X (1903–14), many French clergy considered socialism and Catholicism to be incompatible, condemned strikes totally, rejected the democratic republic of the country, taught that everyone must accept his place in society and put all their trust for the redemption of society in the conversion of the individual. Conservatism was believed to be religious and radicalism irreligious; and at elections the pamphlets and speeches showed this axiom all too plainly.

Yet the more we know of the Christian leaders, the earlier we find traces of social thought. Cardinal Giraud of Cambrai in 1845–46 compared some industrial labour to African slave traffic, talked of the exploitation of man by man and proclaimed the worker's right to a wage that would enable him and his children to live. In 1842 Cardinal Bonald of Lyons denounced the 'economists' view' of man in strong language, on the ground that it treated man as a piece of machinery, trampling on human dignity and neglecting human health. Such bishops wanted industrial legislation, that is, interference by the state. In 1843, Monsignor Affre of Paris, soon to die at a revolutionary barricade, said: 'the doctors of this calamitous science [economics] have tried to make out of the overwhelming majority of the human race a vile tool for accumulating wealth in a small number of hands'.

Religion and revolution

The 1848 revolution caused the reaction. French bishops avoided utterances that could be taken as an approval of socialism. But bolder men continue to denounce oppression. As late as 1960 historians believed that, except for Bishop Ketteler of Mainz, Catholic leaders maintained silence on the industrial question until the papal encyclical *Rerum Novarum* of 1891. Recent investigation of the charges, sermons, speeches and pastoral letters of French bishops, however, shows a very different picture. The social question figured frequently and prominently. Usually, but not quite always, bishops were paternalists rather than democrats, and almost always royalist rather than republican. But they had a clear view of the physical as well as the moral predicament of industrial society. What they seldom did was to follow up words with acts.

The majority of French bishops disliked, and disbelieved, the doctrine that new laws and more interference by the state would cure all. They heard bureaucrats or fanatics promise an earthly paradise if only the state would establish a minimum wage, or abolish capitalism. They had a vivid perception that in large areas of life morality could not be fostered by laws, at least not by laws alone, and they often denounced secular schemes for Utopia. They hated the doctrine that war between classes was inevitable. They disliked liberal economists nearly as much as communists because the doctrines of political laissez-faire caused so many obvious social ills – and they did not yet foresee that communists could produce anything but middle-class anxiety.

There were a number of French bishops, however, who still believed that the chaos affecting doctrine, morality and social structure was entirely due to sin; that no truth existed outside Catholic orthodoxy; that the inequality of classes was a necessary part of creation; that only faith could bring right to society. They were deeply disturbed if their priests committed the church to precise political programmes, both because the priest must be pastor of all his flock and not merely a part, and because political parties were affairs of compromise and selfish interest as well as of ideals. But they seemed to mind less if their priests committed themselves to conservative political programmes. The result was that in France the early Socialist party was fiercely anticlerical.

In Germany the first speech by a Catholic deputy in favour of social action by the state, as an industrialized society understood that action, was delivered as early as 1837 in the upper house of the Baden Parliament by Franz Josef Buss. As in France, however, it was the revolutionary year of 1848 that made such ideas important. In that year, Buss was president of a general assembly of Catholics held at Mainz, where the social question was the main item on the agenda. Buss wanted legal interference in the hours of work, a ban on night work for children, the protection of Sunday as a day of rest, a health service and accident insurance and some provision of insurance for the sick, with employers and employees both contributing. Unlike Lamennais and some of the French, he was not pessimistic about industrialization. Instead of seeing it as the cause of poverty, he saw it as affording a new chance whereby poverty might be cured. What was needed was state intervention to stop industrial development creating those sordid conditions which industry had created in England.

Ketteler, the man whose name came to symbolize Catholic socialism in Germany, went as a simple pastor from the country to the National Assembly at Frankfurt set up after the revolution of 1848. He became famous by preaching a sermon at the funeral of two men who were killed in the revolution, and thenceforth was always to be found delivering courses of sermons with titles like 'The Social Tasks of the Church Today'. The church, he said, had nothing to fear from freedom; but freedom needed the church, it could not stand without the moral and charitable endeavours of the church. The state alone could not solve all the problems of an industrial society because mass poverty and class division were not soluble by legislation alone – they needed a moral transformation of society. At this stage of his life Ketteler's conception of economics was still very naïve; accumulating wealth meant adding house to house and farm to farm. And his first social idea was the old and very simple one that all would be well if everyone could be persuaded to follow the law of Christ and love their neighbours as themselves. Only slowly did he come to realize that this immortal precept was too basic and undeveloped to meet the needs of industrial society.

By 1863 several of Ketteler's Catholic associates were attracted to the socialist critique of Ferdinand Lassalle. This led Ketteler to study the social question afresh; and the result of his study was a book *Christianity and the Worker (Die Arbeiterfrage und das Christentum)*. Under Lassalle's influence, Ketteler came to think that the only way out of the problem of the proletariat was to give the worker a share of the profits. Lassalle proposed to do this by using taxpayers' money; Ketteler at that time refused to accept this because it represented undue interference by government in society. The thing was wrong if the citizen was forced, right if the Christian cared.

By the 1870s his thoughts had become more realistic: you could not help the worker by condemning industry and capitalism; you had to accept industry, and its capital necessities, and use its possibilities critically for the benefit of the worker. It was a significant moment when Ketteler, now no longer a revolutionary curate but the bishop of the most historic see in Germany, preached from his pulpit using words like these: 'Religion and morality alone cannot solve the plight of the worker. The state must help, the church must help, the community must help – every means must be used

to protect that class from destruction.' In a speech given in July 1869 at Offenbach, under the title 'The Workers' Movement and Endeavour in Relation to Religion and Morality', the bishop demanded the formation of German trade unions on the model of the English, with the right to strike. The speech has been called the Magna Carta of the Christian Workers' Movement.

Such ideas were rejected not only by conservatives. Atheist socialists hated them as much or more, because they weakened the theory and therefore the practice of class warfare. August Bebel, the German socialist leader, said bitterly of this Christian Socialist ordering of the world, that 'nobody knows whether it descends from the time when Pope Gregory VII was master of Europe, or from the time when Pope Leo X embezzled money from indulgences'. Nevertheless, Ketteler's ideas were important for the subsequent course of the German Centre Party, and therefore for social legislation in Germany. And they had consequences beyond Germany. When Pope Leo XIII was at last ready to modify the rigid attitudes of his predecessors and to publish a social encyclical of far reaching importance (*Rerum Novarum*, 1891), he called Ketteler his 'great predecessor' from whom he had learned much.

Ketteler's theory was less important than the fact that he, a bishop, was convinced that to interpret the social work of the church simply as almsgiving and charity was hopelessly inadequate – they might cure symptoms but not the disease.

On his way to the Vatican Council of 1869 Ketteler read the first volume of Karl Marx's *Das Kapital*, and it was his theologian, Christopher Moufang, who had the duty of preparing matter on the social question for the Council to consider; but the Council hardly had time to agree on the pope's infallibility before it was ended by the Italian invasion.

Pope Leo XIII began his reign in 1878 with traditional ideas. One of the first things he did was to renew his predecessor's condemnation of socialism (*Quod apostolici muneris*, 28 December 1878). But, though an old man, he learned quickly. In Italy, the national state of the Risorgimento was a middle-class state, and on the whole anticlerical; virtually its first act had been to confiscate the papal lands. The upper class and the working man, on the other hand, were largely Catholic. In northern Italian cities, such as Milan or Bologna, a strong Catholic movement appeared; it was anti-bourgeois, backed by workers and showed signs of radical social thought among its leaders. A pope whose chief enemy was the Italian state, stained at that time by the most corrupt scandals of an ill-ordered capitalism, could not but see the force in a Catholic social programme for the worker. This Italian movement was much the most important influence in changing the attitudes of the papacy.

The United States also had its share in that change. In 1871, an American tailor who had studied for the Baptist ministry created a secret order in Philadelphia called the Noble and Holy Order of the Knights of Labor. The aims of this body were radical. It demanded the nationalization of railways and transport, equal pay for both sexes, more powerful unions among workmen and the right to strike, though it professed a preference for settling labour disputes through arbitration. By 1886 it had 700,000 members and a record of success in several strikes. The question was raised whether it was possible for good Catholics to share in such a body. The bishops in Canada condemned it and refused to allow good Catholics to belong. In the United States, however, the leading Roman Catholic churchman was Cardinal Gibbons of Baltimore, a man with strong concern for the redemption of society. He was determined that the Knights should not be condemned, and achieved from Leo XIII an assurance that they would not. In the end, the Knights faded away and were officially dissolved during the First World War.

In Great Britain, the archbishop of Westminster, Henry Edward Manning, once the most middle class of Anglican archdeacons and still in personal relations stiff and remote, became a champion of the social cause. His flock largely consisted of the poorest people in London, the Irish immigrants. His personal intervention helped to settle the great dock strike of 1889. He was no theorist; nevertheless, since he knew his way among the corridors of power, he became one of the leading Christian minds demanding state intervention for the social welfare of the poor. Yet this cardinal was not highly regarded in Rome and probably had little influence in changing Leo XIII's views.

Germany had a weightier influence in the Vatican. In the era of Bismarck the Centre Party, determined to resist the very Protestant and very upper-class government, became the Catholic party. Its social programme had therefore to satisfy the Catholic workers of Bavaria and the Rhineland, and in its formulation the inheritance of Ketteler was a strong influence.

'Of New Things'

Various influences, of which the Italian carried the greatest weight, thus caused the pope to back the moderate social programme of Christian reformers. The encyclical *Rerum Novarum* (1891) was one of the few great papal pronouncements of the modern era. It spoke of the dignity of the worker as a human being; of the worker's absolute right in the scheme of creation and the Christian ethic not to be treated as a thing; of the right of the state to intervene in private industry and direct the use of capital to protect the worker's rights and welfare; of the worker's right to a just wage; of the right of the worker to organize for protection. The encyclical renewed the condemnation of socialism and communism on the ground that everyone, whether worker or no, had the right to possess private property.

Late though it came, the encyclical released the flood of Christian social thinking and forms one of the foundations of the Catholic democratic parties of the 20th century. That it could not resolve the tension, even in Italy, was shown by the career of Romolo Murri (1870–1944). A priest at Rome university during the 1890s, he adhered with passion to the programme of Christian democracy and resented the conservatism, as he saw it, of the Catholic leaders among the industrial workers of northern Italy. On 14 August 1902, he published a violent article in the review *Cultura Sociale*, which he had founded, against the retiring president of the Congress of the northern Catholic movement. The quarrel resounded throughout Italy. At the Congress in Bologna the next year, the disciples of Murri won extraordinary support for their radical programme at the cost of dividing the meeting and the entire movement into bitterness and faction. When the next pope, Pius X, turned out to be conservative, the young Catholic democrats rebelled against the Congress leadership, seceded and founded at Bologna the National Democratic League. Murri went with them. In 1906, Pius X forbade priests to belong to this League. Murri was further suspect because he approved of the leaders of theological modernism, which Pius X feared as terrible heresy. Murri was elected to Parliament, put off his cassock, married, became a politician of the extreme left and thereafter lost all importance in Italian life.

Because the Protestant churches were more diverse, they were more flexible in coping with the problems of industrial society, but they were not necessarily more successful.

In England, Frederick Denison Maurice was the authentic theologian of the Christian Socialist Movement, and claimed the name of Christian Socialist. His ideas, which included a classless hierarchical society (for he was never frightened of contradictions) and the prohibition of any right to strike, were not compatible with the plans of real socialists, and to disciples of Karl Marx they were contemptible. But they were not contemptible to British working men, who saw a leading churchman stand at their side, and still less to the Anglican middle class. Thus the British generation of the 1880s and 90s, at a time when in Germany and France Christianity and socialism looked incompatible, found the idea of a Christian socialism natural and acceptable, even if their leaders preferred its ideology to be imprecise. Maurice's intellectual programme was supported by the social drive of the English nonconformist churches, with far reaching consequences for British history. The early Labour Party was not in the least anticlerical and was not founded in opposition to churches.

In Germany, the Social Democratic party was founded in opposition to the churches (it said that it was neutral in religion, but its neutrality was decidedly negative). When in 1878 Bismarck made the Socialist party illegal, the governing body of the Prussian Evangelical church supported him. But in the same year a new impetus arrived from an unexpected quarter with the foundation of Adolf Stoecker's Christian Socialist Workers party, perhaps the strangest product of these attempts by churches to meet the needs of industrialized man. Stoecker was really a conservative tribune of the people who hated liberal capitalism and imported into his politics an unpleasant smack of antisemitism. Since the Social Democratic party already commanded the working men's vote unless they were Catholics, he came too late into the field to win many votes. His first flurry of popular support soon faded, and left him head of a little populist fringe at the side of the Conservative party. When the emperor was known to declare that the term Christian Socialist was nonsense, self-contradictory, he lost all importance in politics or among the churches.

The United States: the kingdom on earth

In the United States the churches took up the fight against slavery and this inevitably meant that the message from the pulpit became social and political as well as spiritual. In the years after the end of the Civil War, American churchmen not of the extreme left but of the moderate Protestant centre, developed what came to be called the 'social gospel'. Many of them, as in Europe, were enlightened open-minded conservatives. One of the most astonishing successes of this application of the Puritan ethic to society was achieved by the passing of the Eighteenth Amendment, which enforced Prohibition. The horrors of city life can be remedied by state interference, ran the argument; drunkenness is among the worst horrors of life in a modern industrial city: abolish alcohol.

Unlike Europe, the United States had good cause for optimism: it was a young society, without vested interests and centuries-old habits; it was a society that could be moulded. The Utopia that was being sought in America had its other-worldly aspects, but it was also of this world. God led His people towards His kingdom, and the kingdom upon earth was to be made a reflection of the kingdom of heaven. In interpreting the New Testament kingdom preached by Christ, they talked less about the kingdom in the sky than about the future kingdom here.

The American movement was also stronger because unrestricted capitalism was stronger and belief in the virtues of cut-throat competition more axiomatic. The robber barons not only presided over more powerful baronies but (some alleged) were more successful robbers, and the results produced private wealth on a scale to stir a mixture of wonder, horror and respect. Strike, by all means – this is a free country; break the strike, by all means – this is a free country.

Walter Rauschenbusch was an American descended from a German family of ministers; he was partly educated in Germany and thus provides a link between Christian Socialist thought in Prussia and the American 'social gospel'. At the age of twenty-five he became a Baptist pastor in a sordid district of New York City.

His experience there proved to him that normal Christian attitudes touched only part of life. He arrived in his New York slum with the aim of saving a few souls out of the mass. He would tell them that Christ died for sinners, that the sinner can be reborn, that he can make progress in a holy life, that when he dies he will go to heaven. But in that part of New York and at that social level, the message remained only words, not reality. The convert was still in a situation where the pressures upon him compromised his life. Somewhere in the Gospel must be found a place for the redemption of not only the soul but all society.

Rauschenbusch determined to make it his vocation to find the answer. He read Henry George and Karl Marx and Tolstoy, and from 1889 helped to edit a Christian Socialist periodical in New York, *For the Right*. In 1897 he moved to Rochester, New York, to teach in the seminary, where after five years he became professor of church history. His book of 1907, *Christianity and the Social Crisis*, was the most influential book evoked by the Christian Socialist response to the problem of industrial society and its relation to the churches.

In this book the social order is conceived of as an organism, a living body. If a man sins, others sin with him, sin is corporate, salvation is corporate. Within the body the divine Spirit is ceaselessly at work bringing humanity towards the kingdom of God, which is the kingdom of justice. Capitalism Rauschenbusch regarded as an un-Christian order depriving men of their manhood. He accepted that some social institutions were already Christianized: family, school, church and political structure, when it was democratic. But industry had corrupted society further – it had spawned political corruption, prostitution and the poverty of the proletariat. Somehow the Christian must build a society of which the structure is fraternal and not competitive, and this meant giving the workers a share in the direction of their work; only in this way can class war be brought to an end. The worker must have security in his work (so long as he is honest and does the job), must be protected in sickness and old age and allowed his share in the property of the state so that he can build a decent home. Society, not individuals or corporations, must own the great natural resources.

From all this, Rauschenbusch came very near to identifying Christianity with socialism, though Christianity remained the superior concept because it was the moral and spiritual basis of society as well as containing the principles of its social structure. As early as 1894, he said in Philadelphia that a man would be a better Christian if he were a socialist, and a better socialist if he were a Christian. He held that socialism rightly condemned the present order of society; and because the Christian knows that each life is sacred and that men are equal in the eyes of God, the Christian unites with and deepens this condemnation. But he said that he was a 'practical socialist'. That meant, he explained, that he would not accept the attempt to make a socialist society by violence.

Here was another of the great unresolved tensions in the attitude of the churches to industrial society. If they were Christian Socialists their attitude was, in effect, revolutionary. They called Jesus a social revolutionary, they saw the Christians overthrowing the old structure of the Roman Empire, and Luther overthrowing the structure of medieval society, and themselves overthrowing . . . what? Yet they could not accept class warfare. Almost to a man they disbelieved in violence. They wanted change by evolution, and rejected change by coup. And if they were not willing to accept violence, were they not, for all their talk of revolution, still preaching that men must be resigned under oppression and so, willy nilly, staying on the side of the oppressors? That was what Karl Marx thought, and with some reason.

The politics of salvation

Large cities threw men together and so made them a new political force. The memory of ancient Greek democracy, modified to fit the representative institutions of the United States, inspired the labourer in every Western industrialized society. His vote could remedy his plight. Universal franchise was therefore the goal. It took all the century and more to achieve anything like it, even for males only. In the United States, France, Britain, Italy, and Spain it meant constitutional change of the first importance, always moving a little nearer towards government by a majority in a single chamber, elected by all adult

citizens. In Germany, the special place of Prussia in the federation delayed the process. Nor was progress steady in any country; in all of them, old institutions showed staying power: kings, nobility, upper houses, squires, established churches.

A democratic regime based on a wide franchise was liable to throw up a demagogue and thereby create a dictatorship, and this did in fact happen. France had a dictator from 1851 to 1870, though towards the end his power grew less absolute. Spain made do with military governors from time to time. This historic nemesis, of which Aristotle and the ancient Greeks had warned, finally became evident only after the War of 1914–18 and its aftermath in Europe. But whether the government was a partial democracy – the most usual constitution of the 19th century – or a full democracy, or a popular dictatorship, the development of constitutions threw the historic question of church and state into the melting-pot.

No form of privilege for a particular group – religious, racial, class, family – was compatible with the attitudes of a fully democratic society. For historical reasons, which are reasons of the heart, states often preserved fragments of old forms of establishment. But many established churches were linked to monarchies and soon disappeared when the monarchy was replaced by a republic. The states that composed Germany did not lose their established churches till the revolution of 1918–19, and even then they preserved the right to assess for church taxes, though not the compulsion to pay. Italy suffered a kind of disestablishment between 1850 and 1870, though it simultaneously created a national monarchy. France finally separated church from state in 1905, but because this came (for the circumstances of France) so late, it came with the maximum amount of ill-feeling and anticlerical campaigning. Spain disestablished its church or re-established it according to the swings of politics, for there the church was inherent in the conservative structure and was seen by republicans as an enemy; therefore the fight between clerical and anticlerical was more bitter, and in the end more murderous, than in any other country. Scandinavia and Great Britain preserved their established churches, but only by a process of abolishing what were once regarded as the essence of establishment: public money for churches, special advantages over dissenters in marriage, baptism and funerals and bars against non-Christians in the government of the country.

These constitutional changes were caused not only by the growth of large industrial towns, but by international movements of population. The revolutionary armies of Napoleon overthrew the existing frontiers of Europe. Protestant rulers in Germany found themselves with many Roman Catholic subjects, Roman Catholic rulers with many Protestants. The economic predicament of Italy caused a huge emigration of Italians, which started into western Europe before it turned towards North and South America. Russian persecutions of the Jews created big new Jewish populations in Vienna, Berlin, Hamburg, Amsterdam, London, New York. The expansion of Europe into India and Africa was accompanied by a measure of reciprocal immigration of Indians and Africans into Europe.

All these movements made every European state more diverse in its religious professions. When Napoleon came to power, a grudging toleration barely existed in several European states. By the end of the 19th century the practice of universal toleration was almost complete.

How far these changes affected the social and cultural impact of the churches is hard to determine. Several theories have been proposed, for example, that toleration on any extended scale is a sure sign of a lukewarm faith and therefore of a weakened impact by faith on society. No one has succeeded in propounding any test for judging the truth of such a theory.

Industrial society was not responsible for the leading intellectual problem of the age, which unlike most intellectual problems had a direct effect on the cultural impact of the churches and ultimately upon their social impact: parts of Christianity, as hitherto taught, were proved untrue. In 1800 most Europeans believed that the world was about 6000 years old; a hundred years later most Europeans knew that it was far older. In 1800 most Europeans believed that Adam and Eve were historic characters; by 1900 many educated Europeans accepted that they were legendary. In 1800 a majority of educated Europeans still believed in the possibility of miracles; a century later many educated Europeans would look for any explanation of a strange event rather than miracle.

At one time this intellectual revolution was believed to be an important cause of the de-Christianizing of society. The theory was that if a professor of history read Darwin's *Origin of Species* he stopped going to church, and ceased to set an example to his maids and menservants, and so they, who did not read Darwin, also stopped going to church. The work of social historians has made this old and simple theory very doubtful. At present it looks as though the social causes were far weightier than the intellectual causes.

It is obvious, however, that if a child is taught at the age of five that Adam and Eve were the first people and the garden of Eden the first garden in the history of the world, and then discovers at school that neither people nor garden existed, he may feel an intellectual clash or

Family prayers in mid-19th-century England – from 'The Peep of Day, or a series of earliest religious instructions the infant mind is capable of receiving'.

he may drop the 'knowledge' of the child as easily as he drops the 'knowledge' of Father Christmas and his reindeer. We know of many such cases in middle-class families during the 19th century, usually but by no means exclusively during its second half.

This had a connection with industrial society because it was the new industrial city that first demanded and then made possible systems of national elementary education. The elementary school replaced lore inherited from the family by a basic lore derived from the community at large. In some countries, elementary schools were widely used even before the Industrial Revolution. But industry and city made them more and more common until they were universal. Schools helped to demolish inherited superstition and magic, belief in witchcraft, soothsayers and palmists and astrologers, even though all these things survived among the educated as well as the uneducated. Where religion was associated with ritual performances to secure a better harvest or a pregnancy, it was affected by every scheme of popular education.

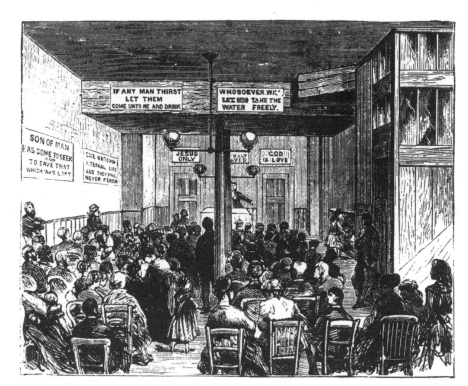

Dr Barnardo's East End juvenile mission, known as Mercy's House – here, destitute children were fed, clothed and educated, and where possible given a suitable industrial training. Great stress was laid on religious teaching, and each child was brought up under the influence and teaching of the denomination of the parents.

Inside the churches

Meanwhile the churches continued their endeavours relatively unperturbed. Internally they were troubled by arguments between liberal and conservative minds, and they needed to spend more time on their internal affairs – readjusting their teaching to new knowledge, and readjusting their constitutions to the new circumstances of the various states. That did not cause them to be unusually introspective compared with previous centuries, because they were confronted with such vast challenges from outside: the expansion of Europe, and European churches, into Asia and Africa and Australasia; the new cities, and especially the new slums. The churches also had to meet the new philosophies that offered themselves to educated men, the materialism of a Marx or a Haeckel, the moral despair of a Schopenhauer, the racial morality of various forms of social Darwinism, the ethical topsy-turveydom of a Nietzsche. Indeed, they coped with such philosophical onslaughts much more willingly and easily than they coped with the indifference and neutrality of urban life.

One way of coping was by raising large sums of money for what we should call plant: new churches, new church halls, new manses, or vicarages, new organizations and new people. Throughout Christendom, the 19th century was the greatest age for building that the church had ever seen; not greatest in terms of art, but in numbers and quality of materials. Medieval churches, Renaissance churches, Baroque churches were restored and decorated, not without loss

in the disappearance of an older art, but with gain in cleanliness and repair, ornament and furnishing. Far more colour was introduced – mosaic, frescoes, filigree – and whole industries developed in stained glass, organ building, woodwork, tombstones.

In such an age of expansion, the builders and church committees needed guidance in matters of taste. The age of neo-Gothic, and the return to the Middle Ages, had perhaps a little to do with reaction against the bleakness of industrial society. Pugin consciously promoted flamboyant colours because these were what helped the common man, coming into church from the drab surroundings of his home and work. Of the guides to taste, the most famous was the Camden Society (originally founded in Cambridge, England), which under the leadership of John Mason Neale systematically analyzed the 'proper' or 'Catholic' modes of furnishing and ornament. The fact that the Roman Catholic Church was centralized in the papacy made Italian habits of ornament or vestment dominant in the Roman Catholic practice of countries outside Italy. But Roman Catholics also needed guides, especially for the practice of liturgy and music. The musical return to the Middle Ages was directed in France by the Benedictine abbot Prosper Guéranger and the abbey of Solesmes. A lot of this work was unscholarly and uncritical, and sometimes demolished ways or rites which were beautiful and precious survivals from an ancient past; but the revival of Gregorian music came out of it, and it stood at the beginning of one of the important movements of renaissance in Christian worship. In

Germany, the old Benedictine abbey of Maria-Laach, near Koblenz, suppressed in the French Revolution, was revived towards the end of the century (1893) and soon grew into a centre for what came to be known as the Liturgical Movement in Christendom.

The churches of the 19th century had a strong feeling that they were advancing. Their morale was high; they felt they could meet the challenge of the new cities. The new cities housed more and more people, and so the congregations grew bigger, but the churches seldom realized that this numerical increase, though large, concealed a fall in percentage of the whole population. They saw Christianity spreading fast overseas and new churches springing up in Africa and India. They could turn into statistics their own new churches and manses and schools. Their morale was so high – they shared in the doctrine of progress and therefore were optimists by nature as well as by grace – that towards the end of the century quite serious Christian statesmen looked forward to 'the conversion of the world' in no distant future:

God is working his purpose out as year succeeds to year,
God is working his purpose out and the time is drawing near,
Nearer and nearer draws the time, the time that shall surely be,
When the earth shall be filled with the glory of God as the waters
cover the sea.

This hymn was written in 1894 by an Anglican, Arthur Campbell Ainger.

One of the fairest products of this flowering of art and music was the Christmas carol; a much older type of song, but now made popular, it elicited some of the best work of Christian composers, and helped to make the Christmas festival far more elaborate, even ornate, among the people – and not only church people.

To get new buildings was easier than to get ministers. A hard effort to raise money could make a church, but could never pay a man a stipend over fifty years. Moreover, the people were less easy to find, mainly because the sons of educated men had other opportunities for professional careers as society grew urban – more bureaucrats, industrialists, managers. Education had always been the special province of the churches. During the century it slowly came to be accepted that a schoolmaster who was a layman was as good as a schoolmaster who was a clergyman. The result was that the increase in ministers could not keep pace with the increase in buildings and congregations.

Protestant churches of the extreme left had long used laymen almost as ministers because they hardly recognized any distinction between a layman and a minister. During the 19th century more conservative churches – Anglican, Lutheran, Reformed, Methodist, even Roman Catholic, though this last was the most

LET HIM THAT HEARETH SAY, COME!

The 19th century foresaw a completely Christianized world, where all men would receive shelter in Jesus Christ, as shown in 'The Pictorial Missionary News' of 1871.

hesitant – began to use laymen for functions hitherto reserved for the ordained: reading lessons, preaching sermons, evangelizing in slums, taking missions to suburbs. The Roman Catholic church saw a parallel growth in the development of new religious orders, men or women under a type of monastic rule and wearing a religious habit, dedicated to caring for the sick or the old or the children.

The contrast between Protestant and Catholic is seen in the two famous providers for the needs of the lost children of the slums. Thomas John Barnardo, a layman, was converted in a Protestant mission at Dublin in 1862, and four years later devoted himself to the care of waifs in the slums of London. By the time he died in 1905 he had helped about a quarter of a million children and left behind him homes to continue the work. In Turin, John Bosco (who was a priest) started a system of schools, boy's clubs, homes and centres for technical training, which was already world-wide before he died in 1888.

One new form of lay power in the churches – like lay

power everywhere – was the press. In the Roman Catholic church of France the editor of *L'Univers*, Louis Veuillot, at one time exercised almost tyrannical power over bishops and priests. The policy of the church was no longer directed by the hierarchy alone. The attitudes of Roman Catholics to moral or even religious questions were made not only by prelates but by such men as Görres in Germany, Lord Acton or W. G. Ward in England and Orestes Brownson in the United States. In the Church of England the editors of the three leading church newspapers exercised the same sort of independent influences upon Christian opinion, as well as contributing to a better knowledge of the current problems and a wider diversity of view among churchmen. This is true also of the Unitarian editor of the *Spectator*, R. H. Hutton, and the religious correspondents of general papers like *The Times*, which during the century first became an organ of national opinion.

The quest for ministers had important consequences for women. The destruction of nunneries and the confiscation of their endowments during the revolutionary wars created a serious problem for unmarried women in Catholic countries, as well as for the nursing and educational services. As the nunneries were slowly restored, more and more women found vocations as nurses and teachers. Urban society displayed the same needs everywhere, leading to the extraordinary phenomenon, in England, Germany, America and France, of Protestant 'nuns'. In Germany the Lutheran pastor Theodor Fliedner dedicated himself to helping prisoners, prostitutes and little children, and soon saw that he needed trained women as ministers. He seized upon the New Testament word 'deaconesses' and founded, in 1836 at Kaiserswerth, a society of deaconesses. By 1850 he had as many as twenty-nine houses served by Kaiserswerth sisters, and from Germany they spread to American cities, Constantinople, Beirut and elsewhere, partly nursing and partly caring for children.

Fliedner's example was followed in England. The desperate nursing need of the Crimean War drew fresh attention to the work of nursing sisters. During the 1860s 'deaconesses' appeared in some London parishes and were commissioned by the bishop of London. The question began to arise whether a deaconess was the same kind of minister as a deacon; that is, whether women could be ordained, at least to certain offices in the church, in the same way as men. In the left wing of American Protestantism women preachers had long been accepted. In the last quarter of the 19th century the number of congregations or denominations accepting women preachers rose steadily. And even in denominations which cared about history and the past practice of the church, the use of women as lay officers or to give addresses in Sunday schools or halls grew slowly. In Catholic-minded denominations it remained unthinkable all through the century that women should administer sacraments (except baptism, long recognized as the right of midwives if a baby's life were in danger) or even preach; but the Church of England accepted a woman as preacher at an official service for the first time in 1919. Women sang in choirs during the 18th century, but only in galleries and in their ordinary clothes. Then, with the ceremonial precision and medieval revival of the early 19th century, they were excluded. In the later 19th century they reappeared, not in the gallery or wearing ordinary clothes, in the Church of England, but near the altar and wearing liturgical costume.

Meanwhile, women began to influence public opinion, mainly by writing novels with a social or cultural message (as with the works of Charlotte Yonge and George Eliot) but also by direct political action. During the 19th century this usually concerned laws touching morality. The classic case was the campaign of Josephine Butler during the 1870s and 80s to reform the law relating to prostitution and the 'white slave traffic', first in Britain and later on the European continent.

Christian churches remembered (hazily) a sunlit past, and an ideal to which they could still hark back. The village of Hursley near Winchester, where John Keble was the vicar, became an ideal of a Victorian parish, and it *was* an ideal parish, but a country parish of the old world, with paternal squire and dutiful peasantry. The ideals of the church, faced with modern urban conditions, changed rather more slowly than their practice, which itself changed more slowly than the speed of social development. The little village of Ars in France had another great priest Jean Vianney, known to posterity not by his name but simply as the Curé d'Ars. The ideal of the saint was still the person remote from the city – Bernadette was a girl who saw her visions of Lourdes, and round her shrine gathered train-loads of pilgrims, almost as though they were escaping from their city into the purer air of the simpler world. Thérèse of Lisieux was a young nun for whom simplicity was all. As the city-dweller needed fresh air at weekends, the religious 'city-dweller' needed a kind of spiritual fresh air, so that he could drink again from some sweeter unpolluted water of life and listen to a silence that was not broken by the clatter of engines.

THE AMERICAN EXPERIENCE

II

Religion at the grass-roots

THE STORY OF CHRISTIANITY in the United States is unique. Alone among nations it was founded with the explicit purpose of providing religious freedom; alone among nations it had no established church, no orthodox tradition. The result has been a proliferation of religious groups without precedent in the Old World. In Europe the founding of a new church was a conscious act of dissent against an old one. In America it was the natural and unremarkable outcome of any new idea or new interpretation. In the early 19th century, the laws of New York State required no more than six persons to constitute a religious society. None of this, incidentally, meant that Americans in general were more religious than other people. Quite the contrary. There were always large numbers – probably more than in other countries – who professed no religion at all.

One way of approaching the plethora of Christian sects in America is to divide them into those that come with the immigrants and those that have originated in America. To begin with, the British Puritan and Anglican strands were uppermost, with the Congregationalists, Presbyterians and Episcopalians. By the late 18th century these had been overtaken by Baptists, Methodists and Roman Catholics, each likewise linked to its European past, and there were numerous other groups, from Russian Orthodox to German Mennonites, also determined to maintain continuity. No group was ever in danger of suppression. Indeed, the churches in America, unlike those in Europe, were marked by a common respect for each other and a common belief in freedom. In such a tolerant climate more exotic growths were not slow to appear: Mormons (founded in 1830), Seventh Day Adventists (1843), Christian Scientists (1879), Pentecostalists (around 1900). . . . In the 20th century new churches have multiplied so fast that it is impossible to list them. Many Christians in America see this as a weakness, and there have been concerted efforts to achieve unity – often leading, ironically, to the creation of one more church – while evangelists like Billy Graham preach a generalized return to spiritual values not tied to any specific group.

One of the most interesting connected themes to the history of Christianity in America has been its relationship to politics, where religious passions may emerge more openly than in the purely doctrinal area. Most American presidents have professed Christianity of some sort, and voters have been concerned to know exactly what. In the ideological ferment that makes the United States today almost a microcosm of the Western world, this religious element is not likely to diminish.

'We . . . having undertaken for the glory of God
and advancement of the Christian faith, and the honour of our king and country, a voyage to plant the first colony in the northern parts of Virginia, do by these presents solemnly and mutually in the presence of God and one another, covenant and combine ourselves together into a civil body politic, for our better ordering and preservation.' The Mayflower Compact, signed by the Puritan settlers of 1620 before they landed at what is now Plymouth, Massachusetts, has become part of national mythology, and the ideal of religious freedom that they represented was to be built into the American constitution. A stained glass window made by Louis C. Tiffany in 1894 for the Congregational Church in Plymouth, depicts the signing. Round the table are Miles Standish, John Carver and his wife, William Brewster and Gilbert Winslow. (1)

SIGNING·THE·COMPACT

Mainstream currents

If the mosaic of American Christianity is complex, there is nevertheless a pattern. The newer sects may attract the publicity, but the older established churches still claim the largest memberships.

The reassuring face of 18th-century Congregationalism, stern but kindly, looks out from a portrait by Winthrop Chandler (*left*) of the splendidly named Reverend Ebenezer Devotion, 1770. (2)

Methodist preachers were expected to travel, braving floods, Indians, alligators and illness to bring the Gospel to the wilderness. This drawing appeared in 1867. (4)

The old Lutheran church of York, Pennsylvania (*left*), could muster a large congregation, nearly all of German descent, in 1800. Note the portraits of evangelists and prophets on the gallery, and the full-length of Luther on the wall. (3)

'The Puritan', by Augustus Saint-Gaudens, 1887, is included here not for its historical accuracy – though it is accurate – but because it is the definitive statement of an American archetype. Stern, unyielding, he embodies the spirit of the *Mayflower*. (6)

Catholics in New York formed a large community, partly Irish, partly Mediterranean. *Above:* drawing of an open-air shrine, 1906. S. Rocco, pointing to his plague sore, and flanked by candles, recalls an Italian street scene. (7)

The Baptists, beginning modestly on the eastern seaboard, grew to be one of the dominant groups, especially in the South. *Left:* baptism near Richmond, Virginia, in the 1890s. *Above:* a Black church in Baltimore, 1882. (5, 8)

267

The moral life

Christianity in America inevitably took some colouring from the prevailing social philosophy which has been called 'the Protestant ethic' – hard work, truthfulness, simple living – with less emphasis on liturgical and sacramental questions.

From the Netherlands came a strain of austere Protestantism that was to remain part of the American heritage. The Rev. Lazard Bayard (*right*) was pastor of the Walloon church of Breda in the early years of the 17th century. His daughter became the wife of Peter Stuyvesant, first governor of New York, then called New Amsterdam. The portrait went with her to the New World. (10)

'The Way of Good and Evil' ▷ (*opposite*), a lithograph of 1826, represents yet another allegory of salvation, this time spelled out more explicitly than ever. Typically, wickedness leads to misery in this world as well as punishment in the next. (12)

The Methodists propagated their church as zealously in America as in Europe. At camp meetings lasting several days (*opposite below*), the participants lived in tents in the forest. (13)

Over the generations the original, deeply felt convictions might fade. The painter Benjamin West (*above*) came from a strictly Puritan family, but whereas his father and brother, in the centre, held to the old way, the artist himself, with his wife and family, relaxed into easy gentility. (9)

The Bible was the foundation of New England religion (*right*, James and Sarah Tuttle, 1835), sufficient for both moral guidance and spiritual understanding, without the need for liturgy or sacraments. (11)

People and policies

Modern revivalists strive to make basic Christianity 'relevant' to young people by the methods of mass entertainment, while the established churches are traditionally patriotic bodies whose presence is expected on state occasions.

Hot Gospellers are an American tradition, though techniques have changed with changing fashions. *Above:* the Rev. Chuck Smith, Baptist and self-styled 'Jesus freak', whose territory is Costa Mesa, California. *Right:* scene from a three-day religious festival held close to Disneyworld at Orlando, Florida. *Below:* Rock'n'Roll in the aisles at the Old South Church, Boston. The inclusion of dancing as part of worship has a long history and is being revived in other countries besides the USA. (14–16)

God and Mammon? A large illuminated sign for a hair-toner dominates the little 'Rainbow Church' in downtown Los Angeles. 'He that believeth not shall be damned', says the billboard by the door. (17)

The religious affiliations of both Martin Luther King and President Kennedy (seen here greeting an Irish cousin who was a nun) had political implications, though in different ways. Kennedy was a politician first, a Catholic second; King's Baptist morality urged him towards the Civil Rights Movement. (18, 19)

'In God we trust': those who drew up the American constitution felt a need to give it a religious endorsement, though in the absence of an established church this had necessarily to be of the vaguest kind. Here President Johnson delivers his State of the Union speech to Congress in 1965. (20)

In wartime the churches of every country have normally supported the national effort. *Right:* a chaplain in Vietnam holds a service for the dead, in May 1968. Such uncritical approval has opened Christianity to the charge of being merely 'State Shinto'. (21)

Churches side by side, of different denominations but
equal status, are a common sight in America, though
surprising to the European visitor. On the Green of New
Haven, Connecticut, stand three elegant early 19th-century
buildings: first (on the left), the Neo-Gothic Trinity
Episcopal Church; second, the Congregationalist Center
Church, modelled on St Martin-in-the-Fields, London;
and third, the United Church, also Congregationalist. In the
far corner facing the Green, upper right, is the United
Methodist Church, with portico and spire, and beyond it is
the apse of the Battell Chapel of Yale University, built in
1876. (22)

II

Religion at the grass-roots

PAUL A. CARTER

SHOULD A TRAVELLER on a first visit to the United States idly leaf through a copy of any classified telephone directory and pause at the section on 'churches', these are some of the many entries he might find:

Refuge Temple of Christ
Elect Gospel Tabernacle Church of God in Christ
Hour of the Deliverance Church
Chinese Conservative Baptist Church
St Michael's Liberal Catholic Church
Burning Bush Pentecostal Church
Church of the Lord Jesus Christ of the Apostolic Faith
Tabernacle of Eternal Life
Church of the Universal Truth

Like countless predecessors, this visitor would have learned that America is a land of rampant sectarianism. Not since imperial Rome, he might reflect, where Mithras and Attis jostled Isis and Mary while the deified Romulus made room for the Black Stone, has a civilization known such jarring juxtapositions of religious faiths. Nor would he find this stimulating cacophony in a metropolis only. He might see, on a leafy back road in rural Ohio, a furious horse-and-buggy race between two bearded, black-garbed, flat-hatted Amishmen relaxing after Sunday service. Or perhaps, in a dusty Utah town, the lone one-storey motel would offer him, in addition to the omnipresent Gideon Bible, a copy of the Book of Mormon.

First impressions can be highly misleading, however, as any experienced traveller knows. On further enquiry our newcomer would discover, in the latest edition of the *Yearbook of American and Canadian Churches*, that this immense variety of sects groups itself naturally into some twenty 'families' of similar, and in some cases nearly identical, religious denominations – Adventist, Baptist, Lutheran, Methodist, Eastern Orthodox – and that these larger groupings claim the allegiance of an overwhelming majority of church members in the United States. Under its colourful surface there is, in short, a 'mainstream' in American Christianity after all. It is a different sort of stream from the one that flows in Europe, where historically established (if nowadays relatively unattended) state churches share religious space with more-or-less recognized modes of dissent, but it is a mainstream nonetheless. Snake-handling or foot-washing services are also authentic expressions of Christian America; but members of Congress, for example, if they go to church, are more likely to participate as conventional Catholics or Methodists.

The course of that American mainstream was fairly clear by about 1850. In 1790, when the first federal census was taken, the three most numerous religious fellowships in the original thirteen states had been the Congregationalists, the Presbyterians and the Episcopalians. All three had been products of the British colonial experience, side-effects of the English Reformation and its Puritan aftermath. What happened in the course of the next sixty years was that American history simply passed these bodies by. The Episcopalians, deriving from the Church of England's colonial state churches and from the missionary activities of the SPG (Society for the Propagation of the Gospel), became a class-linked group of decidedly limited popular appeal; the Presbyterians found their polity and their Calvinist intellectual tradition relatively uncongenial to the broad mass of Americans (excepting those of Scottish descent); and the Congregationalists, highly articulate and influential though they were, remained localized in their New England homeland while most of the American population moved elsewhere. In 1850, in stark contrast to the situation that had prevailed in 1790, the three most populous religious communions in America were the Baptists, the Methodists and the Roman Catholics.

How had this quiet revolution taken place? In the case of Catholicism the answer can be summed up in one word: immigration. This is not to say that Protestantism in the 19th century received no new recruits from overseas; a proverb among American Lutherans has it that the chief theological issue dividing the various synods of Lutheranism in America is whether God is Swedish, Norwegian or German. Largely because of this ingathering, followed by aggressive evangelism among English-speaking Americans, the Lutherans in the 20th century would emerge as the fourth largest of these 'mainstream' Christian groupings. Others – Russian Baptists, German Mennonites, Scandinavian converts to Mormonism – came

A Congregational minister in his pulpit, a rubbing from a gravestone at Paxton, Mass., dated 1769. Congregationalists and Presbyterians were among the most numerous denominations in America at this date.

THE
American Presbyterian
ALMANAC
FOR
1857.

THE PRESBYTERIAN HOUSE.

The Presbyterians remained strongly represented in the eastern states. Their depository (above) in Philadelphia was a substantial house in Chestnut Street.

and made places for themselves in the mosaic of American Christendom. In addition to these Protestant immigrants, Syrians, Greeks, Armenians and Russians added to American religion the wondrous liturgies of Eastern Orthodoxy. However, much the largest and most dramatic of these folk-wanderings that led to America were those of the Jews (whose story falls outside the scope of this study) and the Roman Catholics.

The mainstream: Catholics, Baptists and Methodists

In Protestant America, Catholic newcomers often encountered prejudice and discrimination, but they found no established Protestant state church standing in their path, and they could realistically look forward to a better future. To take the archetypal example, a working-class Irishman migrated to Boston; his son opened a saloon, which in 19th-century urban America functioned as a political clubhouse; his son, in turn, went to Harvard, played the stock market, and was named Ambassador to the Court of St James (a historically ironic appointment!); and *his* son was elected President of the United States, and was installed in a ceremony at which a Catholic prince of the church offered the inaugural prayer. To an unemployed immigrant labourer in the mid-19th century, as he stood reading an employment-office notice that 'no Irish need apply', such a future might have seemed unlikely. Such a person could, at any rate, have taken satisfaction in the stupendous growth of Catholicism itself, from a tiny minority in colonial times to the most numerous group of Christians in the nation: another kind of American success story. In 1847, while the Mormons were entering and settling the valley of the Great Salt Lake where their impressive grey stone temple now stands, Catholics on New York's Fifth Avenue, in the full glory of a Gothic architectural revival, were erecting St Patrick's Cathedral.

Furthermore, for all their difficulties with 'Know-Nothing' Protestant nativists, Catholics in the United States were spared some of the trials that beset their co-religionists elsewhere. The American Revolution had not been, to anywhere near the extent its French equivalent had been, an anticlerical revolution; there had existed no ancien régime with which it was felt that the fortunes of the church must stand or fall. Later, in the burgeoning industrialism of 19th-century America, few workers felt obliged to make an ideological choice between their parish and their trade-union local. The separation of church and state in America was not accomplished by mobilizing politically the state against the church. Quite the contrary; it was the fruit of an unlikely revolutionary wartime marriage between enlightened rationalists – some of whom, Jefferson and Thomas Paine, for example, *were* at least mildly anticlerical – and fervent evangelical Christians, who saw separation not as a way of shutting the church out from secular affairs but as a way of preventing the state from interfering with the free proclamation of God's Word. Those citizens who worked successfully to disestablish the American remnants of state churches (Anglican in Virginia and Maryland; Puritan in Massachusetts and Connecticut) included Baptists, Quakers, Presbyterians, and – logically, in those circumstances – Roman Catholics.

Eventually the separation of church and state in the United States, paradoxically, led to a greater cordiality between religion and government than existed in some Christian nations that retained formal establishments. As one American writer summed up the matter: 'The connection between Church and State in America is intimate and vital. It is not legal ... yet neither can do without the other, ... the State giving freedom of the Church, and the Church giving to the State moral character.' Some critics in our own century have vigorously disputed the moral character of the American state, but such disputants would be among the first to acknowledge that at times that state has shown a messianic and missionary tendency; that its people have constituted, in Sidney Mead's words, a 'nation with the soul of a church'. A Japanese exchange student, attending Christian worship in a small town in Vermont towards the end of the Korean War, on the Sunday nearest the Fourth of July, heard prayers for the armed forces, other patriotic prayers and, at the Offertory, following a common practice at that time in American Protestant churches, a Doxology followed by the last stanza of 'America'. Asked afterwards what he thought of the service, the young Japanese smiled quizzically and said: 'Sounds like State Shinto!'

Catholic clerics in America, despite their church's universalism, have also been capable of utterances as nationalistic as those of any Protestant, from John (afterwards Cardinal) Carroll, preaching timely patriotic sermons during the American Revolution, to Francis Cardinal Spellman, ministering to troops dug in along Korea's hilly battle-line. 'The spirit of America wafts its spell across seas and oceans, and prepares distant continents for the implanting of American ideas and institutions', cried John Ireland, a Civil War military chaplain who was afterwards archbishop of St Paul, Minnesota. 'The centre of human action and influence is rapidly shifting, and at no distant date America will lead the world.'

Such a social polity as America's afforded equally ample scope for both Catholic and Protestant modes of evangelism. To Protestant charges that the Catholic

BIDDY M'FLINN AND FATHER O'QUIGLY.

Catholic ranks were swollen in the mid-19th century by an influx of poor Irish fleeing from the Famine. G. A. Sala's drawing of 1882 casts a sharp but not unfriendly eye on their situation.

Mormonism was a truly American religion, owing nothing to any European precedent. Above: a Mormon confirmation in 1852.

church was 'un-American' in its theoretical opposition to religious toleration and to church–state separation (classically expressed in the Syllabus of Errors of Pius IX), Catholics in the United States often retorted that a church universal was far better suited than caste- and class-bound Protestantism to fulfil the American secular ideal, *e pluribus unum*. At the beginning of the 19th century, however, Protestantism in America was not nearly so caste- and class-bound as it later became. It had, more than Catholicism at that time, the character of a widely dispersed national folk religion, of which the most effective carriers were the Methodists and the Baptists.

Baptist beginnings in Britain's former North American seaboard colonies, like those of Catholicism, were initially modest. Unlike the migrants to America from Catholic countries, however, the Baptists from Europe had been part of a small and usually proscribed minority. They enjoyed a brief flourishing in England under Cromwell, developing the religious culture out of which came John Bunyan's Christian classic *Pilgrim's Progress*. During that period Roger Williams, who in the course of his long life came to profess Baptist views, secured a charter for the colony of Rhode Island; and Henry Dunster, the President of Harvard, scandalized Puritan Massachusetts by becoming a Baptist in 1654. (For this act Dunster was politely but firmly ousted and exiled.) However, Baptist congregations, insisting that the Anglican colonial establishments were hopelessly ensnared in 'popery' and that the Puritan state churches

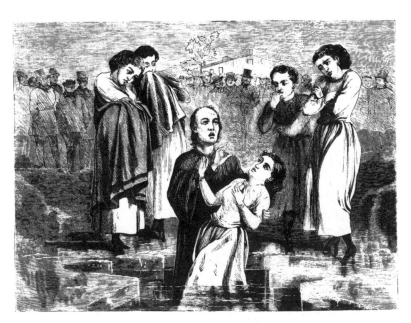

Total immersion at zero degrees centigrade. To the Baptists, successful evangelizers of the Mid-West, enthusiasm and dedication made up for any theological limitations.

were incomplete and inconsistent in their allegiance to the Reformation, continued to appear and thrive. In 1700, no less an establishment Puritan cleric than Cotton Mather – the witch hunter! – assisted at the installation of a Baptist pastor in Boston, and by the time of the revolution the Baptists for all practical purposes had achieved both religious freedom and respectability.

Then came the great internal migration towards the Mississippi Valley. It was a migration primarily of the 'unchurched', for in the 1790 census only five per cent of the citizens of the United States professed any religious affiliation whatsoever. The home missionary need was great, and Eastern seaboard Protestant divines such as Lyman Beecher warned that these unconverted frontier masses might first be reached by popish missionaries, and the West thereby lost to Catholicism – which was, of course, already well entrenched in neighbouring Quebec and in the northern borderlands of Spanish America.

For the vast evangelical task awaiting all the churches in the American hinterland, the Baptists were peculiarly well adapted. Unlike the older denominations they did not, at first, require a university-trained clergy. Typically, the Baptist evangelist on the American frontier was a farmer–preacher who took up his bottom land along the river, cleared it, planted it, and built his house, which served also as a religious meeting place for his neighbours. Baptist clergymen did not have to make long and hazardous journeys back to an episcopal residence to be ordained; they received full ordination from the local congregation of baptized believers. Unlike the intricate theological discourse of many Congregationalist and Presbyterian clerics, the Baptist sermon was likely to be a straightforward exhortation to come forward and be saved – and it was also likely to be punctuated by vehement cries of 'Amen, brother', 'Hallelujah', and 'Praise the Lord', or by still more physical responses, which the settled areas back East would have considered indecorous.

Nationally, the Baptist polity was loose almost to the point of anarchy, yet Baptists back East were able, by tithes and free-will offerings, to support a thriving home missionary enterprise. Most importantly, their rigorously literal insistence upon the priesthood of all believers – or, at any rate, of all adult baptized-by-immersion believers – accorded well with the secular ethos of Jacksonian America, which was similarly levelling and anti-elitist. Moreover, their evangelical fervour, with its insistence upon the primacy of emotional, subjective experience, was a powerful religious variant on a movement that elsewhere in the world at that time was termed Romanticism. In any event, they prospered, and they had an eventual impact on America that is incalculable. In the mid-20th century a Black clergyman from Georgia with roots deep in Baptist tradition became the acknowledged leader of the Civil Rights Movement; and, eight years after Martin Luther King's tragically untimely death, Jimmy Carter, another Georgia Baptist, holding moral-theological views of no little portent for foreign policy, was elected President of the United States.

Methodism, an early 18th-century movement deriving from the Church of England, had its colonial beginnings in the First Great Awakening (*c.* 1740). Separated from their British Methodist brethren – they could hardly have done otherwise, given founder John Wesley's firm Tory view of the War for Independence – the American Methodists in 1784 created a tightly centralized organization that seemed the exact opposite of the informal Baptist polity. Yet they took up the challenge of the expanding frontier with comparable effectiveness. Their method, already employed by Wesley in the industrial Midlands of England, was itinerancy. Every ordained Methodist elder was expected to travel; to be 'located', in Methodist parlance, meant to be retired from active service. Their bishops, instead of presiding over geographic dioceses of the traditional sort, 'circulated freely throughout the Connection'. Edward Eggleston, who grew up on the Indiana frontier and lived the Methodist life, wrote: 'In a true picture of frontier life, neither the Indian nor the hunter is the centre-piece, but the circuit-rider.'

One wandering Methodist evangelist passed on horseback through the pages of Eggleston's factually based novel *The Circuit-Rider* (1874), experiencing 'perils of Indians, perils of floods, perils of alligators, perils of bad food, perils of cold beds, perils of robbers, perils of rowdies, perils of fevers, and the weariness of five thousand miles of horseback riding in a year, with five or six hundred preachings in the same time, and the care of numberless scattered churches in the wilderness'. Methodist religion was as emotional as that of the Baptists; its adherents were known in the 19th century as the 'shouting Methodists', and eye-witness accounts of some of their fire-lit camp meetings in the forests describe people leaping, jerking, barking or rolling on the ground.

In order to carry their gospel to a population much of which was unlettered as well as unchurched, these Methodist pastors had to simplify and vivify. They have, therefore, often been considered as an anti-intellectual force in America. On the other hand, Eggleston believed – as have many social historians since his time – that the circuit-riders more than anyone else, as they started colleges and schools and fought against moral laxness and intemperance, helped to bring cultural order out of the chaos on the frontier. In

Methodism as a missionary religion. Here, in Boston, 1826, a minister preaches to a mixed congregation and an accompanying commentary gives us the thoughts of its members. No. 2, for instance, thinks the style 'very clear and energetic, calculated to influence the lower orders. Such men are useful.' No. 3 is put off by the 'shouting, howling and groaning'. No. 4, a child, thinks what a dreadful thing it is to die and go to hell. But the people in the front, especially Nos 11 and 12, have repented of their sins and go weeping to the altar to pledge themselves to a new life.

any case, Methodist influence upon American society, like that of the Baptists, has been profound. Methodist zeal and piety motivated presidents as diverse otherwise as William McKinley and James K. Polk.

Back in the seaboard cities and the older towns, Methodist and Baptist religious life was more sedate, but at times equally taxing. There the challenger was not the highway robber but the urban slumlord, not fever and flood but epidemic disease and the saloon. Methodists and Baptists, rural as well as urban, faced also the divisions that tore the nation as a whole. As the insoluble quarrel over slavery shattered the Whig and Democratic parties so also it begot a Northern Baptist Convention and a Southern Baptist Convention; a Methodist Episcopal church and a Methodist Episcopal church, South. Nor were the older, more liturgical churches, with the notable exception of Roman Catholicism, immune from this same kind of division. In due course emerged a Presbyterian church in the United States that was northern, and a Presbyterian church that was southern; their descendants remain separated to this day.

Even the Lutherans, although shielded from political–cultural trends to some extent by language barriers (at the time of the revolution one-third of Pennsylvania spoke German, and new German immigration in the 1840s powerfully reinforced American Lutheranism) and by their innate confessional conservatism, found themselves polarizing into a General Synod largely confined to the North, and a General Synod of the South. There were racial as well as regional schisms; separate denominations of Black Methodists, Black Baptists and Black Presbyterians appeared. That process began immediately after the revolution, when a Black Methodist, the Rev. James Allen, was forcibly interrupted at prayer in New York City's John Street Methodist Church; he at once went across the street and founded an African Methodist denomination in protest. Episcopalians held out against these various centrifugal tendencies longer than most; but in 1861, after secession, the southern Anglicans organized a Protestant Episcopal church in the Confederate States of America. One of their bishops, Leonidas Polk, went so far in his militancy as to become a prominent and quite able Confederate general. The paradox was not lost upon Abraham Lincoln, who sadly observed in his second inaugural address that in America's Civil War 'both sides read the same Bible and pray to the same God, and each invokes His aid against the other'.

Civil War and Darwinism

The war came as a religious shock to Americans. The ante-bellum years had been a time, as Professor Mead puts it, 'when wise men hoped'; it had then seemed reasonable to combine a confident prediction of the coming of Christ's kingdom on Earth – perhaps in America itself, as the Mormons, for example, believed it would – with an optimistic secular faith in America as the land of opportunity and progress. Now, suddenly, boys in their teens went out to slaughter one another, and the nation was painfully reminded that some stories cannot have happy endings. 'The prayers of both [North and South] could not be answered', said Lincoln as the war neared its close; 'that of neither has been answered fully'.

The simplest religious explanation, which was indeed offered in many a wartime pulpit, was that the Civil War had come as a divine punishment for the sins and wickedness of men; of grasping, avaricious Yankees, if the sermon was preached in the South, or of overbearing slaveholders, if the pulpit was a northern one. A few Christian Americans saw the fratricidal tragedy more comprehensively, as an appropriate judgment of God upon an entire irresponsible people, who at the outset of national independence had not faced and dealt with racial injustice in accordance with their own revolutionary ideals. However, a just God might yet allow those ideals to prevail. Lincoln, in his brief remarks in 1863 at the blood-soaked field of Gettysburg, hopefully resolved on behalf of his countrymen 'that this nation, under God, shall have a new birth of freedom'. Out of civil strife could come national regeneration, possibly in the form of a war-born fusion of America's wide diversity of regions, classes and cultures into a free, mature, continent-spanning society.

Unfortunately in the post-bellum years that promise was not to be fulfilled. In the reconstructed South, liberty was extended to the former slaves only to be whittled away. On the high plains the native Americans' long and gallant stand against the advancing white civilization was crushed at last. In the bustling, smoky cities, furious collisions between capital and labour – a kind of strife from which many Americans had fondly imagined their country to be immune – convinced some that postwar America was governed by the law of the jungle rather than by Abraham Lincoln's proclaimed national ideal of 'malice toward none, charity for all'. By a malign coincidence, just at that moment in the history of the Western world the law of the jungle was receiving what seemed a scientific rationale, in Charles Darwin's *Origin of Species* (1859) and *Descent of Man* (1871).

Darwinism challenged traditional Christianity at several levels. The rich variety of life as found on this planet was not the created evidence of divine purpose; it was a product of blind chance, filtered through the mechanical process of natural selection. Man had not fallen from a state of primal innocence; he had risen from a state of primal savagery. The Bible was not an infallible record of the origins of the world and of humanity; it was a transcript of the way those origins had been imagined in a pre-scientific age. Worst of all, from a Christian standpoint, the brutal naturalistic doctrine of the 'survival of the fittest' made an absurdity of the Christian injunction to 'love thy neighbour as thyself'.

American responses to these several challenges ranged from whole-hearted acceptance to outright rejection. Evolution was no threat to religion, the genteel Boston philosopher, John Fiske, insisted; it was simply 'God's way of doing things'. The distinguished Princeton theologian, Charles Hodge, disagreed: 'What is Darwinism?' Hodge asked in 1873, and answered himself: 'It is Atheism.' On the evolution question, and more broadly on the interpretation of the Bible in the light of science, Christians in the United States divided deeply, a division that (to a greater extent than is often assumed) persists to the present day.

On many plantations in the South before the Civil War it was common for religious services to be organized for the slaves; a Black preacher, perhaps from a nearby plantation, addressed the workers and their children, and the owner and his family also attended.

'Something to be done'

Christianity in America was ill-equipped to cope intellectually with such questions, for by and large it was not a theologians' or a philosophers' religion. The task, as American churchmen perceived it, was not primarily one of reconciling science or modern philosophy with religion; it was one of preaching, building, organizing. 'Work, for the night is coming', one favourite 19th-century American Gospel hymn enjoined; or, as one nationally prominent pastor later expressed it: 'Christianity first and last is something to be done.'

Above all, it was something to be done in the rapidly growing urban centres. No longer would it suffice to write off the wicked city as fallen and irreligious (as some rural clerics in America continued to do), any more than it would suffice to write off the city politically and continue in Thomas Jefferson's archaic belief that those who laboured in the earth – and they alone – were the chosen people of God. In the turbulent decades of the 1870s and 1880s, when rising entrepreneurs plundered their way to vast new wealth while railway and mine workers fought pitched battles with militiamen, the city, of necessity, displaced the farm as a frontier for religious (as well as political) action; the Methodist circuit-rider dismounted and perforce became something of a social worker. The urgency of the new task was felt to be great; for in America, as in Europe at that same time, churchmen were worried lest, in dealing with urban poverty and industrial unrest, they might lose the initiative to anticlerical radicals, anarchist or socialist. In 1886 – two months before a May Day labour rally in Chicago's Haymarket Square, when some unknown person threw a bomb – the great evangelist to the cities, Dwight L. Moody, declared that the urban masses would either be reached

279

The Five Points Mission in New York (1882) supplemented the Word of God with sustenance for the body – here, one of the mission workers hands out bread to children.

by the Gospel, as the frontier folk had been before them, or else 'the leaven of communism and infidelity ... will break out in a reign of terror such as this country has never known'.

In this potentially revolutionary situation, was the conventional kind of evangelism enough? Some complacent Christians thought so. As the superintendent of the Chicago City Missionary Society declared in 1888: 'Our poor do not need largesses of corn, as old Rome thought, but the Word of God, which is able to make them cleanly, independent, healthy, and righteous.' The Word of God, however, had also traditionally included an injunction to feed the hungry, clothe the naked, minister to the sick – and to drive the money changers out of the Temple. That impulse to widen the Christian evangelical mission beyond simple personal morality, already evident before the Civil War in movements such as the anti-slavery crusade, now manifested itself in criticism of the heartless and exploitative new industrial order. Trade unionists in America, unlike their anticlerical equivalents in some other countries, often used evangelical language, describing Moses and Aaron for example as 'Walking Delegates' who had made an 'attempt at organizing labor' among the oppressed Israelites in ancient Egypt, just as other labour organizers now

sought to unite the working classes in the modern world. Uriah Stephens, the initial president of the Knights of Labor – the first really massive attempt to organize American industrial workers – was a former Baptist minister; his successor, Terence Powderly, was a devout Catholic, who prevailed upon James Cardinal Gibbons to dissuade the Vatican from condemning the Knights (as the conservative French hierarchy in Canada had done); and both Stephens and Powderly presided over a trade union movement whose avowed goal was 'the brotherhood of man under the fatherhood of God'.

Christian activists of every stripe, from Anglo-Catholics in liturgical vestments to Salvation Army workers in severely plain uniforms, took up the challenge of the city. This 'social gospel', as it came to be called, addressed itself not only to the sins of the individual – intemperance, for example – but also to those of society as a whole. It ranged from social settlement work in the cities, inspiring a generation of idealistic activist women, such as Jane Addams, to militant demands for the reform or purgation of capitalism, which 'social gospel' theologian Walter Rauschenbusch termed 'an unregenerate part of the social order'. Occasionally it passed over into socialism, on the assumption that Christian love was absolutely incompatible with the profit motive. That had been said in America before; religious communes flourished in the 19th century, renouncing private property with its implicit sanction for selfishness, in the name of Gospel order and on the precedent of Acts 11:44–45. Some of the more thoroughgoing, such as the Shakers and the Oneida community, pushed that logic on to the abolition of the conventional family as well.

However, as Arnold Toynbee once remarked, nothing fails like success. By pooling their economic resources such communes typically prospered, and in the atmosphere of bourgeois America many of them evolved into ordinary capitalist enterprises. Unlike some that fell by the wayside in this fashion, the Shakers kept their communal faith to the last; but their concept of the equality of men and women on a basis of total celibacy, although not without precedent in Early Christian history, had little appeal as a model for commune founders in the Freud-haunted 20th century. Their plain, severely beautiful buildings and tools have captured the imagination of modern functionalists, but they had little directly to say to the struggle of capital and labour in Victorian America.

The broader social awakening in American religion, however, symbolized in Protestantism by the 'social gospel' and in Catholicism by the quickened social conscience articulated in Leo XIII's encyclical *Rerum Novarum* (1891), did speak to the condition of

A life of celibacy, confession of sin, power over physical disease and separation from the world were the basic Shaker tenets. They lived in 'families' of 30 to 90 individuals, dressed plainly, as shown in this lithograph of 1870, and protested against the fashions of a vain world. In the mid-19th century there were several thousand Shakers, but by the mid-20th century there were fewer than a hundred members.

America's next political generation, commonly called 'progressive'. In the United States at the end of the 19th century, it seemed perfectly natural that an aspiring politician, William Jennings Bryan, should win a major-party nomination for president with a fiery speech whose biblically cadenced conclusion warned the lords of finance capital in America: 'You shall not press down upon the brow of labor this crown of thorns; you shall not crucify mankind upon a cross of gold.'

Witnesses, scientists and speakers in tongues

However, some who agreed with the Christian activists' diagnosis of the ills of American society profoundly disagreed with their prescriptions for its cure. The violent collisions between workers and owners in late 19th-century America, Charles Taze Russell declared in 1886, were but surface symptoms of far more grievous dislocations yet to come. The passing of eleven turbulent years only confirmed Russell in his prophetic pessimism: all the signs of the times, including the rapidly escalating international arms race, Russell wrote in 1897, pointed towards the cataclysm that was to precede Christ's Second Coming. Famine, pestilence, war and death, the Four Horsemen predicted in the Revelation of St John the Divine, were about to ride, and the Christian believer would be well advised to get out of their way.

Out of Pastor Russell's prophecies arose the highly effective modern mass movement known as Jehovah's Witnesses, a new example of the millennialism that had manifested itself periodically throughout Christian history. In America, literal applications of the Books of Daniel and Revelation to current events had long been popular. One specific prediction that the world would end at a definite day and hour in 1843 had led, not to disillusionment as might logically have been expected, but to the creation of a strong new denomination, the Seventh-Day Adventists. The tendency continued; throughout the second half of the 19th century 'prophetic conferences' spread millennialist ideas among representatives of the more conventional denominations, and had a great deal to do with the rise of what, in the early 20th century, came to be known as Fundamentalism.

Far from dying out in a rapidly modernizing world, such ideas were destined to take on renewed vitality as the world experienced social disruption and military catastrophe. Jehovah's Witnesses, when they came to predict an exact date for the calamities forecast in the Book of Revelation to begin, hit upon October of 1914, and they could hardly have picked a more plausible year. On this point, secular rationalism has recently found itself incongruously in agreement with biblical literalism. Barbara Tuchman, a distinguished historian of the dread events in Europe during the summer of 1914, has expressed the belief that the future will look back on the First World War as having been the beginning of the collapse of Western civilization:

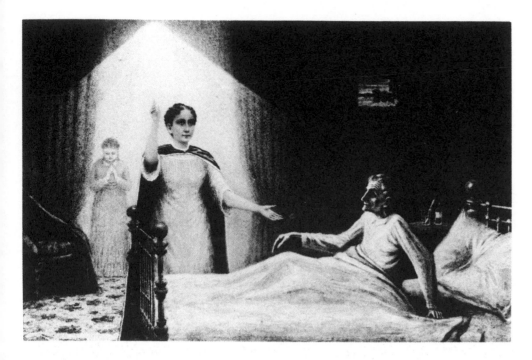

'There is now', Tuchman said in a 1980 interview, 'a pervasive sense of things being out of control.' Exactly so, say the millennialists. Today in American popular religion the interpretation of news events (especially in the Middle East) as the fulfilment of Bible prophecies continues unabated, generating the sale of millions of paperback copies of Hal Lindsay's ominously titled book, *The Last Days of the Late, Great Planet Earth* (1970), and the production of a film with the same title, portentously narrated by Orson Welles.

In gilded-age America, both the new social Christianity and the new millennialism may be seen as critical dissents from that era's complacent materialism; but an even purer dissent from that materialism was embodied in *Science and Health, with Key to the Scriptures*, by Mary Baker Eddy (1875). The notion that matter is evil or nonexistent, a belief basic to many of the religions of the Orient, has lurked throughout Christian history as an ever-tempting heresy. Nurtured in the rich cultural compost of post-Calvinist New England, Mrs Eddy's doctrine of Christian Science went far beyond faith healing or 'mind cure'. Seemingly tangible evils – pain, illness, death itself – were redefined as *errors*; overcoming them was merely a matter of achieving the right point of view. The age-old problem of suffering, which had grieved and perplexed humanity since its classic statement in the Book of Job, was breathtakingly solved by denying its existence altogether.

Attacked by the medical profession, which had only recently elucidated the germ theory of infection and disease, Christian Science was judged more sympathetically as a 'religion of healthy-mindedness' by the psychologist and philosopher William James (in *The Varieties of Religious Experience*, 1902). As modern medicine has flourished and grown, so has the church

founded by Mrs Eddy; and the internationally circulated newspaper that she established, the *Christian Science Monitor*, has earned the respect of many who share none of her religion's distinctive tenets.

Less audacious than Christian Science in its claims, but more pervasive, was the self-help religion that came into prominence at about the same time, urging in a somewhat gnostic fashion that one could think or will one's way to success or happiness. Rarely institutional in form, this very American faith typically spread its message through pep-talk books, of which the best known is *The Power of Positive Thinking*, by Norman Vincent Peale (1952) – a minister, incidentally, in the Dutch Reformed Church, doctrinally considered one of the more conservative of the old-line denominations. This 'positive thinking' gospel has become a major element in modern American Protestantism, and even in the Catholic fold its influence is not unknown.

Yet another challenge to conventional church religion in America was Pentecostalism, which emerged as a distinct movement around 1900. A religion of ecstasy, of spontaneous utterance, such as speaking in tongues, the Pentecostal faith arose in reaction against the deadly formalism its adherents found in the older churches; they sought, in the midst of a modern urban setting, the kind of emotional release in worship that had formerly been known at Methodist and Baptist gatherings on the frontier – or, as the name suggests, at the assemblies of the members of the apostolic generation. It is an ever-recurring theme in Christian history, perhaps in the history of all religions: the 'sect' or 'cult' evolves into a 'church'; the ecstatic prophet metamorphoses into the cautious priest, who slows down the wildness of religious exercise until it becomes formal and sober, which in turn prompts a new prophet to rise in protest. In America, the process was greatly accelerated. Paraphrasing Psalms CXVIII:22, the stone that the builders rejected became the headstone of the corner – regularly, at intervals of about fifty years.

Pentecostalism in America, true to this recurrent pattern, embodied itself at first in new denominations, which in the course of time, as their members prospered in the secular world, acquired robed choirs, Gothic houses of worship and accredited theological seminaries – all the churchly paraphernalia of the Pentecostals' competitors. Thus, by 1960, it would become necessary for a similar movement, this time renamed 'charismatic', to break forth again. This new Pentecostalism, however, would be as likely to arise in staid Episcopalian or even Catholic congregations as in the more previously typical hired store front or Gospel tent. Asked in 1964 why phenomena such as glossolalia (speaking in tongues) or divine healing services should suddenly have appeared in churches that a short time previously would have had nothing to do with such goings-on, a jovial American Anglican bishop answered: 'Obviously, the Holy Spirit just now has a lot to say.'

'Essential oneness'

Challenged by science, by the city and by rival religious life-styles, such as Christian Science and Pentecostalism, religious leaders in America at the turn of the century had to question whether the more traditional kinds of doctrinal and organizational disagreements they had with one another really mattered. In 1908, a delegate to the founding convention of a new national religious confederation, the Federal Council of the Churches of Christ in America, dismissed all denominational differences – however much cherished – as 'bird-tracks in prehistoric mud'. Historic disputes, which the first settlers had brought over in their baggage, as well as quarrels that had broken out in the churches after their arrival in the New World, now seemed, to some, obsolete. The time had come, such witnesses believed, when Christians in a modern world that was increasingly hostile to their way of life ought to emphasize what they held in common rather than to indulge in further separations. 'In the Providence of God', the preamble to the Federal Council's Plan of Federation proclaimed, 'the time has come when it seems fitting more fully to manifest the essential oneness of the Christian Churches of America.'

Earlier generations of Americans had made overtures towards Christian unity, or at least towards Protestant unity; but such overtures commonly had ended in further discord. For example, one entire denomination, founded at the beginning of the 19th century – the largest orthodox Protestant body entirely native to North America, claiming the allegiance of two American presidents (Garfield and Lyndon Johnson) – was the handiwork of former Methodists, Baptists and Presbyterians who consciously cast off their denominational moorings in order to dwell together as 'Christians only'. Ironically, this promising experiment in Christian union evolved into yet one more church alongside all the rest; in fact it became three: the Christian Churches, the Disciples of Christ and the Churches of Christ. Similarly, the great evangelical awakenings tended to cut across and blur traditional denominational lines; a revivalist preacher – in the 18th century, George Whitefield, in the 19th, Dwight L. Moody, in the 20th, Billy Graham – typically waged his evangelistic campaign for an American city's soul with the co-operation of a local interchurch committee. Nonetheless, these same evangelical awakenings just as regularly provoked new disagreements that only multiplied the number of competing denominations.

Furthermore, many American Christians in their more reflective moments praised, rather than condemned, the varieties of their religious experience. James Madison in the republic's early years believed that denominational rivalries were a sign and source of religious vitality, in spite of – or perhaps even *because* of – their intersectarian fierceness. Half a century after Madison's death, the director of the Division of Churches for the eleventh United States Census likened Americans' religious experimentalism to their genius for engineering and technical innovation: 'We have invented more curious and useful things than any other nation', Henry King Carroll observed in 1893. 'In matters of religion we have not been less liberal and enterprising.' Such approval of religious pluralism as a principal source of strength, secular as well as religious, has continued to find powerful champions. 'This country has been singularly blessed', said John F. Kennedy, 'in its ability to take the best of all religions and cultures – not merely tolerating differences but building a new and richer life upon them.'

On the other hand, this high degree of plurality was perhaps a luxury that a shrinking planet could no longer afford. 'Is the great family of man divided by races, and geographical separations, and varying traditions, and habits, and languages?' an American Episcopalian asked, in a Lenten sermon preached near the end of the Civil War. 'The Christianity which is to remedy this [is] still more divided than the human race itself.' The social conscience then awakening in America's churches might indeed be incompatible with traditional Protestant separateness – which commonly in America was along social rather than theological lines. Denominationalism, as H. Richard Niebuhr classically summed it up in 1929, 'draws the color line in the church of God;

it fosters the misunderstandings, the self-exaltations, the hatreds of jingoistic nationalisms ... in the body of Christ; ... it seats the rich and poor apart at the table of the Lord'. This socially premised anti-sectarianism had special urgency for Americans concerned with foreign missions, an activity that in the course of the 19th century had expanded to world-wide proportions. It is said that at one time there existed, on a street corner in Shanghai, a building with a sign proclaiming it to be the 'American Dutch Reformed Church of China'; surely, church union advocates argued, it made little sense to perpetuate distinctions based on historical accidents irrelevant to the local situation, for converts who must find them meaningless.

Dedicated sectarians replied – as they always had – that unity achieved at the price of truth as they understood it was no unity at all. To 'minimize our differences, magnify the cardinal tenets that unite, and consolidate our common spiritual resources', as the Southern Methodist bishops proposed just prior to re-joining the northern brethren from whom they had been separated for a century, might simply be to dilute their Gospel witness into vague platitudes as bland as those contained in a typical American political party platform. The Federal Council of Churches aspired to include all the major branches of at least non-Roman Catholic Christendom in America; but two strong, zealous and rapidly growing denominations – the Southern Baptists and the Missouri Synod Lutherans – refused, on principle, to join. Moreover, those bodies that did join the council soon learned that in the 20th century, conflict *among* denominations in America was going to be far less severe than conflict *within* them.

The optimistic, science-minded, socially conscious liberals who had been moving steadily into positions of authority and control in the churches suddenly found themselves assailed by premillennialists, who were unhappy with the progressive secular Utopianism that seemed to pervade the American branch of Christendom; by biblical literalists, who were opposed both to Darwinian evolution, as inconsistent with Genesis, and to rationalistic explainings-away of Christ's miraculous life and work; and by evangelicals, who were concerned lest the new 'social gospel' mislead Christians into providing for people's material welfare while neglecting the needs of their souls. Between 1909 and 1914, essays containing these several kinds of objection appeared in twelve widely distributed paperback volumes titled *The Fundamentals: A Testimony to the Truth*. Vividly written and often cogently argued, these books constituted a manifesto against most of what had lately been happening to Christianity in America. Shortly the battle lines were drawn within most denominations, between factions that shortly became

known respectively as 'Fundamentalists' and 'Modernists' – and precisely at that moment the guns of August signalled the outbreak of the First World War.

Religious liberals, following the lead of President Woodrow Wilson – a scion of seven generations of Scottish Presbyterian clergymen – hailed the international struggle as a holy crusade to make the world safe for democracy. America was going to war 'for the principles which gave her birth', said Wilson to Congress in his message of Easter Monday, 1917. 'God helping her', the President exclaimed – echoing Martin Luther – 'she can do no other.'

Crisis of faith

In all human history, few hopes have been more cruelly disappointed than those raised by Woodrow Wilson's crusade. Like the United States after 1865, the world after 1918 failed to experience the promised 'new birth of freedom'. In the course of the conflict, to be sure, several mighty empires that had long stood fast against democracy were swept away. However, with a few notable exceptions, such as Finland and Czechoslovakia, the regimes that rose out of the imperial ruins were not democracies but thinly disguised autocracies, some of them having a police efficiency and a control of opinion beyond anything the old autocracies had ever dreamed. Churchmen, insofar as they had committed themselves to the war, inevitably became targets of the resulting disillusionment. 'We trusted our religious leaders', Walter Marshall Horton wrote in 1930, 'when they proclaimed their apocalyptic visions of a new heaven and a new earth, whose coming was contingent upon the military victory of the Allied Powers; and ... we are pretty well convinced that they betrayed us.' Religious conservatives may have been less surprised than the liberals to discover that human beings in this fallen world had learned nothing from tragedy except the desire for vengeance. Yet the hopes of some of the Bible-believing conservatives had been disappointed also; for four terrible years the Four Horsemen had ridden the length and breadth of Europe spreading chaos and destruction, and still in the end Jesus had not come.

'We trusted that God would, somehow, balance the stupendous evils of the war by an equal weight of good,' Horton continued, 'and if faith in God is declining today, it is because many feel that *that* faith, too, has betrayed them.' Armistice Day raised the curtain on a decade during which the scepticism and irreligion formerly professed by elite minorities emerged into wide popular acceptance. According to a YMCA-sponsored study of *Religion Among American Men* (1920), the rank-and-file American soldiers who had served in France – and who, as conscripts in a *levée en masse*, could be regarded as a reasonably representative cross-section of the population at large – considered the church 'a convenient institution for the performance of conventional ceremonies, venerable ... but not much concerned with the real business of life; ... you go there to be married and buried'.

Although the decade of the 1920s also knew religious yearnings, heartfelt if at times vague, it was regularly punctuated by well-received anti-religious tracts having titles like *The Twilight of Christianity*. No doubt, many Americans expressed their non-religiousness less verbally than by writing, reading or discussing such books; in 'mainstream' churches the traditional Sunday evening service and the Wednesday prayer meeting waned to the point of extinction, as people went bowling or to the movies instead – or stayed at home listening to music or comedy on the radio. In 1927 Reinhold Niebuhr, in a book provocatively titled *Does Civilization Need Religion?*, summed up the new mood: 'Religion is not in a robust state of health in modern civilization. Vast multitudes ... live without seeking its sanctions ... and die without claiming its comforts.'

In a sense, American Christians were beginning to experience the drought long known in much of Europe, with its lovely old parish churches that were empty except for throngs of (mostly American) tourists. The prestigious 19th-century clergy – the tireless Methodist circuit-rider, or the dedicated Catholic priest, labouring in what nowadays would be termed the 'inner city' – were giving place to harassed, overworked, underpaid functionaries, whose most important tasks apparently consisted of attending pointless meetings and shaking countless hands. Some of them managed, in spite of all handicaps, to carry forward the social witness of the generation just prior to their own, preaching against the exploitation of labour, racial injustice and war. But they preached these messages from within a vocation less respected by their fellow Americans than in the days of their parents.

Their most concrete political accomplishment, the enactment of Prohibition, turned out to have been a Pyrrhic victory. Alcohol was outlawed in America between 1919 and 1933 from the most high-minded of motives; 'we have fought liquor', the Northern Methodist bishops declared, 'not because it has made men happy, but because it has made men unhappy'. Nevertheless, the legal enforcement of Prohibition, in the youth-conscious, pleasure-loving jazz age, inevitably made it easy for opponents of the measure to caricature all church people as repressive censors and killjoys. 'These glad young folk do not like what they see of the reforming army of the Lord', wrote one anonymous 'old-fashioned parson' in 1920, 'and they say: "We don't want to be like them." ... They think

that the sort of life demanded of them is neither beautiful nor happy.' From this image of the intolerant prude, Protestantism in America has never really recovered, even though Prohibitionists could properly have replied to such critics that there is nothing particularly beautiful or happy about alcohol-induced automobile accidents, drunken wife-beating or the physical and spiritual disease of alcoholism. After the downfall of Prohibition, Alcoholics Anonymous was founded to meet the continuing need, and hundreds of thousands in America and other parts of the world have found in its fellowship and precepts an ultimately religious answer to the problem.

Platforms and persuasions

The struggle for a temperate America also, for the first time, drew the Protestant churches, almost all of which supported Prohibition, into direct political conflict with the Catholic church, which opposed it; especially after a Catholic, Alfred E. Smith, was nominated for president on the Democratic ticket for 1928 and then publicly rejected the Prohibition enforcement plank in the Democratic platform. Historians have been arguing ever since about why Smith lost the presidency to Herbert Hoover, noting such factors as Hoover's high national reputation, the economic prosperity of the 1920s, which redounded to the benefit of the incumbent Republicans, and an acute cultural tension in America between town and country. None of these alternative explanations, statistically examined, really suffices. At the present time, the 1980s, the facts appear to support the conclusion of Allan Lichtman (in *Prejudice and the Old Politics*, 1979) that 'of all possible explanations for the distinctive political alignments of 1928, religion is the best', with the further proviso that 'Catholics as well as Protestants voted their religion' in that election; 'Smith benefited from a pro-Catholic vote and Hoover from an anti-Catholic vote.' For believers in the Federal Council's proclamation of 'the essential oneness of the Christian Churches of America', and in the secular society's continuing motto, *e pluribus unum*, this was a crushing blow.

Equally disruptive of the Christian community during the 1920s in America was the clash, postponed by the war, between Fundamentalism and Modernism. The issues seemed irresolvable: either the Bible was the inspired Word of God and literally true, or it was no more to be trusted than any other old book; either the church must proclaim 'the faith once delivered to the saints', or it must adjust and accommodate its message to the modern world. The scientific and religious question of evolution, which the liberals imagined had been settled back in the 1880s, erupted again. William Jennings Bryan brought the same formidable oratorical talent that had won him three presidential nominations into action against the menace of Darwinism. Several states enacted laws forbidding the teaching of evolution in the public schools, and Tennessee put a young school-teacher on trial for violating it. Bryan volunteered to prosecute, and Clarence Darrow, America's most outstanding criminal lawyer, joined the defence. For a few blazing-hot days in July of 1925 the world – or at any rate the newspapers, wire services, and radio – converged upon the small town of Dayton, Tennessee.

This 'media event' has given rise to considerable misinterpretation of its meaning. Legend has it that the 'monkey trial' of *Tennessee* v. *John Thomas Scopes* was a death blow to Fundamentalism. Darrow, cruelly cross-examining Bryan as a Bible expert, is said to have discredited both the witness and his anti-evolution crusade; Fundamentalism supposedly disintegrated after Bryan's death, which occurred shortly after the trial ended. Few historical generalizations have been further from the truth. The courts, to be sure, including the Supreme Court of the United States, have consistently sided with Darrow in subsequent constitutional testing of anti-evolution laws. Textbook publishers, however, sensitive to mass-market pressures, have just as regularly eliminated material from high school biology texts that community religious forces might find objectionable; such books published after 1925 contained *less*, not more, discussion of Darwinian evolution than they had before the Scopes trial.

Also, Fundamentalists in the 'mainstream' denominations did lose, tactically, the battle for organizational control. But those moderate-controlled denominations in the 1920s and 1930s underwent an actual net membership decline, so severe that church historian Robert T. Handy has termed the decade 1925–35 'the American religious depression'. Meanwhile, the Fundamentalists, through a network of evangelical agencies headquartered especially in Chicago, were regrouping – and growing. 'Fundamentalism was not a defeated party in denominational politics, but a popular religious movement, which in the 1930s developed a separate existence', historian Joel A. Carpenter concludes. 'By the 1950s, this building phase had paid off and Billy Graham, a Fundamentalist favourite son, became the symbol of evangelicalism's new prominence.' Graham in 1968 had so great a national stature that he was the only person to speak from the rostrum at both the Republican and the Democratic national nominating conventions.

The new field of religious radio was one symptom of what was happening. The networks offered free time for 'nonsectarian' broadcasting, but the Fundamentalists gladly paid for programmes of their own, and by 1939 such ecumenical ventures as the CBS Church of the Air were far overshadowed by what was to become America's largest regular prime-time radio broadcast, Charles E. Fuller's Old-Fashioned Revival Hour. As television partially displaced radio, Fundamentalists, such as Graham and Oral Roberts, quickly learned to make sophisticated use of the new medium. It should also be noted that the Gospel song, both old and new – an important component in country-and-Western music, which after World War II soared from regional and cultural obscurity into national acceptance and enjoyment – spoke a theological language that was overwhelmingly evangelical.

The religious depression ended, like the economic one, with the Second World War. Membership statistics and ministerial vocations in 'mainstream' churches turned sharply upward. In the shadow of 'the bomb', some Christian Americans groped for answers that would be neither Modernist nor Fundamentalist. One earnest young curate undertook to instruct President Roosevelt in the mysteries of Søren Kierkegaard, and along the campaign trail Jimmy Carter is said to have read the 'neo-orthodox' theologian Reinhold Niebuhr. Others, following a tradition that ran from Benjamin Franklin to Dwight Eisenhower, opted for a kind of minimal national religion that would cope with sectarian frictions by charitably overlooking them. The 1960s, however, ended the postwar religious revival with renewed demands for clear-cut religious decision, ranging from becoming 'born again' in Christ to proclaiming that 'God is dead'. The 1970s, in contrast, saw a new surge in the gnostic quest for self-help and personal fulfilment, in various forms. If there existed a general religious faith mutually acceptable to most Americans, evidently it was one that was very difficult to put into words. Whereas vigorous political partisans like Edward Kennedy and Ronald Reagan in the campaign of 1980 could speak of an American ideal that transcended their partisanship – an ideal that all heirs of the American Revolution could instantly recognize as their own – the statement of a similarly common religious faith eluded Christian Americans' grasp. Significantly, Reagan in pausing from politics for a religious observance at the end of his acceptance speech asked the listening and watching throng for a moment of *silent* prayer.

MODERNITY AND CHANGE

12
Christianity
in the contemporary
world

IN THE 20TH CENTURY the problems facing Christian churches of all denominations multiplied. The pace of change quickened, the dangers grew more serious – optimists might add that the opportunities for good increased at the same rate.

Some of the 19th-century dilemmas became less acute. If the prevailing image of most institutional churches is still middle class, the gap between classes has narrowed and priests live the same sort of life as their parishioners. Missions to convert the heathen are largely a thing of the past. Christians have reconciled themselves to a world in which theirs is one faith among many, and Christianity is therefore no longer seen as the spiritual face of Western imperialism. The decline in church-going that has occurred in most European countries, whether Protestant or Catholic, has often converted the Victorian problem of a shortage of churches into an equally worrying one of redundancy. On the other hand has come an unexpected revival of interest in and enthusiasm for Christianity among the young, though this is mostly out of sympathy with established institutions.

Theologically, it has been a century of restless re-examination, of controversy and discussion. Churchmen in general have moved closer to secular humanism; whether some of them have actually crossed the borderline, and where that borderline is, are open questions.

In this last chapter of the book, we concentrate on a number of areas where the Christian churches face a challenge and where the response seems to offer fruitful developments for the future. One is modernity, the sheer extent to which people's attitudes and expectations have changed, entailing an equally radical change in the church's methods of ministering. Another is the growth of political ideologies, systems of belief which are closely bound up with moral principles and therefore have much in common with religions: how should the churches regard them? How politically committed should they risk becoming? A third is the new role of Christianity in the world as a whole – no longer aiming at universal conversion but content to offer its own redeeming message to those who need it.

A personal vision

may say more than a public statement. In 1941 the Welsh Catholic poet and artist David Jones was living in Kensington, London, and used to attend services at a Carmelite church near by, which was later destroyed by bombing. In 1947 he moved to Harrow, not far from London, and worshipped at the church of Our Lady and St Thomas of Canterbury. Some years later he wove these scenes into a poem called *The Kensington Mass*. It is a deeply meditated work, in which Jones's experience of two world wars, his Christian faith and his own sense of the church's mission are focused and explored. The painting that is reproduced here is a visual counterpart to the poem. First called by the same name, *The Kensington Mass*, it was later retitled *A latere dextro* – 'from the right side'. The allusion is to an antiphon sung in the Easter liturgy: 'I saw water flowing from the right side of the temple, and all to whom that water came were saved.' Many ideas are contained in the painting: the symbol of the church born from the side of the Saviour as Eve was born of Adam, the sacrifice of the lamb at Easter, the pelican shedding its blood to feed its offspring; together with more personal images – the bombed church, the barefoot Carmelites, St Thomas of Canterbury murdered at his own altar. . . . The picture shows the central Christian mystery as the summing up of a European tradition about whose future Jones had great doubts. At this turning point the wind that blows through the whole picture is ambiguous: wind presaging the end of a civilization, wind also perhaps signifying the spirit that makes all things new. (1)

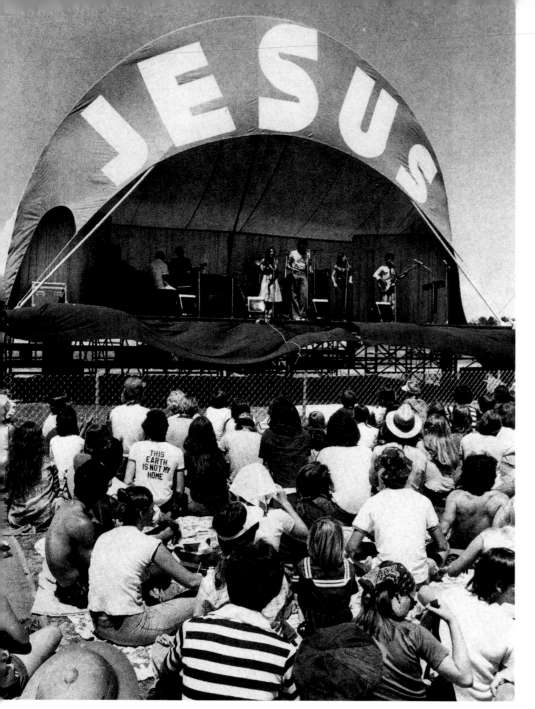

New forms of ministry

Where 19th-century churches sought inspiration in the past, those of the 20th resolutely face the present. Women, the young, the workers, non-European races – all these previously 'under-privileged' groups are being appealed to in their own terms.

The mobile church: a novel idea of an Anglican clergyman in southern England (*below*) for taking religion to the suburbs. (3)

The pop festival has been conscripted into the service of the church, as the drama was by the Jesuits. In this three-day revival meeting, the organizers claimed, '125,000 people of all ages were turned off sin and awakened to God'. (2)

Music in church: a Catholic mass held in New York in 1968 attempts to reach young people by speaking their own language. In the background, slightly incongruous in his liturgical robes, sits the archbishop of New York. (4)

Facing his congregation, in the spirit of the second Vatican Council, a Black priest celebrates mass in America. (7)

In Africa the Catholic hierarchy is firmly in African hands. The first African bishop to be consecrated was Bishop Otunga of Kenya, seen here (*above*) after his enthronement. (5)

The Christian warrior has its modern equivalent in the Lebanon, where religious differences highlight political divisions. (8)

Women priests, mooted in the Reformation, have become a reality in our time. *Left:* Miss Alison Palmer, of the Episcopal church of America, conducts a service in a London Unitarian church. (6)

The face of charity, another theme linking the 20th century with Christianity's long history. *Right:* Mother Theresa of Calcutta visits one of the children being nursed back to health under the care of her order. (9)

Towards unity

Ecumenism – the ideal of unity among all the churches – has been perhaps the most fruitful modern response to Christianity's problems.

Jesus as guerrilla – hero of 'liberation theology' preached in much of the Third World. Is this, in St Paul's words, 'another Christ', or merely a new version of an age-old image, Christ the defender of right against the forces of evil? (10)

John Paul II – the first non-Italian pope for centuries – has devoted himself energetically to the task of reconciliation and peace. Here he greets African followers, in front of a church watched over by a Black St Peter. Yet there are strict limits, in both morality and dogma, beyond which the Catholic church refuses to go, and the pope's appeal is essentially for a return to traditional discipline. (12)

The World Council of Churches represents ecumenism at its most international. Nearly all Christian churches, except the Catholic, belong to it. Beginning as a movement of interchurch co-operation, it has adopted an increasingly political stance. This poster (*below*) was designed for its Study on the Ecumenical Sharing of Resources, and expresses 'the wholeness of the ecumenical fellowship in which this sharing must take place'. (11)

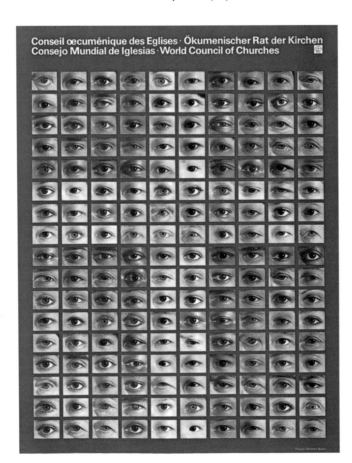

Conseil œcuménique des Eglises · Ökumenischer Rat der Kirchen
Consejo Mundial de Iglesias · World Council of Churches

Pro et contra

Where should a Christian stand politically in the modern world? Do the teachings of Christ imply any particular attitudes on such issues as democracy, equality, feminism or human rights? How far may the churches compromise with an unjust regime?

To the radical left, during the 1920s and 30s, Christianity was identified with the forces of reaction. *Above:* in a Mexican revolutionary fresco, the cross appears as part of the formula of oppression: capitalist Christianity plus totalitarianism equals slavery. (13)

A divided world: between the wars, the churches came under heavy attack from Communism, driving them sometimes to ally themselves with the right. *Top right:* crosses being taken down from a church in the Kremlin, 1918. *Centre: A Satisfied Priest* by André Masson, Spain, 1936. *Bottom:* Catalan anarchists burning the contents of a church, 1936. (14–16)

294

The church's dealings with the dictators did in fact lend some colour to the anticlerical view. In Italy, Pope Pius XI came to an agreement with Mussolini, and the Lateran Treaty of 1929 (*above*) ensured the autonomy of 'the City of the Vatican'. In Spain the church and Franco's Falangist party (*right*, the Falange symbol is the yoke and the arrows) became inescapably linked. (17, 19)

The middle way: the Catholic church today is tending to withdraw both its support for the right and its antagonism to the left. *Above:* Dom Helder Camara, the 'Red Bishop' of Brazil, champion of the people and leader of a campaign against terrorism. In Poland the church has become a focus for patriotism, intensified since the election of a Polish pope. *Right:* mass held at Staszia coal-mine in Silesia, December 1980. The miners wear caps with crossed hammers. (18, 20)

The image of Christ continues to represent an ideal for modern man, though there is less agreement about the nature of that ideal. One of the themes of this book has been his progressive 'humanization'. Where he is no longer a divine principle incarnate, he has become a figure standing for universal man, embodying aspirations that can be purely of this world. The Mexican Communist painter José Clemente Orozco makes him a militant leader impatiently destroying his own cross with an axe; the religion of suffering belongs to the past, together with the whole history of Western culture. To the Englishman Stanley Spencer, by contrast (*right*), he is a symbol of peace, holding in his massively gentle hand the poisonous cruelty of the scorpion and taking no harm. (21, 22)

12
Christianity in the contemporary world

ADRIAN CUNNINGHAM

OVER THE LAST forty years the Christian churches have had to adjust themselves to world political change. They have now to accept that Europe is no longer the centre of the world and to disentangle themselves from largely conservative establishments. They have to adjust to a situation where, for example, the majority of members of the Anglican communion are Black, where in a decade or two the majority of the world's Catholics will be Latin Americans.

The ending of the Second World War seems an obvious date from which to examine recent history. The defeat of Nazism and of Fascism; the partition of Germany, the incorporation of countries to the east and south-east into a Soviet-dominated bloc; the realignment of Japanese politics, are all events that have left a permanent mark on world history. In other ways, however, the postwar world was the continuation of an earlier period. Franco in Spain, Salazar in Portugal, Stalin in Russia were all confirmed as the saviours of their people. Huge areas of the world continued as colonies of Belgium, Britain, France and Portugal. By the mid-1960s it was apparent that a deeper and more lasting change had come. Stalin was dead, Franco aging, Castro in command in Cuba. Decolonization was virtually complete. Cities had been transformed by high-rise blocks. Dress, cinema, popular art – all proclaimed a new age. In the specifically Christian context, the year 1965 marked the end of the Vatican Council that gave birth to a 20th-century Catholicism, sixty years delayed.

Four things dominate the development of Christianity since the Second World War: modernization, secularization, the increasing strength of non-European Christianity and the new politicization of the churches. In the following pages I shall consider some of the main Christian responses to modernity: ecumenism and the Vatican Council; the challenge to inherited views in the advent of worker-priests and the ordination of women; the political realignment of the churches and their relation to Communism; the growth of new styles of basic Christian community in the Third World. All these areas show the bitter problems of Christianity trying to maintain continuity with vital elements of its own history and to adjust to a vastly changed world.

Christianity in a secular world

However one measures the processes of modernization and of secularization and whatever their long- and short-term prospects, one thing has become clear: Christianity is not going to convert the world. In its traditional areas of greatest strength in Europe, secularization has meant a decline in the numbers of Christians and in the overt social and political influence of the churches, a *reversal* unprecedented in the previous history of European Christianity. In its 'mission' territories, Christianity either meets the insuperable resilience of other world religions, such as Hinduism and Islam, or where it has taken root, in Latin America and parts of Africa, it may be unable to prevent the process of modernization from leading to secularization, as it has done in the West.

To highlight this situation is not necessarily to consider it as a 'failure' of Christianity. There may be a lot of important things to do short of, as it were, ruling the world – this indeed has turned out to be a mistaken goal for Christianity to have set itself. Nonetheless, a revolution in thought is required, because, with minor exceptions, Christian groups in the past were expansionist, seeing an indefinite horizon for evangelization. When the Catholic church 'lost' great 'territories' in the 16th-century Reformation, the response was one of internal reform and consolidation undertaken in total confidence that such a setback could not last. Under the further blows of the French Revolution, the loss of the Papal States and the Russian Revolution, the view of the church as the only stable element in a chaotic world was reinforced. The only ground for hope was a reunification of Christendom focused upon Rome and slow but irreversible evangelization outside Europe. Of course this essentially monarchical and imperial view was seen by Protestants as a direct threat, yet they too shared the idea of a steady expansion of Christianity outwards from Europe and North America.

The definitive end to these assumptions of Eurocentrism and expansionism has been traumatic. For some people there is the sense of relief that a burden has been lifted, but they also are involved in the crisis of identity. There are strong links between the dynamic of Christianity and the origins of the process of modernization which, however, now seems to be bypassing it.

Some theologians have attempted to see secularity as the legitimate end-product of Christianity, as something issuing from the essence of the tradition; to others this has seemed merely a baptizing of the inevitable. It is in the area between secularity as an end-product of Christianity and secularity as the end of Christianity that new positions are being sketched out. In the 1960s and 1970s Christians increasingly came to realize that preaching the Gospel may not mean that the world should become Christian.

There are as many definitions of secularization as there are ways of measuring it. Basic to all of these, however, is a sense of the diversification of the different spheres of life, the separating out of education, work and politics from under the overarching canopy of an explicit religious world-view and its institutional influence; the validation of social life is increasingly technical rather than moral. One effect of the first wave of industrialization from the mid-18th century onwards was the breaking up of what can be called the 'vertical' relationships of traditional society (i.e. relationships between classes) and the growing antagonism between classes focused upon authority in work. The second wave of industrialization in this century has tended to erode the 'horizontal' relationships of the extended family, the stable locality and voluntary associations, upon which Christian movements, with their exclusion from the world of work, had tended to concentrate their resources. The sphere of effective Christian moral influence became increasingly narrowed to the morality of the individual and of the family, and thus to the morality of private, and more especially sexual, life. Christianity has often determined moral change in society, but, as the philosopher Alasdair MacIntyre has argued, changes in religious thought and discipline can also be preceded and determined by moral changes in society. And this is very much the case with contemporary sexuality, the family and the struggle for women's rights. The older patterns of domestic life have reached a point of crisis and it will be a long time yet before the Christian assimilation of the new situation becomes clear.

What I shall be examining here are attempts to find new forms of Christian life responsive to the impact of modernization. Though it seems an odd thing to say, modernity is modern and recent. Religious life has many of its deepest roots in a traditional, agricultural world. The single greatest crisis of contemporary Christianity is that the world of modern working relationships is almost wholly lost to it, and the variety of attempts at a Christian social ethic – industrial chaplaincies, Christian worker groups and so on – have had little long-term impact. It was often said by the worker-priests that the modern working class had not

been 'lost' by the church, it had for the most part grown up outside it.

In many cases the basic unit of the parish no longer covers both the world of work and that of domestic life as it did in earlier periods. Increasingly, the parish has come to mean only the place to which people come home after work, and thus religion has tended to be seen as a leisure-time activity. Geographical mobility has also made the parish and the continuing family relationships upon which it was based less meaningful. Many of the most vital modern Christian developments are efforts to re-engage with the worlds of work and politics and to rebuild new, and necessarily less permanent, forms of 'horizontal' relationships. Some of the attempted responses to modernity include worker-priests, 'village Christianity' and basic communities in the Third World, experimental forms of liturgy and groups based on working or professional activities. All these represent experiments to find a less triumphalist and experientially more real Christian life, with smaller, grass-roots communities. The upsurge of Pentecostalism in mainstream churches is one potent index of this search, for although charismatic phenomena may become routinized they are incompatible with any uniform bureaucratic organization. In other ways, the notion of the church as the people of God and as a pilgrim church reflects the same concern. It is another sign of reconstruction upon unfamiliar bases that a very small monastic development on the historically improbable soil of the French Reformed Church, the Taizé Community, should have acquired world-wide fame and touched the lives of thousands.

Ecumenism: from theology to politics

One response to the erosion of Christian institutions in the 20th century is ecumenism, the ideal of unity between all Christian churches. While the divisions between the Christian churches are a scandal, they also represent distinct traditions of thought, feeling and practice lasting over centuries, which will not easily be given up. In part, ecumenism is a response to the pressures of modernization as seen, in another sphere, in the bureaucratic rationalization of governments and big corporations, the uniformity of city centre architecture and the tendency towards a flattening of regional forms of speech and custom. Here one has to balance what is gained by the breaking down of outmoded barriers to achieve a greater communication of people on the large scale, against the wiping out of important small-scale differences, which help form a person's identity. Ecumenism, too, has to find a balance between the liberating effects of release from parochialism and prejudice, and the dulling of specific valued resonances and loyalties. It is not surprising, then, that ecumenism has involved great stress and even division within particular churches, as, say, certain Methodists and Anglicans can feel threatened by rapprochement between their churches.

At the same time, it is all too easy for the believers to see their tradition in too simple terms. The clearest example here would be the supposedly monolithic nature of Catholicism. In fact, the idea of a single centrally controlled and smoothly uniform organization is modern and largely mythical. The actual history of Catholicism differs from this imperial and bureaucratic dream, being of wide diversity and of competing and often bitterly conflicting schools of thought. The same is true of many other churches. What should be looked for, perhaps, in ecumenism is recognition and respect for different styles of thought and practice within as well as between the Christian churches.

Ecumenism as part of the process of modernization can, in part, be quite convincingly explained in terms of a market model. Protestant denominations have an increasingly homogeneous middle-class population: suburban, mobile, literate and selective. With this catchment area the room for expansion is restricted, while direct poaching of members from other congregations is deprecated. At the same time economic inflation affects many aspects of church life, from the costs of building to ministers' salaries. The result is the formation of cartels, reducing the number of competitors by ecclesiastical mergers and sharing out the market among the remaining larger units. This, in turn, leads to standardization of the product, together with the development of 'marginal differentiation' – largely functionally irrelevant embellishments and packaging. This irreverent analysis is not applicable to Black Protestant churches in America and does not help with understanding relations among major traditions – Protestant, Catholic or Jewish. Nevertheless it may prompt a more worldly-wise view of a phenomenon which is often over piously recorded.

In organized form ecumenism derives ultimately from the International Missionary Conference, held in Edinburgh in 1910, which surveyed the missionary work of the reformed churches. Much of the energy in ecumenism has remained linked to traditional missionary fields. While Europe of the 1920s and 1930s was divided by denominational theological conflict, many churches in Africa and Asia were forming multidenominational unions. The best known of these is the Church of South India, formed in 1947, after thirty years of discussion, by a union of Anglican, Methodist, Presbyterian and Congregational churches. Such a proposal to remedy the evils of division in missionary work by the creation of a united ministry without

'Ecumenism' comes from the Greek word 'oikoumene', meaning the whole inhabited world. Together with the symbol of the cross and the ship, it serves as the logo of the World Council of Churches.

reordination underlines the mixture of practical and theological factors in ecumenism.

Ecumenism can exist at many levels. There is often a tension between ecumenism from above – arrangements between leaders and administrators – and ecumenical contacts that spring up in a more informal way from below, in shared use of buildings, occasional joint services and intercommunion, study groups and joint ventures in social and political action. At its most international, ecumenism is represented by the World Council of Churches, inaugurated in Amsterdam in 1948. The World Council brings together almost all the Christian churches with the exception of the Catholic, though close relations with the latter have developed since the 1960s. While retaining its concern with doctrine and with interchurch co-operation, the council has increasingly assumed a political role. In this way it meets the misgivings of some Christians that energy poured into ecumenism is an inwards-turning distraction from the even more painful division of the social and political world and the call to act in it. The continuing importance of the extra-European impetus in ecumenism can be seen in the disputes over the council's special fund, the 'Programme to Combat Racism', which has supported non-military parts of liberation movements in southern Africa. The history of the World Council of Churches and its concerns points to the deliberate intertwining of the religious and the political, characteristic of the last two or three decades, and the controversy this can provoke.

At a national level, in Europe and the United States as well, some churches have actually unified, for example the United Church of Christ, which brought together Evangelical, Reformed and Congregational churches, with widely differing styles of churchmanship, in America; and the United Reform Church in

Le Corbusier's pilgrimage church of Ronchamp, France, marked a break with traditional church design. Organic, emotive, mysterious,

it unites an irregular, dimly lit interior with a dramatically composed external form.

Britain, formed by an amalgamation of Congregationalists and Presbyterians. In other cases there has been an increased unity of practices and doctrines, and, at grass-roots, we find communities pooling resources in times of need. The gains of ecumenism are obvious if Christian groups can turn from expending a great part of their energies on defending denominational boundaries, and co-operate freely, sharing prayer and worship without seeking any stricter uniformity.

New doctrines, new liturgies

A vital strand in 20th-century Christianity is provided by Pentecostalism, which has come to have a strong influence on the mainstream churches and the Ecumenical Movement. Pentecostalism (see Chapter 11) takes its name from the traditional feast of Pentecost (Whit.Sunday), when forty days after the death and resurrection of Christ the apostles experienced the outpouring of the Spirit and preached ecstatically. It is a specifically American contribution to the modern development of Christianity and is the fastest growing of Christian movements; it is reckoned that there are four million Pentecostals in Latin America alone, in Chile one person in seven. With its stress upon personal experience of the Holy Spirit, apart from sacraments and church institutions, its strong belief in the Second Coming of the Lord and in baptism in the Spirit, with the associated phenomena of healing and speaking in tongues, it represents a late mutation of Reformation radicalism.

In modern form it derives from the Holiness Revivals in 19th-century America, which came increasingly to diverge from official Methodism and took recognizable shape in the Azusa Street meetings in Los Angeles in 1906. As successor to 18th-century Methodism and the 19th-century Salvation Army, and with very little in the way of hierarchical organization, it spread rapidly among the poor and in Black communities. Developing outside, and in opposition to, the mainstream churches, it slowly came to be recognized by the World Council of Churches as a 'third force' in Christianity alongside the Protestant and Catholic traditions.

A further transformation took place when Pentecostal beliefs and practices developed in Episcopalian congregations in California in 1960 and then spread with extraordinary rapidity within the established churches – something that, on historical grounds, would have seemed improbable in the extreme. The growth of charismatic renewal within the established churches gave an intellectual strength and diversity to the fundamentalist cast of traditional Pentecostalism and provided a distinctive grass-roots element in ecumenism, feeding new energies back into mainstream Christianity. Charismatic groups, meeting in houses rather than churches for periods of singing, silent meditation, spontaneous prayer and testimony, and with little emphasis if any upon clerical leadership, form a contrast to usual patterns of church authority. This may be of considerable significance for women, nuns in particular, who can speak more confidently and assume positions of leadership outside the more standard and male-centred structures of church life.

Analogous changes in terms of authority and participation can be seen in Christian liturgy and art from the mid-century onwards. Changes in liturgy are important for they affect not only what is said and seen in worship but how it *feels* to worship, and they are thus capable of stirring deep emotions. Changes in worship can be experienced by some as the access of a new vitality and dreaded by others as the selling of a birthright for pottage. One can see this in the move from the mass in Latin to the vernacular or the alternatives to the old prayerbook services in Anglicanism. Liturgy involves very direct senses of how and where people stand with regard to one another, whether they touch one another or not, whether they look at one another or not. The increased involvement of the body in worship has not yet moved very far in the use of liturgical dance but even tentative experiments here would have been inconceivable until very recently.

Many previous upheavals in Christianity had changed what was said and done in churches and their decoration but it is not often that the basic customary shape of the building has changed. New buildings show a preference for the circular, as in Le Corbusier's church at Ronchamp or the new Liverpool Cathedral, and even with traditional oblong or cruciform buildings there is an attempt to make the internal shape circular or semi-circular, narrowing the distance between minister and congregation and between both and the focus of worship. This change of shape represents the open assembly of the people rather than their all facing in one direction as a solid body. The new style encourages more active participation, face to face, than the old.

Something similar can be seen in Christian art. Major works of art, such as the stained glass of Chagall, Piper and Rouault, or the linear decorative shapes of Matisse, represent a break with lifeless and degenerate styles, seeking new forms of expression with new materials. Complementing the idea of liturgical art as the highest and most lavish offering to God, there is also a new emphasis upon offering something representative of the local community. Stereotyped mass-produced images distantly modelled on the great masters have often been replaced by individually commissioned and experimental work by little known artists. Churches may also be decorated with the drawings of children. Again, this is an attempt at authentically expressing the life of the community, its abilities and its shortcomings, and a turning away from the dispensation of standardized and anonymous images.

A desire for greater popular immediacy is also evident in music. There are major works designed for church use or inspired by Christian motifs, such as Britten's *War Requiem* or Menotti's *Amahl and the Night Visitors*; but the outstanding feature of the contemporary scene is the burgeoning of folk and popular music, of hymns, modern in lyric and sentiment, showing the influence of Pentecostalism and the musical style of Black churches.

Cinema and theatre have also responded to and helped create the new mood. Up to the 1960s films with a religious interest tended to stay within fairly safe conventions. There were heroic spectaculars, *The Ten Commandments, The Greatest Story Ever Told*, or *The Robe*; for power and seriousness compare any of these with the Marxist Pasolini's remarkable *Gospel According to Matthew*. Other conventional forms were the lives of religious women (*Song of Bernadette, The Inn of the Sixth*

Design for St Dominic, to be carried out in painted and glazed tiles in the chapel of Vence, by Matisse: another example of bold innovation in religious art.

Happiness, or, with a strong romantic interest, *The Nun's Story*), and homely tales of tough-guy priests (*Boystown*). The idea of a religious musical was new. In *The Sound of Music* this was developed in a familiar and sentimental way, but a different note was struck by such immensely successful musicals as *Joseph and the Amazing Technicolor Dreamcoat, Godspell* and *Jesus Christ Superstar*, which were free and easy with their scriptural sources and appealed to the diffuse, non-institutionalized, religious feeling of the period. There is also the peculiar popularity in a modern and technically complex society, with an updated Christianity, of films full of motifs from the archaic and

301

peripheral folklore of Christianity and the pagan past; hauntings, black magic, demonic possessions, were-wolves and vampires, with quantities of exorcisms, crucifixes, stakes and silver bullets.

Vatican II: the 'bringing up to date' of Catholicism

In the Catholic church the major changes in worship and in basic stance towards the world date from the Vatican Council of 1962–65. On his election in 1958 as John XXIII, seventy-seven-year-old Cardinal Roncalli was thought of as a caretaker pope, an interim appointment. In fact his five-year reign started a transformation of the Catholic church and the office of the papacy. He had no detailed plans of his own for the council he summoned, setting it the two general aims of the promotion of Christian unity and the renewal of the church – his happily chosen term *aggiornamento* (bringing up to date) avoided the pitfalls of 'reform' or 'modernization'.

War had brought a halt to the first Vatican Council in 1870 and it had not reconvened. Its definition of papal authority had thus been left in isolation from consideration of the rights of bishops and the laity, and this distorted view of authority prevailed until the second Vatican Council called by John XXIII.

Some 42,000 written proposals were submitted. These were drawn up into draft schemata by ten commissions and then debated. Of the seventy schemata prepared, sixteen were finally voted upon and accepted. Decisions in large religious institutions emerge not only from the co-operation of reason and grace but also from the exercise of power and political skill. Initially, the ten commissions were controlled by permanent officials of the corresponding Vatican departments but John had the foresight to set up separate secretariats for Christian unity and for relations with non-believers on more independent lines. Later, they and the central co-ordinating commission were of key significance.

As important as political astuteness was the simple fact of communication among the church fathers. It had been a common pattern for bishops to deal individually with Rome; the Italian bishops, for instance, had rarely met collectively in modern times. Much of the speed of change at the council derived from the pooling of experience, and willingness to learn. The bishops of 'the Rhine countries' – Germany, France, Switzerland and the Low Countries – were particularly well organized and came prepared with shadow schemata of their own, and their theological experts gave hundreds of influential open lectures.

The first two schemata to be discussed, on liturgy and on revelation, were to be decisive for the council

and, in turn, for the church as a whole. In rejecting the schema on revelation, the bishops were rejecting not only the ultra-conservatism of its theology but also the means by which the Curia, the permanent officials of the Vatican, were attempting to control proceedings. The way was opened for greater diversity in the preparation of later documents and, most importantly, for the authority of the college of bishops to complement that of the pope, thus balancing the 19th-century declaration of papal infallibility. The changes in the pattern of worship, most obviously the change from Latin to vernacular, brought something of the new theology to the daily lives of the great mass of believers and gave the work of the council an effective symbolic backdrop. Equally important in its long-term consequences was the opening up of discussion and debate, and the recognition of long-repressed differences about the nature of Christian belief. The idea of the church as a form of monarchy in which decisions filtered down to believers from the monarch-pope was severely damaged. The widespread opposition, both public and private, to Paul VI's restatement of the official position on birth control (*Humanae Vitae* 1968) is a clear index of this change of attitude. In the council the protest at the triumphalism, legalism and clericalism of the church was loud and clear. This image came to be replaced by that of the church as the people of God, a sign of mankind seeking unity.

The council's decisions about the doctrine and government of the church were far more radical than could have been imagined in 1960 or 1962. The years since 1965 have seen a struggle between, on the one hand, those in positions of central authority who assumed that the council was essentially pastoral, implying that the preceding conservative theological position remained intact and that *aggiornamento* came to an end with the close of the council, and, on the other hand, those who came to believe that the renewal of Catholicism started by John is a continuing process. The advent of John Paul II as the first non-Italian pope in centuries was as much a mark of the new thinking and of shifts of power in the church away from Italy, as his forceful traditional attitudes represent resistance to change.

New forms of ministry: the worker-priests

Of the many changes that have taken place in Christianity in the contemporary world, with shifting patterns of authority and participation, those affecting the idea of the ministry are particularly important. The two to be examined here concern the attempt to overcome the mutual isolation of the world of the church and the world of work, and the attempt to change the status of women in the church. Both of these can produce severe problems of divided opinion and conflicting desires in churches that have seen themselves as all-embracing and smoothly functioning.

Significant historical developments are often best represented in relatively small events. The crisis over the worker-priests in France in 1952–54, involving a 'sociologically insignificant' total of fewer than one hundred men (without a uniform policy), was just such an apparently small-scale event. In a larger perspective, all the major issues of contemporary Christianity were focused in it: the experience of the Second World War (and more especially of the occupation and the resistance); the falling away of numbers; the question of how the church can make contact with an urban industrial world; the relation between the church establishment and conservative or oppressive regimes; the genuineness of the 'unity' of the church in a society deeply divided by class antagonisms; the role of the priest as a 'man apart' or as a worker alongside others. These issues were common to all churches in the 1970s and early 1980s – most obviously in South America. Looking at the question of the worker-priests helps to crystallize many of the issues that confront Christianity in very different locations today.

Self-conscious secularism and organized Catholicism had, in France, been in a state of confrontation for a century and a half, producing a vigorously defensive Catholic milieu, which tended to see the period between the 14th and the 20th centuries (with the three 'Rs' of Renaissance, Reformation and Revolution) as the reign of a second Fall.

France had also registered in striking form some of the characteristic features of early 20th-century Christian development. It had a large social movement outside the direct control of clerical authority (the *Sillon*). The currents of historical and biblical research of the Modernist crisis of the 1900s were strongly represented in France. However, although Modernism had been an affair of intellectuals, having little connection with the body of the faithful, its suppression and the reverberations that followed created a theological and political climate between 1910 and 1950 that was, for all its signs of assured self-confidence, temporary and artificial.

As with the Modernists, so with the worker-priests, it was only in the misleading retrospective light of their suppression that they came to be seen as a coherent movement. At their origins lay several distinct initiatives of the early 1940s. In 1941, Père Augros made a comprehensive study of the training of priests throughout France, following which the hierarchy sanctioned the establishment of a seminary of the Mission de France, recruiting on a national basis for

especially difficult ministries, in particular that to the working class. France, the eldest daughter of the church, was now regarded as mission country. This conception needs to be seen in the context of the alliance among the army, the nobility and the hierarchy, under the Pétain regime at Vichy, for its daring and dangerous nature to be appreciated. In 1943 the rather differently conceived Mission de Paris was under way and priests were sent clandestinely to accompany deported workers in German labour camps.

The experience of *le monde ouvrière* of the later 1940s led beyond new styles of mission (sermons in the Métro or at factory gates), in which the priest might teach the old message more effectively, to a need to learn the language of a new world and to demonstrate this by actually earning a living as a worker. The sense of identification with the world of the worker occurs again and again in the writings of the worker-priests, themselves largely from the milieu of orthodox lower-middle-class Catholicism. Their understanding of *le monde ouvrière* took them beyond identification with particular Christian individuals and families, within what appeared to be an amorphous religiously uninterested mass. That this world was one of very sharp perceptions and political organization with resilient values of its own created tensions that were to seal the fate of the worker-priests. The priests came increasingly to be engaged actively in trade unions and working-class politics, occasionally under Communist aegis. This 'change of side' by the priests brought into prominence not only the issues of secularization and the traditional role of the priest, but also the question of the relation between membership of the church and the class struggle. The German author Gregor Siefer commented: 'The ghetto wall which had previously separated the "church" and the "world" had not been broken down. Instead it had been pushed into the middle of the church, and now separated right and left, conservatives and progressives, parish clergy and worker-priests of the one church.' This confrontation of sharp political divisions and the claim of the church to speak to all members of all social classes has remained one of the most serious unresolved issues in contemporary Christianity.

Sensitive to Italian political realities and desiring a united anti-Communist front, Rome demanded the recall of the worker-priests, in August 1953, and the ending of what it saw as a limited experiment and what the worker-priests saw as an unlimited commitment. Father Henri Perrin, a leading figure in the strikes at the Arc-Isère dam project in 1952–53, wrote: 'With God's help I still believe in God, in Christ and in the church; but something has been broken that cannot be mended.' Half the priests refused to obey and in the years that followed many of them left the church. Some initiatives continued in a quiet way as late as July 1959, when, with the Italian Christian Democrats in danger from the left, a complete ban on priests taking any part in industrial work was made. The circumstances of political polarization in France during the Cold War and the homogeneity of working-class life before the Algerian War were, of course, specific; the long-term issues for Christianity were not. Much of the dynamism and dedication of the worker-priests, as well as some of their tragedy, was seen again in the involvement of clerics and nuns, some of them joining armed guerrilla groups, in liberation movements in the Third World from the late 1960s onwards.

The role of women

Another disturbance in received ideas of the clerical state and its authority came with the great numbers leaving the priesthood to marry, and the growth of demands for a married clergy by those who sought to distinguish the celibate state of monasticism (which may not involve priesthood) from the role of the priest (which may not require celibacy). In churches where a married clergy is normal the issue seems puzzlingly simple; in churches where the celibate priest has been pivotal to the system, a change of this kind means a profound transformation, as does the ordination of women.

The traditional exclusion of women from the Christian priesthood has been challenged by small groups of Christians since the women's suffrage campaign at the turn of the century. The reformed churches took a lead on the issue of women's activity in the service of the church. The Lutheran church in Denmark ordained three women ministers in 1948 and today nine per cent of parish priests there are women. Swedish and French reformed churches followed; and, by 1975, seventy-five of the constituent members of the World Council of Churches admitted women as full ministers. A particular turning point was the ordination of eleven women to the Episcopalian ministry in the USA, on 29 July 1974, for the Episcopal church is a member of the Anglican Communion and catholic in its theology. It seems improbable that the exclusion of women from ministry in the world-wide Anglican church can be maintained for more than a few years. However, it is likely that on this issue the pressures for change in Catholic and Greek and Russian Orthodox practice might take decades to work through.

The rapid change of the traditional position on female ministers is a response to the widespread women's liberation movements in the contemporary world. It is part of the core of these movements that what is at issue in such matters is not the substitution of a female for a male official, in an otherwise unchanged role, but the fundamental rethinking of roles defined in sexual terms and of the experiences that they both reflect and constrain.

The exit from the religious life of nuns in tens of thousands is an obvious and dramatic event. In Australia and the USA it had immediate practical consequences not only for the individuals and the religious orders they had left, but for those other religious institutions, like schools, which had often depended upon this source of cheap labour. The long-term consequence of the changes in female self-consciousness and power, however, if sustained, will far outrun these initial upheavals in areas that, because of the historical continuity of western religion, are deeply masculine. Ordination is one sign among many of the beginning of a transformation of relations between men and women and of the cultural forms – some of them of millennial duration and depth – in which they are expressed, the consequences of which are (since by the nature of the case there are few precedents) quite incalculable. In a very long perspective this issue may prove to be the most significant of all the developments of the Christian churches discussed here.

Christians and politcs

In the area of Christianity and politics it might be remarked, at least before the 1960s, that the Protestants tended to have the better ideas – the clarity and force, for instance, of Paul Tillich's *The Protestant Era* – and the Catholics the larger movements. The latter's effectiveness, however, was limited by the organization of the church itself, which was both highly centralized and ideologically isolated from modern conditions – conditions that had given rise to trade unionism, socialism, and Communist parties. The church proclaimed a theoretical indifference to the form of any actual state while in practice it maintained a very clear option in favour of governments of the right, including Fascist ones. The heritage of an essentially monarchical system remained.

In Pius XII, Catholic pessimism about the modern world, according to the English historian E. E. Y. Hales, 'reached a perfection of philosophical expression and sad and beautiful dignity which raise it to the sublime atmosphere of great tragedy'. Pius's Christmas message of 1954 still quoted Leo XIII's grudging concession, at the end of the last century, that it was 'not forbidden to give preference to moderate forms of popular government'. The clue to understanding the outdatedness of official thinking here lies in the relation between the diplomatic strategy of the Vatican and the question of the role of the laity in the church.

A key feature of complex and all-inclusive institutions like churches is the ability to provide creative channels for dissent and discontent. One of the channels by which energy is turned to advantage is the religious order, but the last major form of this canalization was the formation of the Jesuits in response to the Reformation. The right-wing Opus Dei organization, founded in 1928 and given official Vatican approval in 1950, can be seen as an attempt to form a modern equivalent body with an intense spiritual life and a lay and political emphasis. Of Spanish origin, it was very important in the modernization of the Spanish economy and the preparation of a succession to the Franco regime. It is involved in higher education in Australia, Kenya, Japan and Mexico, and has more than two hundred student residences throughout the world. Opus Dei's activities continue to arouse suspicion and hostility, but its really effective power remains limited to Spain.

The real heirs, perhaps, to the religious orders were the Christian Democratic parties. The rise of modern states and, in particular, the unification of Italy and the loss of the Papal States meant that to hold its own the church needed to mobilize believers directly, in political terms. A pattern of tension between centre and periphery developed. The central authority needed to engage sufficient lay political interest to ensure its own support, but not enough to threaten overall clerical control.

Although started in very different circumstances, the Christian Democratic parties reached the peak of their influence in the early 1950s. Those with a predominantly Catholic membership tended to occur in countries where Catholics constituted between 30 per cent and 60 per cent of the population; strong enough for organization to pay dividends, and weak enough for it to be necessary.

By the 1890s Catholic parties had emerged in Austria, Belgium, the Netherlands and Germany, to some extent in France, but not in Italy, for domestic reasons, until the first decade of the 20th century. With shifts of population, the Catholic factor was often important in English-speaking countries, although it rarely took the form of an explicitly named Christian party. Rather, with the exceptions of Canada, in the 1870s and 1880s, and Ireland, the tendency was for Catholics, who in such situations were apt to belong to the poorer sections of society, to support the coalition of forces that comprised the more left wing of the major parties.

A lot of the initial impetus in Christian Democratic parties was concerned with the retention of as many of the old legal rights of the church as the new republican and democratic circumstances would allow. Typical issues were the question of divorce or the disestablish-ment of the church, the most basic and intransigent of all often being education. By the early 1930s these issues had usually either been resolved by political compromise and concordat or there had been a reinstatement of the old regime and traditional forms of clerical influence (Salazar in Portugal, Vargas in Brazil).

A concern that was limited to specifically ecclesiastical issues was now politically insufficient, and a distinctive feature of the modern period was the presentation of a coherent Catholic social theory. This emerged as decentralist and corporatist, i.e. suspicious of big organizations and the modern state, supporting anything that would conserve the economic power of the family. From the papal encyclical *Rerum Novarum* (1891) to *Quadragesimo Anno* (1931) and on into the 1950s, this stance covered an untidy melange of political options. These were fundamentally conservative but could be interpreted either (unfavourably) as a last-ditch attempt to prevent modernization and democratization, or (favourably) as a final effort to strengthen the values and social organization of rural populations, which were being swamped by those of the city. At one end of the political spectrum there were links with Salazar and Mussolini and at the other with the anarcho-syndicalists of the Spanish Civil War, despite their anticlericalism.

The German situation gives a useful example of the complexity of relations between religious and political issues. The Vatican Council was something of a trade fair for German Catholicism, yet many of those who presented themselves there as ecclesiastical radicals were staunch conservatives in secular politics. The postwar period was one of particularly anguished self-examination by German Christians, but the debate extended far beyond Germany. Why had the churches, with a small number of heroic exceptions, failed to respond adequately to Nazism? And how was it that just those elements that had compromised then survived now? Carl Amery, active on the postwar German political scene, has argued that even if their leaders had declared against the Nazis the churches would still have capitulated. German Catholicism in particular was dominated by the values of the urban and rural lower middle class. Those values are summed up by the word *Anstand* – the virtues of diligence, honesty, cleanliness, reliability, mistrust of all excess or ambiguity, obedience to authority. These are not specifically Christian virtues, like charity or humility, nor are they major virtues of any kind: rather, they are secondary virtues that imply no end in themselves but only come into play when subordinated to some particular end. 'Punctuality' can be as efficient in the service of evil as of good. Attacks by Amery and others on the canonization of secondary virtues, and the continued reliance on such virtues in the interdenominational Christian Democratic Union of today, were not only a feature of a specifically German development but led to the questioning of what *exactly* constituted a Christian social and political ethic in the general political shake-up of the 1960s. Surely it must be more than an extra and peculiar reason for doing the same as other respectable or well intentioned people were already doing?

The restoration of democratic government in many parts of Europe at the end of the Second World War saw the Catholic forces more prominent than ever. An example of the appeal of traditional Catholicism linked with vigorous anti-Communism is provided by the Catholic activist B. A. Santamaria's movement in Australia, which split the Labour Party in the 1950s. But the period of peak influence was brief. With the exception of countries like Canada, Ireland and Poland, where nationalism and religion were still identified, the political world was no longer so clearly organizable in terms of religious constituencies. Further, some of the personal, family and moral issues that were basic to the church were already showing signs of transformation. In the wake of the war several Christian Democratic parties tried to widen their recruiting base by loosening their ties with the institutional church. In Germany, the bulk of Catholics transferred their support from the old Centre party to the new interdenominational Christian Democratic Union. In Belgium, Holland and Italy, however, the bishops stepped in to discourage the dispersion of the Catholic vote, although this dissuasion did not last long. Old political lines were being redrawn: the socialists, for instance, were also interested in widening their base and tended to drop much of their earlier anticlericalism, so that by 1960 even in Italy there was a rapprochement between the major socialist group under Nenni and the Christian Democrats.

These political realignments were accelerated by the Vatican Council. Pope John XXIII's social encyclical *Mater et Magistra* was greeted as innovatory, largely perhaps for what it did *not* say. It marked the end of a distinctively Catholic social philosophy rooted in corporatism. In its positive recommendations, the encyclical only followed the kind of positions that the World Council of Churches had taken a decade earlier, but its significance lay in the implicit admission that the Catholic church had ceased to present the old monolithic front to the world. The opening of dialogues with other Christian bodies and with Marxists aided this process, as did the spread of dissent within the church over religious and moral issues. Reiteration of the ban on most forms of birth control, when vast numbers had long resolved this issue in favour of control, only weakened ecclesiastical authority, particularly as this practical dissent was widely known – an important consequence of modern communication. While many may have left the church over this issue, many clerics as well as laity stayed, putting to one side this clear ruling of the central authority. The change of position on this single issue by large sections of the laity, most marked among the younger age groups, easily leads to diversity of opinion and lack of strict conformity on a whole range of moral issues, and this transformation of attitude in turn also affects political habits.

All the Christian denominations were affected by differences over religious priorities. One can see this in the Christian contribution to the struggle for civil rights in the USA and also in the resistance to it, and in the upsurge of conservative Christian lobbying in the 1980 presidential election. In South Africa, on the other hand, it was only recently that the position of any of the churches became one of clear and effective opposition to apartheid.

The churches and Communism

From Pius IX's encyclical *Qui Pluribus*, in 1848, to the 1960s, popes had consistently seen that 'sect of men who are known by the diverse and almost barbaric name of socialists, Communists and Nihilists' (Leo XIII, 1878) as intent upon the destruction of the fabric of human society, and of religion in particular. Such an official attitude was hardly surprising. Throughout the greater part of the world, church authority had been intimately linked with established economic and social power, and there was little impetus to consider whether there might be a difference between a world organized on these lines and a truly human society. The revolutionary changes of the 20th century, in particular the Russian Revolution and the Spanish Civil War, compounded this view of the Catholic church as locked in mortal combat with the forces of atheism and modernity.

Seen from this position, the church's attitude was one of defence and extreme pragmatism. As Pius XI had put it in 1929, where 'there is the question of saving souls or preventing greater harm to souls we feel the courage to deal with the devil in person'. On this basis concordats were made with Nazis, Fascists and, later, Communists. As is often the case, in the longer run pragmatism tended to alternate between astuteness and moral stupidity. Thus, in responding to Roosevelt's supply of arms to Russia in 1941, Pius XII observed that Communism was more of a threat to the church than Nazism, and therefore the best outcome of the war would be a defeated Communism and a weakened Nazism that could be defeated later. Despite his secret

John XXIII's last letter, 'Pacem in Terris' of 1963 was addressed not just to Catholics but 'to all men of good will'. The English cartoonist Vicky saw him as taking up the banner of nuclear disarmament and marching in protest against the atom bomb.

diplomacy on behalf of Jews, his public silence on the attempted destruction of European Jewry, in the belief that public denunciation would worsen the situation, will permanently mark his reputation.

Pius's official neutrality ended abruptly at the end of the war. The Soviet advance in eastern Europe, the growth of the Italian and French Communist parties and the elimination of Catholic missions in China strengthened the pope's support for the formation of NATO. Paul Higginson, in 'Vatican and Communism', summed up the situation: 'An unholy alliance of United States finance, the propertied sections of the European community, and the Vatican, combined to oppose Communism in any and every way possible, and in Italy particularly, Vatican influence kept the Catholic vote in firm opposition to all the left wing parties.' In July 1949, in the wake of the trial of Cardinal Mindszenty in Hungary, Pius excommunicated Catholics who joined or assisted the Communist party. It was an arid time for radicals in the church. During the Cold War, when all manner of 'non-conservative' activity would be labelled 'communist' or 'communizing', the French worker-priests were perhaps lucky to survive as long as they did.

While in Russia the position of Baptists and other Christian minority groups was extremely precarious the response of Protestant bodies to the Soviet expansion of influence was, in the nature of the case, different. They were not as widely represented in the dominated countries nor as closely involved in so many of the anciens régimes. In Czechoslovakia, where there

was a sizable Moravian population, and in what became East Germany, where there was a Lutheran majority, theologians made a heroic effort to understand the failure of the churches to withstand the Nazis during the 1930s and 1940s. In this task they looked back to the few dissenting voices in the Reformed church, notably to Dietrich Bonhoeffer, and to the Swiss theologian, Karl Barth, who saw the war and subsequent Communist takeover as a prophetic judgment upon a Christianity that had fused itself with German civilization and enthusiastically christened its armies. If the churches were to avoid repeating their old errors, it was necessary to accept Barth's judgment, particularly his radical separation of religion and politics. This position left open limited possibilities of co-operation in the rebuilding of society.

Two years before he died in 1958, Pius XII denounced the bad faith of those who attempted any dialogue with Communism: 'What is the use of a discussion without a common language?' Within a few years such dialogue was to be actively encouraged. The pronouncements (or lack of them) on Communism by Pope John XXIII and his successor Pope Paul VI marked the first real change in more than a century of official thought. The change can be illustrated dramatically in the career of the fiercely anti-Communist cardinal, Mindszenty. When released from prison in the Hungarian uprising of 1956 he was acclaimed as one of the church's heroes. By 1974 he was an embarrassment to the Vatican in its search for detente and was unceremoniously dismissed as primate of Hungary.

Given the key role of the papal office, these changes of attitude are in part linked with the personalities of successive popes. The autocratic Pius XI had been papal representative in Warsaw during the Communist upheavals of 1918–21 and persecution of Catholics; the aristocratic professional diplomat Pacelli (Pius XII) suffered throughout his life from the memory of a confrontation with gun-toting Spartacists while papal nuncio in Munich in 1919; John XXIII gave little public sign of radicalism before his late sixties and elevation to the papacy, but his Italian traditionalism sprang from peasant rather than aristocratic or professional roots; he was personally acquainted with some of the disasters of the suppression of modernism, and he had been a notably quiescent papal nuncio in Paris up to 1953, when the repression of the worker-priests began.

The first months of John's reign saw him assent both to the reinforcing of the 1949 condemnation of Communism and to the refusal of any relaxation in the worker-priest situation – moves that were dictated by the Italian political climate of the time. However, the more characteristic marks of John's five years were the 'opening to the left' of the Italian Christian Democrats and the clear down-playing of anti-Communism in the preparatory schemata of the Vatican Council. Formal and informal contacts between the Kremlin and the Vatican became more frequent and more cordial.

The address of his final letter, *Pacem in Terris* (1963), to 'all men of good will', and not just to Catholics, is indicative. John distinguished not only between erroneous beliefs and the inviolable humanity of the person holding them, but 'between a false philosophy of the nature, origin and purpose of men and the world, and an economic, social, cultural and political pro-gramme, even when such a programme draws its origin and inspiration from that philosophy'. The change was very much part of the conciliar openness to the world, the ending of a long period of isolation. It also had highly practical consequences. The election of Bishop Montini as Paul VI, in 1963, saw diplomatic confir-mation of the new policy. Paul's restatement of the traditional position on birth control, which so divided the church, tends to overshadow the more adventurous nature of his diplomacy. In the following years important agreements were reached with Hungary and Yugoslavia. In 1967 and 1968 Paul met the Soviet president, the Romanian prime minister, and Marshal Tito. The first papal representative since the revolution visited Moscow in 1971. In western Europe the new policy was probably a factor in the increase in Communist and socialist votes in Italy. The dialogues between Christians and Communists that had been forbidden only a few years earlier now sprang up in

several countries. In English-speaking countries, where neither side had any real political pull, the dialogue was a marginal and largely theoretical issue. With regard to Portugal and Spain, it was of great importance, for neither side could be confident of outright success when the Franco and Salazar regimes came to an end. The way was thus prepared for the Portuguese bishops' initial support for the socialist government of 1975, and for the co-operation of the Spanish church in the political changes following Franco's death. The new policy also gave an impetus to the bishops and missionaries of South America and Africa to disentangle themselves from conservative establishments and was thus a factor in processes of decolonization and politicization in the two continents.

The papal election in 1978 saw not only the first non-Italian for centuries but a Pole formed by his experience of east European Communism. As would be expected from such a background, his position is theologically conservative. His priorities are the guaranteeing of the church's independence of any particular political party and the consolidation of the clerical office so greatly weakened in numbers and influence in Europe in the 1960s and 1970s. This latter strategy became particularly clear in his summoning of a special synod of the Dutch church, the most progres-sive in Europe, in January 1980. Such priorities are not necessarily incompatible with the commitment of Christians to emancipatory social and political change but there are bound to be strains – for instance in the considerable political involvement of clerics in Latin America. John Paul seems to find no conflict between his insistence that clerics should not be involved in politics and his own far reaching political activities. In the early 1980s it is not yet clear how far John Paul's desire to strengthen the morale and status of the clergy will spill over into an attempt to reclericalize the church and thus run the risk of splitting it further.

Christianity in the Third World:
Africa and Latin America

In a period of accelerated change for Christianity, the greatest changes of all have taken place in Africa. On some estimates, the number of African Christians quadrupled between 1950 and 1980, from 25 million to 100 million. The changes in religious institutions have been just as great and as rapid. Different patterns of colonial rule, Belgian, British, French and Portuguese, were accompanied by differing styles of missionary activity. Attitudes to the autonomy of indigenous clergy varied considerably; the African voice was far more evident at an earlier date among Protestants than Catholics. There was a great diversity of Christian experience and organization in the conflicts, triumphs and disasters of the ending of colonial rule and the establishment of independent African states. The churches faced civil war in the Congo, Burundi, Nigeria and Sudan, and hostile dictatorships, as in Uganda and Zaire. Within the framework of the nation-state tribal loyalties and divisions remained. Burundi was, in statistical terms, the most Christian country in Africa. And yet, when in 1972 the slaughter took place of more than one million of the majority Hutu, the leading Catholic bishops, both Tutsi, identified themselves along tribal lines, wholly with the government repression.

From the end of the last century, in reaction to the missions, there had developed a variety of independent African Christian churches, combining traditional indigenous beliefs and Christian ones, and usually organized around a charismatic leader. They were particularly evident in areas of Protestant influence and in southern Africa generally. Two major forms can be described: the 'Ethiopian', which desires to keep something like the existing church practice and organization, free from white domination, and later the 'Zionist' type, with an emphasis on healing and prophecy. Some analogies can be drawn between these churches and the Anabaptists of 16th-century Europe. In the 1970s the growth of these new churches seems to have slowed considerably. Rather surprisingly, perhaps, in most areas the mission churches were rescued from decline by the triumph of Black nationalism and the irritant of the independent churches. Though originally closely tied to the European and North American headquarters of the missionary bodies, and without the spur of progressive theologians to harry them, Black church leaders in the 1960s and 1970s came to take vigorous and independent lines of action. Both independent and mainstream churches have often found themselves at odds with their governments.

Seen from the orderly missionary perspective of, say, 1950, the complexity and diversity of contemporary African Christianity would seem chaotic. In fact, it is an index of the degree to which Christianity has really taken root and is capable of developing styles of its own. These have been tested in political crises. In periods of dictatorship, the mainstream churches often offer the only alternative source of information and of moral and political authority. They have thus proved their independence of *both* local and European authority.

In all parts of Africa, the diminution of European missionary power and the strains of political independence had made ecclesiastical control over the official structure of church buildings, seminaries, priests and schools precarious. In both urban and rural areas, however, basic communities were thriving. The churches in the 1970s had to struggle with the contrasting claims of structure and *communitas*: a structure largely derived from above, a communion from below. In his comprehensive account of modern African Christianity, Adrian Hastings says: 'If in many countries in the past the mission churches must have struck observers as networks of schools, today they can hardly continue at all as other than a network of prayer houses.'

The withdrawal of many missionaries compounded the already acute shortage of ministers, and this has produced a 'village Christianity' of prayer groups serviced by lay leaders and catechists with relatively infrequent sacramental celebration. Village Christianity has come to replace mission Christianity and is more loosely structured. Although they have lost many of their institutions the churches are in many ways less vulnerable; the power they have is more locally based and enjoys more popular credibility. While far harder to chart than the official world of colleges, seminaries, ecumenism and development projects, this underlying social life of Christianity in Africa, which is now an African Christianity, contains the real seeds of the future.

If it is hard to speak of a *typical* South American country, it is reasonable to take the largest, Brazil, as an example. While the greatest area of Christian growth has been in the phenomenal spread of Pentecostalism, which has claim to be the only Latin American Christian movement with real indigenous roots, Brazil is the largest of the Catholic churches, with some 330 bishops to serve it. The stand of the Brazilian church moved from 19th-century church-state symbiosis, through separation of church and state in the First Republic, to restoration of its influence under Vargas in the 1930s. It began to show signs of real change in the late 1950s. The church became concerned with the improvement of economic and social conditions without which – so ran the thesis – the achievement of religious salvation would be impossible.

In August 1967, a widely publicized document by sixteen Third World bishops, 'Gospel and Revolution', argued that Christians have a duty to prove that 'true socialism is a full Christian life that involves a just sharing of goods, and fundamental equality'. Paradoxically, while radical Christians in Europe often used theological arguments to urge their fellows towards the political left, in South America as much effort had to go into showing that Christian theology was not actually a barrier to desired social changes. The 'liberation theology' of the 1970s was an attempt to rediscover basic categories of active Christian prophecy and judgment in dire situations of human misery. The South American bishops' conference at Medellin,

One of the paradoxes of a world-wide Catholic church is that without shifting its basic position it can seem left wing or right wing according to the context in which it operates. Long identified with the right – or at least with anti-Communism – in Europe, its concern with social justice leads it to adopt an opposite stance vis-à-vis the ultra right wing regimes of South America. The pope's visit in 1980, though cautious in the pronouncements that accompanied it, could only strengthen this radical (to some governments revolutionary) programme.

Colombia, in 1968, took up this theme: 'God has sent his Son so that in the flesh he may come to liberate all men from slavery which holds them subject, from sin, ignorance, hunger, misery, oppression.' Taking recent papal teaching as their point of departure, but necessarily radicalizing it by applying it in regions of desperate poverty and inequality, theologians and activists produced a consistent reading of Christian social understanding as radical as it was orthodox. This in its turn provided inspiration for progress in Europe. Liberation theology took organizational shape in 1972 with the founding of 'Christians for Socialism' in Santiago, Chile, in support of the ill-fated Allende government.

In Brazil, concern with the material preconditions for religious salvation led to increasing conflict with the government after the military coup of 1964. In part, the church had been radicalized by the experiences of the Vatican Council, but the major factor in its transformation was the complete reversal in government policy on economic and social justice, and the use of repression and torture as normal instruments of policy, numbering clerics among its victims.

With only 25,000 priests, a quarter of whom are foreign born, to 120 million Brazilians, experimental and unorthodox pastoral methods have had to be developed. Over twenty years Brazilians have attempted forms of grass-roots political and evangelistic political action. One of the best known of these, the Movement for Basic Education, grew from a 1961 agreement between the government and the bishops' conference to expand the basic literacy programme of several of the diocesan-owned radio stations to the less developed parts of the country as a whole. The hallmark of the movement was *conscientizacão*, the arousing of consciousness among peasants and the urban poor of the socio-economic and political roots of their impoverishment. Its most famous product was the booklet *Viver é Lutar (To Live Means to Struggle)*. After the coup of April 1964, many organizations of the Brazilian Catholic left were suppressed. The Movement for Basic Education, with its strong episcopal links, survived for some while in a substantially modified form.

In recent years there have been further developments of 'base communities' in the poor areas of the cities; in 1980 there were as many as eighty thousand base community workers. The scale of what is involved can be seen in the bishop of Volk Redonda's actual suppression of the parishes in his diocese to give more scope for some 1,600 basic Christian communities. The communities are a means of getting self-help organizations going among desperate and often ignorant people and of putting pressure on civil authorities. In all this the existence of a strong national bishops' conference, as the main policy-making body, has been vital and has allowed the church to be the regime's most feared critic. The remarkable political transformation of the Brazilian church in the 1960s can be contrasted with the state of the church in Cuba in the early years of Castro's revolution – a church that, in the terms of its severest critics, simply failed.

The Christian diaspora

The Third World is a term encompassing such diverse countries and civilizations that it can only be applied provisionally, but nevertheless it registers an important shift in our perception of the human world. Reflecting on the developments outlined in these pages, one can underline the point made by Geoffrey Barraclough in the introductory chapter of this book: Christianity is from the outset a missionary religion whose greatest successes have been in the countries of Europe and the countries originally colonized by Europeans. It reaches its limit when it encounters such other world religions as Buddhism, Hinduism and Islam, with which it now has to learn to enter into dialogue rather than confrontation. Professor Barraclough also underlines the thousand-year duration of the image of the church militant in the figure of the armed crusader. Such powerful images do not die easily, but the image of the church as the people of God, as pilgrim and itinerant without abiding city, shows signs of replacing the image of the crusader. This is particularly important in a world where the demand for the recognition of the human rights of individuals and minorities also draws upon the resources of the Christian tradition, and is one of the most hopeful signs of our times.

It is important to remember that mission is not always a one-way process. In a long period of turmoil the main line of classical and Christian culture was preserved in the missionary outpost of Ireland whence it returned to spread throughout Europe. We have seen the importance of Pentecostalism in 20th-century Christianity deriving in significant ways from the experience of Black Americans, and it may not be too much to expect that the fundamental reconstruction of Christian community, involving great suffering as well as great joy, in Latin America and in Africa will feed similar disturbing energies into European and North American Christianity.

Another of the questions that run through this book concerns not only the extent of Christianity's world but the degree of Christianity's impact within that world. As Professor Barraclough observes, the Christianization of Europe was completed only with the conversion of Lithuania in 1387, and if we consider Siberia as now partially European this date would have to be shifted towards the 17th century. One description of the Reformation is that it was the Christianization of the northern European peasantry. A controversial description, but it alerts us to the persuasive error of seeing the record of the political power of shifting elites and the written, artistic and architectural record as evidence of a coherent and popularly rooted Christian civilization. For those who talk of a 'Christian past which we have lost', the present age may seem one of

'God is love is peace': a message that in Europe would be purely religious carries in South America the overtones of a political manifesto.

complete decline; on a more careful reading of the evidence a more balanced and realistic picture might emerge.

As it approaches its third millennium, Christianity's composition and influence are in a state of flux. While the major Christian traditions seek closer doctrinal and organizational ties, the pressures of social divisions between classes and economic divisions between nations are straining the individual churches' inherited sense of coherence and unity. In this chapter some emphasis has been put on political developments in contemporary Christianity. It is worth emphasizing that Christianity has *always* had a political impact; the current trends examined here represent an open recognition of the fact that they are not so much introducing politics into Christianity as striving to change the direction of its existing political influence. It is also worth emphasizing that Christianity's strength, like that of all the world religions, lies in its diversity, and that amidst political turmoil the contemplative and otherworldly elements of its heritage will also be represented.

The speed and ease of modern communications have greatly affected the churches. A considerable part of the sharp decline in Christian practice, and the practice of the ministry in particular, follows from the fact that what might earlier have been private and silent doubts are now openly acknowledged ones. Many of the forces making for continued external conformity have now vanished. Ease of communication, however, has also meant that centralized control, which thrives when monopoly of the channels of communication can be effected, is more difficult to enforce and that minority groups are less easily ignored or silenced. The days of mainstream church institutions as we know them may be numbered, but it would be misleading to take this as the only index of Christian vitality. Against the clear evidence of institutional decline one should set the qualitatively significant numbers of Christians active outside the formal structures, the appeal of the more extreme forms of Christian sectarianism and the remarkable, if diffuse, general interest in religion stimulated by the growing presence of Western adherents of Eastern religions.

The past impact of Christianity on Europe has been so profound that there are obvious grounds for doubt about the survival of the humane strengths of that culture with Christianity now in a position of declining importance. Against this, one can say that it is precisely the profundity of that past influence that may allow this culture to survive as an autonomous achievement, continuing on its own momentum. If this were to be

so then the diaspora situation of contemporary Christianity could contain its new strength. The resilient complex nature of advanced societies, their apparent ability to continue functioning through major shifts of power and extreme differences of belief and practice, might mean that it is a mistake to continue to look to Christianity as their integrating force. It has been said that religion is incapable of unifying modern societies because nothing can unify them. This failing, if it is such, is not a peculiarity of religion. It may be that modern societies require far less uniformity of values for their continued operation than had previously been supposed. In a sense, the order of Christian life continued surprisingly longer than underlying social changes would have indicated. Thus the scale and speed of contraction are delayed reactions, which may or may not mean a continuing collapse. It is this that will eventually be decided in the remaining decades of the century.

Extremes often go together. A world balanced on the edge of a man-made apocalypse of nuclear destruction also contains an unprecedented awareness that we inhabit a single world; there is a growing respect for the rights of individual humans and for diverse quests for the meaning of human life. In this perspective Christianity has much hope and much doubt, as much rootedness in the past and commitment to the future as at any time in its history.

'Shadow play' by Tomi Ungerer.

Select bibliography

General bibliography

There are several good general histories of Christianity: the Pelican History of the Church, ed. Owen Chadwick, in 6 volumes (Harmondsworth 1964), covers the history of the western church from its origins to the present day; Paul Johnson, *A History of Christianity* (Harmondsworth and New York 1978) is a popular summarizing history and covers the eastern church as well; Kenneth Scott Latourette, *A History of Christianity* (New York and London 1975) is in two volumes, the first dealing with Christianity from its origins to 1500, the second with the period from 1500 to the present day. All these histories are in paperback. More massive works are the *New Catholic Encyclopaedia* (15 vols; New York 1967); A. Fliche and V. Martin, *Histoire de l'Eglise depuis les origines jusqu'à nos jours* (8 vols; Paris 1934); and Kenneth Scott Latourette, *A History of the Expansion of Christianity* (7 vols; London 1939–55) which begins with the background to Christianity in the Greco-Roman world and traces the history of its expansion through to the first half of the 20th century. The history of Christianity and the church seen in terms of lives of the popes can be studied in H. K. Mann, *Lives of the Popes in the Middle Ages* (18 vols; 2nd ed. London 1925), covering the period 590–1304, and Ludwig Pastor's famous *History of the Popes from the Close of the Middle Ages* (40 vols; 6th ed. Nendeln/Liechtenstein 1969) which covers the period 1305–1799 and is 'drawn from the secret archives of the Vatican and other original sources'.

I
Christianity in the Roman Empire

The rise of Christianity has attracted an enormous literature since Gibbon wrote his *Decline and Fall of the Roman Empire*. Good up-to-date general works include: R. M. Grant, *From Augustus to Constantine: the thrust of the Christian movement into the Roman world* (New York 1970 and London 1971). H. C. Frend, *The Early Church* (London 1965), and Henry Chadwick, *The Early Church* (vol. 1 of the Pelican History of the Church; Harmondsworth 1967), may guide the reader through the external history and history of Christian thought up to AD 451. For the Church and the Roman Empire, see H. C. Frend, *Persecution and Martyrdom in the Early Church* (Oxford 1965), H. B. Workman, *Persecution in the Early Church* (repr. Oxford 1980), and R. A. Markus, *Christianity in the Roman World* (London and New York 1974). For the Gnostics, Elaine Pagel, *The Gnostic Gospels* (London 1979) is a fast-moving survey of the recently published Nag Hammadi Gnostic library but it tends to over-emphasize the feminist element among the Gnostics. Constantine and his religious policy are well summed up by N. H. Baynes, *Constantine the Great and the Christian Church* (2nd ed. Oxford 1972), Ramsay Macmullen, *Constantine* (New York 1969) which is rapid and concise, and A. H. M. Jones, *Constantine and the Conversion of Europe* (Teach Yourself History; London 1948). For the later Empire, *The Conflict between Paganism and Christianity in the Fourth Century*, ed. A. Momigliano (Oxford 1963), contains a series of excellent studies of aspects of the conversion of the pagan world. On the Fathers, J. N. D. Kelly, *Jerome* (New York 1975), and Peter Brown, *Augustine of Hippo* (London 1967), are excellent biographies; Peter Brown's *Religion and Society in the Age of St Augustine* (London 1972) and his *World of Late Antiquity* (London and New York 1971) should be consulted by all interested in the development of a Christian civilization on the eve of the barbarian invasions. For the heretics, see H. C. Frend, *The Donatist Church* (2nd ed. Oxford 1971) and the same author's *Rise of the Monophysite Movement* (2nd ed. Cambridge 1979). On the development of Christian thought, see J. N. D. Kelly, *Early Christian Doctrines* (5th ed. London 1979), and R. A. Markus, *Saeculum: history and society in the theology of St Augustine* (Cambridge 1970); for the later period, including the papacy during the pontificate of Gregory I, see R. V. Sellers, *The Council of Chalcedon: an historical and theological survey* (London 1961), and J. Richards, *The Popes and the Papacy in the Early Middle Ages* (London 1979); for early monasticism, Owen Chadwick, *John Cassian* (2nd ed. Cambridge 1968) is valuable. For the documentation of the period up to AD 461, J. Stevenson's two works, *A New Eusebius* (London 1957) and *Creeds, Councils and Controversies* (London 1966) are indispensable guides.

2
The rise of Christian art

Two volumes by A. Grabar, *The Beginnings of Christian Art* (London 1967) and *Byzantium from the Death of Theodosius to the Rise of Islam* (London 1966), present the most comprehensive recent survey of Christian art from the 3rd to the 7th century. E. Kitzinger's *Byzantine Art in the Making* (Cambridge, Mass. 1977) emphasizes the historical dynamics of stylistic developments in the same period. The origins of Christian subject-matter in art are studied by A. Grabar in *Christian Iconography* (Princeton 1968). The best book on architecture is by R. Krautheimer, *Early Christian and Byzantine Architecture* (2nd rev. ed. Harmondsworth and Baltimore 1975). W. Weidlé, *The Baptism of Art* (London n.d.) is an excellent brief essay on the significance of catacomb painting. W. F. Volbach, *Early Christian Art* (London 1961), and P. du Bourguet, *Early Christian Art* (New York 1971), are well illustrated summaries. A concise introduction to manuscript illumination is offered by K. Weitzmann, *Late Antique and Early Christian Book Illumination* (New York 1977). The technique of mosaic painting is traced from the antique to the Middle Ages by H. P. l'Orange and P. J. Nordhagen, *Mosaic* (London 1966). The most detailed study of the monuments of Ravenna is by F. W. Deichmann, *Ravenna, Hauptstadt des spätantiken Abendlandes*, vols 1–3 (Wiesbaden 1969–76), while an abridged but superbly illustrated account is given by G. Bovini and L. von Matt in *Ravenna* (New York 1972). The subject of icons in Christian worship is treated by E. Kitzinger, 'The Cult of Images in the age before Iconoclasm' in *Dumbarton Oaks Papers*, 8 (1954) pp. 83 ff. This is reprinted in E. Kitzinger, *The Art of Byzantium and the Medieval West*, ed. W. E. Kleinbauer (Bloomington and London 1976) pp. 90 ff.

3
The conversion of the barbarian peoples

General surveys of Christianization in the Dark Ages are surprisingly few and far between, although more general works on the history of Christianity, such as Stephen Neill, *A History of Christian Missions* (London 1964), usually include a survey of the period. Fuller treatments of the whole are to be found in a number of collections of essays, most notably in *Die Kirche des früheren Mittelalters*, ed. K. Schäferdiek (vol. 2 of *Kirchengeschichte als Missionsgeschichte*; Munich 1978), and in the conference proceedings *La Conversione al Christianesimo nell' Europa dell' Alto Medioevo, Settimane di Studio del Centro Italiano di Studi sull' Alto Medioevo*, vol. 14 (Spoleto 1967). By contrast there is much covering particular periods and invididuals, including collections of translations of original sources. Of these the most wide ranging is J. N. Hillgarth, *The Conversion of Western Europe, 350–750* (Englewood Cliffs 1969), while C. H. Talbot translated a number of saints' lives in *The Anglo-Saxon Missionaries in Germany* (London and New York 1954). The early contacts of the barbarians with Christianity are most easily studied in E. A. Thompson, 'Christianity and the Northern Barbarians' in *The Conflict between Paganism and Christianity in the Fourth Century*, ed. A. Momigliano (Oxford 1963) and in E. A. Thompson, *The Visigoths in the Time of Ulfila* (Oxford 1966). There is much of importance on the English, both as recipients of Christianity and as missionaries; particularly useful are Henry Mayr-Harting, *The Coming of Christianity to Anglo-Saxon England* (London 1972), S. J. Crawford, *Anglo-Saxon Influence on Western Christendom* (Oxford 1933), and Wilhelm Levison's magisterial *England and the Continent in the Eighth Century* (Oxford 1946). Finally, the relationship between the Carolingian Renaissance and missionary activity is one of the many problems broached by Rosamond McKitterick in *The Frankish Church and the Carolingian Reforms 789–895* (London 1977).

4
The Greek church and the peoples of eastern Europe

The best general studies dealing with the whole theme of the Orthodox church throughout its history are S. Bulgakov, *The Orthodox Church* (London 1935); P. Evdokimov, *L'Orthodoxie* (Neuchâtel 1965); J. Meyendorff, *The Orthodox Church* (London 1965); S. Runciman, *The Orthodox Churches and the Secular State* (Auckland and Oxford 1971); A. Schmemann, *The Historical Road of Eastern Orthodoxy* (London 1963); T. Ware, *The Orthodox Church* (Harmondsworth 1963); and N. Zernov, *Eastern Christendom* (London 1961). Two further books cover the theological and liturgical aspects in greater detail: V. Lossky, *The Mystical Theology of the Eastern Church* (London 1957), and S. Salaville, *An Introduction to the Study of Eastern Liturgies* (London 1938). For the significance of icons in the Orthodox church, see L. Ouspensky and V. Lossky, *The Meaning of Icons* (Boston 1952). N. H. Baynes, *Constantine the Great and the Christian Church* (2nd ed. Oxford 1972), and G. Every, *The Byzantine Partriarchate* (2nd ed. London 1962) provide excellent accounts of the church in Byzantine times. Essential for an understanding of the iconoclastic controversy is P. J. Alexander, *The Patriarch Nicephorus of Constantinople* (Oxford 1968). J. M. Hussey, *Church and Learning in the Byzantine Empire* (London 1937); J. Meyendorff, *Byzantine Theology* (London 1975); and B. Tatakis, *La Philosophie byzantine* (Paris 1949) are recommended for the intellectual background. There are also useful chapters on the Byzantine church in the following books: *Institutions de l'empire byzantin* (Paris 1949) and *La Civilisation byzantine* (Paris 1950) (vols 2 and 3 of L. Brehier, *Le Monde byzantin*); *Cambridge Medieval History*, vol. 4, part ii (new ed. Cambridge 1966); A. Fliche and V. Martin, *Histoire de l'Eglise*, vol. 4, parts i and ii (Paris 1934–); G. Ostrogorsky, *History of the Byzantine State* (Oxford 1956); A. A. Vasiliev, *History of the Byzantine Empire* (Madison 1952). Literature on the history of the Orthodox church after Byzantium and during the Turkish domination is less plentiful; the following provide useful information, though differing in their emphases: W. F. Adeney, *The Greek and Eastern Churches* (Edinburgh 1908); P. Hammond, *The Waters of Marah* (London 1956); N. Jorga, *Byzance après Byzance* (Bucharest 1935); T. H. Papadopoullos, *Studies and Documents Relating to the History of the Greek Church and People under Turkish Domination* (Brussels 1952); M. Rinvolucri, *Anatomy of a Church* (London 1966); S. Runciman, *The Great Church in Captivity* (Cambridge 1968); T. Smith, *An Account of the Greek Church* (Oxford 1980); T. Spencer, *Fair Greece, Sad Relic* (London 1954); G. Waddington, *The Present Condition of the Greek or Oriental Church* (London 1829). For the expansion of the Orthodox church into the Balkans and Russia, see especially M. Bourdeaux, *Patriarch and Prophets* (London 1969); L. Hadrovics, *Le Peuple serbe et son Eglise sous la domination turque* (Paris 1947); B. Leib, *Rome, Kiev et Byzance* (Paris 1924); W. K. Medlin, *Moscow and East Rome* (Geneva 1952); J. Meyendorff, *Byzantium and the Rise of Russia* (Cambridge 1981); D. Obolensky, *The Byzantine Commonwealth* (London 1971); and M. Spinka, *A History of*

Christianity in the Balkans (Chicago 1933). W. C. Fletcher, *A Study in Survival* (London 1965) is also recommended. The subject of the church in Russia has been treated from various points of view: F. C. Conybeare, *Russian Dissenters* (Cambridge, Mass. 1921); M. Rouet de Journel, *Monachisme et monastères russes* (Paris 1952); A. Soloviev, *Holy Russia* (The Hague 1959); N. Zernov, *Moscow, the Third Rome* (London 1927), and the same author's *The Russian Religious Renaissance* (London 1963). Finally, a number of interesting studies have been made tracing the relations between eastern and western churches, concentrating mainly on the schism with the Roman church, but also covering contacts with Protestant denominations. The following are scholarly and authoritative: E. Benz, *Die Ostkirche im Licht der Protestantischen Geschichtsschreibung* (Freiburg 1952); J. Douglas, *The Relations of the Anglican Church with the Eastern Orthodox* (London 1921); F. Dvornik, *Byzantium and the Roman Primacy* (New York 1966); A. Florovski, *Le Conflit des deux traditions* (Prague 1937); D. J. Geanokoplos, *Byzantine East and Latin West* (Oxford 1966); J. Gill, *The Council of Florence* (Cambridge 1959); W. Norden, *Das Papsttum und Byzanz* (Berlin 1903); S. Runciman, *The Eastern Schism* (Oxford 1955); P. Sherrard, *The Greek East and the Latin West* (London 1959); N. Zernov, *Orthodox Encounter* (London 1961).

5
Medieval Christendom

General introductions to medieval society may be found in Marc Bloch, *Feudal Society* (London 1961); R. W. Southern, *The Making of the Middle Ages* (London 1953); and in the collection of studies edited by Joan Evans, *The Flowering of the Middle Ages* (London and New York 1966). A general history of the church during this period is R. W. Southern, *Western Society and the Church in the Middle Ages* (vol. 2 of the Pelican History of the Church; Harmondsworth 1964). On the papacy, G. Barraclough, *The Medieval Papacy* (London 1968) is much the best short introduction. The popular interest in relics and pilgrimages is examined in P. J. Geary, *Furta Sacra: thefts of relics in the Central Middle Ages* (Princeton 1978); and in Jonathan Sumption, *Pilgrimage: an image of mediaeval religion* (London 1975); and there is a lively account of the financing of the cathedrals in H. Kraus, *Gold was the Mortar* (London 1979). Ideals of poverty influenced the life of the church and of society as a whole, and they are examined in L. K. Little, *Religious Poverty and the Profit Economy in Medieval Europe* (London 1978), and M. Mollat, *Les Pauvres au Moyen Age: étude sociale* (Paris 1978). C. Brooke, *The Monastic World* (London 1974) provides a valuable survey of the changes which were taking place in these centuries, and contains references to some of the very voluminous literature on the subject. It is also splendidly illustrated by the photographs of Wim Swaan. On the ideology of the papal reform movement, a classic work is G. Tellenbach, *Church, State and Christian Society at the Time of the Investiture Contest* (Oxford 1940). The role of the laity in Christian society is examined by J. Gilchrist, 'Laity in the Middle Ages', *New Catholic Encyclopaedia*, vol. 8 (New York 1967) pp. 331–35, and G.

Duby, *Les Trois Ordres ou l'imaginaire du féodalisme* (Paris 1979). Useful information about the development of the hospital service is provided by J. D. Thompson and G. Goldin, *The Hospital: a social and architectural history* (New Haven and London 1975). The best starting-point for a study of the changing character of marriage is G. Duby, *Medieval Marriage: two models from twelfth-century France* (Baltimore 1978). The classic discussion of attitudes to warfare and knighthood is C. Erdmann, *The Origin of the Idea of Crusade* (Princeton 1977). On the development of chivalry, there are good surveys by S. Painter, *French Chivalry* (Ithaca 1957), and G. Duby, *The Chivalrous Society* (London 1977); forthcoming is J. Bumke, *The Concept of Knighthood in the Middle Ages*.

6
Popular religious movements
in the Middle Ages

Some of the best writing, including the best general surveys, on popular religion in the later Middle Ages is in French. Francis Rapp, *L'Eglise et la vie religieuse en occident à la fin du Moyen Age* (Paris 1971), and E. Delaruelle, E.-R. Labande and P. Ourliac, *L'Eglise au temps du Grand Schisme et la Crise Conciliaire (1378–1449)* (vol. 14, part ii of the *Histoire de l'Eglise* founded by A. Fliche and V. Martin; Paris 1964) offer rich coverage of the field, with full documentation. Two volumes of collected papers add insights on particular topics: Etienne Delaruelle, *La Piété populaire au Moyen Age*, ed. P. Wolff, introd. R. Manselli and A. Vauchez (Turin 1975), contains the collected papers of one who made a large contribution to the field; *La Religion populaire en Languedoc du XIII⁰ siècle à la moitié du XIV⁰ siècle*, ed. Edouard Privat, introd. M.-H. Vicaire (Toulouse 1976), is a collection of studies by different authors. A comparable collection in English, *Popular Belief and Practice*, ed. G. J. Cuming and Derek Baker in *Studies in Church History*, 8 (1972), contains several valuable papers on the period covered by this chapter. Two good recent studies of pilgrimage are: Ronald C. Finucane, *Miracles and Pilgrims: popular beliefs in medieval England* (London 1977), and Jonathan Sumption, *Pilgrimage: an image of mediaeval religion* (London 1975). E. W. Kemp, *Canonization and Authority in the Western Church* (Oxford 1948) remains the best on this subject. For the influence of the Franciscans see M. D. Lambert, *Franciscan Poverty: the doctrine of the absolute poverty of Christ and the Apostles in the Franciscan Order, 1210–1323* (London 1961). The best general survey of heresy (with bibliographies) is M. D. Lambert *Medieval Heresy: popular religious movements from Bogomil to Hus* (London 1977). Emmanuel le Roy Ladurie, *Montaillou: Cathars and Catholics in a French village, 1294–1324*, trs. Barbara Bray (Harmondsworth and Baltimore 1980), though singularly lacking critical apparatus (even an index), presents much vivid material drawn from inquisitorial records. On the Inquisition, the major work is still that of H. C. Lea, *A History of the Inquisition of the Middle Ages* (3 vols, New York 1888 and subsequent reprints). Richard C. Trexler, 'Florentine Religious Experience: the sacred image' in *Studies in the Renaissance*, 19 (1972), pp. 7–41, is illuminating on the use of imagery.

7
The age of the Reformation

Of the immense literature on the Reformation, we note two useful general histories, H. J. Hillerbrand, *The World of the Reformation* (New York 1973), and S. Ozment, *The Age of Reform 1250 to 1550* (New Haven and London 1980). Conditions before the Reformation are discussed very perceptively in B. Moeller's essay on 'Piety in Germany around 1500' in S. Ozment, *The Reformation in Medieval Perspective* (London 1971). B. Moeller, *The Imperial Cities and the Reformation* (Philadelphia 1972) is a brilliant and seminal essay which stresses the importance of the urban Reformation. Why the urban centres proved congenial to the Reformation is also discussed in S. Ozment, *The Reformation in the Cities* (London and New Haven 1975). Among the outstanding studies on specific towns, we note R. Walton, *Zwingli's Theocracy* (London 1967), and T. Brady, *Ruling Class, Regime, and Reformation at Strasbourg, 1520–1555* (Leiden 1978). None of the recent Marxist interpretations are available in English, so reference needs to be made to Friedrich Engels's seminal work, *The Peasant War in Germany* (Eng. ed. Chicago and London 1967), and the thorough historiographical survey by A. Friesen, *Reformation and Utopia: the Marxist interpretation of the Reformation and its antecedents* (Wiesbaden 1974). Martin Luther has received continuous attention, the best introduction being the biography of A. G. Dickens, *Martin Luther and the Reformation* (London 1967). A highly controversial attempt to relate Luther to personality theory is E. Erikson, *Young Man Luther* (London 1959). G. Strauss, *Luther's House of Learning* (London and Baltimore 1978) surveys the massive evidence for the pedagogical effort (and failures) of the Lutheran Reformation in Germany, while *The German Peasant War of 1525*, ed. B. Scribner (London 1979), contains several splendid essays. On the radicals of the Reformation there is C. P. Clasen, *Anabaptism: a social history 1525–1618* (Ithaca and London 1972), and J. Stayer, *Anabaptists and the Sword* (Lawrence 1972). The best introduction to the English Reformation is G. R. Elton, *Reform and Reformation: England 1509–1558* (London 1972). The most useful recent work on Calvin is T. H. L. Parker, *John Calvin: a biography* (London 1975), while the influence of Max Weber's *The Protestant Ethic and the Spirit of Capitalism* (London 1930), a highly controversial and much maligned thesis, continues. A panoramic survey of the richness of the popular religion in England is Keith Thomas, *Religion and the Decline of Magic* (London and New York 1974).

8
The social impact of Puritanism

For the early history of Puritanism, see Marshall M. Knappen, *Tudor Puritanism* (Chicago and London 1968); Patrick Collinson, *The Elizabethan Puritan Movement* (London 1967); and William Haller, *The Rise of Puritanism* (New York 1938). The doctrinal side of Puritanism is thoroughly examined in Perry Miller, *The New England Mind: the seventeenth century* (New York 1939). Miller analyzes the relationship between Puritanism and society in *The New England Mind: from colony to province* (Cambridge, Mass. 1953). Robert Middlekauff's *The Mathers: three generations of Puritan intellectuals* (New York 1971) explores religion and society through the lives of three prominent American Puritans, Richard, Increase and Cotton Mather. Edmund S. Morgan's *Puritan Dilemma* (1958) is a fine, readable biography of John Winthrop. Several books have examined the local history of Puritan New England. Among the best are Philip J. Greven, Jr, *Four Generations: population, land, and family in colonial Andover, Massachusetts* (Ithaca and London 1970); John Demos, *A Little Commonwealth: family life in Plymouth Colony* (New York 1970); and Kenneth A. Lockridge, *A New England Town: the first hundred years* (1970). Christopher Hill's *Society and Puritanism in Pre-Revolutionary England* (London 1969) is an exhaustive survey of its subject. William Haller's *Liberty and Reformation in the Puritan Revolution* (New York and London 1963) explores Puritan ideas in the Civil Wars. And Christopher Hill's *The World Turned Upside Down* (Harmondsworth and Baltimore 1978) describes the radicals in the Revolution. Hill has also written a fine biography of Oliver Cromwell entitled *God's Englishman: Oliver Cromwell and the English Revolution* (London 1970). On the local history of Puritanism in England see Christopher Haigh, *Reformation and Resistance in Tudor Lancashire* (London 1975) and Margaret Spufford, *Contrasting Communities: English villages in the sixteenth and seventeenth centuries* (London 1974).

9
Religion in the age of the Baroque

The best introduction is G. R. Cragg, *The Church and the Age of Reason (1648–1789)* (vol. 4 of the Pelican History of the Church; Harmondsworth 1960), which includes a chapter on Baroque art. For Baroque civilization itself, two important introductions are V. L. Tapie, *The Age of Grandeur: Baroque and Classicism in Europe* (London 1960) which deals with the visual arts, and P. Skrine, *The Baroque: literature and culture in seventeenth century Europe* (London 1978) which is concerned with literary questions. Standard reference works on the arts are A. Blunt, *Art and Architecture in France 1500–1700* (London 1953); G. Kubler and M. Soria, *Art and Architecture in Spain and Portugal and their American Dominians* (London 1959); R. Wittkower, *Art and Architecture in Italy 1600–1750* (London and New York 1958); and N. Powell, *From Baroque to Rococo* (London 1959). For music, the best introduction is M. F. Bukofzer, *Music in the Baroque Era* (London 1948). Two particularly stimulating approaches to the problem of Baroque sensibility are R. A. Kann, *A Study in Austrian Intellectual History* (New York 1960) and R. T. Petersson, *The Art of Ecstasy* (London 1970). The latter discusses the works of St Theresa, Bernini and Crashaw. On the Jesuits the most useful work is that of J. de Guibert, *The Jesuits, their Spiritual Doctrine and Practice* (Chicago 1964). *Baroque Art: the Jesuit contribution*, ed. R. Wittkower and I. B. Jaffe (New York 1972) brings together a number of essays of varying quality and has an excellent introduction. On Rome, the most important introduction to the Baroque era is T. H. Fokker, *Roman Baroque Art* (New York 1972).

10
Christianity and industrial society

For England, E. R. Norman, *Church and Society in England 1770–1970: a historical study* (Oxford 1976) has been much controverted for its conclusions but contains valuable material. Christian Socialism in England is discussed in P. N. Backstrom, *Christian Socialism and Co-operation in Victorian England* (London 1973); P. d'A. Jones, *The Christian Socialist Revival, 1877–1914* (Princeton 1968); and T. Christensen, *The Origins and History of Christian Socialism 1848–54* (Aarhus 1962). H. U. Faulkner, *Chartism and the Churches* has useful material on the radicals' attitude to religion, but still more useful are E. Royle, *Victorian Infidels* (Manchester 1974); K. S. Inglis, *Churches and the Working Classes in Victorian England* (London 1963); W. R. Ward, *Religion and Society in England 1790–1850* (London 1972); and S. Mayor, *The Churches and the Labour Movement* (London 1967). K. Heasman, *Evangelicals in Action* (London 1962) describes social work carried out in the cities by the evangelicals. For America, see *The Social Gospel in America*, ed. R. T. Handy (Oxford 1966); C. H. Hopkins, *The Rise of the Social Gospel in American Protestantism in 1865–1915* (New Haven 1940); R. T. Handy, *A History of the Churches in the United States and Canada* (Oxford 1976); H. F. May, *Protestant Churches and Industrial America* (New York 1949). For France, J. B. Duroselle, *Les Débuts du catholicisme social en France, 1822–1870* (Paris 1951) is the fundamental book. Roman Catholicism in general during this period is discussed in *The Church in a Secularized Society*, ed. R. Aubert (London 1978) and A. R. Vidler, *A Century of Social Catholicism 1820–1920* (London 1964). R. L. Camp, *The Papal Ideology of Social Reform: a study in historical development, 1878–1967* (Leiden 1969) describes the evolution of papal ideas. For the growth of Catholic democratic parties, see M. P. Fogarty, *Christian Democracy in Western Europe, 1820–1953* (London 1957), and for Cardinal Manning's work there is V. A. McLelland, *Cardinal Manning: his public life and influence, 1865–1892* (London 1962). *Christianisme et monde ouvrier*, ed. F. Bédarida and J. Maitron (Paris 1975), contains essays on recent Christian work, and Emile Poulat, *Eglise contre bourgeois* (Paris 1977) is an important work.

11
Religion at the grass-roots

Sydney Ahlstrom, *A Religious History of the American People* (New Haven 1972) is comprehensive and judicious. On the 19th-century matrix, see William Warren Sweet, *Religion in the Development of American Culture* (New York 1952), and another book which has profoundly influenced church historians, Sidney E. Mead, *The Lively Experiment* (New York 1963). For the post-Civil War reform impulse, see C. H. Hopkins, *The Rise of the Social Gospel in American Protestantism* (New Haven 1940) and Robert D. Gross, *The Emergence of Liberal Catholicism in America* (Cambridge, Mass. 1958). The origin of a major challenge to 'mainstream' American Christianity is studied by Ernest R. Sandeen, *The Roots of Fundamentalism* (Chicago 1970). The 'mind-cure' movement is perceptively examined in Donald Meyer, *The Positive Thinkers* (New York 1965). A classic account of non-religious reasons for religious differences is H. Richard Niebuhr, *The Social Sources of Denominationalism* (New York 1929), a judgment later qualified by Niebuhr in his essay 'The Protestant Movement and Democracy in the United States' in *The Shaping of American Religion*, ed. James Ward Smith and A. Leland Jamison (Princeton 1961). By far the best study of Prohibition is Norman H. Clark, *Deliver Us from Evil* (New York 1976). R. T. Handy has written on 'The American Religious Depression, 1925–1935' in *Church History*, 29 (March 1960), a judgment to which partial exception is taken by Joel A. Carpenter, 'A Shelter in the Time of Storm: fundamentalist institutions and the rise of evangelical Protestantism, 1929–1942' again in *Church History*, 49 (March 1980).

12
Christianity in the contemporary world

A concise account of the phenomenon of modernization is given by Peter Berger and others in *The Homeless Mind: modernization and consciousness* (Harmondsworth and Baltimore 1974). *The Social Reality of Religion* (London 1969; the American edition is called *The Sacred Canopy*), also by Berger, is an excellent study of the impact of modern sociology on Christian thinking. The main issues in the debate about secularization are presented in concise form in Bryan Wilson, *Contemporary Transformations of Religion* (Oxford 1979); David Martin *The Dilemmas of Contemporary Religion* (Oxford 1978); and Alasdair MacIntyre, *Secularization and Moral Change* (London 1967). A fuller account is given in David Martin, *A General Theory of Secularization* (Oxford 1978). Detail on the ecumenical movement can be found in *The Ecumenical Advance*, ed. Harold E. Fey (London 1970). The standard work on Pentecostalism is Walter J. Hollenweger's *The Pentecostals* (London 1972). A good introduction to recent Catholic history is given in E. E. Y. Hales, *The Catholic Church and the Modern World* (London 1958), and a short account of the second Vatican Council in George Bull, *Politics at the Second Vatican Council* (London 1966). The best study of the worker-priests is by Gregor Siefer, *The Church and Industrial Society* (London 1964). On developments in Germany, Carl Amery's *Capitulation* (London 1967) is polemical and searching. The best study of Christian responses to Communism remains Charles West's *Communism and the Theologians* (London 1958); Paul Higginson, 'Vatican and Communism' in *New Blackfriars* (April 1980) is also useful. In his *History of African Christianity 1950–1975* (Cambridge 1979), Adrian Hastings gives a careful assessment of present trends, and T. C. Bruneau, *The Political Transformation of the Brazilian Catholic Church* (Cambridge 1977), offers an account which is of relevance to other Latin American countries.

Sources of
Illustrations

Introduction: A Christian World?

9 1. *The Harrowing of Hell*. Alabaster relief, Nottingham, 15th century. Victoria and Albert Museum. Photo: John Webb.
10 2. *The Trinity*. Detail from painting by Lucas Cranach the Elder, 1516. Museum der bildenden Künste, Leipzig.
3. God depicted as a pope. From French Book of Hours, 15th century. Bodleian Library, Oxford.
4. *The Trinity*. Tyrolean folk painting, early 17th century. Tiroler Volkskunstmuseum, Innsbruck.
5. God as a judge. Miniature from Flemish Book of Hours, late 15th century. Bodleian Library, Oxford.
11 6. God the Father. Stained glass window, 15th century. Church of St Mary and St Clement, Clavering, Essex. Photo: Alfred Lammer.
12 7. *Virgin with the Milk Soup*. Painting by Gerard David (1450–1523). Musée Royale, Brussels.
8. *Virgin of the Immaculate Conception*. Detail from silver gilt statue by J. L. Saler, Olten, 1750. Landesmuseum, Zürich.
9. *Pietà*. Painting by Sebastiano del Piombo, *c*. 1517. Museo Civico, Viterbo.
13 10. *The Virgin of Mercy*. Painting by Jean Mirailhet, *c*. 1425. Musée Massena, Nice. Photo: Giraudon.
14 11. Head of Christ. Detail from terracotta bust by Giovanni della Robbia, *c*. 1500. Victoria and Albert Museum, London. Photo: Istvan Racz.
15 12. *Christ Taking Leave of the Three Marys*. Painting by Lucas Cranach the Elder, 1520. Kunsthistorisches Museum, Vienna.
13. *Christ Crucified*. Detail from altarpiece by Rembrandt, 1631. Church at Le Mas d'Amgenais. Photo: Giraudon.
14. *Christ on the Mount of Olives*. Altarpiece by Goya, 1819. Church of S. Antonio, Madrid. Photo: Mas.
16 15. Christ Resurrected. Easter procession in Sicily. Photo: F. Scianna.

18 *Above*. Pantocrator, mosaic from the presbytery, Monreale Cathedral.
Below. Christ the Judge, from the west front of Chartres Cathedral, *c*. 1150. Drawing by IM-K.
20 *Left*. Printer's device, Murcia, 1578, from a historical account of the reign of Ferdinand and Isabella.
Right. Woodcut, 1489, from Ulrich Molitor, *De laniis et phitonicis mulieribus*, Cologne, 1489.
21 Woodcut from *Improbatio alcorani*, Barcelona 1500.
22 Tombstone from Fayum, Egypt, Staatliche Museen, Berlin. Drawing by IM-K.
23 Relief from the church of the Holy Cross, Aghtamar, Turkey, 10th century. Drawing by IM-K.
25 North cross in Co. Tipperary, 8th century.
26 *Left*. Engraving from F. du Halde, *Description de la Chine*, Paris, 1735.
Right. Japanese woodcut.

26 *Below*. Engraving from A. Kircher, *La Chine illustreé*, Amsterdam, 1667.
Below left. Cross from Mexico with the instruments of the Passion, National Museum of History, Mexico City. Drawing by Elizabeth Wickham.
27 *Above left*. Bronze processional cross from Ethiopia, British Museum, London.
Below left. Carved wooden crucifix from the Congo, Musée de l'Afrique Centrale, Tervuren. Drawing by Georgie Glen.
Above right. Queen Victoria, *Illustrated London News*.
Below right. Bible group in Latin America. Drawing by Sue Coe.
28 German single woodcut, Nuremberg, 1470–80, British Museum, London.
29 Woodcut from *La Mer des Histoires*, Lyons, 1506.
30 Printer's tailpiece, Paris, 1630.

1, 2. The Ancient World

33 1. Constantius IV grants Bishop Reparatus Privileges. Mosaic from S. Apollinare in Classe, Ravenna. Photo: Scala.
34 2. Catacomb of the Jordani, Rome, 4th century. Photo: Pontificia Commissione di archeologia sacra.
3. Baptism. From the Catacomb of S. Callisto, 3rd century. Photo: Pontificia Commissione di archeologia sacra.
4. Three Young Men in the Furnace. Catacomb of St Priscilla, Rome, 3rd century. Photo: Pontificia Commissione di archeologia sacra.
35 5. Orant figure, called 'Donna Velata'. Catacomb of St Priscilla, Rome, mid-3rd century. Photo: Pontificia Commissione di archeologia sacra.
6. Bread and fish. From the Catacomb of S. Callisto, Rome, early 3rd century. Photo: Pontificia Commissione di archeologia sacra.
7. The sacrifice of Isaac. Catacomb of Via Latina, Rome, 4th century. Photo: Pontificia Commissione di archeologia sacra.
8. The heavenly banquet. Catacomb of SS Pietro and Marcellino, 4th century. Photo: Pontificia Commissione di archeologia sacra.
36 9. *Thebaide*. Detail from painting by Starnina, 15th century. Uffizi, Florence. Photo: Scala.
10. Caves in Göreme, Cappadocia. Photo: Emily Lane.
36, 37 11. St Catherine's monastery, Sinai. Photo: Roger Wood/Camera Press.
38 12. Jonah, orant figure and philosopher. Detail from Early Christian sarcophagus, S. Maria Antiqua, Rome. Photo: Hirmer.
13. Peacock and vine. Marble relief from S. Apollinare Nuovo, Ravenna, mid-6th century. Photo: Hirmer.
14. Lamb of God. Detail from Christian sarcophagus, S. Apollinare in Classe, Ravenna, 6th century. Photo: Leonard von Matt.
15. Baptismal font in mosaic. Kelibia, Tunisia, 6th century. Photo: Tunisian Embassy.
39 16. Christ-Helios. Mosaic from the crypt of St Peter's Rome. Photo: Pontificia Commissione di archeologia sacra.
17. Head of Christ. Floor mosaic from Hinton St Mary, Dorset, 4th century. British Museum, London.
18. Christ as the Good Shepherd. Mosaic from the mausoleum of Galla Placidia, Ravenna, 5th century. Photo: Scala.
19. Christ as emperor. Mosaic from S. Pudenziana, Rome, 4th century.
40 20. Mosaic on the triumphal arch, S. Maria Maggiore, Rome, 432–40. Photo: Scala.
21. Moses and the daughter of the Pharaoh. Detail of mosaic from S. Maria Maggiore, Rome, 432–40. Photo: Scala.

40 22. Rebecca giving Eliezer water to drink. Detail from the Vienna Genesis, early 6th century. Osterreichische Nationalbibliothek, Vienna.
23. The entry into Jerusalem. From the Rossano Gospels, 6th century. Museo Diocesano, Rossano, Calabria. Photo: Hirmer.
41 24. Apse mosaic from S. Apollinare in Classe, Ravenna, mid-6th century. Photo: Scala.
25. The transfiguration. Mosaic from the church of the monastery of St Catherine, Mount Sinai, *c*. 600. Photo: Roger Wood.
42 26. Sarcophagus of a child, Constantinople, *c*. 400. Archaeological Museum, Istanbul.
27. The ascension. Ivory panel, *c*. 400. Bayerisches Nationalmuseum, Munich. Photo: Hirmer.
43 28. Interior of the mausoleum of Galla Placidia, Ravenna, 5th century. Photo Alinari/Mansell Collection.
29. The procession of the Magi. Mosaic from S. Apollinare Nuovo, Ravenna, 6th century. Photo: Hirmer.
30. Mosaics in the nave, S. Apollinare Nuovo, Ravenna, 6th century. Photo: Hirmer.
31. Ceiling and south-west wall of the presbyterium, S. Vitale, Ravenna, 532–47. Photo: Hirmer.
32. Interior of S. Vitale, Ravenna, 532–47. Photo: Hirmer.
44 33. Dome mosaic from the Orthodox Baptistery, Ravenna, 5th century.
34. Dome mosaic from the Arian Baptistery, Ravenna, 5th century. Photo: Scala.

47 Gnostic gem, Staatliche Museen, Berlin. Drawing by Trevor Hodgson.
50 Medal of Diocletian, British Museum, London. Drawing by Paula Brown.
51 Epitaph of Simplicius and Faustinus, Vatican Museums. Drawing by Paula Brown.
53 Roman calendar, Biblioteca Apostolica Vaticana.
55 Tombstone of Coptic abbot, by courtesy of Christies, London. Drawing by IM-K.
59 Papyrus, 15th century, Sopr. Antichità d'Etruria, Florence.
60 Plans of Hagia Sophia, Old St Peter's, the church of the Holy Sepulchre and the church of the Nativity, Thames and Hudson Archives.
63 Reconstruction of a martyrium, Thames and Hudson Archives.
65 The sarcophagus of Junius Bassus, Vatican Museums. Drawing by IM-K.
66 'Christ of Psammatia', Staatliche Museen, Berlin. Drawing by IM-K.
67 Mosaic from S. Constanza, Rome.
69 Dome mosaic of St George, Salonica.
73 Gold solidus of Justinian II, British Museum, London. Drawing by IM-K.

3. A Conquering Mission

77 1. Baptizing two heathen noblemen. Sandstone relief from Grosskirbach, Upper Franconia, *c*. 1040. Photo: Hirmer.
78, 9 2–5. Story of the mission of Poppo. Gold plaques from Tamdrup, Denmark, *c*. 1200. National Museum, Copenhagen.
80 6. Floor mosaic from Teurnia, in Carinthia, *c*. 500.
7. Stele with crucifixion scene, Rhineland, 7th century. Rheinisches Landesmuseum, Bonn.
8. Christian tombstone, Niederdollendorf, late 7th century. Rheinisches Landesmuseum, Bonn.
9. The Jelling stone, Jelling, Jutland, 965–85. National Museum, Copenhagen.
81 10. Silver crucifix pendant from Birka, Sweden, Viking Age. National Museum, Stockholm.

Index

Page numbers in *italic* refer to the illustrations.

images, iconoclasm, 111–12, 169; religious, 162–64; *see also* art
'Imago Primi Saeculi', *233*
imitatio Christi, 166
Incas, *223*
India, 259; Christianity in, *26*; Church of South India, 299; conversions to Christianity, 261; cult of the Sacred Heart of Jesus, 236; missionaries in, 225, 234; North American, 214
indulgences, 164, 174, 188; *189*
Industrial Revolution, 240, 249–62, 298
Ine, 96
Ingeld, 96
Innocent, Metropolitan of Moscow, 121
Innocent III, Pope, 140, 145, 162, 166
Inquisition, 57, 166
International Missionary Conference (1910), 299
Investiture Contest (1076–1122), 140
Iona, 87
Ireland, 305; church and politics, 252, 306; conversion to Christianity, 19, 58, 87, 95–96; emigration to America, 274; *275*; missionaries, 88; monasticism, 76; stone crosses, *25*
Ireland, John, 275
Irenaeus, St, 48, 68
Irene, Empress, 74, 112
Irminsul, 88, 92
irreligion, 19th-century, 253
Isidore, Archbishop, 119
Isidorus of Miletus, 72
Islam, 19, 25, 28, 297, 311; conquest of Byzantium, 114; European conquests, 133
Israel, kingdom of, Christian missionaries, 45
Istanbul, *see* Constantinople
Italy, anticlericalism, 254; Catholicism, 225; Christian Democrats, 308; Christian Socialism, 251, 255–56; church primary schools, *246*; Lombard invasions, 59; monasteries, 136; 19th-century Christianity, *246*; Ostrogoths conquer, 58; pilgrimages, *152*; relics of saints, 135; religion and politics, 258–59, 306; universal franchise, 258; worker-priests, 303–4
Ivan III, Tsar, 119
Ivan IV the Terrible, Tsar, 120
Ivan V, Tsar, 121; *107*
Ivo, Bishop of Chartres, 138

JACOBITES, 25
James I, King of England, 202, 204, 209
James the Great, St, 135, 151; *84, 150*
James the Just, St, 46
James, William, 282
James Bar'adai, 59
Januarius, St, *217*
Japan, 297; Christianity in, 25; *26*; Jesuit missionaries, 225; *238*; Opus Dei, 305; persecution of Christians, *231*
Jassy, 115
Jefferson, Thomas, 275, 279
Jehovah's Witnesses, 281
Jelling, 93, 98; *80*
Jeremias I, Patriarch, 116
Jeremias II, Patriarch, 116
Jerome, St, 54, 55–56; *82*
Jerpoint Abbey, *131*
Jerusalem, 100; Acacian Schism,

58; fall of (AD70), 47; Holy Sepulchre, 64, 68; *60*; patriarchate of, 117; pilgrimages, 135, 158; *150*
Jesuits, 216; churches, 234, 237; *224, 227*; education, 115, 234; formation of, 305; influence of, 228; interest in the theatre, 232–34; *235*; missionary work, 29, 225, 230, 232, 234; *26, 222, 238*; relations with Orthodox church, 116
Jesus Christ, *see* Christ
Jews, 45–46, 133, 259, 274, 307; *see also* Judaism
Joachim, Patriarch, 121
Joachim, Prince of Anhalt, *175*
Job, Book of, 282
John, St, *Gospel*, 62, 95
John VIII, Emperor, 113
John XXII, Pope, 165, 166
John XXIII, Pope, 302, 306, 307, 308; *307*
John of Damascus, 74
John of Kronstadt, Father, 122
John of Salisbury, 144
John of the Cross, St, 227, 230
John of Wallingford, *139*
John the Baptist, St, 46, 135; *9, 77*
John Cantacuzenus, Emperor, *106*
John Chrysostom, St, 112, 121
John Frederick the Magnanimous, Elector of Saxony, *173*
John Paul II, Pope, 19, 302, 308; *293*
Johnson, Lyndon, 283; *271*
Jones, David, *289*
Joseph, Abbot of Volokolamsk, 120
Joseph of Arimathea, 46
Josephians, 120
Josephus, 45
Jouarre, *84*
Judaism, 19; Christianity and, 45–48, 53; influence on Christian art, 62; *see also* Jews
Julia Mammaea, 49
Julian, Emperor, 54
Julian, presbyter, 59
Julius I, Pope, 53
Justin I, Emperor, 59
Justin Martyr, 47, 48
Justinian I, Emperor, 42, 43, 58, 59, 70, 71, 72, 111, 139; *106*
Justinian II, Emperor, 73
Jutes, 57

KAISERSWERTH, 262
Kappel, 227
Kartashev, Professor, 122
Keble, John, 262
Keldby church, *149*
Kempe, Margery, 158
Kempis, Thomas à, *The Imitation of Christ*, 167, 228; *167*
Kennedy, Edward, 286
Kennedy, John F., 283; *271*
Kent, 87
Kenya, 305
Kerensky, Alexander, 122
Ketteler, Bishop of Mainz, 254, 255, 256; *Christianity and the Worker*, 255
Kierkegaard, Søren, 286
Kiev, 119
King, Martin Luther, 277; *271*
Kings, Book of, 94
kingship, power increased by Christianity, 97–98; and the Reformation, 198
Kingsley, Charles, 250
Kirkeby church, *131*
Klephts, 116–17

knights, medieval, 142–44; *130, 131, 143*
Knights of Labor, 256, 280
Koblenz, 261
Konstanz, 88
Korais, Adamentios, 116
Korean War, 275

LABOUR PARTY (Britain), 257
Lactantius, 51
la Hale, Thomas de, 162
laity, medieval, 140–45, 146, 148; and the Reformation, 199; and the religion of the people, 157–70; use in 19th-century church, 261
Lallemand, Louis, 227
Lamennais, Hugues Felicité Robert de, 251, 254; *251*
Lançon, A., *250*
Languedoc, 166
Laon, 134
La Rochelle, 230
Las Casas, Bartolomé de, 30
Lassalle, Ferdinand, 255
Lateran Council, Third (1179), 166
Lateran Council, Fourth (1215), 146
Lateran Council, Fifth (1512), 186
Lateran Treaty (1929), *295*
Latin America, 19, 297, 300, 308, 311
Latin language, 49, 95–96, 109, 302
Laud, William, Archbishop of Canterbury, 209; *209*
Lausanne, Treaty of, 117
Lawrence, St, 70, 246
League of Schmalkald, 194
Lear, Edward, *103*
Lebanon, 117; *291*
Lebuin, 94
Le Corbusier, 301; *300*
Le Fèvre, Jacques, 195
legislation, canon law, 139, 140–41, 142, 145; matrimonial, 144–45
Legros, *244*
Leibniz, Gottfried Wilhelm, 228
Leipzig, 188
Lemercier, 226–27
Lenin, 122
le Nobletz, Michel, 236
Leo I, Pope, 57, 58
Leo III, Emperor, 74
Leo V, Emperor, 112
Leo VI, Emperor, 109
Leo IX, Pope, 136, 142
Leo X, Pope, 255
Leo XIII, Pope, 256, 304, 306; *Quod apostolici muneris*, 255; *Rerum Novarum*, 254, 255, 256, 280–81, 305
Leovigild, King of the Visigoths, 98
leper-houses, 142
Lerins, 58
Levant, 117
Levellers, 213; *213*
Liber Miraculorum, 159
Liber Pontificalis, 64
'liberation theology', 292, 299, 309–10
Libri Carolini, 74
Lichtman, Allan, 235
Licinius, 51
Limoges, *155, 178*
Lincoln, Abraham, 278
Lincolnshire, 209
Lindisfarne, 87
Lindsay, Hal, *The Last Days of the Late, Great Planet Earth*, 282
Lipany, battle of (1434), 168
literacy, in the Dark Ages, 196; in the Middle Ages, 157–58
Lithuania, 19, 230, 311

Liturgical Movement, 261
liturgy, modern developments, 300–1; Orthodox church, 112; Vatican Council, 302
Liutprand, King of the Lombards, 96
Liverpool Cathedral, 301
Locke, John, 225, 231
Lollards, 148, 155, 164, 167–69
Lombard, Peter, 145
Lombardy, Lombards, 59, 86, 88, 96, 140, 160, 166
London, churches, 135; deaconesses, 262; Jewish population, 259; in the 19th century, 256, 261; *247*; Puritanism, 209; St Augustine and, 59; St Mary Magdalen, *243*; Temple Church, *131*; Westminster Abbey, 135; *152*
Long Island, New York, 210
Long Parliament, 211, 212
Longobards, 70; *see also* Lombards
Los Angeles, *270*; Azusa Street meetings, 300
Lothair I, Emperor, *82*
Lotto, Lorenzo, *154*
Louis VI, King of France, 143
Louis IX, St, King of France, 155
Louis XIII, King of France, 230
Louis of Anjou, St, 159, 162
Louis the Pious, Emperor, 88, 94, 96
Louis Napoleon (Napoleon III), 251
Lourdes, 262
Low Countries, Anabaptists, 192; *Devotio Moderna*, 167; Flagellants, 165; monasticism, 96; and Vatican Council, 302
Loyola, St Ignatius, 161, 216, 222, 228; *The Spiritual Exercises*, 232, 234; *236*
Lucca, 135
Ludlow, John Malcolm Forbes, 250
Ludmilla, St, 237
Ludovisi, Cardinal Ludovico, 228, 234
Ludwig IV of Bavaria, *138*
Luke, St, 47; *Gospel*, 62
Lull, Raymond, *151*
Lupus of Tours, 58
Luther, Martin, 172, 185, 188–92, 194–96, 199, 226, 258, 284; *173–77, 180, 217, 266*; *Against the Murderous and Plundering Hordes of the Peasants*, 190; *Deudsch Catechismus*, 188; *To the Christian Nobility of the German Nation*, 190
Lutheranism, 24; in America, 273, 278; *266*; incompatability, with politics, 251; and the Reformation, 185, 190–91, 192, 194, 195; relations with Orthodox church, 116; role of women, 304; use of laity, 261
Luxeuil, 88, 98
Lvov, Prince, 122
Lydney, temple of Nodens, 54
Lyons, 48, 230; *179*
Lyons, Council of (1274), 113, 160

MAASTRICHT, 88
Macarius, Archbishop of Cyprus, 117
Macarius, Metropolitan, 120
Macedonia, 118
MacIntyre, Alasdair, 298
McKinley, William, 277
Madison, James, 283
Magdeburg, 90, 94
Magnificat, 253
Magno, Paolo, 222